The State of Rhode Island:
Politics and Government

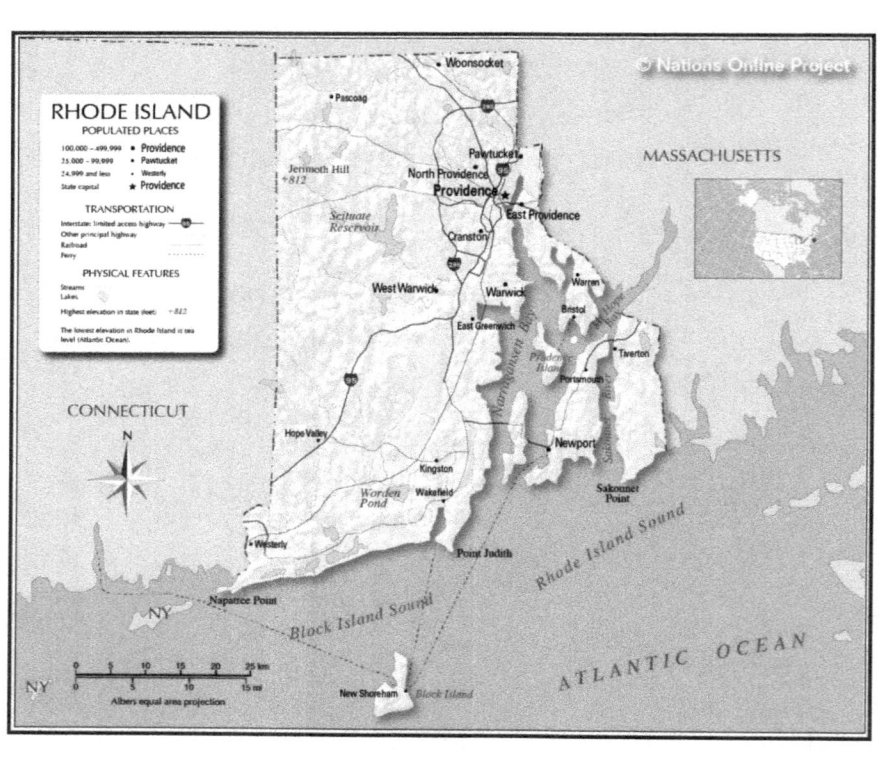

The State of Rhode Island: Politics and Government

Edited by

Maureen Moakley
and
Emily Lynch

Rhode Island Publications Society
East Providence, RI
2023

Copyright 2023 Rhode Island Publications Society

All rights reserved. No part of this book may be reproduced in any form whatsoever without permission in writing from the publisher, except for brief passages in connection with a review.

For information write:
The Rhode Island Publications Society
1445 Wampanoag Trail, Suite #201
East Providence, RI 02915
Tel: (401) 273-1776
Fax: (401) 273-1791

Printed in the United States of America
ISBN: 978-1-930483-08-8

Typeset in Minion Pro, Clarendon, and Neue Haas Grotesk Pro

Book design and typesetting by Clifford Garber

Contents

PREFACE   vii

1   Politics and Culture in the Ocean State   3
2   Rhode Island Constitutional Development 1636–2020   25
3   Rhode Island and the Federal System   49
4   Voting and Elections   63
5   Political Parties   85
6   Interest Groups   105
7   Media   125
8   The General Assembly   143
9   The Executive Branch   163
10   The Rhode Island Judiciary   179
11   Local Government   197

Policy Essays   219

A   The Legacy of Women in Rhode Island Politics: From the State House to Governor   221
B   Taxing and Spending   231
C   The Politics of Rhode Island Education   241
D   Health Policy in Rhode Island   251
E   Overview of Environmental Policy in Rhode Island   267
F   Transportation Policy in Rhode Island   279

ABOUT THE CONTRIBUTORS   290
INDEX   293

Preface

As Rhode Island drivers wind their way through the narrow curves of I-95 in the capital city of Providence, they might catch a glimpse of the statue of the Independent Man above the State House on Smith Hill. The brief sighting of this historical golden statue may lead Rhode Islanders to reflect on how this state symbol relates to the political life of the state and their experiences in the Ocean State. The Independent Man, placed upon the State House at the turn of the 20th century, is often incorrectly labeled as Roger Williams, the state's founder. Williams's dedication to religious freedom is an important reason for our individualistic political culture that set Rhode Island apart from most other states, even among other New England states. The Independent Man, with an anchor resting on his legs, serves as a beacon of hope for the state. Recent changes over the past twenty years—such as the adoption of true separation of powers among Rhode Island's branches of government as well as the state's official name change—suggests that Rhode Island's political culture, while still echoing the independent spirit, can be collaborative and inclusive. Our book focuses on the current state of Rhode Island politics and government

We edited this book with the intent to update the *Rhode Island Politics and Government* book published over twenty years ago. It has been the only book about Rhode Island written from a political science perspective for students and the interested general reader. Since over twenty years have lapsed since its publication, there was a need to for an updated publication to provide a comprehensive overview of political change and continuity in the Ocean State.

This project was truly a team effort where the book's authors include scholars and experts at public and private universities and public policy organizations from across the state. Our distinguished authors are researchers, teachers, and practitioners at The University of Rhode Island, Community College of Rhode Island, Rhode Island College, Brown University, Providence College, Roger Williams University and the Rhode Island Public Expenditure Council.

The new edition is comprised of eleven chapters that give insight into the major political institutions, policy, and behavior in the state. The chapter beings with Maureen Moakley's overview of the state's political culture to set the stage for the rest of the book. The next chapter focuses on the historical development of Rhode Island's constitution from Patrick Conley. Adam Myers describes Rhode Island and the federal system in Chapter 3. Emily Lynch covers voting, elections, and political parties in Chapters 4 and 5. The role of interest groups (Matthew Ulricksen) and the media (Rob Horowitz) is covered in Chapters 6 and 7. The three branches of government, The General Assembly (Adam Myers), The Executive Branch (Gary Sasse), and the Judiciary (Maureen Moakley), are discussed in Chapters 8–10. The concluding chapter gives an overview of the local government in Rhode Island (June Speakman).

The final portion of the book includes six policy essays. The first section covers the legacy of women in Rhode Island politics (Wendy Schiller). The next five sections cover specific policy areas, including taxing and spending (Michael DiBiase), education (Dian Kern and Shanna Pearson-Merkowitz), health policy (Robert Hackey, Colleen Kennedy, Michaela Szymczak), environmental policy (Aaron Ley), and transportation policy (Barry Schiller).

We want to give special recognition to Patrick Conley, who met with us early in 2021 during the COVID-19 pandemic to discuss our initial book proposal. Since then, Dr. Conley and the Rhode Island Publications Society have been incredibly supportive of the project. We are indebted to the exceptional editorial work of Heather Dubnick and Cliff Garber, who helped us finally reach the finish line, and we'd also like to thank Sabrinna Fogarty for her footnote editing.

This book is for all our students. Their inquisitiveness and interest in Rhode Island politics have motivated all of us to consider new perspectives, and they are a constant reminder of the true purpose of examining the politics of the Ocean State—to help our state become a better place for future generations. Although this was written with a student audience in mind, we believe political actors and interested general readers across the state will enjoy a fresh perspective on contemporary Rhode Island government and politics. We hope any Rhode Islander or individual interested in the Ocean State will find this an informative book on state politics. So, head to the coast with a Del's in one hand and our book in the other and enjoy learning more about the politics of Lil' Rhody.

The State of Rhode Island:
Politics and Government

1 / Politics and Culture in the Ocean State

MAUREEN MOAKLEY[1]

Rhode Island, since its founding, had been known as The State of Rhode Island and Providence Plantations. The name reflected the fact that during colonial times, the city of Newport, located on Aquidneck Island, that was named Rhode Island by early explorers, was the political and economic center of the colony. Providence Plantations referred to the farming plantations in and around the environs of Providence.

Founded by Roger Williams in 1636, the colony was an outlier. During the period of Puritan settlements in New England, a strict theocracy was established wherein church and state set adherence to religious and political norms. Williams rejected this belief, was exiled, and then settled the colony of Rhode Island and the Providence Plantations, which distinguished itself as a sanctuary for religious and political freedom. With no established church it became a refuge for dissidents, a place where Quakers and Jews settled and prospered. In contrast to the rest of more communitarian New England, the state ethos was highly individualistic.

The state continued to use Rhode Island and Providence Plantations as its official name on all official government buildings, documents, references, and checks; it is one of the quirky distinctions, related to its history, in which many Rhode Islanders take pride. In this tiny state, with population of just over one million, the lore of the founding and early history runs deep; a university, local schools, a hospital, the zoo, federal and state parks, various healthcare and non-profit facilities, businesses, streets, and boulevards around the state are named for Roger Williams.

During the early 2000s, growing awareness of racial injustices and the history of the slave trade in Rhode Island emerged and the question of changing the state's name—eliminating Providence Plantations from the title—came to the fore. The issue was put to the voters in 2010 to approve a constitutional change. Many argued that plantations alluded to slavery, noting the state's prominent role in the slave trade. Others countered that Rhode Island referred to Aquidneck Island and the port of Newport, which was the center of trade and commerce in the seventeenth and eighteenth centuries, while the Providence Plantations, then a backwater, referred to the farming plantations—a common title for such enterprises—around Providence where Roger Williams settled, reflecting our early founding.

The question was put on the ballot in 2010. While one can assume that some voters opposed the change based on racial bias, others took umbrage that we would alter our history. The question was roundly rejected by 78 percent of the voters.[2]

Energized by the growing minority voice in the state, and subsequent events that highlighted the deep and enduring injustices endured by Black and Native Americans in the state and the nation, sentiment began to change. These groups were also part of the founding history that was usually overlooked. The question was again put to the voters in 2020; it was approved by 53 percent of the voters.[3] This represented a significant shift in attitudes from the first referendum. It was the first time in US history that a state altered its name without territorial changes. "I'm very impressed. It's monumental to us African Americans," noted a leader from the Black community. Rhode Island is changing. Hugely. It makes me feel great that there is room for change."[4]

Into the Twenty-first Century—Change and Continuity

Change has come to Rhode Island. While enduring aspects of the political landscape remain, state and national events and marked demographic changes have altered perceptions and expectations about state politics among Rhode Islanders and their elected representatives.

This chapter presents an overview of the social and political milieu of the state looking at the historical background and the contour of politics and public policy. It also explores the underlying dynamics of demographic and attitudinal changes that have affected the political culture of the state. Subsequent chapters and policy essays will provide a comprehensive picture of the institutions, political processes and key policy issues that define the current shape of politics in Rhode Island.

Little Rhody, the smallest state in the union, has a land mass of just over 1,200 square miles: north to south it is 48 miles: east to west 37 miles. With a population of just over one million,[5] it is the second most densely populated state in the country, yet nearly 50 percent of the state is forest. It is called the Ocean State as, given its small size, it has over 400 miles of shoreline.

One can drive from New York to Boston on Interstate 95 and pass through Rhode Island in about an hour. Heading north, to the west one encounters scrub pines, beyond which are stretches of forests, state parks, nature preserves, and an array of lakes. The rural part of the state extends northwest, through old colonial settlement towns, farmland, and increasing patches of new development. To the east one catches glimpses of the coastal shoreline. En route to Providence there are of stretches of brown fields and many older gritty residential and industrial areas before the Providence skyline comes into view. The city center experienced a shabby decline in the 1970s and 1980s, but a remarkable rebound known as the Providence Renaissance, began by rerouting railroad tracks and a massive river relocation, creating an urban jewel. Just a few miles away lies the Massachusetts state line.

Beyond the city center and the surrounding urban environment are older middle-class areas and declining urban neighborhoods where the poor, immigrant, and minority populations struggle with a lack of economic and occupational opportunities.

Providence sits at the confluence of three rivers at the head of Narragansett Bay. From there one can travel down the east bay route past waterfront vistas, old colonial towns, and suburbs, and arrive in Newport. This storied town was the center of commerce and trade during the colonial era but declined after the Revolutionary War. In the late 1880s, it became a summer retreat for a wealthy, Gilded Age elite, mostly from New York, who provided new life and glamour to the city. The famous America's Cup race, an international sailing event, made the city a world sailing capitol; the cup remained in Newport until 1987. While most of the high glamour is gone, the city remains a wealthy enclave and a popular tourist attraction. Nearby, workers, mostly Irish Catholics, who originally served as servants to wealthy residences, formed neighborhoods that still exist as working-class neighborhoods nearby. More recently, minorities and undocumented immigrants have settled there for service work opportunities; poverty rates and the need for housing are growing problems.[6]

Water is everywhere. Along the west bay beyond the requisite waterfront homes, there are colonial villages, suburbs, and declining neighborhoods. Shoreline bungalows, commercial fishing enterprises, and public beaches provide residents of the state with a summer refuge, especially for urban populations.

Given this topography, Rhode Island is considered a gem that has been rediscovered in the 2020s. Pushed by the onset of COVID-19, when many were looking for less confining and more distant locations, as well as waterfront properties, the state become a preferred destination, especially for wealthy buyers. "The secret is out," one realtor noted; out-of-state buyers, mostly from Massachusetts, New York, and Connecticut—purchased almost half the sales in the state in the luxury market.[7] The wildly inflated cost of high-end homes and increased the value of all real estate has created difficulties for buyers in the general market, where the average price of homes rose by 16 percent.[8] Providence has also been discovered by many professionals who work in Boston and find that they can commute to work and still enjoy the benefits of less expensive real estate and rents. A thriving arts and cultural scene and communities of rich ethnic diversity—in and around Providence have made the city a vibrant urban locale.[9]

Little Rhody

The state population of 1,097,379 has grown by 44,812 since 2010; It has the fifteenth highest median income in the country.[10] Regarding higher education, residents with a college or post-graduate degree are 38.4 percent of the population, just above the national average of 33 percent. The most significant demographic change is the increase of the Hispanic population, which has grown by about 40 percent since 2010 and is now 16.6 percent of the population.[11]

Rhode Island, as the saying goes, is a state where everybody knows everybody else. Given its size and population, this idea has real currency; or as one *Providence Journal* editor noted, "... here in Rhode Island, take six degrees of separation and divide by two."[12] From this perspective, one can become a real Rhode Islander if one wears the "everyone knows everyone coziness of our state like a badge of honor."[13]

Given its small size, such coziness creates tight-knit communities and lends itself to a certain parochial ethos. During the roll call at the National Democratic convention in 2020 via zoom, many states recorded their vote with references to historical or current political issues. The state roll-call vote for Rhode Island featured the chair of the state Democratic party on a beach in Rhode Island touting a plate of calamari, the state's official appetizer, while announcing the vote. The *Washington Post* noted it was certainly the "most irreverent" and the "characteristically Rhode Island way to make an appearance on the national stage."[14]

There is, however, a darker side to these quaint observations. Among political folk, everybody *does* know everybody, and this dynamic lends itself to a certain insider advantage.[15] It is the basis of the "I know a guy" syndrome that critics note about the culture. As historian Patrick Conley acknowledged, "There is a unique degree of coziness between political leaders, labor leaders, social leaders. It's the result of living in a city-state."[16] Steve Brown, the head of the state's American Civil Liberties Union, notes that, "Everybody knows everybody else; everybody has relatives involved in something. It's the inbred nature of the state."[17]

Rhode Island has a legacy of political corruption. The machinations of Republican Boss Brayton in the 1880s, scandals associated with the Democratic political machine, to the reign of the Mafia during the postwar period and the escapades of colorful politicians like Mayor Buddy Cianci in the early 2000s, it is the stuff of legends.

During the early 1900s, to forestall the ascendency of working-class populations that were becoming a majority, the Republicans devised strategies to sustain GOP rule that included severe voting restrictions and malapportionment lines that were upheld by a compliant court system. Their efforts were able to block working class and immigrant voters. That is until a masterful maneuver know as Bloodless or Green Revolution of 1935.

Democrat Governor Theodore Francis Green was elected in 1932 and reelected in 1934 when the party achieved a majority in the Rhode Island House of Representatives with tight results in the State Senate. At the post-election annual reorganization meeting, which occurred in 1935 when the legislature convenes for the opening session, the Democrat lieutenant governor, who then presided over the RI Senate, accepted challenges to the results of two Republicans senate elections. With a Democrat the lieutenant governor controlling the floor, they were able to invalidate GOP claims and install two waiting Democrats in the seats, achieving a majority. The Democrats then proceeded to vacate all seats on the Supreme Court and install judges who would not be inclined to veto the subsequent political changes. All in one day.[18]

Although the Democrats passed significant administrative and political reforms, they too used political office to sustain patronage, government bloat, and the "I know a guy" ethic that also involved their share of political scandals.

Another dubious legend was the reign of the Italian Mafia in Providence. Along with a base in Boston, New England Mafia emerged around the time of Prohibition and created a base on Federal Hill in Providence; the Mafia continued its nefarious activities, including influence in politics, until its decline in the late 1980s. While petty extortions and briberies still occur, the Mafia days are over. Rhode Islanders, however, still have a perverse fascination with the Mafia, fueled in part by continued media focus on its corrupt past, which reinforces dated stereotypes.

Data over the past decades shows Rhode Island ranks in the middle range of states in number federal convictions for corruption which is how these rankings are made.[19] Yet the media still reference old stories and old pictures— and in some cases create their own impressionistic scores that are well off the mark as to where Rhode Island ranks.[20]

This history has had a somewhat deleterious effect on Italian Americans. Around the turn of the nineteenth century, thousands of Italians immigrated to the state. Because of language differences and their Mediterranean background, they had more difficulty assimilating. Communities of strong families with guild orientations settled around the state. As they moved up the socioeconomic ladder, they were slower to break into politics. No doubt the Mafia association, as well as pushback from earlier groups like the Irish who wanted to sustain their standing, contributed to this delay. Italians often became the butt of humor in ubiquitous Mafia jokes that include an ethnic connection. This type of humor probably wouldn't be tolerated about other ethnic groups, but these references are still part of the jargon of some in the state.

The lore of Buddy Cianci continues to fascinate. Cianci was a savvy and charismatic politician first elected mayor as a Republican in 1974. In 1983 he was convicted of crimes related to brutalizing his wife's lover and was forced to resign. He was reelected as mayor in 1990 and applied his energies to promoting and facilitating the Providence Renaissance; he was a cheerleader for the city and ably managed the public's business. Apparently, his management included unseemly activities, and in 2002 he was convicted of racketeering and sentenced to five years in federal prison. After he was released, he ran unsuccessfully for mayor in 2014. In the end, he noted, "...The city of Providence is my significant other."[21]

Scandals still emerge, and bribes and kickbacks are revealed, but overall, these instances are less frequent and, as the data indicates, on a par with many other states. The change is in part the result of vigorous enforcement by the state's attorney generals, increased political clout of the state's ethics commission, and requirements of greater transparency in public transactions.

The Political Landscape

Rhode Island is a Democratic state. Since the Green or Bloodless Revolution in 1935, beyond blips of Republican successes, Democrats have dominated state politics. One reason is that the state has been relatively moderate in its political orientations. This balance is kept in check by a small minority GOP that can occasionally win statewide office or a congressional seat when the Democrats move to far too the left. From 1995 to 2011, Republicans controlled the governor's seat for four terms as a result of the Democrats nominating a progressive woman candidate three times, which was a reach at the time and the reelection of a GOP incumbent. These GOP governors represented policies that were more fiscally conservative but within the mainstream of the state's politics.

In the early 2020s, many GOP elected local and legislative officials were boxed in by a relatively small but vocal number of Trump voters who exercised disproportionate influence on this minority party and could make a difference in rural local and legislative elections. Trump picked up support of about 20, 000 votes in the 2020 election.[22] While not supporting extreme far-right policies, most of these candidates and officeholders were forced to placate their constituencies and walk a fine line by offering muted support for Trump but essentially engaging in moderate Republican politics with a libertarian edge.

State politics continues to be dominated by an overwhelming Democratic General Assembly. Rhode Island has one of the most powerful state legislatures in the country, while Rhode Island governors are among the weakest in the fifty states. With no line-item veto and limited appointment authority, the nexus of power often lies with the General Assembly.[23]

The internal dynamic within the legislature has changed. Leadership is less conservative and new progressive legislators have joined the ranks. Legislative leaders, while keeping a firm grip on power, have given voice and space to members. As one legislator noted, "the vibe is different." These changes are more manageable as national studies have found Rhode Island legislators are some of the least ideologically divided representatives in the country.[24]

Another critical factor that sustains Democratic dominance is that Rhode Island is a labor state. During the early twentieth century, labor was a powerful advocate for the rights of workers and immigrant groups that provided the labor to fuel the industrial growth that contributed to the state's prosperity and a rising middle class. Private sector unions remain influential, but the power of the unions is centered in the state's public service unions. Thousands of state worker unions, including teachers, unions and state and municipal public service unions like fire fighters and police, collectively wield considerable influence.

When the state passed pension reform, some of the more excessive aspects of union agreements involving excessive disability pension provisions and costly work allowances for public service workers were curtailed.[25] However, many over-burdened cities and towns still face costly work rules and high accumulated pension obligations. The city of Providence has an unsustainable pension obligation of over one billion dollars. As yearly payout costs continue to escalate, voters in Providence approved a $515 million obligation bond to ameliorate the debt.[26] As interest rates escalated, the proposal was put on hold. Whatever the outcome, the unions are in a position of strength, as they are confident that while other municipalities might be forced into bankruptcy, the state would not allow the capitol city to go under.

Union power derives from the unions' ability to influence primary elections in legislative and municipal races, where they can be a critical factor. Statewide primary candidates also court the union vote. In 2022, in a highly contested Democratic primary for governor, Dan McKee, was one of the more moderate political candidates in the gubernatorial race. Yet, relying on federal funds for COVID-19 relief, he endorsed a policy, at the union's request, offering all state workers a $3,000 bonus for getting a COVID-19 vaccination. The blowback was considerable, so the policy was reconfigured to offer these bonuses to all state workers as part of a retention effort to keep them on the job. The policy included bonuses for judges in the state system who have lifetime tenure.

Political Culture and Politics

Political culture is defined as a common understanding of the orientations and expectations of the public and officeholders about the purpose and conduct of government. These orientations are rooted in a state's early history and are still reflected in attitudes about politics and government. Within this context, however, expectations evolve based on significant events, and demographic changes alter the conduct of government.

These characterizations are drawn from a study of American political culture by Daniel Elazar who posits that, in addition common basic principles of representation, states and regions, from their founding, developed distinct orientations based on their political, religious, and demographic histories.[27] He identifies these orientations as moralistic, individualistic, and traditionalistic. Such cultures are not pure literal types but dominant strains that mutate over time. To a remarkable extent, however, studies have shown that a state's founding and early demographic patterns remain evident in a state or region's current politics and policy.[28] Moreover, intuitively one understands that Rhode Island is not Georgia or Texas and that many of the differences are rooted in the early development of these states.

A moralistic political culture was formed in Puritan New England; it derived from the Puritan understanding of a commonwealth where a strict theocracy of church and state promoted the ideals of a good society. This culture was dominant in the homogeneous settlements in New England.

An individualistic political culture sees the public sphere as more secular —a utilitarian marketplace akin to a business where individuals and groups participate in politics to advance themselves socially and economically.

A third strain, a traditionalistic culture, evolved from the plantation hierarchy of the South. It fostered a paternalistic concept of politics, where an elite controlled political and economic decision making; the object of politics was to preserve the status quo.

Rhode Island shared many of the early ideals of the good society of the New England region; it was the first colony to abolish slavery in 1652, and contrary to the ethos of the Puritans, the state was founded on ideals of tolerance of thought and religion. But it was an outlier in that strains of individualism were evident early on. Historian Gordon Wood notes that by the late 1700s, commerce, trade, and freedom of religion created the "most liberal, the most entrepreneurial and most modern of the eighteenth-century colonies."[29]

This concept of politics is consistent with the ideas of James Madison, who rejected the idea of a state religion and defined interest group politics as the "principal task of legislation, [that] involves the spirit of party and faction in the necessary and ordinary operations of government."[30] Moreover, it represented the inclination of the steady succession of immigrant groups throughout its history that settled in Rhode Island. Their interests are mainly transactional in that they are interested in promoting their claim to a share of the political, economic, and social pie that was initially denied them.

A shift in the political ethos is evident in the acknowledgment of and reckoning with injustices visited upon minority populations. The unsettling events surrounding the murder of George Floyd created heightened awareness of long simmering racial inequities—particularly for Blacks and Native Americans in the state. These racial groups are among the oldest in the state, yet their history and culture were either obfuscated or ignored.

Until recently, Rhode Island's role in the slavery and the slave trade was muted. While it involved a small number of Africans to the colony—there were some enslaved workers on colonial plantations in South County and, in towns like Providence, prominent families owned house slaves. But the fortunes that prominent families like the Brown's reaped were the result of their role in the slave trade, whereby they funded expeditions to Africa, bought slaves, and then transported them to the Caribbean to be sold.[31] Slavery was banned in the state in 1843, and the General Assembly passed anti-discrimination laws in 1885, but rampant discrimination against Blacks continued. Exclusion from employment and fair housing opportunities, segregation in neighborhoods with inferior schools, and denial of equal access to public and private facilities[32] resulted in the marked disparities in social/economic indicators like higher poverty and unemployment and lower income and home ownership among Blacks.[33]

While the Black population in the state has declined, they are a stronger voice in the public square. Funds from federal monies designated to educate, employ, and empower minority groups are a part of the public agenda. Groups like Black Lives Matter have had a notable impact on public perceptions, and political action committees have been successful in recruiting Blacks to run for office and promote a progressive agenda. A thoughtful attempt to consider reparations for Blacks was undertaken, looking primarily at housing and educational opportunities for this community.[34] Disparities remain but their place in the public square suggest progress.

After the Indian colonial wars, many Narragansett survivors were driven into servitude or slavery. In subsequent years, most of the tribal land was taken by force or deceit, impoverishing, and marginalizing the remaining Narragansetts for generations to come. They are now just over one percent of the population—a meager constituency. A telling indication of their status was a maneuver to block the ability of Native Americans to benefit from economic opportunity created by 1988 Federal Indian Regulatory Act allowing Native Americans to operate casinos. In 1996, the late Senator John Chafee attached a rider to a federal bill that essentially blocked gambling initiatives by the Narragansett tribe.[35] A subsequent attempt of the tribe to sell cigarettes on tribal land events was shut down by the state police.[36] After these incidents, there was outcry to "do something for the Indians," but nothing much came of it.

The current reckoning has begun to acknowledge Narragansetts' history and the taking of their lands. Scholarship funds have been established, small portions of tribal lands have been restored to the Narragansetts, tribal museums have been expanded, and universities and other public entities acknowledge their presence on former tribal land and offer programs that pay tribute to their history and culture.

Substantial change has been stalled by local municipalities demands they sign away their sovereign immunity before gaining permits to build on their lands. Housing and economic opportunity remain critical problems for tribal members, but nearby municipalities have retained solicitors to keep any development on their land at bay.[37]

Other minorities have been empowered to advance their status and interests. Public interest groups and foundations invest their research, influence, and money into projects to support minority populations and create avenues for diverse leadership. Corporate and small businesses actively promote diversity in employment and other institutions have helped secure political and policy appointments. Minorities hold positions of influence in government, nonprofits, education, and private industry, and they are becoming a respected contingent of new leaders in the state.

The Immigrant Experience

Rhode Island, the birthplace of the Industrial Revolution in the United States, generated early and continuous demands for mill and manufacturing workers, who contributed to the colorful history of various ethnic groups that settled in the state. French Canadian workers, Irish laborers, Italians, and Russian Jews, along with the Portuguese from the mainland, the Azores, and Cape Verde— made their mark on the state's development. These groups were joined by Greeks, Armenians, Germans, Poles, and other European groups. Most endured prejudices and discrimination, located in neighborhoods with their compatriots, and worked hard to achieve a measure of prosperity for their families and communities.

The Immigration Act of 1965 lifted many of the race-based quota restrictions, allowing more Asians, Latin Americans, and Africans entry to the country. These groups had a less burdensome plight than earlier immigrants. The Civil Rights Movement not only affected civil rights for Blacks but also infused the political climate with expectations and demands from other groups facing discrimination, including women and minorities. Various laws were passed to protect and expand rights that gave legitimacy to their place in society. Policies like food stamps, Medicaid, rent control, public housing, and other forms of public assistance, as well as anti-discrimination laws, mitigated the harsh environment that earlier immigrants had endured.

In Rhode Island, one significant change was the growth of the Latino population and their ascendency into the economic and political ranks. From 2010 to 2020 the Latino population doubled; they are now the second largest ethnic group in the state. As one historian notes, "For earlier immigrants, it sometimes took decades or even a century for them to become full participants in the Rhode Island community."[38] Not so for Latinos.

There had been pockets of Puerto Ricans, Cubans, and Mexicans immigrants in Rhode Island, particularly in the postwar period, but a surge of Latino immigrants occurred from the 1970s to 1990s, and in one generation, they have become a political force. Many migrated from urban areas of New York City for the more open and supportive environs of Rhode Island. A few of these emigres from New York brought with them a strategy for creating a cohesive political force in their new home. "We didn't want to be like New York or Boston" where immigrant power was diffuse and competitive, noted one leader. Infighting between Puerto Ricans and newcomer Dominicans prevented overall political progress for Latinos. In Boston, he noted that attempts to organize "didn't quite jell."[39] These leaders organized outreach efforts with different Latino communities to encourage voting turnout. They created a political action committee to help fund and endorse candidates from various Latino backgrounds. They established a Latino Leadership Institute that avoided entrenched leadership and ethnic competition by mandating rotating term limits. The Institute groomed civic leaders, especially women, who have been remarkable successful in breaking into Rhode Island politics.[40]

One factor was a political vacuum in Providence and other urban cities was a somnolent political landscape provided opportunities that Latinos were ready to fill. The city of Central Falls is an example. In the 1980s this small city of one square mile was in steep economic decline. Manufacturing jobs had dried up; almost half the population lived below the poverty line, and crime, drug trafficking, and addiction were rampant. Some of the poverty was the result of large cohorts of poor immigrants, many of whom were undocumented, who settled in the area. The decline was compounded by inefficient and corrupt leaders of city government—part of an ossified political class.[41] The state took over the public schools in 1991, and in 2011, the city was forced to file for bankruptcy. After a difficult period that saw pension, salary, and workforce cuts, the city began to recover. Competent Latino leaders were elected and by 2021 median income has begun to rise. Sixty-six percent of the population is Latino, and Central Falls is transitioning to diverse and productive city on the rebound.

Latinos have been elected to city councils, mayoral offices, the state legislature and served as statewide general officers. In 2022, two of five general offices were held by Latinas, and state legislature estimates of all minority representation (which include other minorities) runs near 20 percent.[42] Their voice sustains the transactional culture, but it also contributes an ethos that is willing to mitigate social and economic inequality and expand social services, employment, and housing opportunities.

While there is a strong political establishment that enhances Latino political clout, they are not a monothetic group. As elsewhere in the country, some

Latinos are more conservative and religious and do not support some progressive positions. In the 2020 presidential election, Trump picked up support in Latino communities.[43] In some elections, political divisions among individual candidates emerge, but they remain a relatively cohesive group; there is still a strong pull to support members of the Latino community.

The issue of undocumented immigrants remains. Estimates are that there are about 30,000 undocumented residents, which is 9 percent of the immigrant population and 1 percent of the total state population.[44] Many are from Latino communities. While there are inevitable instances of drug trafficking, gangs, and violent crime that accompany poverty and displacement, most of this population is generally accepted as productive residents. Formerly undocumented immigrants are in the state legislature and other elected office and are productive and respected members of the political elite.

The media is sensitive to their presence in the state; in coverage of various community activities as well as crime, street fights, or other disruptive happenings, the immigration status of individuals or groups involved is rarely implied or mentioned.

Non-profit community organizations offer assistance, and some public policies are crafted to support them. During the height of the COVID-19 crisis in 2021, Governor Gina Raimondo advocated for a program of donations to supplement incomes for the undocumented population who were denied public assistance to federal benefits. In 2021, Governor McKee signed legislation that entitles residents, regardless of immigration status, to be eligible for in-state tuition at the state colleges and universities. The Student Success Act requires these students to have a high school equivalency degree, reside in the state, and have applied for lawful immigrant status.[45] The state also passed legislation providing child health care and driving privileges for this population.[46]

One impressive drive among minority community activists was efforts to get an accurate census count, particularly in poorer urban areas where undocumented residents and other limited English-speaking residents resided. Estimates were that there was a significant undercount in these communities in the 2010 census and mid-decade census data indicated that, given current census population estimates, Rhode Island was overrepresented in and would lose one of two members of the US House. in 2022.

After the attempt by the Trump administration to add a citizenship question to the forms was put aside, state activists and minority groups pulled out all the stops and mounted an aggressive campaign to find residents and get them counted. They hired staff, organized volunteers, set out stations at food banks and COVID vaccination sites, and went door to door to individual residences, triple-deckers, and basement apartments. The effort added about 38,000 people to the count, which put the state over the top in retaining both US House seats. These efforts may have been too robust, as a subsequent analysis by the US Census Bureau indicated that Rhode Island was one of eight states that were overcounted.⁴⁷ The state, however, was still able to keep the two congressional seats.

Asians, Native Hawaiians, and Pacific Islanders have also emerged on the political scene. In the post-Vietnam era, most Asians were not active in the public square, but successive generations and new immigrants are emerging as elected officials, and state and nonprofit administrators. While under 4 percent of the population, they are a voice in politics. In 2023, members of the Black Latino legislative caucus renamed itself the Black, Latino, Indigenous, Asian American pacific Islanders caucus.

Women and Politics

Gina Raimondo, the first elected female governor in the state, changed expectations about the capacity of elected women in public office. In the early 2000s, there remained a national reluctance to vote for a woman as the chief executive. When Raimondo was elected governor in 2014, she was only one of nine elected governors in the country, and as of 2022, there were still just nine states with a woman chief executive. A commentary from *Politico* noted, "…Women in many states have yet to shatter the highest glass: the governorships."⁴⁸ Raimondo broke that barrier in Rhode Island.

During her first term in office, she had some notable policy successes, yet her polling numbers were weak; national polls ranking all state governors indicated women governors had most of the low rankings—with Raimondo among them. Statewide polls indicated a significant gender gap. She received strong support among women but lower rankings from men.⁴⁹

She was reelected in 2018, and sentiment began to change. Although many did not agree with her policies, she displayed strong and decisive policy leadership. She also found her footing with legislative leadership and during the COVID-19 crisis at her daily press briefings, where she presented an informed and transparent voice that was reassuring to the public. While resentment from public unions continued,⁵⁰ polls during that period gave her positive rankings and the gender gap in polling on her COVID-19 management disappeared.⁵¹ She resigned in 2020 to take a position with the Biden Administration.

Women have been making a strong showing in other elected and appointed offices. In 2021, women were over 44 percent of legislative membership, making Rhode Island the state with the fourth highest number female legislators in the country.⁵² In that year, women reached parity with men in the state senate being 50 percent of that body. In 2022, two of five statewide offices were held by women.

The state ranks twelfth in the nation for the number of elected women executives in the state.⁵³ In the judiciary, women's ranks have increased significantly; in 2021 women judicial officers were 38 percent of all judicial officials, and women are now a majority on the State Supreme Court.

The Current Contour of Politics

Events in the past few decades have encouraged some transformative policy initiatives. Pension reform was a political watershed in Rhode Island in that it broke encrusted assumptions about what policy initiatives were possible.

Rhode Island struggled for years with a with an underfunded state pension liability exacerbated by the financial crisis and recession of 2008. A shrinking and older public service workforce resulted in diminished revenues and escalating pension debts. A common problem in other states and cities across the country, the shortfall was the primarily the result of generous pension concessions that, over the years, politicians supported to shore up their electoral support and avoid dealing with the long- term pension issues, regarded as a "third rail" of state politics.[54]

Given the political heft of public service unions, there was faint political will to make fundamental changes. The standard remedy was to amortize the debt, which would provide a short-term fix but incur significant interest and additional debt; essentially it was a strategy of kicking the can down the road. There was every expectation that this would continue to be the solution.

Gina Raimondo, elected state treasurer in 2008, raised questions about the growing costs of the state pension liability and began to articulate the need for reform. She released a report, *Truth in Numbers*, that clearly laid out the consequences of inaction and invited debate on the topic.[55] It was received tepidly and while some elected officials quietly agreed with the analysis, it was considered a non-starter; this kind of change couldn't happen.

Raimondo also noted that many municipal pension funds, that were not under her purview, were critically vulnerable. Shortly thereafter, in August 2011, the city of Central Falls was forced to filed for bankruptcy. Everything changed. One aide to the governor noted, now "the stars were aligned," as the governor, the speaker of the house, and the senate president went along with Raimondo and worked to pass the Rhode Island Retirement and Security Act in 2012, completely revamping the state pension system.

There was a fierce pushback from public service unions, whose members' cost-of-living adjustments were suspended, and from current state workers whose benefits would be affected by the stringent reforms. After a flurry of lawsuits and some research studies that suggested the change was an overreach,[56] the law remained intact. Nationally it was regarded as a "shining example"[57] and a model that other states should emulate.

Over the next decade, the legislature took on a more progressive agenda. In this most Catholic state in the Union,[58] Rhode Island passed a law in 2019 to codify the right to an abortion into state law. That same year, the legislature took over the Providence school system after an independent study report deemed these schools some of the worst performing in the country.[59] In 2021, the General Assembly passed the Act on Climate, a sweeping regulatory reform to reduce carbon emissions with strict monitoring and accountability provisions.

Drawing on COVID-19 funds, the state provided multiple assistance programs to address economic and social displacements during the health crisis. Temporary cash assistance, emergency housing programs and homeless shelters, extended unemployment benefits, and grants to small businesses were part of that effort. These programs encouraged efforts at longer-term solutions.

Grants and programs to support educational programs to complete secondary education and provide access to higher education were extended. Robust efforts to expand job-training programs—Like Real Jobs RI and Back to Work RI that have received increased attention and support.[60]

The crisis in housing remains high on the political agenda. A long-term solution appears to be a priority in the legislature. Multiple state and foundation programs were dedicated to tackling the housing crisis, but the need for a centralized entity became evident. In 2022, legislation was introduced to use 300 million dollars of federal recovery monies to create a centralized, cabinet level Department of Housing. Advocates, reflecting on this changing paradigm, noted the need for government infrastructure that could put some muscle behind these efforts.

The state has long been progressive on energy issues. In addition to the Act on Climate, Rhode Island is heavily invested in wind power. It was the first in the country to install wind power turbines in Rhode Island Sound. If plans live up to expectations, Rhode Island could get 80 percent of its electricity from renewable sources and come close to getting 100% of its energy from non-fossil sources by 2030.[61] In addition to the Act on Climate, the legislature approved other far-reaching environmental policies, including the establishment of a Forest Conservation Commission to protect the state's forests from clear cutting for solar panels. The goal is to encourage incentives to support renewable solar energy on preferred sites like brownfields, carports, and rooftops.[62]

To be sure, the expanding agenda encouraged a very different view among many Rhode Islanders and some state legislators. They resent government intrusions about mask mandates and protocols, consider environmental policies like The Act on Climate an overreach, and object to the proliferation of new programs that they see as an extension of the "nanny state." Generally, these conservative voters have a libertarian perspective. They want the government to stay out of the way and limit new programs. Their voices will remain a vocal part of the ongoing debate, and at times a corrective voice, on major initiatives in the state.

Rising Expectations and Citizen Engagement

Rising expectations about state government performance as well as more voices in the public square have created a new dynamic. During the COVID-19 pandemic, state government briefings and increased funding for groups and individuals impacted by the economic fallout appear to have created higher expectations about the role and responsibilities of government. People expect government to work. Groups with broader interests were energized to push for resolution of longstanding contentious issues they supported.

One example is the rights of shoreline property owners and the shoreline access for fishermen, surfers, and the public. The state constitution allows that the people "shall continue to enjoy and freely exercise all rights of fishery, and the privileges of the shore."[63] What these privileges *are* has been an unresolved issue, with beachfront property owners' intent on limiting shore access. While this debate has been ongoing for over a decade, in 2021 the beach access issue "got legs" as more activists became involved. Parking restrictions were modified to give access to surfers. The politics of shoreline communities' fire districts—districts funded by beach communities, whose purpose is to maintain the beach and prevent public access rather than fight fires—have come under scrutiny.[64] A bipartisan legislative commission developed a plan to clarify and extend public shoreline access. In 2022 it passed by unanimous consent in the RI House, and although it did not get a vote in the Senate, the public's right to shore access is being defined and expanded.[65]

State officials have also responded to the changing environment. There is more scrutiny of administrative agencies; the legislature has become more active in examining lax performance, particularly in the field of Health and Human Services and in the Department of Youth and Family Services, where poor outcomes, misspent monies, administrative failures, and leadership turnover have hobbled these agencies for years.[66]

They have also tightened oversight provisions of state contracting bids, which have long been subject to insider deals and neglect of performance goals. A federal grading system devised to monitor state spending and performance of states using monies from a trillion-dollar infrastructure grant indicated that in 2022 Rhode Island made progress. Although the ranking mechanisms had some critics, Rhode Island ranked first among the states to meet these target areas.[67]

Lobbyists still have influence at the Statehouse, and labor unions remain a strong force. Insider deals still get done; in the end-of-session rush, many insider bills are pushed through quietly, in the hopes of avoiding public scrutiny. Interest group politics is still the norm, but the process has broadened as more activists, foundations, and other citizens get involved in policy process.

More open and participatory norms can be challenging. Federal monies with permitting and regulatory mandates can stall development for both public and private projects. New federal programs' requirements for community input and municipalities' yielding to public demands for participation have generated more voices, pro and con, in the public square. While public input is critical, there are more public hearings that become contentious—more protests, demonstrations, and invidious debates even among groups with common interests.[68] Zoom meetings for executive and legislative hearings expanded the public audience but often stymied the capacity of elected officials to get timely resolutions through personal negotiations on policy debates. In addition, the pushback from more conservative Rhode Islanders, with different perspectives, remains part of the dialogue.

Whatever the drawbacks, change has come to Rhode Island. The following chapters and essays will explore in greater depth the institutions, processes and politics that define the political life of the state.

Notes

1. The author thanks Elaine Cali and Rob Horowitz and especially Amy Logan for their thoughtful review of this chapter.
2. Tom Mooney, "In Close Vote, RI Appears Poised to Drop 'Plantations' from State Name," *The Providence Journal*, November 4, 2020, https://www.providencejournal.com/story/news/politics/2020/11/04.
3. Mooney, "Close Vote."
4. Tom Mooney, "We're Just Rhode Island Now: Voters Decide to Drop 'Plantations' from State Name," *The Providence Journal*, November 4, 2020, https://www.providencejournal.com/story/news/local/2020/11/04/close-vote-ri-does-away-plantations-state-name/6159803002/.
5. America Counts Staff, "Rhode Island's Population Grew 4.3% Last Decade," United States Census Bureau, August 25, 2021. census.gov/library/stories/state-by-state/rhode-island-population-change-between-census-decade.html.
6. Antonia Ayres-Brown, Antonia and Pearl Marvel, "As Newport Home Prices Rise, Undocumented Families Struggle to Find Secure Housing," The Public's Radio, December 6, 2021, https://thepublicsradio.org/article/as-newport-home-prices-rise-undocumented-families-struggle-to-find-secure-housing.
7. Wheeler Cowperthwaite, "RI's Housing Market Is Still Hot, but Is It Starting to Cool off?" *The Providence Journal*, July 30, 2022, https://www.providencejournal.com/story/news/local/2022/07/30/rhode-island-housing-market-data-brokers-slowing-sales-price-increases/10162671002/.
8. "This May Be the Major Reason Why RI Real Estate Prices Continue to Skyrocket," *GoLocalProv*, January 30, 2022, https://www.golocalprov.com/business/this-may-be-the-major-reason-why-ri-real-estate-price-continue-to-skyrocket.
9. Amy Russo, "'Providence Is Reborn': PVDFest Hiatus Ends with Dancing in the Streets," *The Providence Journal*, June 11, 2022, https://www.providencejournal.com/story/news/local/2022/06/11/providence-pvdfest-hiatus-ends-dancing-streets/7595925001/.
10. Edward Fitzpatrick and Daigo Fujiwara, "What's the Wealthiest Town in Rhode Island? See Census Data on Income in the Ocean State," *The Boston Globe*, April 22, 2022. https://www.bostonglobe.com/2022/04/22/metro/whats-wealthiest-town-rhode-island-see-census-data-income-ocean-state/?et_rid=589784446&s_campaign=rhodemap:newsletter.
11. Edward Fitzpatrick, "R.I. Latino Population Grew by Nearly 40 Percent in the Past Decade, Census Shows," *The Boston Globe*, August 13, 2021. https://www.bostonglobe.com/2021/08/12/metro/ri-latino-population-grew-by-nearly-40-percent-past-decade-census-shows/.
12. David Ng, "Opinion/Ng: For a RI Doctor and Me, It's Only Three Degrees of Separation Instead of Six," *The Providence Journal*, January 16, 2022, https://www.providencejournal.com/story/news/columns/2022/01/16/providence-journal-editor-david-ng-shares-nyc-childhood-connection-miriam-hospital-doctor/9103245002/.
13. Ng, "Degrees."
14. Teo Armus and Antonia Noori Farzan, "Calamari, Rhode Island's Controversial State Appetizer, Becomes an Unexpected Star of Democratic Convention," *The Washington Post*, August 19, 2020, https://www.washingtonpost.com/nation/2020/08/19/calamari-rhode-island-comeback-dnc/.

15. Katherine Gregg, "Political Scene: 3 Tales from RI 'Where Everybody Knows Everybody Else,'" *The Providence Journal*, March 14, 2021, https://www.providencejournal.com/story/news/politics/2021/03/14/political-scene-3-tales-ri-where-everybody-knows-everybody-else/4601847001/.
16. Gregg, "Scene."
17. Ibid.
18. Patrick T. Conley, "Robert E. Quinn and the Political Revolution of 1935." *Small State Big History*, n.d., http://smallstatebighistory.com/obert-e-quinn-and-the-political-revolution-of-1935/.
19. Harry Enten, "Ranking The States From Most To Least Corrupt," *FiveThirtyEight*, January 23, 2015, https://fivethirtyeight.com/features/ranking-the-states-from-most-to-least-corrupt/.
20. "RI Ranked 6th Most Corrupt by Bezos-Owned Washington Post—Who Often Paid Zero in Fed Income Tax," *GoLocalProv*, August 13, 2021, https://www.golocalprov.com/news/ri-ranked-6th-most-corrupt-by-bezos-owned-washington-post-who-often-paid-ze.
21. Tom Mooney, "Vincent 'Buddy' Cianci, 1941–2016," *The Providence Journal*, January 28, 2016, https://www.providencejournal.com/story/news/politics/2016/01/28/vincent-buddy-cianci-1941-2016/32593767007/.
22. Phil Eil, "When Trump — and Trumpism — Came to Rhode Island," *Uprise RI*, November 18, 2020, https://upriseri.com/2020-11-18-phil-eil/.
23. For a fuller discussion of this dynamic, see Adam Myer's account on the legislature in chapter 8.
24. Borris Shor and Nolan McCarthy. "The Ideological Mapping of American Legislatures," *The American Political Science Review* 105, no. 3 (2011): 530–51.
25. "The National Congress of American Indians Resolution #FTL-04-103," National Congress of American Indians, 2004, https://www.ncai.org/attachments/Resolution_buDYanHCsyhfXdwrXDLiqJAvlMtFApovgfXbkaPJnnKwGPFbZEi_ftl04-103.pdf.
26. Chip Barnett, "Providence, Rhode Island, Voters Approve $515 Million of Pension Bonds," *The Bond Buyer*, June 8, 2022, https://www.bondbuyer.com/news/providence-rhode-island-voters-approve-515-million-of-pension-bonds.
27. Daniel J. Elazar, *American Federalism: a View from the States*, 1st ed (New York: Thomas Y. Crowell, 1966).
28. Thomas Anton, *American Federalism and Public Policy: How the System Works* (New York: Random House, 1989).
29. Gordon Wood, *The Radicalism of the American Revolution* (New York: Vintage Books, 1991).
30. "Madison #10," in *The Federalist Papers* (New York: Bantam Books, 1982).
31. For an excellent account of the slave trade in Rhode Island see Charles Rappleye, *Sons of Providence: The Brown Brothers, the Slave Trade and the American Revolution* (New York: Simon and Schuster, 2006).
32. Geralyn Ducady, Geralyn. "African American Civil Rights in Rhode Island," EnCompass, n.d., http://library.providence.edu/encompass/african-american-civil-rights-in-rhode-island/african-american-civil-rights-in-rhode-island/.
33. "African Americans in Rhode Island 2015," Rhode Island Department of Health, The Office of Minority Health, 2015, https://health.ri.gov/publications/factsheets/minorityhealthfacts/AfricanAmerican.pdf.
34. Amy Russo, "New Providence Board Weighs How to Offer Reparations, from Housing to Education," *The Providence Journal*, April 19, 2022. https://www.

providencejournal.com/story/news/local/2022/04/19/providence-weighs-reparations-payments-housing-education/7356501001/.
35. National Congress of American Indians, "Resolution."
36. Tom Wanamaker, "Let the Games Begin: Casinos, Cigarettes and Rhode Island," ICT, September 12, 2018, https://indiancountrytoday.com/archive/let-the-games-begin-casinos-cigarettes-and-rhode-island.
37. Alex Nunes, "In Charlestown, Critics Say Special Solicitor Position Is 'Discriminating against One Group of People,'" *The Public's Radio*, January 18, 2022, https://thepublicsradio.org/article/in-charlestown-critics-say-special-solicitor-position-is-discriminating-against-one-group-of-people.
38. Marta Martinez, *Latino History in Rhode Island: Nuestras Raices* (Gloucestershire, UK: The History Press, 2014).
39. Interview with Pablo Rodriguez by the author, June 8, 2022.
40. Martinez, *Latino History*.
41. "Former Central Falls Mayor Pleads Guilty to Soliciting and Accepting a Bribe; Court Vacates Conviction for Accepting Gratuities," United States Attorney's Office District of Rhode Island, February 28, 2014, https://www.justice.gov/usao-ri/pr/former-central-falls-mayor-pleads-guilty-soliciting-and-accepting-bribe-court-vacates.
42. Rhode Island General Assembly, Black and Latino Caucus, https://www.rilegislature.gov/commissions/blackandlatincaucus/Pages/welcome.aspx.
43. Eli Sherman and Ted Nesi, "Biden Outperforms Clinton; Trump Makes Gains in RI Latino Communities," *WPRI*, November 4, 2020, https://www.wpri.com/news/elections/biden-outperforms-clinton-trump-makes-gains-in-ri-latino-communities/.
44. "Immigrants in Rhode Island," American Immigration Council, August 6, 2020, https://www.americanimmigrationcouncil.org/research/immigrants-in-rhode-island#:~:text=More%20than%2018%2C000%20U.S.%20citizens,total%20state%20population%20in%202016.
45. Melanie DaSilva, "McKee Signs Bill Ensuring in-State Tuition for RI Students, Regardless of Immigration Status," *WPRI*, October 18, 2021, https://www.wpri.com/news/local-news/providence/bill-ensures-in-state-tuition-for-ri-students-regardless-of-immigration-status/.
46. Katherine Gregg, "Senate Panel Approves Driver's Permits for Undocumented Immigrants," *The Providence Journal*, April 28, 2022, https://www.providencejournal.com/story/news/politics/2022/04/28/drivers-licenses-undocumented-immigrants-ri-senate-vote/9569857002/.
47. Ted Nesi, "RI Overcounted Population in 2020 Census, Federal Study Finds," *WPRI*, May 19, 2022, https://www.wpri.com/news/politics/ri-overcounted-population-in-2020-census-federal-study-finds/.
48. Liz Crampton, "There Are Just 9 Female Governors. Both Parties Want Change," *Politico*, September 2021, https://www.politico.com/news/2021/09/29/the-fifty-women-governors-499533.
49. See Maureen Moakley, "A Gender Gap Against Raimondo," Op-ed in *Providence Journal*, November 13, 2019, https://www.providencejournal.com/story/opinion/2019/11/13/my-turn-maureen-moakley-gender-gap-against-raimondo/2299144007/
50. Dan McGowan, "Gina Raimondo Isn't Here to Talk about the Past. But the Failed Hospital Merger and the Providence School Takeover Should Haunt Her," *The Boston Globe*, March 15, 2022, https://www.bostonglobe.com/2022/03/15/metro/

gina-raimondo-isnt-here-talk-about-past-failed-hospital-merger-providence-school-takeover-should-haunt-her/?p1=StaffPage.
51. Alexa Gagosz, "Boston Globe/Suffolk University Poll of Likely Rhode Island Voters: Explore the Data," *The Boston Globe*, June 27, 2022, https://www.bostonglobe.com/2022/06/27/metro/explore-data-boston-globesuffolk-university-poll-likely-rhode-island-voters/.
52. "Rhode Island," Rutgers Eagleton Institute of Politics, Center for American Women and Politics, n.d., https://cawp.rutgers.edu/state_fact_sheets/ri.
53. "2022 Women in Municipal Office," Rutgers Eagleton Institute of Politics, Center for American Women and Politics, n.d., https://cawp.rutgers.edu/2022-women-municipal-office.
54. Jim Leech and Jacquie McNish, "How the Rhode Island Treasurer Slayed Her State Pension Dragon," *The Globe and Mail*, November 2, 2013, https://www.theglobeandmail.com/globe-investor/retirement/how-the-rhode-island-treasurer-slayed-her-state-pension-dragon/article15225383/.
55. Gina M. Raimondo, "Truth In Numbers: The Security and Sustainability of Rhode Island's Retirement System," National Association of State Retirement Administrators, State of Rhode Island Office of the General Treasurer, June 2011, https://www.nasra.org/files/State-Specific/Rhode%20Island/TIN-WEB-06-1-11.pdf.
56. Monique Morrissey, "Truth in Numbers? A Brief History of Cuts to the Employees' Retirement System of Rhode Island," Economic Policy Institute, June 20, 2013, https://www.epi.org/publication/bp363-brief-history-of-cuts-to-the-employees-retirement-system-of-rhode-island/.
57. John G. Dickerson, "Gina Raimondo's Shining Example—Pension Reform In Rhode Island." California Policy Center, January 28, 2013. https://californiapolicycenter.org/gina-raimondos-shining-example-pension-reform-in-rhode-island/.
58. "US States By Population of Catholics," *World Atlas*, n.d., https://www.worldatlas.com/articles/us-states-by-population-of-catholics.html.
59. Kevin Mahnken, "Johns Hopkins Report Offers 'Devastating' Findings for Providence Schools, Sparking Talk of State Takeover," *The 74*, June 26, 2019, https://www.the74million.org/article/johns-hopkins-report-offers-devastating-findings-for-providence-schools-sparking-talk-of-state-takeover/.
60. "Job Training Programs," State of Rhode Island Department of Labor and Training, n.d., https://dlt.ri.gov/individuals/job-training-programs.
61. "100 Percent Renewable Electricity by 2030," State of Rhode Island Office of Energy Resources, n.d., https://energy.ri.gov/renewable-energy/100-percent-renewable-electricity-2030#:~:text=In%20January%202020%2C%20Executive%20Order,with%20renewable%20energy%20by%202030.
62. Meg Dalton, "Rhode Island Looks to Spare Green Space with Brownfield Solar Projects," *Energy News Network*, December 10, 2018, https://energynews.us/2018/12/10/rhode-island-looks-to-spare-green-space-with-brownfield-solar-projects/.
63. "Rhode Island Constitution Art. I, § 17, "Fishery Rights—Shore Privileges—Preservation of Natural Resources," *FindLaw*, January 1, 2019, https://codes.findlaw.com/ri/rhode-island-constitution/ri-const-art-i-sect-17.html.
64. Patrick Anderson, "Political Scene: Beach-Access Politics Heating up This Summer," *The Providence Journal*, June 28, 2021, https://www.providencejournal.com/story/news/politics/2021/06/28/political-scene-beach-access-politics-heating-up-summer/5343990001/.

65. Antonia Noori Farzan, "Shoreline Access Bill Unanimously Passes RI House; Awaits Senate Action," *The Providence Journal*, June 2, 2022, https://www.providencejournal.com/story/news/politics/2022/06/02/ri-house-passes-shoreline-access-bill-awaits-senate-action/7482398001/.
66. Tom Mooney, "Months after DCYF Got Money to Fill 91 Positions, No One Has Been Hired," *The Providence Journal*, October 18, 2021, https://www.providencejournal.com/story/news/local/2021/10/18/dcyf-slow-fill-91-positions-approved-ri-lawmakers/8512420002/.
67. Ian Duncan, "Under Federal Rules, 'Significant Progress' on Infrastructure Can Mean More Road Deaths and Decrepit Bridges," *The Boston Globe*, March 17, 2022, https://www.bostonglobe.com/2022/03/17/metro/under-federal-rules-significant-progress-infrastructure-can-mean-more-road-deaths-decrepit-bridges/?et_rid=589784446&s_campaign=rhodemap%3Anewsletter.
68. Alexa Gagosz, "Senator Mendes and Others Have Slept in Tents Outside the R.I. State House for a Week. Now, a Storm Is Coming," *The Boston Globe*, December 8, 2021, https://www.bostonglobe.com/2021/12/07/metro/senator-mendes-others-have-slept-tents-outside-ri-state-house-week-now-storm-is-coming/.

2 / Rhode Island Constitutional Development 1636–2020

PATRICK T. CONLEY*

The Colonial Era: to 1763

Government in Rhode Island began when religious exile Roger Williams and about a dozen disciples founded Providence in the spring of 1636. During the town's early months, a fortnightly meeting of "masters of families," or "householders," conducted civic affairs, considering matters relating to the "common peace, watch, and planting." As the number of settlers increased, a formal government became necessary, so Williams and the initial settlers drafted articles of self incorporation in 1637.

These documents were the fundamental papers of Providence town government. The major features of these first governmental agreements were the vesting of administrative control in a majority of the householders and the all important proviso that they were to exercise such control "only in civil things." This latter clause reflected the desire of Roger Williams to establish a colony based on the then revolutionary principles of religious liberty and the separation of church and state.[1]

Legal title to the lands on which the early towns were planted rested only upon deeds from the Narragansett chiefs, or sachems, because Williams had been so bold as to declare that the king of England's authority to grant these New World lands to English colonists rested upon "a solemn public lie." This view, though just, was unacceptable to the neighboring colonies of Plymouth, Massachusetts Bay, Connecticut, and New Haven. The more orthodox Puritans who resided therein, angered by the defiance of Rhode Island's religious outcasts,

---

*This chapter is an abridged version of "Rhode Island Constitutional Development" by Patrick T. Conley, which served as the introduction to Patrick T. Conley and Robert Flanders, *The Rhode Island State Constitution: A Reference Guide*, Praeger, 2007 and reprinted by Oxford University Press in 2011.

began to cast covetous eyes upon the beautiful Narragansett Bay region, which, they said, had been transformed by Williams and his kind into "a moral sewer."[2]

To unite the towns against this threat, and to secure parliamentary protection for his holy experiment, Williams journeyed in 1643 to an England on the verge of civil war to secure a patent that would unite the settlements of Portsmouth, Newport, and Providence into a single colony and officially confirm the settlers' claims to the lands they held by Indian purchase. Williams obtained the desired patent from Robert Rich, earl of Warwick, and his parliamentary Committee on Foreign Plantations.

The patent of March 14, 1644—or 1643 using England's old style calendar—was the first legal recognition of the Rhode Island towns by the mother country and served as an embryonic constitution. It authorized the union of Providence, Portsmouth, and Newport under the name of "the Incorporation of Providence Plantations in Narragansett Bay in New England," and it granted these towns "full power and authority to govern and rule themselves" and future inhabitants by majority decision. It specifically conferred political power upon the inhabitants of the towns. The repeated emphasis of the document upon "civil government" gave implicit sanction to the separation of church and state. Williams was greeted with great enthusiasm when he returned to Providence, patent in hand, in September 1644.[3]

The towns embraced the legislative patent and initially met on Aquidneck Island in November 1644. After this and three subsequent sessions, they held the momentous Portsmouth Assembly of May 1647 to organize a government and to draft and adopt a body of laws. They further declared that the form of government for the colony was "democratical," in that it rested on "the free and voluntary consent of all, or the greater part of the free inhabitants." According to Charles McLean Andrews, the leading historian of colonial America, "the acts and orders of 1647 constitute one of the earliest programmes for a government and one of the earliest codes of law made by any body of men in America and the first to embody in all its parts the precedents set by the laws and statutes of England."[4]

The 1647 Assembly, which by then included Samuel Gorton's Warwick settlement, elected officers, established a system of representation, and devised a legislative process containing provisions both for local initiative (repealed in 1650) and popular referendum. Then it enacted the remarkable code, an elaborate body of criminal and civil law prefaced by a bill of rights. Finally, for the administration of justice, the productive Assembly established a General Court of Trials with jurisdiction over all important legal questions.

The president, who was the chief officer of the colony, and the assistants, who represented their respective towns, were to constitute this high tribunal. By inference, the existing town courts were to possess the jurisdiction they heretofore exercised in matters of minor and local importance.

There were still stormy seas ahead for the Rhode Island ship of state, for no sooner had a semblance of internal unity and stability been created than two external dangers arose, one of which menaced the colony's landed possessions and the other its very existence. The first danger resulted from the claims of the Connecticut based Atherton Land Company to much of present day Washington County; the second and greater threat arose from the restoration of the Stuart dynasty to the throne of England in 1660. The Restoration rendered doubtful the legal validity of the parliamentary patent of 1644 and placed Rhode Island in a precarious position because of her close ties with the antimonarchial Commonwealth and Protectorate of Oliver Cromwell.

Fearful for its legal life, the colony commissioned the diligent Dr. John Clarke to obtain royal confirmation of its right to exist. Clarke, with the assistance of Connecticut agent John Winthrop Jr., secured from Charles II the Royal Charter of 1663. This coveted document was immediately transported to Rhode Island, where it was received by the grateful colonists in November 1663.

The 6,500 word constitutional instrument had the legal form of a corporate or trading company charter. It devoted relatively brief space to the organization of government, but it did provide for the offices of governor, deputy governor, and ten assistants. The original holders of these positions were named in the Charter itself, but their successors, called magistrates, were "to be from time to time, constituted, elected, and chosen at large out of the freemen" of the colony (or "company").

The Charter also provided that certain of the freemen should be "elected or deputed" by a majority vote of fellow freemen in their respective towns to "consult," to "advise," and to "determine" the affairs of the colony together with the governor, deputy governor, and assistants. It specified that Newport was entitled to six of these "elected or deputed" representatives; Providence, Portsmouth, and Warwick received four each, and two were to be granted to any town that might be established in the future. This was an equitable apportionment in 1663, but in the early nineteenth century it would become a source of grave discontent.

The governor, deputy governor, assistants, and representatives (or deputies) were collectively called the General Assembly. Rhode Island's legislature was endowed by the Charter with extraordinary power, much of which it retained until 2004. It could make or repeal any law, if such action was not "repugnant" to the laws of England; it could exercise extensive powers over the judicial affairs of the colony, prescribe punishments for legal offenses, grant pardons, regulate elections, create and incorporate additional towns, and "choose, nominate and appoint such . . . persons as they shall think fit" to hold the status of freemen.

The Royal Charter also mandated annual elections for all at large officers of the colony, provided for the raising and governing of a militia, and granted rights of commerce and fishery. The Charter's most liberal and generous provision bestowed upon the inhabitants of the tiny colony "full liberty in religious concernments." The document commanded that no person shall be "molested, punished, disquieted, or called in question for any differences in opinion in matters of religion" that "do not actually disturb the civil peace of our said colony." As Williams observed, this liberality stemmed from the king's willingness to "experiment" in order to ascertain "whether civil government could consist with such liberty of conscience."

This was the "lively experiment" on which the government of Rhode Island rested—an experiment that prompted some to observe that Massachusetts had law without liberty, but Rhode Island now had liberty without law.

The Charter of 1663 won the overwhelming approval of the colonists, and with good reason: as the nineteenth century American historian and longtime summer resident of Newport George Bancroft remarked, with only slight exaggeration, "Nowhere in the world were life, liberty and property, safer than in Rhode Island."[6]

During the last three decades of the seventeenth century, Rhode Island's governmental progress was halting and uneven. In 1675 and 1676 King Philip's War—a fierce struggle with the Wampanoag, Nipmuck, and Narragansett Indians—caused racial embitterment, drained the colonial treasury, disrupted civil government, caused widespread property damage, and took a high toll of human lives. From 1686 to 1689 Rhode Island's Charter was suspended as King James II attempted to consolidate the coastal colonies from New Jersey to Maine under one regional government called the Dominion of New England.

That the seventeenth century ended with Rhode Island intact was a minor miracle. Despite freewheeling dissenters, jealous neighbors, internal secessionists, hostile Indians, avaricious land speculators, and imperial reorganizers, Rhode Island survived.

From 1696 onward, however, the colony began to achieve a measure of stability. In that year the General Assembly developed more systematic and workable procedures and formally became bicameral, dividing into the House of Magistrates, or Senate, and the House of Deputies, or Representatives. Then, in 1719, the Assembly issued its first printed compilation of Rhode Island's general laws. On the debit side, this digest contained a statute banning Catholics and Jews from voting or holding office—a violation of the spirit, if not the letter, of the Charter of 1663.

An important territorial development was the creation of the county system in 1703. The five counties created between 1703 and 1750 influenced the operations of Rhode Island's government for more than a century. The county system served mainly to systematize judicial proceedings. Because legislative and judicial functions were for a time combined in the same body of men (namely, the governor, deputy governor, and assistants), the General Assembly often exercised functions now considered the exclusive domain of the judicial branch. Almost any part of the judicial process was open to its inspection and possible correction.

The development of executive power under the Charter of 1663 was comparable to the growth of judicial autonomy: both were repressed by the powerful legislature. Apart from making the governor the presiding officer of the General Assembly and granting him the right to convene special sessions of that body, the Charter bestowed upon him few exclusive powers of significance. As little more than the executive agent of the Assembly, he had no appointive power, for that important prerogative resided in the legislature. Even the governor's Charter-conferred position of commander-in-chief was carefully circumscribed by the Assembly.

A final significant implementation of the Charter concerned the creation of freemen and their consequent power to vote. In 1723 a statute was passed by the Assembly that set the first specific landed requirement for town freemanship. The law stipulated that a person must be a "freeholder of lands, tenements, or hereditaments in such town where he shall be admitted free, of the value of one hundred pounds, or the [rental] value of forty shillings per annum, or the eldest son of such a freeholder." In 1729 the real estate requirement was increased to £200, and in 1746 to £400, but by 1760 it had been reduced to £49 (about $134.)

While the incentive to participate politically was not widespread, it was strong in some quarters, as evidenced by the development of an extraconstitutional system of two party politics in the generation preceding the American Revolution. Opposing groups, one headed by Samuel Ward and the other by Stephen Hopkins, were organized with sectional overtones; generally speaking (though there were notable exceptions), the merchants and farmers of southern Rhode Island, led by Ward, battled with their counterparts from Providence and its environs, the faction led by Hopkins. The principal goal of these groups was to secure control of the powerful legislature in order to obtain the host of public offices—from chief justice to inspector of tobacco—at the disposal of that body. In these circumstances the governor, as party leader, acquired an informal influence far beyond his meager official power.

The salient and most significant feature of Rhode Island government under the Charter was that the crucial electoral arena was the colony—and later the state—as a unit. The governor and deputy governor, together with a secretary, an attorney general, and a treasurer, were elected annually in April on a colony wide or at large basis, as were ten "assistants" who constituted the upper house. Only the deputies, elected semiannually in April and August, were chosen on a local basis. Thus, there existed an obvious inducement to form colony-wide parties in order to elect a full slate of general officers.

The Revolutionary Era: 1764–1790

In the eyes of the colony's conservative critics, the land of Roger Williams, on the eve of the American Revolution, was "dangerously democratic." Chief Justice Daniel Horsmanden of New York, in a 1773 report to the earl of Dartmouth during the investigation into the June 1772 burning of the English customs sloop *Gaspee*, disdainfully described Rhode Island as a "downright democracy" whose governmental officials were "entirely controlled by the populace," and conservative Massachusetts governor Thomas Hutchinson lamented to George III that Rhode Island was "the nearest to a democracy of any of your colonies."

Rhode Islanders of the Revolutionary generation and their individualistic forebears knew well that they enjoyed near autonomy within the empire and broad powers of self government within their colony, and they were also keenly aware that their self determination flowed in large measure from the munificent Charter of Charles II. Thus, they harbored a passionate attachment to that document and defended it against all challenges. Allowed to weather the Revolutionary upheaval, the Charter would remain the basic law of the state until 1843—a point far beyond its useful life.

The Revolution was a blow from which Newport never fully recovered. British occupation adversely affected both its population and its prosperity. From this period onward, numerical and economic ascendancy inexorably moved northward to Providence and the surrounding mainland communities.[7]

The Revolution did not alter Rhode Island's governmental structure, but it did prompt some legal and political changes. For example, the Revolution and the reform sentiments it generated influenced legislation affecting Catholics and Black slaves. Whatever anti-Catholicism existed in Rhode Island was mollified by assistance rendered to the struggling colonials by Catholic France and by the benevolent presence of large numbers of French troops in Newport under General Rochambeau, some of whom remained when the struggle was over. The General Assembly in February 1783 removed the disability against Roman Catholics, imposed in 1719, by giving members of that religion "all the rights and privileges of the Protestant citizens of this state." In 1798 a legislative bill of rights removed the voting restriction for those of the Jewish faith.

The most significant of several statutes relating to Blacks was the Emancipation Act of 1784. With a preface invoking sentiments of Locke, that "all men are entitled to life, liberty, and property," the manumission measure gave freedom to all children born to slave mothers after March 1, 1784.[8] The Emancipation Act was followed by a concerted effort of Rhode Island reformers—the influential Quaker community—to ban the slave trade. This agitation had a salutary result when the General Assembly enacted a measure in October 1787 prohibiting any Rhode Island citizen from engaging in this barbarous traffic. The legislature termed the trade inconsistent with "that more enlightened and civilized state of freedom which has of late prevailed."[9]

In 1778 the state quickly ratified the Articles of Confederation, with its weak central government, but when the movement to strengthen that government developed in the mid-1780s, Rhode Island balked. The state's individualism, its democratic localism, and its tradition of autonomy caused it to resist the centralizing tendencies of the federal Constitution. This opposition was intensified by an agrarian debtor revolt in support of the issuance of paper money. Suspicious of the power and the cost of a government too far removed from the grassroots level, it declined to dispatch delegates to the Philadelphia Convention of 1787, which drafted the United States Constitution. Then, when that document was presented to the states for ratification, this faction delayed (and nearly prevented) Rhode Island's approval.[10]

In the period between September 1787 and January 1790, the rural dominated General Assembly rejected no fewer than eleven attempts by the representatives from the mercantile communities to convene a state ratifying convention. Instead, the Assembly defied the instructions of the Founding Fathers and conducted a popular referendum on the Constitution. That election, which was boycotted by the supporters of stronger union (called Federalists), rejected the Constitution by a vote of 2,714 to 238.

Under strong federal and internal pressure, Rhode Island finally called a ratifying convention in January 1790 by a one-vote margin. The first session met in South Kingstown in March and adjoined in May offering 36 amendments to the new basic law.

Enraged Federalists threatened Rhode Island with tariffs and made other financial demands; Providence threatened to secede from the state if ratification did not occur. This pressure brought compliance. On May 29, 1790, Rhode Island ratified the Constitution by a vote of 34 to 32, the narrowest margin of any state. The approval was accompanied by 21 suggested amendments to the founding document.

Rhode Island's course during this turbulent era—first in war, last in peace—is attributable in part to its tradition of individualism, self reliance, and dissent. Most of its residents feared the encroachment on local autonomy by any central government, whether located in London, Philadelphia, or Washington. This ideology, coupled with the economic concerns of the agrarian community, explain Rhode Island's wariness toward the work of the "Grand Convention."

Because the Constitution three times gave implied assent to slavery, the influential Quaker community also denounced it. These factors explain the strength of Antifederalism. Small wonder that "Rogue's Island," as Federalists called it, withheld ratification.[11]

The Early National Period: 1790–1840

The year 1790 marked the state's grudging acceptance of the new federal Constitution and also saw an event that served as a catalyst in Rhode Island's transition from a mercantile and agrarian economy to one based principally upon industry. That event, which some have lavishly termed "the beginning of America's Industrial Revolution," was the reconstruction of a cotton-spinning frame and its employment in a mill at Pawtucket Falls, the last plunge of the Blackstone River on its course to the Seekonk and thence to Narragansett Bay.

The men chiefly responsible for this promising venture were Providence merchant Moses Brown, who was seeking to diversify his business interests, and Samuel Slater. The latter was a young Englishman with technical knowledge and managerial experience acquired in the Derbyshire cotton industry, hired by the enterprising Brown for this industrial experiment. This combination of capital and craftsmanship was successful; in December 1790 cotton yarn was spun by waterpower for the first time in America. Gradually, almost imperceptibly at first, from this event began a metamorphosis in Rhode Island that would alter not only the state's economy but its political, constitutional, and social complexion as well.

By 1840 Providence was the industrial leader in a rapidly industrializing state and the possessor of the best-balanced and most-diversified manufacturing economy. It owed this primacy to its superior financial resources and banking facilities, its development of steam power, its position as the center of the base-metal industry, and its emergence as the hub of Rhode Island's transportation network, hosting a railroad terminal and serving as the outlet for the Blackstone Canal. As the 1830s drew to a close, Providence (then only one third its present geographical size) was well on the way to becoming the metropolitan center of southern New England.

The transition and expansion of Rhode Island's economy had a profound impact upon the political culture of the state and upon what one might term its constitutional demography. Industrialization not only effected significant changes in the distribution of population and the rate of population growth; these changes in turn precipitated demands for constitutional reform, especially in the area of legislative apportionment, because the Charter's allocation of representatives was not only rigid but, as successive census reports revealed, increasingly inequitable.

Population and immigration trends pointed to the rise of a landless class of artisans and factory workers in crowded mill villages. In Rhode Island the statutory freehold qualification disfranchised this group, and as industrialization progressed, the number of these second-class citizens multiplied.

Politically, declining rural populations jealously guarded the prerogatives of their community and watched the rise of the northern towns with awe and apprehension. They were estranged economically and socially from the native-born factory operatives of the mill villages, and they were worlds apart from the immigrant Irish laborers who began to add to the burgeoning industrial population in the decade of the 1830s. The outnumbered rural folk regarded reapportionment and "free suffrage" as their political death knell. Their position on these issues strengthened and stiffened with each passing year and reached unparalleled intensity by 1840, as it became clear that the mounting though landless industrial population would increasingly be composed of such "undesirables" as Irish Catholic immigrants. The stand of these agrarians was diametrically opposed to majoritarian principles and the powerful national trends toward suffrage extension and equal representation.

By 1840 the battle lines were drawn. Although the categories were far from rigid, generally the expanding towns were arrayed against the static and declining, the industrial sectors against the agrarian, the north and east against the south and west. A dynamic and irresistible force struggled against a reactionary and seemingly immovable object, with political ascendancy the prize.

During the fifty years (1790-1840) when these political battles were occurring, the structure of Rhode Island's government remained virtually unchanged, owing to the inflexibility of the colonial Charter, which was still the state's basic law. Sustained agitation for reapportionment of the General Assembly and for a diminution of its powers, beginning in 1817, led the reluctant legislature to authorize two constitutional conventions, in 1824 and 1834. Both failed. The legislature's tactic was obvious: by requiring constitutional conventions to be apportioned in the same ratio as decreed by the Charter and to be manned by delegates qualified and elected under the existing, restrictive suffrage statute, the legislature contrived to prevent any significant change in its structure or power.[12]

The Dorr Rebellion and Its Aftermath: 1841-1854

Reformers such as Thomas Wilson Dorr attacked this system and those who supported it. Industrialization and its corollary, urbanization, combined by the 1840s to produce an episode known as the Dorr Rebellion, Rhode Island's crisis in constitutional government. The state's Royal Charter, nearing its 180th anniversary with hardly a change or a blemish, gave disproportionate influence to declining rural towns, conferred almost unlimited power on the General Assembly, and contained no procedure for its own amendment. State legislators, regardless of party, insisted upon retaining the old real estate requirement for voting and officeholding, even though it had been abandoned in all other states. As Rhode Island grew more urbanized, this freehold qualification became more restrictive. By 1840 about 60 percent of the state's free adult males were disfranchised.

Because earlier moderate efforts at change had been virtually ignored by the General Assembly, the reformers of 1840-43 organized as the Rhode Island Suffrage Association, embraced a radical theory called "popular constituent sovereignty," bypassed the legislature, and convened a People's Convention, equitably apportioned and chosen by an enlarged electorate. Thomas Wilson Dorr, a patrician attorney, assumed the leadership of the movement in late 1841 and became the principal draftsman of the progressive People's Constitution, which was ratified by a popular referendum in December 1841 by a margin of 13,944 to 52.

The People's Constitution remedied many of the abuses that existed under the Charter regime. It eliminated the statutory landholding requirement by a clause that extended suffrage to white male citizens with one-year's residency in the state. Its reapportionment provision increased the House representation of Providence and other urbanized centers; it contained a secret ballot clause, made education a fundamental right in a progressive bill of rights, diminished the power of the General Assembly by providing for a clear separation of powers in a three-branch system, and established a workable amendment process. Dorr was elected governor under this document in April 1842, while the Charter adherents reelected Whig incumbent Samuel Ward King of Johnston in separate balloting.

With the two rival governments preparing to assume power on May 3–4 under their respective basic laws, a clash appeared imminent. On Tuesday, May 3, the suffragists prefaced their accession to office by staging a colorful parade to the Providence statehouse on North Main Street. The eventual setting of the People's legislature diminished the luster and triumph of the occasion. Since the Law and Order faction (as the defenders of the Charter government were called) had locked the statehouse—which contained the state's seal, its archives, and other symbols of sovereignty—the suffragists were forced to retreat to a preselected alternative site, an unfinished foundry building on Eddy Street near Dorrance, to conduct their legislative deliberations.

Dorr ruefully observed "that it was here that the cause was defeated, if not lost." In Dorr's view, therefore, the failure to possess the statehouse as a symbol of legitimacy loomed large in deciding the unhappy fate of the People's Party. The reformers were resisted by a Law and Order coalition of Whigs and rural Democrats led by Governor King and a "council of war," consisting of Democratic former governor James Fenner and six prominent Whigs. Operating from the Newport statehouse, they authorized the use of force and intimidation to prevent the implementation of the People's Constitution. At the Providence arsenal and at Acote's Hill in Chepachet such force was effective.

Although the Dorr Rebellion had been effectually ended, the turmoil and popular agitation against the Charter forced the victors to consent to the drafting of a written state constitution. Their Law and Order coalition held its officially sanctioned convention in Newport's statehouse during September 1842. It reconvened in East Greenwich in early November and sent its handiwork to the General Assembly, then meeting in that town, which set November 21–23 as the referendum dates.

Arthur May Mowry, the first major historian of the Dorr War, calls this instrument "liberal and well-adapted to the needs of the state" because it improved House apportionment, contained a comprehensive bill of rights, and removed the real estate requirement for native-born citizens. Mowry's appraisal, however, neglects one important item: this constitution established a $134 freehold suffrage qualification for naturalized citizens, and this anti-Irish Catholic restriction—not removed until 1888—was the most blatant instance of political nativism found in any state constitution in the land. Other defects included the stranglehold on the Senate that the document gave to the rural towns (there was to be one senator from each town, regardless of its population), cumbersome amendment procedures that made reform of the document a very difficult task, the lack of a mechanism for the call of future constitutional conventions, and the absence of a secret ballot. This constitution, overwhelmingly ratified in November 1842 by a margin of 7,024 to 51, became effective in May 1843. Despite the margin of victory, the turnout was meager, for there were more than 23,000 adult male citizens in the state. That the opposition, in mute protest, refrained from voting explains in part the constitution's apathetic reception and the lopsided vote.

In 1849 Dorr's attempt at vindication was dashed when the United States Supreme Court refused to decide if the People's government was legitimate. In the case of *Luther v. Borden*, Chief Justice Roger B. Taney devised the Political Question Doctrine, asserting that the Supreme Court was not the proper authority to conduct a retroactive investigation of the rival claims to sovereignty. That determination, said Taney, was not vested with the Court but rather with the political branches—Congress and the president, the state legislature, and the governor. To Dorr's chagrin, Taney simultaneously placed primary responsibility for the Constitution's guarantee of a republican form of government (which Dorr claimed the Charter regime was not) on Congress and the president and withdrew the courts from playing any role in its enforcement.

The Republican Ascendancy: 1854–1935

The Know-Nothing, or American, Party was a political aberration formed during the early 1850s in many northeastern states to curb the recent heavy influx of Catholic immigrants and to delay the citizenship applications of those already here. The rise of the American Party was a byproduct of the disintegration of the second national party system (Democrats vs. Whigs) and the emergence of a third. By 1854 the Whig party—split nationally over the issue of slavery into "Cotton" and "Conscience"—was fragmented locally. Those who considered the spread of slavery the country's greatest evil embraced the newly formed Republican Party, while those who saw Catholic immigration as the main menace joined the American (KnowNothing) Party, at least temporarily.

* * *

During the turbulent 1850s two notable governmental changes occurred. In November 1854 the quaint but cumbersome custom of rotating General Assembly sessions among the five county seats was abolished by Article of Amendment III to the state constitution. This revision stated that "there shall be one session of the General Assembly holden annually on the last Tuesday in May at Newport and an adjournment from the same shall be holden annually at Providence." The smallest state thus progressed from five capitals to only two.[14]

In 1856 the new constitution's nebulous language pertaining to the independence of the judiciary was clarified. In the landmark case of *Taylor v. Place*, Chief Justice Samuel Ames once and for all rejected the power of the General Assembly to review or reverse decisions of the highest state court.[15]

During the last third of the nineteenth century and the first third of the twentieth, the GOP skillfully maintained its political dominance. Such party stalwarts as US senator and *Providence Journal* publisher Henry Bowen Anthony (1815–84) and his protégés Charles Ray Brayton (1840–1910) and US Senator Nelson W. Aldrich (1841–1915) consistently deflected attempts by Yankee reformers and Irish Catholic Democrats to dislodge the Republicans by altering the state constitution.

For a quarter century after the arch-nativist Anthony's death in 1884, Aldrich and Brayton ran the Rhode Island GOP. Of this dynamic duo, Aldrich was "Mr. Outside," operating for thirty years on the national stage in concert with John D. Rockefeller Sr., J. P. Morgan, and other giants of business and finance. Officially, he was majority leader of the US Senate; unofficially, he was by common estimation "the general manager of the United States." Brayton, on the other hand, stayed home. As "Mr. Inside" he took charge of the nuts and bolts of GOP organization and discipline. His boldness was legendary. From 1901 until he was ousted by Democratic Governor James Higgins in 1907, Brayton, who was never a legislator, directed the actions of the General Assembly from the sheriff's office in the newly constructed (and present) statehouse. With the completion of that structure in 1900, Article of Amendment IX mandated that an annual session of the General Assembly convene at Providence beginning on the first Tuesday of January 1901—an enactment that left Providence the state's sole capital from that date onward.

The Republican organization of the Brayton-Aldrich era owed its ascendancy to many factors;, including (1) a malapportioned Senate that gave a legislative veto to the small rural towns; (2) a cumbersome amendment process to frustrate reform; (3) the absence of procedures for the calling of a constitutional convention; (4) the absence (until 1889) of a secret ballot; (5) a General Assembly that dominated both the legislatively elected Supreme Court and the weak, vetoless (until 1909) governorship; and (6) a real estate voting requirement for the naturalized citizen.

This last-mentioned check was eliminated by the Bourn Amendment (Article VII) in 1888, but it was replaced by a $134 property tax paying qualification for voting in city council elections. This requirement had the practical effect of preventing those at the lower socioeconomic levels, usually Catholic immigrants, from exercising control over the affairs of the cities in which they resided. This was true because the mayors, for whom all electors could vote, had very limited powers, while the councils, for whom only property owners could vote, were dominant, controlling both the purse and the patronage.[16]

The Equal Rights Movement of the 1880s, led by Irish American attorney Charles E. Gorman, demanded a constitutional convention to effect sweeping reforms in Rhode Island's basic law, especially in the area of voting rights. That effort was stymied in 1883 by a Republican-dominated state Supreme Court, which rendered an advisory opinion to the Senate declaring that a constitutional convention could not be convened either by the people (as the Dorrites had done) or by the General Assembly. This incredible and reactionary ruling endured until after the Democrats seized control of state government in the "Bloodless Revolution" of 1935.

As if constitutional checks were not sufficient to ensure Republican control, Boss Brayton for good measure engineered the enactment in 1901 of a statute designed to weaken the power of any Democrat who might back into the governor's chair by virtue of a split in Republican ranks. With a few limited exceptions, this "Brayton Act" placed the ultimate appointive power of state government in the hands of the Senate. In the aftermath of its passage, a governor could effectively appoint only his private secretary and a handful of insignificant state officials.[17]

By 1920 the Senate—the possessor of state appointive and budgetary power—was more malapportioned than ever. For example, West Greenwich, population 367, had the same voice as Providence, population 237,595! The twenty smallest towns, with an aggregate population of 41,660, outvoted Providence 20 to 1, although the capital city had over 39 percent of Rhode Island's total population.

The Progressive Era (ca. 1898–1917) was an age of national reform—political, economic, and social—but Rhode Island's reactionary political and constitutional system survived the period relatively intact. The Brayton-Aldrich combine even survived a national exposé by noted muckraker Lincoln Steffens, who described Rhode Island as "A State for Sale" in a 1905 article for *McClure's Magazine*.

Although nearly all the reforms associated with the Progressive Era bypassed Rhode Island, one that finally succeeded after more than fifty years of local effort was women's suffrage. The battle, begun in Providence in 1868 by Paulina Wright Davis, Elizabeth Buffum Chace, and Anna Garlin Spencer, was won on January 6, 1920, when the state Senate (voting 38 to 1) and the House

(89 to 3) ratified the Nineteenth Amendment to the federal Constitution. The wide margins were deceptive, however, for the Assembly yielded only when it appeared that nationwide approval of women's suffrage was unavoidable. The Democrats lost no time in recruiting women candidates. In 1920 they ran Elizabeth Upham Yates for lieutenant governor and Helen I. Binning for secretary of state, and in 1922 and 1924 they nominated Susan Sharp Adams for the latter office. All four efforts were unsuccessful, and so the Democrats waited until 1982 to endorse another woman for the state ticket. With both major parties nominating women for secretary of state that year, Providence Republican Susan Farmer prevailed to become Rhode Island's first female general officer.

Despite their early failure to gain statewide elective office, women did register an important breakthrough in 1922 when Mrs. Isabelle Florence Ahearn O'Neill became Rhode Island's first female legislator. When she was elected in 1922 as a Democratic representative from the Broadway district of Providence, she was a teacher of elocution and physical education. Mrs. O'Neill served four terms as a member of the House education committee and two terms as state senator prior to retiring undefeated from elective office in 1935.

With the return of peace in Europe, Rhode Island's political wars resumed. The stormy decades of the 1920s and 1930s witnessed a major transition from Republican to Democratic control in state government. Economic unrest—stemming from such factors as the decline of the textile industry, the stock market crash of 1929, the ensuing Great Depression, and the local rise of organized labor—coupled with the development of cultural antagonisms between native and foreign stock weakened the normal allegiance of local Franco-Americans and Italian Americans to the Republican Party.

Simultaneously, vigorous efforts by the Irish-led Democratic Party to woo ethnics, key constitutional reforms such as the removal of the property-tax requirement for voting in council elections (by Amendment XX to the RI Constitution in 1928), a shift in control of the national Democratic Party from rural to urban leadership, the 1928 presidential candidacy of Irish Catholic Democrat Al Smith, and the social programs of Franklin D. Roosevelt's New Deal all combined by the early 1930s to pull the newer immigrant groups towards the Democratic fold.

The Bloodless Revolution and Its Aftermath: 1935–1939

By the General Assembly session of January 1935, Democratic leaders—especially Governor Theodore Francis Green, political boss Thomas P. McCoy of Pawtucket, State Senator William Moss, and Lieutenant Governor Robert Emmet Quinn—were on the verge of achieving political ascendancy by staging a governmental reorganization now known as the "Bloodless Revolution."

This bizarre coup made possible by a controversial scheme that gave the Democrats narrow control of the state Senate in defiance of election day returns, resulted in the repeal of the Brayton Act, the reorganization of the state government through the replacement of the commission system with the present departmental structure, the seizure of state patronage by the Democrats, and the dismissal of the entire five-member Republican Supreme Court.

The Democratic Ascendancy: 1940–85

In the four and a half decades from 1940 to 1985, the Democratic Party enjoyed its era of political dominance. Of the ten governors who served during that span, eight were Democrats; so too were all the members of the state's congressional delegation from 1940 until 1976. In addition, Republican control of Rhode Island's smaller towns was weakened by the large-scale influx of urban ethnics and the application of the "one man, one vote" principle to state legislatures by decisions of the US Supreme Court (*Reynolds* v. *Sims* and *Wesberry* v. *Sanders*). Prior to that time Senate apportionment gave small rural Republican towns an undue influence in state affairs. After the 1965 redistricting statute was enacted, however, the 50-member state Senate, like the 100-member House, became overwhelmingly Democratic.

By the three and a half century mark, Rhode Island's three branches of government were closer to parity, but the General Assembly remained dominant. Although the office of governor was little strengthened by the constitution of 1843, several subsequent amendments had enhanced the power of the chief executive. In 1909, Article of Amendment XV endowed him with veto power, subject to a three-fifths override by the General Assembly. Two years later his term (together with that of the other four general officers) was lengthened from one to two years by Amendment XVI. The reorganization act of 1935 greatly enlarged the governor's appointment powers and his control over the state budget, both advances being made at the expense of the Senate.

Though the constitution of 1843 mandated a Supreme Court, the framers retained a close legislative check on the judiciary. In its *Taylor* v. *Place* ruling (1856), the not-so-high court asserted a measure of independence by terminating the Assembly's long-standing habit of reviewing and remanding its decisions. In 1903, Amendment XII ratified the *Taylor* rule and paved the way for the Court Reorganization Act of 1905. This statute, the root of our present system, established the county-based Superior Court and relieved the Supreme Court of its trial duties.

Constitutional Conventions and Amendments

The decades of Democratic ascendancy were quite active in a constitutional sense. One full-scale convention and five limited gatherings were held between 1944 and 1973. These limited sessions were called principally to effect constitutional change in a more rapid and less demanding manner than that provided in the cumbersome amendment procedures of the state's basic law. From 1843 through 1973 a constitutional amendment that originated in the General Assembly required passage by two successive assemblies, a general election intervening, and then ratification by a three-fifths vote of the qualified electors. The limited convention became a device to circumvent this difficult, time-consuming process, because an amendment proposed by such a body only required a majority vote of the qualified electors voting thereon for ratification.

The 1944 convention drafted Article of Amendment XXII, exempting servicemen from voter registration requirements while on active duty. The 1951 body, called to consider eight proposed amendments, produced six changes in the basic law; these included amendments repealing the poll tax (Article XXVII), establishing a system for the permanent registration of voters (Article XXIX), allowing a veterans' exemption from the taxpaying requirement for voting in financial town meetings (Article XXX), increasing the borrowing power of the state (Article XXXI), and providing for the use of eminent domain to acquire off-street parking (Article XXXII). In addition, this gathering drafted the municipal Home Rule Amendment—now Article XIII of the state constitution; designed to strengthen local self-government, this measure established a procedure whereby a city or town could draft its own charter to replace the legislative enactment under which all municipalities were then governed. Rhode Island's municipal system was fixed by the legislature to 8 cities and 31 towns, the last, West Warwick, created in 1913.

In December 1964 Rhode Island's first open, unlimited constitutional convention since 1842 convened. Its call had been approved and its delegates had been selected (81 Democrats and 19 Republicans) in the November 1964 general election. Former governor Dennis J. Roberts secured election as convention chairman.

The convention's blueprint for action was the well-crafted *Report of the Commission on Revision of the Rhode Island Constitution*, prepared in 1962 by a 13-member blue-ribbon legislative panel chaired by prominent Providence attorney and legal scholar William H. Edwards. For more than three years the convention dragged on, hampered by factionalism and extremely cumbersome rules that made delay the order of the day. Since the Democrats controlled the convention by a lopsided majority, both the *Providence Journal* and incumbent Republican Governor John H. Chafee repeatedly criticized the gathering and made political hay from its controversies and its conservatism. Ironically, such prodding encouraged some significant reforms.

Though the 1968 document was rejected by the voters, its defeat could be ascribed more to the opposition of the popular Republican governor, the terrible image of the previous convention that sat more than four years (probably the longest such conclave in the history of constitution making), and the reluctance of Democratic conservatives in that body to make innovations that might upset the status quo until forced to yield by public and, especially, media pressure. The voters, in effect, judged that constitution not by its content but by its parentage.

Though constitutional change was stymied in 1968, such persistent issues as legislative pay, lotteries, four-year terms for state officials, suffrage, and grand jury reform prompted a call for a limited constitutional convention in 1973 to consider these specific items. The enabling statute called for each political party to nominate one candidate in each of the fifty senatorial districts. Democrats cheated the system and gave their party a 56-to-41 delegate margin, with 3 independents, in the 100-member convention.

Ironically, the proposed convention was nearly aborted by the voters. Experts attributed opposition to the convention call to several factors: (1) the poor image of the recent 1964–69 convention; (b) a fear that the amendments proposed by the 1973 convention would be submitted to the voters as a package— an all-or-nothing proposition; and (c) public coolness toward a proposed legislative pay increase that the convention was authorized to discuss.

The fears of those who opposed the convention were largely dispelled by the efficient, workmanlike, bipartisan nature of the body. It opened on September 4 and adjourned on October 4 in accordance with the instructions of the General Assembly; it rejected the package ballot in favor of an item-by-item referendum; and it took a broad view of its powers in the four areas opened to it by the General Assembly and the people (viz. the grand jury, lotteries, election laws, and legislative compensation). This broad interpretation was especially evident in the delegates' response to the directive that they effect a "revision in the election laws." The convention regarded this instruction as enabling it to advance proposals dealing with such topics as financial disclosure of election contributions and election requirements for constitutional revision.

This convention ran smoothly, efficiently, and rapidly under the leadership of William E. Powers, a former attorney general and recently retired Supreme Court justice, and Professor Patrick T. Conley, the convention's secretary. It removed the last vestige of the ancient property qualification by eliminating the property-taxpaying requirement for participation in financial town meetings, and it enacted a campaign finance disclosure amendment (now Article IV, Section 9, of the state constitution). In addition, the convention expanded the role of grand juries, gave eighteen-year-olds the vote, and removed the ban on state lotteries. Its proposals for a legislative pay increase and four-year terms for general officers were narrowly rejected by the voters.

Its most important achievement, however, was the proposal that became

Article of Amendment XLII, and is now Article XIV, of the state's basic law. Sponsored by Secretary Conley, it streamlined the amendment process by requiring only a simple majority of the whole membership of each house of the General Assembly together with a majority of those electors voting thereon at a general election, and it set up a mechanism for the regular call of state constitutional conventions.

Article of Amendment XLII was the proximate cause of the highly productive 1985–86 open convention, ably presided over by attorney Keven McKenna. That assemblage, authorized in 1984 and elected in 1985, integrated the 44 amendments to the 1843 constitution into a concise, streamlined, "neutral rewrite" and created a new basic law for Rhode Island. Of this convention's proposals, the people ratified not only the neutral rewrite (and gender-neutral language) but also such political provisions as those creating an ethics commission, conferring budgetary power upon the governor, and banning felons from holding office for three years after their sentence has been completed. Perhaps the most significant changes emanating from that conclave were the environmental protection provisions of Article I, Sections 16 and 17.

Proposals for increasing legislators' pay (from the five dollars per day stipend that dated from 1900) and for giving the governor and general officers four-year terms were defeated by the electors in the 1986 general election, when the convention's handiwork appeared on the ballot. Also rejected were proposals creating a commission on judicial selection and discipline, the implementation of voter initiative, increased home rule for municipalities, and a controversial "paramount right to life" provision containing a ban on government funding of abortions and limiting the abortion procedure only "to prevent the death of a pregnant woman."[18]

The Modern Era

From 1986 to the present, Rhode Island's political system has survived several traumatic events. Two successive chief justices (Joseph Bevilacqua and Thomas Fay) resigned to avoid impeachment, and a governor (Edward DiPrete) served jail time for bribery and extortion, as did House Speaker Gordon Fox. In addition, the state's credit union system collapsed in 1991 because of lax regulation and fraudulent lending practices—all this despite a constitutionally created Ethics Commission and the activities of such citizen watchdog groups as Common Cause, Operation Clean Government, and Red Alert.

During the 1990s the legislature initiated several structural reforms via the amendment process, affecting all three branches of government; they included an amendment to Article IV, Section 1, lengthening the term of general officers from two years to four and making them subject to recall (ratified November

3, 1992); a change in Article VIII, Section 2, extricating the lieutenant governor from the legislative process by relieving him or her from the duty of serving as presiding officer of the Senate and the Grand Committee (ratified November 8, 1994, and effective in January 2003); an amendment increasing legislators' pay to ten thousand dollars per year and downsizing of the House of Representatives from 100 to 75 members and the Senate from 50 members to 38 (ratified November 8, 1994, effective January 2003); the addition of Article VI, Section 22, requiring both statewide and local referenda on any expansion of gambling; and the 1994 amendment to Article X, Sections 4 and 5, relating to judicial selection, which took the election of Supreme Court justices from the Grand Committee of the General Assembly and placed it in the hands of the governor acting in response to the recommendations of a judicial nominating commission—a long overdue reform. Briefly stated, it transferred the election of Supreme Court justices from the Grand Committee to the governor, and it directs the governor to fill any Supreme Court vacancy by nominating, on the basis of merit, a person from a list submitted by a judicial nominating commission with the consent of the House and Senate, acting separately. In addition, the justices so appointed hold their positions "during good behavior."

Separation of Powers Amendment

Article III, Section 8, of the 1986 constitution directed the General Assembly to establish an Ethics Commission, which it did. This commission, however, eventually turned on its creator by enacting both conflict-of-interest and separation-of-powers regulations to prevent legislators from serving on state administrative boards and commissions, and it thereby launched the momentous separation-of-powers controversy of the present era. In November 1997 Governor Lincoln Almond requested an advisory opinion from the Supreme Court regarding the constitutionality of these proposed commission regulations in light of the long-standing General Assembly practice to the contrary.

This attempt by the Ethics Commission to bar members of the General Assembly from making appointments to, or serving on, state administrative boards and commissions, styled Regulation 5014, posed a major constitutional question. In this century only the 1935 Supreme Court advisory opinion relative to the power of the General Assembly to call a constitutional convention rivaled this issue in significance.

In the actual argument before the justices on November 10, 1998, seven attorneys, including those representing the House, the Senate, the attorney general, and the American Civil Liberties Union, spoke on behalf of legislative power, while five advocates, including attorneys representing the governor, the Ethics Commission, Common Cause, the State Council of Churches, and the Environmental Council, urged the high court to uphold Regulation 36-14-5014.

On that day professor and attorney Patrick Conley argued a historically oriented *amicus* brief tracing the appointive power of the Rhode Island legislature from its origins in the Royal Charter of 1663 through two constitutions to the present. The Supreme Court agreed, but it was an uneasy settlement.[19]

The concrete case and controversy were not long in coming. The governor chose to fight the legislatively dominated Rhode Island Lottery Commission, which controlled millions of dollars in gambling revenue. In this high-visibility case, wherein the governor challenged the power of the commission to extend video gambling, Conley spoke as an expert witness at the Superior Court hearing before Judge Michael Silverstein. In that forum he testified first as a historian documenting absolute legislative control over state lotteries from their inception in 1744 for financing public improvement projects and private endeavors to their ban in the constitution of 1843. Then he testified as secretary of the 1973 constitutional convention concerning the intent of that body in removing the constitutional ban on state-run lotteries. Clearly, said Conley, that convention intended that the legislature create and control an agency to run a state lottery.

The Supreme Court agreed. In 2000, Chief Justice Joseph Weisberger for the majority (with Justice Maureen McKenna Goldberg abstaining and Justice Robert Flanders dissenting) upheld the power of the Lottery Commission to authorize an expansion of video gambling at Lincoln and Newport (the action that gave rise to the case). "The Rhode Island Constitution," said Weisberger, "does not prohibit the appointment of legislators to administrative boards and commissions." The Rhode Island General Assembly, he concluded, "unlike the federal Congress, need not look to the state Constitution as a source of authority by virtue of its historical plenary power (preserved in both the 1843 and 1986 Constitutions). It may exercise any power unless prohibited in this Constitution," and its delegation of power to the Lottery Commission was proper.

In the aftermath of his two decisive judicial setbacks, Governor Almond and his principal legal counsel, Joseph S. Larisa Jr., tried their luck in the court of public opinion. They boldly swayed that court by crafting advisory referenda that created an apparent mandate not only for the implementation of separation of powers but also for a major diminution of legislative power.

It contained no standards for a referendum's phraseology; hence it allowed leading questions that could be subjective, slanted, or argumentative and thereby give potentially false or exaggerated readings concerning the will of the electorate.

The 2002 referendum, Governor Almond's parting shot at the General Assembly, took direct aim at the legislature's historic powers. It read as follows:

QUESTION 5: QUESTION PROPOSED BY THE GOVERNOR (Rhode Island General Laws Section 17-5-2) CO-EQUAL BRANCHES OF GOVERNMENT (ADVISORY REFERENDUM) Should the Rhode Island Constitution be changed to eliminate Article 6, Section 10, which preserves to the General Assembly today broad powers granted to it by King Charles II of England in 1663 and also be changed to expressly provide that the legislative, executive, and judicial branches of Rhode Island government are to be separate and co-equal consistent with the American system of government?

This leading question linked Article VI, Section 10, the potent residual powers clause, to a seventeenth-century British monarch and concluded by suggesting that Rhode Island's three branches were not "consistent with the American system of government." Seventy-six percent of Rhode Island's electors rallied against king and for country by voting to approve the advisory referendum. This vote was hailed as a "mandate" for reform. Nevertheless, the same electors who desired to divest the legislature of its powers by a 3-to-1 margin simultaneously elected a General Assembly that was 85 percent Democratic.[20]

When the new General Assembly, downsized to 75 representatives and 38 senators, convened in January 2003, the incoming Republican governor, the influential *Providence Journal*, and several determined and insistent citizens' groups—especially Common Cause led by Phil West—demanded that the purported popular mandate in favor of separation of powers be implemented. Fearful of retribution at the polls on election day if they ignored the people's will, senators then voted unanimously to relinquish its time-honored powers. After a contest for power no less significant than the Bloodless Revolution of 1935, separation-of-powers amendments were approved by the General Assembly and sent to the people for ratification. They were easily ratified (257,308 to 71,236), but the convention call failed again (162,296 in favor to 175,601 against). The legislature not only vacated its role on all state boards and commissions that exercise executive power (the issue that sparked the separation controversy); it also relinquished the source of its residual powers by allowing the repeal of Article VI, Section 10.

Although the procedure to amend the 1986 constitution has been frequently used and has wrought substantial changes in Rhode Island's basic law, no convention has been held in over three decades since 1986. In fact, two convention referenda have been rejected by the electorate. In 1994 three important amendments were already on the ballot, and in addition the spirit of Article XIV, Section 2, was violated when the mandated bipartisan preparatory commission "to assemble information on constitutional questions" formed too late to meet or give the voters instruction regarding the need, if any, for constitutional reform.

As the General Assembly began its 2005 session, it soon became evident, however, that the power struggle among all three branches of government was far from resolved by the adoption of the separation-of-powers amendment. The judiciary soon claimed the right to prepare its own budget, and the General Assembly pondered its continued role, if any, in such traditional and constitutionally referenced areas of legislative activity as education, lotteries, the environment, and control over cities and towns. The General Assembly did however initiate a ballot question that was put to the voters in 2020 that eliminated "Providence Plantations" from the official state name.[21]

Looking back on 370 years of government, one is impressed with both the durability of Rhode Island's basic law and the volatility of its political system. If one regards the patent of 1644 as merely a license to survive, the colony and state have had but three fundamental laws: the corporate Charter of 1663, which endured for 180 years; the constitution of 1843, which enjoyed 143 years of life; and the 1986 constitution, under which Rhode Island has been governed since November 1986. These documents have been like the granite walls of a Grand Canyon, through which has rushed the agitated and turbulent stream of Rhode Island parties and politicians—and the view has often been spectacular. Both tradition and turmoil have been hallmarks of Rhode Island's constitutional and political culture, and most Rhode Islanders seem to relish, or at least to accept, this fascinating dichotomy.

Notes

1. The "householders" compact has been lost, but Williams expressed his intention to institute the above-described system in a letter to John Winthrop [n.d., ca. Sept. 1636], published in the Narragansett Club Edition, *The Complete Writings of Roger Williams* (Providence, 1866–74), 6:3–7. The submission agreement is printed in Horatio Rogers, George M. Carpenter, and Edward Field, eds., *The Early Records of the Town of Providence* (Providence, 1892–1915), 1:1.
2. Patrick T. Conley, *Democracy in Decline: Rhode Island Constitutional Development, 1776–1841* (Providence: Rhode Island Publications Society, 1977), contains copious documentation for this entire narrative from 1636 through the Dorr Rebellion and its aftermath in the 1850s. The reader is referred to that volume for substantiation of the statements and conclusions made in this constitutional summary.
3. Howard M. Chapin, ed., *Documentary History of Rhode Island* (Providence: Preston & Rounds, 1916–19), 1:214–17, contains the British State Paper Office copy of the patent, which is the most accurate draft.
4. Charles McLean Andrews, *The Colonial Period of American History* (New Haven, CT: Yale University Press, 1934–38), 2:26.
5. See note 3.
6. The Charter is published in *Rhode Island Colonial Records*, 2:1-21. See also Sydney V. James, *John Clarke and His Legacies: Religion and Law in Colonial Rhode Island, 1638–1750*, edited by Theodore Dwight Bozeman (University Park, PA: Pennsylvania State University Press, 1999).
7. Conley, *Democracy*, 72–73
8. Christian McBurney, "Rhode Island Acts to Prevent an Enslaved Family from Being Transported to the South," *Journal of the American Revolution*, May 19, 2022, https://allthingsliberty.com/2022/05/rhode-island-acts-to-prevent-an-enslaved-family-from-being-transported-to-the-south/.
9. *RICR*, 9:674-75 10:7 (Manumission Act).
10. Irving H. Polishook, *Rhode Island and the Union* (Evanston, IL: Northwestern University Press), 1969, passim.
11. Polishook, *Union*, 163–230; Patrick T. Conley, *First in War; Last in Peace: Rhode Island and the Constitution, 1786–1790* (Providence: Rhode Island Bicentennial Foundation and Rhode Island Publications Society, 1987); Frank Greene Bates, *Rhode Island and the Formation of the Union*, 149–216 (New York: AMS Press, 1898).
12. Conley, *Democracy*, 184–268; "Journal of the Convention . . . 1824," Rhode Island State Archives. *The Manufacturers' and Farmers' Journal*, a Whig newspaper published in Providence, printed a draft of the 1834 constitution in its issue of September 18, 1834.
13. *Luther v. Borden* 7 Howard 1 (1849); William M. Wiecek, *The Guarantee of the U.S. Constitution* (Ithaca, NY: Cornell University Press, 1972), 78–129; Peter C. Magrath, "Optimistic Democrat: Thomas Wilson Dorr and the case of *Luther* v. *Borden*," *Rhode Island History* 29 (1970): 94–112; Michael Conron, "Law, Politics, and Chief Justice Taney: A Reconsideration of the *Luther v. Borden* Decision," *American Journal of Legal History* 11, no. 4 (1967): 377–88. Ironically, Taney had foreshadowed this formulation of the Political Question Doctrine in an 1838 dis-

sent from a ruling in a case involving a dispute between Rhode Island and Massachusetts over Rhode Island's northern boundary when he asserted that "rights of sovereignty and jurisdiction between states over any particular territory, are not . . . the subject of judicial cognizance." *Rhode Island v. Massachusetts*, 37 U.S. 657 (1838).

14. See Patrick Conley, Robert Owen Jones, and William McKenzie Woodward, *The State Houses of Rhode Island* (Providence: Rhode Island Publications Society and Rhode Island Historical Preservation Commission, 1988 and 2013).)

15. Taylor v. Place, 4 R.I. 324 (1856); Peter C. Magrath, "Samuel Ames: The Great Chief Justice of Rhode Island," *Rhode Island History* 34 (July 1965): 65–76; Patrick T. Conley, "Putting Taylor in Its Proper Place." in *Neither Separate Nor Equal: Legislature and Executive in Rhode Island History*, 83–88 (Providence: Rhode Island Publications Society, 1999).

16. Chelsea Clifford Hubbard, "Constitutional Development in Rhode Island [1636–1926]" (Doctoral diss. Brown University, 1926); Conley, *Neither Separate*, 89–112; Edward L. Rondeau, "Charles Ray Brayton: A Study in Bossism" (Master's thesis. University of Rhode Island, 1966); Robert C. Power, "Rhode Island Republican Politics in the Gilded Age—The G.O.P. Machine of Anthony, Aldrich, and Brayton" (Honors thesis. Brown University, 1972).

17. *Advisory Opinion to the Senate*. 14 R.I. 649. 1883; *Report of Joint Select Committee on Changes in the Constitution* . . . Providence, 1882; Report of the Commission to Revise the Constitution . . . Providence, RI, 1898; *Proposed Revised Constitution of the State of Rhode Island*. Providence, RI, 1898; *Report of Joint Special Committee on Constitutional Amendments* . . . Providence, RI, 1899; *The Proposed Revised Constitution of the State of Rhode Island* . . . Providence, RI, 1899; *Report of Commission to Consider the Amendment and Revision of the Constitution*. Providence, RI, 1915; Richard P. Ironfield, "The Constitutional Reform Movement in Rhode Island from 1895–1905" (Doctoral diss. Providence College, 2002); Charles Carroll, essay, in *Rhode Island: Three Centuries of Democracy*, 2:666–69 (New York, 1932).

18. Mario R. DiNunzio et al., *Annotated Edition: Constitution of the State of Rhode Island and Providence Plantations Done in Convention at Providence on the Fourth Day of December, A.D. 1986* (Providence: Secretary of State of Rhode Island, 1988).

19. Conley published his successful brief titled *Neither Separate nor Equal: Legislature and Executive in Rhode Island's Constitutional History* along with summaries of other briefs submitted.

20. See Patrick T. Conley, "The 'Elephant Gun': Governors' Advisory Referenda," *Providence Journal*, June 10, 2006, F7.

21. "Rhode Island Question 1, Name Change Amendment (2020)," *Ballotpedia*, https://ballotpedia.org/Rhode_Island_Question_1,_Name_Change_Amendment_(2020). Conley's strong but futile opposition, "Why R.I. Should Keep Providence Plantations in Its Name," was published in the *Providence Journal* on October 25, 2020.

3 / Rhode Island and the Federal System

ADAM S. MYERS

Introduction

As the 2019 regular session of the Rhode Island General Assembly was drawing to a close, the attention of the state's political community was on the always-contentious issue of abortion. With the recent confirmations of two conservative justices (Neil Gorsuch and Brett Kavanaugh) to the US Supreme Court, abortion rights supporters around the country feared that the Court's rightward shift might portend its reversal of the landmark 1973 *Roe v. Wade* decision guaranteeing legal abortion in every state. Scrambling to respond to these developments, abortion rights advocates in Rhode Island worked to pass the Reproductive Privacy Act (RPA), which codified *Roe*'s protections into state law. The highly controversial bill passed the state House only to become mired in conflict between progressive and conservative Democrats in the Senate. Eventually, a compromise between the factions was reached and a revised bill was passed by both chambers and then signed into law in 2019 by Governor Gina Raimondo. We now know that the warnings of the RPA's strongest proponents were prescient: the Supreme Court in 2022 announced its decision in *Dobbs v. Jackson Women's Health Organization* overturning *Roe* and thereby allowing states to regulate abortion as they see fit. Because the General Assembly passed the RPA, abortion rights in Rhode Island will be unaffected by the Court's decision.

The battle over abortion rights in the State House that followed the confirmation of two justices to the *national* Supreme Court is just one example of how Rhode Island politics and policy are highly influenced by political and policy developments in Washington, DC, pointing to the importance of *federalism*—the division of authority between the US national government and the states—in understanding Rhode Island government. This chapter examines how federalism affects government and politics in the Ocean State across an array of public policies and from a variety of theoretical perspectives. Because federalism is an enormous topic whose many aspects cannot be satisfactorily covered in a book chapter, the chapter does not attempt to cover federalism comprehensively. Instead, it focuses on what the author has deemed to be the most important events, themes, and issues of state-national relations as they relate to Rhode Island. The chapter begins with an abbreviated historical overview of American federalism, focusing especially on Rhode Island's place in the federal system, from the Founding to the present day. It then proceeds to examine the contemporary relationship between the national government and Rhode Island in the areas of taxing and spending (what scholars call *fiscal federalism*). Lastly, it considers the intersection between federalism and contemporary political conflict over social and cultural issues, examining Rhode Island's recent policy actions on matters such as abortion, gay rights, and marijuana legalization within the context of the interstate "culture wars."

American Federalism and Rhode Island: A Brief Historical Overview

Any discussion of American federalism must begin with the Founding Era, and particularly with the framing and ratification of the US Constitution in 1787–88. In the eight years prior to the adoption of the Constitution, the United States functioned as a loose confederation of sovereign states under its original governing document: the Articles of Confederation. During this period, the vast bulk of political power lay with the thirteen states; the US Congress's ability to raise revenue, conduct foreign policy, and legislate on domestic matters was highly circumscribed. For a variety of reasons that need not detain us here, many (though not all) of the country's political leaders viewed this decentralized arrangement as dysfunctional and potentially disastrous. With the goal of rectifying the "vices" of the Articles and creating a stronger central government, these leaders issued a call for each state to select delegates to a convention to be held in Philadelphia during the summer of 1787. The charge of this convention would be to revise the Articles to render them "adequate to the exigencies of Government & the preservation of the Union."[1]

Uniquely among the thirteen states, Rhode Island rebuffed this call and refused to send delegates to the Philadelphia convention. The state's objections to the gathering had deep ideological underpinnings. To a degree that most contemporary Americans would find surprising, it was Rhode Island—not the southern states with which notions of "states' rights" would come to be associated in the future—that most vociferously stood for the principle of state sovereignty during the Founding. As the historians Patrick Conley and John Kaminski have noted, Rhode Island's fierce resistance to surrendering power to a central government in the Founding Era had to do with its long tradition of local democracy and individualism. Indeed, by the standards of the time, Rhode Island's political system was remarkably egalitarian: religious freedom was guaranteed, all local officials were chosen directly by eligible voters, and elections were highly frequent.[2] The obviously elitist undertones of the movement to establish a stronger central government that was blossoming in other parts of the country worried Rhode Islanders. On top of that, many of the movement's leading forces had regularly expressed strong disapproval of Rhode Island's paper-money program, leading to (as it turns out, accurate) fears that the convention would target the state's monetary policies.[3] Because the convention seemed likely to pursue changes deemed contrary to Rhode Island's sovereignty and economic interests, the state's leaders chose not to take part in it.

Whether Rhode Island's decision to boycott the convention was a sound strategic move is a question historians have long debated. Many have argued that, by not sending delegates to the convention, Rhode Island's leaders lost their ability to shape its proceedings to their liking. In the absence of voices (from Rhode Island and elsewhere) strongly promoting the state-sovereignty perspective, the Convention became dominated by nationalists whose main disagreement concerned not whether the powers of the central government should be increased (and those of the states diminished) but rather just how far to move in a centralizing direction. When the convention delegates finally revealed their work to the public in September 1787, it became clear that they had decided to move far indeed. Rather than revising the Articles (as they had said they would do), the delegates proposed replacing them with a new governing document—the United States Constitution—that would create a far more robust and capacious central government with a long list of powers, including a nearly unlimited power to tax and a power to independently raise a standing army. Besides vastly increasing the central government's powers, the Constitution would also significantly curtail those of the states, preventing them from issuing their own currencies (again, a direct response to Rhode Island's much-criticized monetary policies) or regulating interstate commerce. Although the document did not go as far as the most staunchly nationalist delegates would have wanted (i.e., it preserved the states as entities with independent authority and, through the Senate and electoral college, gave them a voice in national institutions), the overall centralizing thrust of the Constitution, at least as compared with the Articles, was plain for all to see.

Following the unveiling of the Constitution, the United States entered one of the most dramatic and high-stakes moments in its history: the battle over the Constitution's ratification, fought out in conventions in each of the states. True to form, Rhode Island resisted ratifying the Constitution longer than any other state. At first, the state legislature repeatedly defeated attempts to call a state-ratifying convention. After months of temporizing, the legislature opted for the highly democratic approach of submitting the ratification question to a popular referendum in lieu of a convention. This referendum, the only one of its kind during the Founding period, resulted in the state's citizens rejecting the Constitution. The state's resistance continued through 1789; by 1790, all other states had ratified the Constitution, and the newly empowered US Congress had convened, but Rhode Island was still outside the constitutional union. Congress subsequently began putting pressure on Rhode Island, threatening it with major economic sanctions and hinting at the potential dismantling of its territory.[4] Against this backdrop, the state's leaders finally gave in and called for a ratifying convention, which ratified the Constitution on May 29, 1790—but by a vote of only 34 to 32.[5] Regardless, after years of self-imposed isolation, Rhode Island was back in the union of states.

With the ratification of the Constitution, a new American regime was created, one with an independent and robust national government operating alongside state governments maintaining a largely unspecified amount of political autonomy. Because the Constitution's language concerning the boundary between national and state authority is ambiguous, federalism has taken a wide variety of forms—and served as the focal point for many conflicts—ever since. During the period between the Founding and the Civil War, the dominant understanding of federalism was that, under the Constitution, the national government and the states are mutually sovereign within their respective policy spheres—an idea that scholars call *dual federalism*.[6] While a highly nationalist Supreme Court issued several important rulings expanding national power during this period, the basic view that state governments retain autonomy in matters of "internal police" largely predominated. Thus, even amidst a more active national government (particularly in foreign affairs), the states of this period were highly vital and self-contained entities that featured widely varying policies and political dynamics.

In Rhode Island's case, these early years featured a dramatic shift away from the populist, democratic spirit that defined the state during the Founding Era. Whereas the Rhode Island of the 1780s was well ahead of other states in terms of the openness of its political system, by the 1830s it was far behind. In the intervening years, most other states had adopted new constitutions and then revised them to abolish property-based suffrage restrictions, but Rhode Island continued to be governed by its unamendable colonial charter, which limited voting rights to property owners.[7] The growth of an unpropertied urban population in the early nineteenth century meant that, by the 1830s, less than half of white men in the state were eligible to vote. This situation, combined with a highly malapportioned state legislature (discussed extensively in Chapter 8), led a group of political dissidents representing the urban working classes to declare the people's right to abolish the colonial charter and form a new state government under a new, more democratic state constitution. The result was the most famous event in Rhode Island history—the Dorr Rebellion—in which two different governments claimed to rule over Rhode Island for a period of time. The dispute over which of these governments was legitimate eventually made its way to the US Supreme Court, which (in the landmark 1849 decision *Luther v. Borden*) affirmed two key notions of dual federalism: one, the US Constitution is largely silent on the question of how state governments should be organized; two, the federal courts have little to no role in supervising state political processes.[8]

The dominance of the dual federalism view of the US Constitution largely ended with the Civil War, which, as with so much else, constituted a profound juncture in the history of state-federal relations. In addition to settling the paramount question of whether states have a right to secede from the Union, the Civil War resulted in the addition of three new constitutional amendments that further expanded the national government's powers and limited those of the states. The Thirteenth Amendment banned slavery, an area that was previously subject to state control. The Fourteenth Amendment established national citizenship, clarified that Americans have due process rights against state governments, and prevented states from denying individuals the "equal protection of the laws." The Fifteenth Amendment established a right to vote for all men across all states. Each of these amendments gave Congress the power of enforcement, effectively bestowing on the national government new authority in many areas of domestic policy previously understood to be in the states' sphere.

Hence, from the end of the Civil War to the 1930s, American federalism was in a transitional era defined by weaker fealty to the principles of dual federalism and stronger acceptance of national supremacy. Many of the federalism-related questions of this era concerned the respective roles of the national government and the states in regulating capitalism and responding to the vast inequalities in wealth and political influence that emerged during the industrial age. Compared to other northern states, Rhode Island functioned as a highly reactionary state on these and other matters. Throughout much of this period, the Ocean State was what political scientists would today call an "authoritarian enclave": in addition to having a highly malapportioned legislature dominated by a rural minority, Rhode Island continued to feature one of the country's most restrictive electoral systems, with property requirements for voting in local elections staying on the books until 1928.[9] These undemocratic features helped facilitate the rise of a rural political machine that controlled the state throughout much of the late nineteenth and early twentieth centuries, as well as a political culture largely tolerant of corruption. The famed muckraker journalist Lincoln Steffens famously called Rhode Island a "state for sale" in 1907.[10] Rhode Island's highly closed political system meant that, unlike other northern states, it was not a major engine of policy innovation during the Progressive Era (1897–1920), when states played an important role in modernizing American government and regulating industrial economic activity.

The next major juncture in the history of American federalism occurred in the mid-twentieth century, specifically in the 30 years between the 1930s and the 1960s. During this period, the United States finally shed the remaining vestiges of dual federalism and became a thoroughly consolidated regime in which the principle of national supremacy was (mostly) unquestioned. Several developments during this highly tumultuous period led to this outcome. First, during the New Deal Era of the 1930s, the national government dramatically expanded its activities in the realm of economic regulation; after initially resisting these interventions, the US Supreme Court ultimately blessed them, thereby indicating that it would no longer restrict the national government from making policy in areas once understood to be in the states' sphere. Second, the size and taxation capacity of the national government grew enormously in response to World War II. Third, the postwar period saw a big increase in national government grants to states and localities for numerous domestic purposes. Lastly, postwar congressional statutes on civil and voting rights, as well as numerous US Supreme Court decisions on legislative apportionment, the rights of criminal defendants, and civil liberties, showcased a national government eager to supervise the states and force them to conform to national norms and priorities. All these developments suggested to observers that the United States had entered an era of unrivaled national power devoid of fixed boundaries between national and state authority. Scholars took to describing the national-state relationship established during this era as *cooperative federalism*; rather than working in separate spheres (as in dual federalism), the national government and the states were now cooperating with each other on the same issues, though with the former usually taking the lead.[11]

The transformation of US federalism in the mid-twentieth century is closely related to major changes in Rhode Island state politics that occurred during this same period. In many ways, the outcomes discussed in the previous paragraph helped to bring about Rhode Island's transition from a closed political fiefdom to the modern democracy that it is today. First, the rise of the Democratic Party in the urban northeast during the New Deal Era led to the Democrats' takeover of Rhode Island government in 1935 and the belated arrival of two-party competition in the state. Second, the Supreme Court's reapportionment rulings in the early 1960s (discussed more extensively in Chapter 8) ended the massive overrepresentation of the state's rural minority in the General Assembly and created a political system in which every vote carries equal weight. Third, the growth of conditional grants from the national government to the states in the postwar era (discussed in greater detail below) helped modernize Rhode Island's government and forced its leaders to upgrade the state's taxation capacity. In all these ways, Rhode Island's modern state government—to a larger extent than most states outside the South—was arguably facilitated by national intervention.

Federalism and Rhode Island in the Twenty-first Century

Federalism in the twenty-first century is a highly complex arrangement influenced by America's constitutional structure, the historical events and paradigms discussed above, as well as modern trends in American government and politics. The cooperative federalism that dominated American politics in the mid-twentieth century lives on in the form of numerous federal grants and programs that shape the affairs of state governments, including that of Rhode Island. At the same time, nineteenth-century notions of dual federalism (particularly the idea that states are or should be sovereign within their policy spheres) have been making a comeback in the US Supreme Court, which has issued a variety of recent decisions restricting the national government's ability to influence the states. More importantly, the rise of intense partisan polarization in contemporary American politics has resulted in the layering of a stark new federalism reality on top of the old patterns: while the national government is increasingly beset by partisan gridlock and policy rigidity, the states (many of which are dominated by one party or the other) have regained the status they enjoyed in the nineteenth century as vital engines of policymaking. But because state-level policymaking in the modern era is so heavily influenced by national party priorities, many worry that today's state governments are exacerbating polarization's most harmful effects on the country as a whole.[12]

All these trends are evident when one examines present-day Rhode Island politics and government, though in occasionally surprising ways. Here, I examine federalism's influence on modern Ocean State government in two important areas: fiscal policy and cultural policy.

Fiscal Federalism and the Rhode Island Budget

Fiscal federalism refers to the relationship between the national government and the states in the areas of taxing and spending. Of these two areas, the spending relationship receives the lion's share of attention from public finance experts. This is because national government and the states interact fiscally primarily through the vast network of national government expenditures that flow through the states. Most of these expenditures, often referred to as "conditional grants," were established in the mid-twentieth century during the heyday of cooperative federalism. By far the largest conditional grant in the twenty-first century is for Medicaid, the joint federal-state health insurance program for low-income Americans. Additional important conditional grants include Federal Aid for Highways, Temporary Assistance for Needy Families (i.e., welfare), the Supplemental Nutrition Assistance Program (i.e., food stamps), the State Children's Health Insurance Program, Section 8 Housing, and many others.[13]

Figure 3.1 (below) plots the percentage of state government revenue coming from national government grants between 2000 and 2019. As it shows, there was a slight upward trend in the share of state revenue coming from the national government over this time period, for all states as well as Rhode Island specifically. In particular, the share of state revenue coming from national grants increased following the 2008 financial crisis, when state tax revenue plummeted, and national stimulus funds helped states shore up their budgets. The figure also shows that Rhode Island has consistently relied on national grants to a somewhat larger extent than other states. To be clear, the Ocean State is nowhere near the most reliant on federal funds of the fifty states; with nearly half of their revenues regularly coming from the national government, the poor states of the Deep South (i.e., Mississippi, Louisiana) are far more reliant. Nonetheless, it is noteworthy that Rhode Island is more fiscally reliant on the national government than any other state in the Northeast.

It is also important to note that the data in Figure 3.1 stop in 2019, before the COVID-19 pandemic and the subsequent glut of national grants to state governments as a part of Congress's various COVID relief packages. The effect of these grants was to substantially increase the national grant share of state revenue in 2020 and 2021, including in Rhode Island. At this time, it appears that the national government's efforts to shore up state budgets during these years was a temporary response to emergency circumstances, and that the national share of state revenue will revert back to previous levels in the future.

Figure 3.1: National Grant Share of State Revenue for Rhode Island and All States, 2000–2019

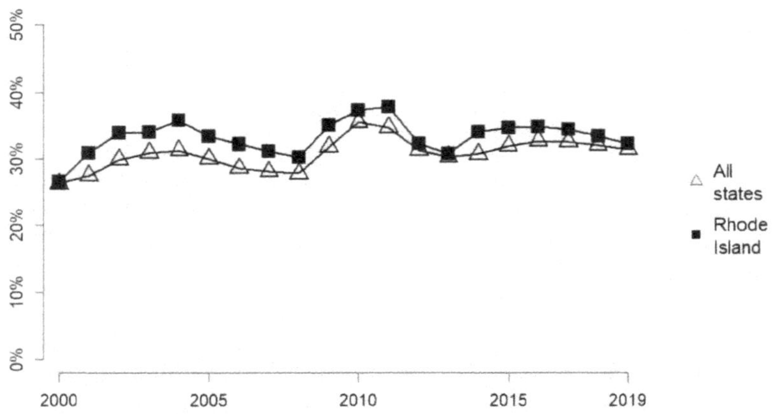

Source: Pew Research Center, State Fiscal Health Project

While national government grants clearly have a major impact on state budgets, it nonetheless bears emphasizing that all states (certainly including Rhode Island) raise most of their revenue from their own sources. In other words, much like the national government, they have to tax their residents and businesses. This points to the second, and often-ignored, fiscal federalism issue: the relationship between the national government and the states in the area of taxation. In sharp contrast to other countries with a federal system of government (i.e., Australia, Canada, Germany, and Switzerland), the national –state taxation relationship in the United States is largely *uncoordinated*: i.e., the national government and the states tax independently of each other.[14] While the national government overwhelmingly relies on the personal income tax for its revenues, states rely on a broader mix of taxes, including income taxes, sales taxes, severance taxes, and others.

Historically, state taxation policy was not heavily influenced by partisanship, but as with much else, party control of state government has become a leading indicator of state tax choices in the twenty-first century. This is especially the case regarding state income taxes: whereas Republican-controlled states have been regularly cutting their income taxes over the past 20 years (particularly for the highest earners), Democrat-controlled states have been increasingly raising them. The result is that a significant gap has opened between Democrat-controlled and Republican-controlled states in terms of tax progressivity (i.e., the degree to which a state places a greater share of its tax burden on the wealthy), with the former now exhibiting significantly more progressive tax systems than the latter on average. So far, however, Rhode Island has resisted this trend. The state's top income tax rate is 5.99 percent, significantly lower than that of many leading "Blue States" like California (top rate of 13 percent), New Jersey (top rate of 10.75 percent), New York (top rate of 8.82 percent), or Oregon (top rate of 9.9 percent).

Rhode Island's overall tax burden on its wealthier residents is important because of its consequences for what has been the most politically sensitive area of the national–state taxation relationship: the State and Local Tax Deduction (SALT). Stated briefly, SALT allows taxpayers to deduct the amount of taxes paid to state and local governments from their federal income tax liability. This has historically worked to the benefit of wealthy taxpayers from high-tax states, who have taken advantage of SALT to lower their federal income tax payments significantly. In 2017, however, congressional Republicans capped the SALT deduction at $10,000 per taxpayer, thereby significantly limiting the ability of Americans to utilize it. GOP leaders argued that the SALT cap was necessary to reduce the impact of the tax cut they also passed on the national government's deficits. Observers noticed that it had a political side benefit: in adversely affecting wealthy taxpayers from high-tax states like California, New York, and New Jersey, the SALT cap put pressure on these Democrat-controlled states to reduce their tax burdens, lest their wealthy taxpayers flee to less-taxed and usually more Republican jurisdictions.[15] Since 2017, repealing the SALT cap has become a central focus of many lawmakers from high-tax states (including a number of Republicans), but these efforts have so far not borne fruit. With SALT (effectively a national subsidy to states with high taxes) being severely restricted, it will be difficult for advocates of raising taxes on the wealthy in Rhode Island to gain support for their cause.

Rhode Island and the Interstate Culture Wars

One of the most prominent areas in which federalism exercises major influence on twenty-first-century US politics is in the broad arena of hot-button cultural issues like abortion, LBGTQ rights, marijuana legalization, and others. Throughout most of American history, states were primarily responsible for making policy on such matters, which were viewed as falling clearly within the states' "police powers" (i.e., those areas of domestic policymaking reserved for the state governments under the dual federalism understanding of the Constitution). During the highly centralizing period between the 1930s and the 1960s, however, the country moved toward national uniformity on a wide array of cultural issues. While Congress played a role in imposing this uniformity (particularly in regard to racial and sex equality), the institution that led the move toward a consistent national approach to cultural issues was the Supreme Court. Through a large set of decisions striking down state laws sanctioning various public expressions of religion or regulating private conduct, the Court of the mid-twentieth century advanced a national approach to cultural issues that prioritized liberal conceptions of public secularism and individual autonomy. The Supreme Court's decisions of this era played a major role in triggering the conservative backlash of the 1970s and the rise to power of the Republican Party under Ronald Reagan in the 1980s.

In sharp contrast to the mid-twentieth century, the early-twenty-first century appears to be a period of rapid *decentralization* of cultural policy. The American public is deeply and closely divided on current cultural flashpoints such as abortion, gun control, transgender rights, the teaching of America's racial history in public schools, and others. Aware of the strong emotions surrounding these issues, Congress appears to be largely staying away from them. Meanwhile, the current Supreme Court, stocked with conservative appointees, has started overturning the nationalizing decisions of the liberal, mid-twentieth-century Court (case in point: the *Dobbs* decision, which returns the issue of abortion to the states).

With the country divided and the national government adrift on cultural matters, state governments have been stepping into the breach. As noted above, unified party control of government has been far more prevalent in the states than at the national level in the twenty-first century, and, as with tax policy, this has had major consequences for cultural policy as Democrat-controlled and Republican-controlled states have been increasingly moving in opposite directions. Thus, the culture wars are increasingly being fought not in Washington, DC, but in the corridors of the nation's statehouses.

Rhode Island has generally moved in the same direction as other "Blue States" in the interstate culture wars, having passed laws codifying abortion rights, protecting LGBTQ residents from employment discrimination, restricting gun access, providing driver's licenses to unauthorized immigrants, among other policies. In general, however, the state has not been at the forefront of liberal cultural policymaking. For example, Rhode Island's codification of *Roe* v. *Wade* came relatively late, and the state has still not expanded abortion access to the same degree as other Democratic states like California, Illinois, or New York.[16] Likewise, the Giffords Law Center, an anti-gun research and advocacy group, gave Rhode Island a "B" grade in its 2021 gun law scorecard while nearby Connecticut, Massachusetts, New York, and New Jersey all received A minuses.[17] Rhode Island similarly lagged behind other Democratic states in marijuana legalization.

Given the lopsided Democratic advantage in both chambers of its legislature, the fact that Rhode Island consistently exhibits more conservative cultural policies than those of other "Blue States" may be surprising to those who are unfamiliar with the intricacies of the state's politics. But in fact, Rhode Island's more conservative approach to cultural issues is quite easily explained by the unusually strong power of cultural conservatives within the state's Democratic Party. Indeed, for much of the twenty-first century, the leaders of both the State House and Senate have been Democrats with conservative views on cultural issues. Whether on abortion, gay rights, or guns, these leaders have often sought to stall efforts emanating from the state's progressive activist community to change the state's cultural policies. Time and again, however, political pressures have eventually forced the House Speaker and Senate President to relent and pave the way for a major progressive policy change, the effect of which has been to mostly if not completely align the Ocean State with other Blue States in the culture wars. If and when the progressive activist community succeeds in its goal of taking over the state Democratic Party and, with it, the General Assembly, we can expect that Rhode Island will shift from being a laggard to being a leader in Blue-State cultural policymaking.

Conclusion

This chapter has provided an overview of how federalism has affected Rhode Island politics and government from the time of the Founding to the present day. While it has sought to cover many historical and contemporary issues, there are a wide variety of others in which federalism and Rhode Island government intersect, including environmental protection, criminal justice, education, and Native American relations. In fact, upon careful examination, one can find evidence of federalism's influence in nearly every issue handled by state and local government. To understand Rhode Island politics, therefore, it is necessary to understand federalism.

Additionally, the chapter has sought to show how the federal system *has been affected* by Rhode Island across American history. Here, the clear takeaway message is that the state's role was once highly significant but also that it has shrunk dramatically over time. During the Founding Era, Rhode Island was just one of thirteen states, and its strong defense of state sovereignty played a major role in the resistance to the Constitution and the development of a states' rights ideology that has pervaded American politics ever since. During the antebellum period, the biggest political crisis in Rhode Island history—the Dorr Rebellion—helped influence early American understandings of dual federalism, a doctrine that—like state sovereignty—continues to occasionally appear in constitutional debates. Since the Civil War, however, Rhode Island's role in shaping the federal system has not been nearly as large. As the smallest state, and one with a highly insular political culture, Rhode Island's position in modern federalism struggles has often been ignored. In our current era of polarized federalism, larger Blue states where the Democratic party is primarily controlled by progressive forces (e.g., California, Oregon, New York, Illinois) tend to be the leaders of progressive policy innovation; Rhode Island is, more often than not, a follower. Given its small size, it seems unlikely that Rhode Island will regain the prominence it enjoyed in the federalism-related conflicts of the eighteenth and nineteenth centuries (and this may be a good thing), but the state's history has been full of surprises. One can envision various ways (a progressive takeover of the state's Democratic Party is one that has already been mentioned) by which Rhode Island could become a policy leader to which other states would look as a model in the future. In short, Rhode Island's evolving role in the federal system is something worth watching as the 21st century continues to unfold.

Notes

1. "Report of Proceedings in Congress; February 21, 1787," The Avalon Project, Yale Law School, n.d. https://avalon.law.yale.edu/18th_century/const04.asp.
2. Patrick T. Conley and John P. Kaminski, "First in War, Last in Peace: Rhode Island and the Constitution, 1786–1790," in *The Constitution and the States* (Madison, WI: Madison House, 1988), , 269–94.
3. Michael A. Gillespie and Michael Lienesch, "Rhode Island: Protecting State Interests," in *Ratifying the Constitution*, edited by John P. Kaminski and Patrick T. Conley (Lawrence: University of Kansas Press, 1989), 368–90.
4. Conley and Kaminski, "First in War, Last and Peace."
5. Pauline Maier, Pauline. *Ratification: The People Debate the Constitution, 1787–1788* (New York:Simon and Schuster, 2010, 458–59.
6. Ernest A. Young, "The Puzzling Persistence of Dual Federalism," *Nomos* 55 (2014): 34–82.
7. Patrick T. Conley, *Democracy in Decline: Rhode Island's Constitutional Development, 1776–1841*, (Providence: Rhode Island Publications Society, 1977).
8. Alexander Keyssar, *The Right to Vote: The Contested History of Democracy in the United States* (New York: Basic Books, 2009), 56–60. The dual federalism principles laid down in *Luther v. Borden* were eventually overturned by the Supreme Court in the reapportionment decisions of the early 1960s.
9. Alexander Keyssar, *The Right to Vote*, 105, 183.
10. Lincoln Steffens, "Rhode Island: A State for Sale," *McClure's Magazine*, February 1905
11. Joseph F. Zimmerman, "National-State Relations: Cooperative Federalism in the Twentieth Century," *Publius: The Journal of Federalism* 31, no. 2 (2001): 15–30.
12. See, for example, Jacob Grumbach, *Laboratories against Democracy: How National Parties Transformed State Policymaking* (Princeton, NJ: Princeton University Press, 2022).
13. "Federal Grants to State and Local Governments: A Historical Perspective on Contemporary Issues § (2019)," Congressional Research Service, May 22, 2019, https://sgp.fas.org/crs/misc/R40638.pdf.
14. Thomas O. Hueglin and Alan Fenna, *Comparative Federalism: A Systemic Inquiry* (Toronto: University of Toronto Press, 2015), 174–76. For more on the unique aspects of American fiscal federalism, particularly regarding taxation, see my forthcoming book *Coordination Failure: State Taxation and Federal Response from the New Deal to Today* (forthcoming in 2023/2024).
15. Susan Milligan, "The War Against New Jersey (and Other Blue States)." *US News*, November 26, 2021, https://www.usnews.com/news/the-report/articles/2021-11-26/democratic-states-battle-over-salt-tax-rules.
16. "What If Roe Fell?" Center for Reproductive Rights, June 30, 2022, https://reproductiverights.org/maps/what-if-roe-fell/.
17. "Annual Gun Law Scorecard." Giffords Law Center, hhytt 2021, https://giffords.org/lawcenter/resources/scorecard/.

4 / Voting and Elections

Emily K. Lynch[1]

Over the past couple decades, elected officials, interest group leaders, and other election reform advocates have attempted to improve access to voting in Rhode Island. Despite these efforts, it took a worldwide pandemic in 2020 to implement a temporary universal mail ballot system in Rhode Island. The Rhode Island Department of State (DOS) was not alone in their efforts; many other states shifted their electoral systems with guidance from the US Election Assistance Commission to help them prepare for the increase in mail-in voting due to the COVID-19 pandemic.[2]

The Rhode Island Secretary of State's office first sent out mail ballot applications before the presidential primary in June 2020 due to pandemic concerns. Amidst criticisms of the mail ballot process, and despite skipping mail ballot applications for the September primary, in fall 2020, Secretary of State Nellie Gorbea decided to send out a mail ballot application to every active registered Rhode Island voter for the general election. Secretary Gorbea assured the public that all voting options in the state were safe and secure.[3] Mail ballots were considered secure in Rhode Island due to safeguards that required signature verification, allowed voters to use drop boxes in secure locations, and gave voters the ability to track a mail ballot. Also, voters had the option to hand deliver their mail ballot to the Board of Elections. Changes in voting options created a national debate over access to voting, where one side focused on the ability of the mail ballot system to ensure voters could participate in the election during a pandemic, while others were concerned about election security. Current debates over mail ballot voting exemplify contemporary politics of enfranchisement in Rhode Island and elsewhere. Nearly 33 percent of Rhode Islanders chose to vote by mail on election day (see Table 4.1). In comparison, 43 percent of the nation voted by mail in the 2020 election.[4]

TABLE 4.1 2020 Voter turnout by Voting Method

Polls on Election Day	202, 014
Early Voting	149, 611
Mail Ballot	170, 611
Total Turnout	522,014

Data retrieved from RI Department of State.

The chapter begins with a brief examination of Rhode Island's history of suffrage. The next section explains the current electoral system in Rhode Island with a discussion of voter registration, primary voting, and voting methods, with an emphasis on evolving debates about the accessibility and integrity of the electoral system. The next section outlines election administration followed by a brief examination of recent trends in voting and other forms of participation. The final segments cover the process for running for political office, party endorsements, and campaign finance.

Suffrage in Rhode Island

The historical roots of suffrage in the Rhode Island and Providence Plantations colony were embedded in the liberal colony charter in 1663. The 1663 charter designated that "freemen" had the power to elect general assembly members. Sixty years later, the general assembly defined freemen as property owners.[5] The charter was adopted as the state's constitution after Rhode Island became the first colony to declare independence from Britain in May 1776. Since Rhode Island never updated its constitution, voting was limited to white male landowners and their sons through 1841, making the vast majority of Rhode Islanders ineligible to vote.[6] Disenfranchisement was the impetus for the Dorr Rebellion where Thomas Dorr and his followers created their own Rhode Island government through the People's Constitutional Convention in 1841, which approved universal male suffrage, yet the Dorrites were ultimately defeated, and Dorr fled from the state. Although the Dorrites did not survive, the rebellion left a lasting impression on Rhode Island leaders, who made sweeping changes to the new constitution like easing some of the voting restrictions.

In 1843, the new state constitution granted suffrage to all native-born men with property. During this time, voters rejected a ballot measure restricting voting rights to whites only.[7] While Blacks were granted suffrage, the new constitution specifically prohibited members of the Narragansett Tribe from voting. Native-born men without property could vote if they paid a poll tax. In addition, there was still a property requirement if you were a naturalized citizen.[8] It was clear that the new constitution explicitly discriminated against indigenous people as well as disproportionately impacted the voting rights of immigrants who primarily rented in urban areas. In 1888, the Bourn Amendment ended the poll tax, but certain property qualifications remained.

Even though voters who did not meet property qualifications were granted the right to vote in elections, they were still restricted from voting in certain elections. For example, only citizens with property could vote in local financial meetings.[9] Property qualifications were officially eliminated in Rhode Island 40 years after the Bourn Amendment passed. Easing voting restrictions paved the way to the Democratic Party's rise in power in the Green Revolution of 1935.

Beginning in the 1860s, women's suffrage groups submitted petitions to the General Assembly to enfranchise women. Despite these efforts, a woman's right to vote was only achieved once the federal constitutional amendment was ratified in 1920. It took another 30 years for all Rhode Islanders to achieve full suffrage when the Narragansett tribe gained suffrage in 1950. The Democratic Party, once in power after the Green Revolution, is mainly credited for the push for universal suffrage because Democrats needed the working-class votes. Universal voting rights were not fully guaranteed across the country until the Voting Rights Act of 1965. Today, advocacy groups and some members of the General Assembly focus their efforts on making voting easily accessible to all.

Apportionment is a significant component to providing equal representation in the elections process. Apportionment is defined as the process of distributing legislative seats in districts based on population. The 1663 charter specified the number of representatives from each town. The 1843 constitution included limited apportionment reforms, and the state adopted constitutional amendments in 1909 and 1928, yet these limited reforms failed to address the overrepresentation of "Yankee" interests in rural areas and the underrepresentation of the urban immigrant working class (see Constitution and General Assembly chapters for more discussion on the evolution of the apportionment). Most urban areas were underrepresented until the 1960s when all states had to ensure that each district was equal in population after a series of Supreme Court cases related to this matter.[10]

Voter Registration

In 2016, Secretary of State Gorbea implemented online voter registration. Eligible Rhode Islanders can also register by mail, or in-person at their local board of canvassers. Under current law, individuals must register at least 30 days before a primary or election. There are additional laws about the proper polling place when a voter moves within the same town or a different town in Rhode Island and their address wasn't updated.[11] Same-day registration is only allowed in presidential elections where individuals may only vote for president and vice president, and their vote is counted as a provisional vote until registration is verified.

In 2015, Oregon became the first state to enact an automatic voter registration. This means an individual is automatically registered when they interact with DMV (Department of Motor Vehicles). Several states followed suit, including Rhode Island in 2017, where Secretary Gorbea implemented automated voter registration where voters are automatically registered to vote at the DMV unless they decide to "opt-out." If an address is updated at the DMV, the voter registration information is also updated, which may reduce the potential for voter fraud.

In order to register to vote, applicants must complete a form that requires a license number, state ID card number, or Social Security number. Individuals may indicate their party affiliation (Democrat, Republican, unaffiliated, other) and interest in serving as a poll worker. The registration form is used for new voters, updating information, and party change. The forms include additional questions about citizenship, residency status, and age.

Individuals must be at least 16 years old to register to vote, based on a relatively new law. Legislation on lowering the age requirement passed in 2006 through 2009 but was vetoed by Governor Donald Carcieri until the General Assembly overrode his veto in January 2010. Once the preregistered individuals turn 18, their registration becomes active, and they are automatically registered to vote. Thus, preregistration would allow young adults who are applying for learner's permits to participate in the motor voter program. Proponents suggest that this will lead to more accurate voter rolls and encourage youth to participate in politics right away, although critics argue that preregistration can be costly and reflect inaccurate registrations since young adults are more mobile.[12] As of 2019, 14 states and Washington, DC, allow preregistration beginning at age 16.[13]

A Rhode Islander is unable to register to vote if "legally judged mentally incompetent by a court of law" or a convicted felon still in prison. That means an individual is eligible to register and vote under the following circumstances: (1) if they have been released from prison, (2) if they were charged with a felony or misdemeanor, and (3) if they were convicted of a misdemeanor. If they are awaiting trial, sentencing, or incarceration, they can register to vote and vote by absentee ballot. They are also eligible to vote if sentenced to home confinement, probation, or parole. A referendum passed in 2006 (51.5 percent approval) that stated no incarcerated individual shall be allowed to vote until discharged. Once discharged, the person's right to vote would be restored. After being released from prison, an individual can notify their local board of canvassers in writing or submit a new voter registration form.

If any official elections mailing is returned and marked as "undeliverable," then names are marked "inactive" on registration lists. Once made "inactive," names are completely removed from the voter registration list if the voter does not cast a vote in one of the next two federal elections.

Voting in Primaries

A primary is necessary when two or more individuals from the same political party qualify for ballot placement for the same office. Rhode Island's primary system is defined as a "semi-closed" primary. Open primaries permit any voter—no matter their party affiliation—to participate in a primary election, and participation in closed primaries is restricted to party affiliates. Semi-closed primaries allow unaffiliated voters to declare a party affiliation to participate in that party's primary. Once an individual votes, they can disaffiliate by filling out a registration document with the local board of canvassers at the polling place, updating their voter registration record online, or downloading a new voter registration form and mailing/bringing it in. The disaffiliation process is completed within 30 days. Recent attempts to expand the electorate by allowing seventeen year olds to vote in a primary if they turned eighteen by the general or special election have not been successful in the General Assembly. Nineteen states allow 17-year-olds to vote in primaries or caucuses for presidential elections through state laws or party rules.[14]

Voting Methods

Convenience voting has been at the top of the agenda for election reformers in Rhode Island. As early as 2008, a group of House members and Senator Michael McCaffrey introduced legislation in each chamber to relax restrictions on mail ballot procedures.[15] The following year, legislators introduced bills to allow early voting. Similar bills continued to be introduced and tabled. Then, in 2011, the General Assembly passed legislation that changed the mail ballot procedure so anyone could vote by absentee ballot without providing any specific reason for requesting the mail ballot. At the same time the General Assembly loosened mail ballot voting, legislators tightened requirements for in person voting by requiring voters to present photo identification.[16]

Photo identification may be one of several forms with a photograph as long as they are not more than six months expired, including:

- driver's license/permit
- RI voter ID card
- US passport
- ID card issued by any federally recognized tribal government
- ID card issued by any US educational institution

- US military ID card
- ID card issued by US government or state of RI (e.g., RIPTA bus pass)
- government issued medical card.

Although identification is required, there are a couple caveats. First, identification is not needed when voting by mail ballot (instead, there are multiple signature verifications). Second, Rhode Islanders have the right to request a provisional ballot even if their name is not on the voter list or if the voter does not have acceptable photo identification. The vote will be counted when local board of canvassers validates the voter's eligibility.

Rhode Island made national news for its implementation of the photo identification law, making it the only state in New England that requests photo identification at the polls.[17] These elections reforms, one more liberalizing and the other more restrictive, exemplifies the balancing act of "independent" politics in Rhode Island, where, although the state is considered a liberal stronghold, there is a conservative pull that cannot be ignored.

2020 Election Procedures

Due to the pandemic, Rhode Islanders had the opportunity to vote without having to go to a polling place. While many Rhode Islanders still voted in person on election day during the designated times (7 a.m. until 8 p.m.) at a polling place, others took advantage of temporary options like mail ballot voting or early voting. Individuals had to return a mail ballot application to vote by mail. Mail ballot voters could mail in the ballot, hand deliver their mail ballot to any local board of canvassers as long as it was received by 8 p.m. on election day (see introduction to chapter for a lengthier discussion about politics of early voting in Rhode Island), or turn in the mail ballot at a drop off location.[18] Before COVID-19, an individual was required to include the signatures of two witnesses or a notary on the mail ballot envelope. These requirements were waived because of COVID-19. If a voter changed their minds from voting through mail ballot to in-person voting, then the voter would have to vote a provisional ballot. If a voter missed the mail ballot application deadline for any reason, they also had the option to vote through an emergency ballot process beginning 20 days before an election.

Politics of Voting

Mail ballot voting has been an option for some voters since the 1800s.[19] Only recently, however, has mail ballot voting become more prevalent, with some states like Oregon implementing full-scale mail ballot voting. Concerns have been raised about the integrity of mail ballot voting, including worries about vote harvesting. While evidence of election fraud is rare, mail-in voting may lead to other election administration problems like lost ballots or processing errors.[20]

Studies have shown that mail ballot voting increases accessibility to vote, especially for people of color, the disabled, young adults, and senior voters. Data based on early voting or absentee ballot from the Census also showed that older voters (65+), women, Asian Americans, individuals with a bachelor's degree or higher, and those with the most income had higher percentages of voting by mail than other groups. Election studies suggest that there is little-to-no partisan difference with mail ballot voting.[21] Yet other recent national survey analyses show the partisan nature of voting method choice during the pandemic, when 60 percent of Democrats chose mail-in-voting versus 30 percent of Republicans.[22]

Regardless of voting methods, ensuring the integrity of elections has been a priority for RI government officials and watchdogs. Ken Block, a former gubernatorial candidate, was an outspoken critic of election methods in Rhode Island. Block served as a guest speaker at President Donald Trump's election integrity commission in 2017, where he voiced his concerns about voter fraud in the form of duplicate voting or voting from locations other than residences. Secretary Gorbea refuted his points by explaining how voter fraud is rare in Rhode Island elections.[23] In 2021, Rhode Island legislators introduced several bills related to election integrity that never made it to a floor vote in both chambers. Some of these bills focused on allowing mail ballot certification to begin 20 days prior to election day, requiring "more comprehensive mail ballot voter signature verification process," conducting extensive cybersecurity assessment of our election systems and facilities, establishing a cybersecurity review board, examining the post-election audit of mail ballots, and identifying and canceling voter registration of registrants who change residence without notifying authorities.[24]

In 2015, Secretary Gorbea convened a voting equipment taskforce to modernize outdated voting infrastructure. In 2016, Rhode Island selected new optical scan voting machines. These machines allow for safe and secure voting measures to be in place that include paper receipts, scanned images, and paper ballots. Beginning in 2018, voters check in by using electronic poll books which makes the process more efficient. In addition, 33 other states use the e-poll books, and they are deemed safe to use with multiple levels of security in place. In 2017, Rhode Island adopted a system that authorizes risk limiting audits, making Rhode Island the second state in the country to use statistics to determine whether the election outcome was accurate. This was implemented in 2017 because of the concern over election security during the 2016 presidential election and because of raised awareness in Rhode Island of how a misalignment on a North Kingstown ballot could lead to an inaccurate vote count.[25]

Voting reform discussions have continued as the Rhode Island General Assembly considered legislation related to allowing electronic voting for overseas and military voters as well as voters with disabilities. This legislation passed in the House but was held for further study in the Senate during the 2021 session.[26] Currently, Rhode Island laws allow for overseas and military voters (voters covered by the Uniformed and Overseas Citizens Absentee Voting Act) to return their ballots via fax, although the RI Board of Elections has counted emailed ballots from these voters.[27] Comparatively, there are 31 states that allow some form of electronic voting (mobile voting app, email, fax, or web-based portal) for mostly overseas and military voters, and 19 states that restrict any electronic submissions of votes.[28]

The Let RI Vote campaign, initiated in March 2021 by the Rhode Island Voting Access Coalition, included over 25 community groups and organizations to promote legislation that supported convenience voting in Rhode Island.[29] Legislation supported by this campaign would have changed requirements for voter registration (ending the requirement for RI registered voters to live in the state for 30 days before voting and same day registration), mail ballot voting, and early voting, among other goals. Despite the efforts of this massive interest group bloc, in 2021 the General Assembly tabled bills related to expanding voting rights. Yet the General Assembly passed voting reform legislation in the next session so the temporary changes to remove the requirement for two witnesses or notary signatures for mail ballots and early in-person voting became permanent when Governor McKee signed legislation into law in June 2022.[30]

Election Administration

Under Article II, Section 2, of the Rhode Island Constitution, the General Assembly has the power to enact law related to the nomination of candidates, voter registration, absentee voting, conduct of elections, and residency requirements. These laws are implemented through the tripartite elections system. Rhode Island is one of seven states where election administration is handled by a combination of entities that includes the State Board of Elections, the local board of canvassers, and the Department of State (DOS) (see Figure 4.1 from the website of the Rhode Island Department of State). Although each entity is mentioned in the state constitution, most of their responsibilities are listed under state law.[32]

Figure 4.1 Election Administration

Agency	Main Duties
State Board of Elections	• Oversees campaign finance • Oversees election operations across the state • Tallies results • Certifies election results
Local Board of Canvassers	• Maintains voter records • Identifies polling locations • Oversees local operations
Department of State	• Maintains registration system • Certifies candidates • Prepares ballots • Provides voter information

Source: Rhode Island Department of State

The State Returning Board, established in 1901, was renamed the Board of Elections in 1941. The Board of Elections plays an important role in every election stage. In the pre-election stage, the Board trains poll workers. The Board is also responsible for testing and preparing voting machines and e-poll books. On election day, the Board of Elections is responsible for overseeing operations across the state and tallying initial results. They are also responsible for certifying the election results. Although the state constitution designates campaign finance oversight duties to the Secretary of State's office, state law gave this responsibility to the State Board of Elections in 1974.[33]

The local boards of canvassers maintain voter records throughout the year. During the pre-election stage, the local boards are responsible for certifying nomination papers, processing mail ballot applications, recruiting poll workers, and identifying polling locations. During elections, the local boards process emergency ballots and oversee operations locally.

The final segment of the election organization is the Elections Division at the DOS. The DOS manages the ballots, certifies candidates, prepares the elections calendar, provides voter IDs, disseminates election information to the public, and maintains the statewide database of registered voters and online voter registration, which was implemented in 2016.

Registered Voter Turnout

In 2020, the number of Rhode Island voters was the highest in the past 50 years. Yet, the percentage of those who voted out of the number of registered voters was at 64.1 percent, making it the twelfth highest total turnout based on percentage of registered voters who voted since 1970 (see Figure 4.2 from the Rhode Island Department of State website).[34] Comparatively, the US voting-eligible population turnout was at 66.8 percent.[35] Levels of voter turnout are influenced by several factors, such as registration requirements, demographic factors, and party composition in the states.

Figure 4.2 Voter Turnout in Rhode Island General Elections (1970–2020)

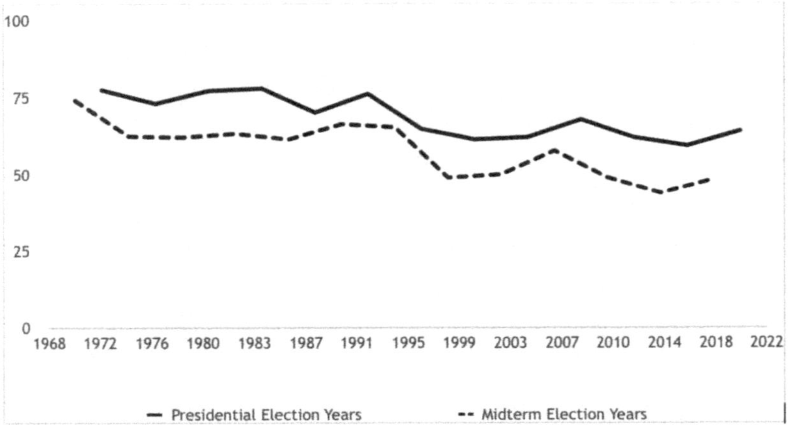

Source: Rhode Island Department of State

Socioeconomic factors like education and income are related to voter turnout. The lack of survey data, especially exit poll data at the state level in Rhode Island, makes it nearly impossible to complete a full analysis of voter turnout based on socioeconomic and demographic factors. However, Census data and the Current Population Survey can give us insight on Rhode Island voters. For instance, in the 2020 election, 67.2 percent of females and 65.3 percent of males in Rhode Island voted as a share of the voter population.[36] There was no sufficient data for the percent of voter population that voted by race and ethnicity other than whites (66.1 percent).[37] Although there is no RI voter turnout data based on education, we can examine the education levels of Rhode Island's voting eligible population in 2019. In Rhode Island, the voting eligible population (based on residents 18 and older) consisted of the following education breakdown: 9.4 percent had some high school or less, 38.4 percent had a high school diploma or less, 29.2 percent had an associate's degree or some college, and 32.4 percent had a bachelor's degree or higher.[38]

There are important voting trends based on age. Baby Boomers (born between the years of 1946 and 1964) made up the largest proportion of the number of voters in 2016, 2018, and 2020, and had the highest percentage of voters of their generation that turned out to vote (77 percent in 2020).[39] With the exception of the Greatest Generation (those born in 1927 and earlier), the rest of the generational groups of the electorate increased in voter turnout in 2020 compared to 2018 and 2016.[40]

The percent of voters who voted by mail increased substantially for each generation in 2020. A supermajority of the Greatest Generation (83 percent), and a majority of the Silent Generation (those born between 1928 and 1945) voted by mail (55 percent), making them the largest groups to use this method of voting, which suggests that alternative forms of voting may be particularly useful for older voters who are unable to make it to the polls. All generations took advantage of other methods of voting (voting by mail, voted early), with Baby Boomers having the largest percentage of their generation that voted early (32 percent of Baby Boomer turnout). Although examining voting method based on age is useful, new survey data is necessary to develop a better understanding of additional voter characteristics in Rhode Island.

Special Elections

Special elections are held at the state and local level to fill a vacancy or, on rare occasions, to recall an elected official. According to the RI Constitution, a special election for a General Assembly seat is held within three months of the vacancy or later if the vacancy occurs at the end of January. There is no special election if the vacancy occurs after the beginning of February during an election year. The Constitution does not require a special election for general office vacancies. When there is a vacancy for secretary of state, attorney general, or general treasurer, the General Assembly in grand committee (all House and Senate members) elects an individual for a temporary appointment. The RI constitution and statutes do not address cases when the lieutenant governor leaves office. General Assembly members have attempted to clarify the process to fill lieutenant governor vacancies by introducing bills that give this power to the Grand Committee. Other legislators have supported the implementation of a special election to fill the lieutenant governor vacancy.[41] These attempts have been unsuccessful. Discussion about the need to review this process came up in 2021 when President Joe Biden nominated Governor Gina Raimondo to be Secretary of Commerce. When Governor Gina Raimondo was replaced by Lieutenant Governor Daniel McKee in early 2021, McKee selected his own replacement, Providence Councilwoman Sabina Matos, and she was unanimously confirmed by the state Senate. A similar event occurred in 1997 when Governor Lincoln Almond appointed Bernard Jackvony to Lieutenant Governor Robert Weygand's seat after he won a US House election.

Special elections can also take place for bond measures, such as the recent March 2021 series of seven bond measures. The General Assembly refers constitutional amendments, statutes, and bond measures to be placed on the ballot. Examining the vote returns for higher education facilities funding for one of the 2021 measures highlights two important points: the low level of voting in special elections (14.7 percent of total active registered voters) and how voters took advantage of the multiple ways to vote because of the pandemic. Individuals who approved the measure voted through mail ballots (74 percent), at the polling place (18 percent), and emergency ballots (7 percent). Those who rejected the measure voted via mail ballot (60 percent), at the polling place (29 percent), and through emergency ballots (10.6 percent).

Initiative, Recall, and Referendum

The Rhode Island Constitution permits one direct form of participation: the recall. Rhode Islanders can vote to remove general officers only at these set times during their term, and if they were "indicted or informed against for a felony, convicted of a misdemeanor, or against whom a finding of probable cause of violation of the code of ethics has been made by the ethics commission."[42] A minimum number of signatures are required for a special recall election, and a majority of voters must support the removal of the officer. Although no Rhode Island general officer has been recalled to date, every so often campaigns have emerged, such as a short-lived campaign to remove Governor Lincoln Chafee due to his ban on members of his administration going on talk radio shows.

Other major forms of direct participation, the initiative and referendum, are not options in Rhode Island. When voters propose a ballot question for approval, it's called an initiative; when they decide whether they approve of a statute, it's called a referendum. Both forms of direct participation are initiated by submitting a petition with a set number of signatures. The state Constitution requires statewide referendums to amend the Constitution (or amendments can be made through a constitutional convention) and statewide and local referendums for gambling. The state legislature must initiate the process for a measure to be on the ballot. Governors may add advisory opinion questions on the ballot as a tactic to gauge public opinion and raise awareness on an issue, but the election result does not lead to any changes in laws. One example occurred during the early 2000s when Governor Lincoln Almond put pressure on the legislature to add a ballot measure to change the Constitution to ensure checks and balances among the branches of government. Local cities and towns have the power to adopt their own ordinances related to initiative, recall, and referendum. Some cities, such as Providence, have used the recall to remove city council members from office.

Political participation

Political participation can take many forms. Bumper stickers adorn cars with political mottos in like "Keep Hopkinton Country" in rural areas or "No New Stadium" in urban cities like Providence. Residents participate in town and city council meetings, especially when there is a hotly debated issue. In summer 2020, thousands participated in peaceful rallies and marches across the state to support Black Lives Matter. Due to the size of the state, it is relatively easy to directly access most RI politicians. Perhaps the size of the state also makes it more manageable for Rhode Islanders to stay on top of political news. Based on recent survey data, a majority of Rhode Islanders follow state and local politics most of the time (60 percent).[43]

While the level of engagement based on news consumption in Rhode Island is impressive, comparative state statistics place Rhode Island around the middle of the pack for other indicators of civic engagement. For instance, the youth engagement in Rhode Island was lower than the national rate, with 43.6 percent of young adults ages 18 to 29 discussing political or social issues with friend or family.[44] Other forms of engagement, including sharing views on social media, contacting public officials, and belonging to a group were lower than the national rate as well. Rhode Island ranks thirty-first (2020) based on eleven indicators of political engagement ranging from the number of registered voters to the number of participants in local groups or organizations.[45] Rhode Island was recently ranked the twenty-sixth state for political engagement, based on voter registration, contributions, and voter turnout.[46] Furthermore, Rhode Island is thirty-third among all states for volunteering rates.[47] Together, these rankings indicate that Rhode Islanders level of civic participation is about average compared to other states.

A Rhode Island survey conducted in April 2020 indicates how the coronavirus pandemic has affected the decision to be civically engaged in the future compared to levels of engagement before the pandemic. Although Rhode Islanders lost interest in donating and volunteering, they now express a stronger likelihood to engage in voting and express views to elected officials.[48] High levels of voting in the 2020 presidential election support this survey data.

Running for Political Office

Candidates must file a Declaration of Candidacy form to run for political office. The local board of canvassers handles these forms for local and state offices, and the Department of State handles forms for federal and statewide offices. Candidates must fill out a form with personal information (address, birth date, place of birth, length of residence in city or town) and party affiliation (Democrat, Republican, non-partisan local office, independent, other).[49] The individual must attest they are not imprisoned upon a felony sentence, they must not have served a sentence within the past three years, they are not on probation or parole for a crime committed after 1986, they have not been convicted of a felony or misdemeanor for a sentence of imprisonment for six months or more, they have never been lawfully declared as having an unsound mind, and they have not been a member of a different political party within 90 days of the filing date. The form must be turned in on the last consecutive Monday, Tuesday, or Wednesday in June before the primary election.

In order to run for political office in Rhode Island, an individual must collect a minimum number of signatures of registered voters. The required number of signatures varies by seat. For example, a candidate running for US Representative must collect 500 signatures. It is relatively easy to add your name to the RI ballot. Montana has a similar population size as Rhode Island, but sets the threshold of petition signatures at 5 percent of the votes cast for the last successful candidate. A candidate for US representative in Montana has to attain over 12,000 signatures, whereas a Rhode Island candidate only needs 500. For the General Assembly, a state representative candidate needs only 50 signatures in Rhode Island, and a candidate for Montana state representative ranged from 70 to 265 votes.[50] Rhode Island is one of 17 states that do not require any filing fees for general assembly candidates.

Ballot Placement

In a large primary, party candidates benefit from a party endorsement since this factor determines ballot placement. For multiple unendorsed primary candidates, the order of ballot placement is based on lottery by the Department of State. Party candidates are also given the benefit of appearing first on the ballot in a general election. The order of candidates on the general ballot is determined by the lottery system, and the independent candidates are always placed below the party candidates.

Endorsements

Endorsements serve as one of several heuristics individuals use to make vote decisions. Candidates can be endorsed by a party's local, district, or state committee. An asterisk is placed by the endorsed candidate's name on the ballot for primary elections. It is not unusual for candidates to win without a party endorsement. In 2020, a quarter of the Democratic candidates won the primary election without the endorsement of the Democratic Party. On the Republican side, about 10 percent of the Republican candidates won their primary without the endorsement of the Republican Party.[51] Recent research suggests party endorsements have a limited influence on state election outcomes, but future studies should examine the extent to which the party endorsement is useful in Rhode Island, especially given the lack of intra-party competition in General Assembly elections.[52] For example, in 2020, 67 percent of the Democratic candidates and 97 percent of the Republican candidates ran unopposed in the primaries. The lack of any competition is apparent even in the general elections, where 55 percent of senate seats were unopposed and 59 percent of House seats were unopposed, with only six of those unopposed seats being Republican candidates in 2020.

Campaign Finance

The Board of Elections is responsible for overseeing campaign finance. Every candidate must register with the Board of Elections before raising or spending funds. Based on the most recent Campaign Finance Annual General Assembly report, there were close to 900 active candidates and committees.[53] The majority of candidates, political action committees, and political party committees (60 percent) submit campaign finance reports electronically. Even "write-in" candidates must follow the campaign finance laws.

The Constitution allows gubernatorial candidates and other general officer candidates to voluntarily accept public financing if they qualify and follow the limitations on total campaign expenditures of campaigns. Rhode Island is one of 14 states that provide public financing options.[54] Rhode Island sets limits for maximum matching funds and maximum total amount spent and raised for candidates for general office. Also, there are statutory restrictions on how to use the public funds.[55] The total public funds for 31 candidates since 2002 is at about nine million dollars.[56] Every four years, several candidates for general state offices have made use of these public funds. For example, in 2018, the amount of public funding provided for general office candidates included $141,812 for Secretary Nellie Gorbea, $220,355 for Attorney General Peter Neronha, and $293,586 for former Lieutenant Governor Dan Mckee. Allan Fung, a Republican, used $1,175,245 of public funds for his gubernatorial campaign. There has not been any proposals or legislation from the Board of Elections to offer public funds to General Assembly members. In 2019, Common Cause worked with General Assembly members to introduce legislation to implement a public financing system for state legislators.

According to the state constitution, the General Assembly has the power to adopt limitations on contributions for state and local offices of any type of election. All candidates, political action committees (PACs), and political party committees must file quarterly campaign reports and periodic reports about campaign activity, including contributions and expenditures that exceed $100.[57] Candidates must keep records of the donors (even if they are less than $100) in case of an audit or account reconciliation. If a contribution is less than $100, then a candidate can list the contribution in the aggregate. If a contribution is more than $100, then the contributor must be itemized by disclosing the name, address, and place of employment.

Candidates can receive up to $1000 in a calendar year from an individual or PAC. Candidates can receive up to $25,000 and unlimited in-kind (non-monetary contribution like goods and services) from state political parties. All other sources of contributions are prohibited, including businesses, unions, non-profit organizations, and anonymous sources. Candidates can file an exemption from filing if they have a small campaign that spends less than $1000 in a year from small donations (less than $100 per source) so they only have to submit an annual summary at the end of the year.

If campaign reports are not filed on time with the Board of Elections, a candidate must pay a fine that continues to grow even once the election is over. In the first half of 2018, 15.9 percent of the campaign finance reports were filed late.[58] In September 2021, the Rhode Island Board of Elections published a three-page list of past candidates with outstanding fines, ranging from $25 to over $500,000.[59] In 2018, the Campaign Finance Division attempted to establish a maximum late filing fine for these reports, but the corresponding bill was held for further study.

The Board of Elections does not calculate the average candidate spending for General Assembly campaigns. However, based on anecdotal evidence, it is relatively inexpensive to run for political office in Rhode Island. General Assembly candidates typically spend around $8,000 for a low-stakes race. Efforts to win elections at the town level can be successful for under $1,000. If there is a high-stakes vote anticipated for that legislative session, a candidate in a competitive district may spend closer to $40,000 on their campaign. General Assembly leadership may spend more, perhaps due to the fact that they have larger campaign coffers.

Campaign funds must be used for campaign purposes, including advertising, consulting, donations, employee services, travel, and food, among others. Volunteers for the campaign do a lot of canvassing for candidates. One General Assembly member described how they used campaign funds to host house parties, visit coffee shops, printing, logos, yard signs, local newspaper ads, and mailers, but the largest expense was to pay a campaign manager. Use of campaign funds for personal use are restricted, although a 2021 law allows campaign contributions to be used for childcare expenses, which may make it more feasible for young mothers to enter the political pipeline.

Conclusion

While it is relatively easy to run for office in a small state like Rhode Island, there is clearly a lack of competition in state primary and general elections. Similarly, competitiveness in many other state legislative elections has been declining since the 1970s.[60] The high rate of uncontested elections in Rhode Island should continue to be a topic of discussion for party leaders and voters alike to promote the health of democracy in Rhode Island.

The RI electoral system began to change dramatically when voting access temporarily expanded due to the COVID-19 pandemic. Senator Alana DiMario, a co-sponsor of the "Let RI Vote Act" argued that "if in current times, we have the technology to allow for early in-person voting and sending mail ballot applications for people who want them, why would we not do that if the voters are liking it?"[61] In contrast, House minority leader Blake Filippi publicized the concern over election integrity, stating that "elections are all about trust and we feel many people will lose trust in our election system if this passes."[62] Yet, despite initial debates, it took a relatively short time for the General Assembly to pass legislation that permanently expanded voter accessibility through mail voting and early voting reforms. It is expected that Rhode Islanders will continue to grapple with additional election reforms that reflect the debate over balancing accessibility to polls with ensuring safe and secure elections.

Notes

1. The author thanks Rhode Island Director of Elections Rob Rock for his thoughtful review of this chapter.
2. Kate Rabinowitz and Brittany Renee Mayes, "At Least 84% of American Voters Can Cast Ballots by Mail in the Fall," September 25, 2020, https://www.washingtonpost.com/graphics/2020/politics/vote-by-mail-states/; "Vote By Mail Project Timeline," U.S. Election Assistance Commission, accessed December 17, 2021, https://www.eac.gov/sites/default/files/electionofficials/vbm/VBMProjectTimeline.pdf.
3. Nellie M. Gorbea, "Opinion/Gorbea: Rhode Islanders Will Have Safe and Secure Options to Vote," October 3, 2020, https://www.providencejournal.com/story/opinion/2020/10/03/opiniongorbea-rhode-islanders-will-have-safe-and-secure-options-to-vote/42720709/.
4. Zachary Scherer, "Majority of Voters Used Nontraditional Methods to Cast Ballots in 2020," April 29, 2021, https://www.census.gov/library/stories/2021/04/what-methods-did-people-use-to-vote-in-2020-election.html.
5. In 1723, landownership worth $134 became a requirement for voting. See Maureen Moakley and Elmer Cornwell, *Rhode Island Politics and Government* (Lincoln: University of Nebraska Press, 200), Chapter 4.
6. Steve Mintz, "Winning the Vote: A History of Voting Rights," The Gilder Lehrman Institute of American History, October 14, 2018, http://inside.sfuhs.org/dept/history/US_History_reader/Chapter2/Winning%20the%20VoteA%20History%20of%20Voting%20Rights%20Gilder%20Lehrman%20Institute%20of%20American%20History.pdf.
7. Erik J. Chaput and Russell J. DeSimone, "My Turn: Erik J. Chaput and Russell J. DeSimone: How Rhode Island Expanded Black Rights," September 16, 2017, accessed December 17, 2021, https://web.archive.org/web/20170917155413/http://www.providencejournal.com/opinion/20170916/my-turn-erik-j-chaput-and-russell-j-desimone-how-rhode-island-expanded-black-rights.
8. Chilton Williamson, "Rhode Island Suffrage since the Dorr War." *New England Quarterly* 28, no. 1 (1955): 34–50, https://doi.org/10.2307/362359.
9. Ibid.
10. In *Reynolds* v. *Sims* (1964), the Supreme Court ruled that state legislative districts must be equal in population under the equal protection clause of the Fourteenth Amendment.
11. "Guide to Address Affirmation on Election Day," State of Rhode Island Board of Elections, accessed December 17, 2021, https://elections.ri.gov/publications/Election_Publications/Voter_Info/voter_affirmation_chart_11_2008.pdf.
12. "Rhode Island Legislature Passes 16-year-old Voter Pre-registration Bill," *FairVote*, June 26, 2006, accessed December 17, 2021, https://www.fairvote.org/senate-passes-16-year-old-voter-preregistration-bill-in-rhode-island; "Preregistration for Young Voters." National Conference of State Legislatures, June 28, 2021, https://www.ncsl.org/research/elections-and-campaigns/preregistration-for-young-voters.aspx.
13. Ibid.
14. "Voting in Primaries at 17 years old," Ballotpedia, accessed December 17, 2021, https://ballotpedia.org/Voting_in_primaries_at_17_years_old#cite_note-fairvote-1; "Primary voting at Age 17," FairVote, accessed December 17, 2021,

https://www.fairvote.org/primary_voting_at_age_17#facts_17_year_old_primary_voting.
15. H7420, https://status.rilegislature.gov/; S2815, https://status.rilegislature.gov/.
16. Governor Lincoln Chafee signed the photo identification bill into law in 2011, and the requirement became effective in 2014.
17. Spencer Woodman, "The Strange Case of Rhode Island's Voter-ID Law," Vice, April 26, 2016, https://www.vice.com/en/article/qbx7j5/the-strange-case-of-rhode-islands-voter-id-law.
18. "Mail Ballot Drop Off and Early Voting Locations," accessed December 20, 2021, https://ristate.maps.arcgis.com/apps/instant/nearby/index.html?appid=72c6ecd6bddd44cbbd3f007969fb1c35.
19. "Voting By Mail and Absentee Voting," Election Lab, last modified March 16, 2021, accessed December 20, 2021, https://electionlab.mit.edu/research/voting-mail-and-absentee-voting for more information on the history of absentee voting.
20. "Research on Vote-by-mail," Stanford-MIT Healthy Elections Project, accessed December 20, 2021, https://healthyelections.org/research-vote-mail.
21. Warren Cornwall, "Do Republicans or Democrats Benefit from Mail-in Voting? It Turns Out, Neither," *Science Magazine*, August 26, 2020, https://www.sciencemag.org/news/2020/08/do-republicans-or-democrats-benefit-mail-voting-it-turns-out-neither.
22. Charles Stewart III, "How We Voted in 2020: A First Look at the Survey of the Performance of American Elections," Election Lab, December 15, 2020, http://electionlab.mit.edu/sites/default/files/2020-12/How-we-voted-in-2020-v01.pdf.
23. Katherine Gregg, "Block's Voter-Fraud Charges Fall on Deaf Ears," *Providence Journal*, September 3, 2017, https://www.providencejournal.com/news/20170903/political-scene-blocks-voter-fraud-charges-fall-on-deaf-ears; Katherine Gregg, "Block Brings Voter-fraud Allegations before Trump's 'Election Integrity' Commission," *Providence Journal*, September 12, 2017, https://www.providencejournal.com/news/20170912/block-brings-voter-fraud-allegations-before-trump-commission.
24. H5890 SUB A, H6042, S835, H5756, H6316, H5896, https://status.rilegislature.gov/.
25. Rhode Island RLA Working Group, "Pilot Implementation Study of Risk-Limiting Audit Methods in the State of Rhode Island," Brennan Center, https://www.brennancenter.org/sites/default/files/2019-09/Report-RI-Design-FINAL-WEB4.pdf.
26. S738 and H6004, https://status.rilegislature.gov/.
27. Katherine Gregg, "House Approves Electronic Voting Bill over Opposition from Board of Elections, Others," *Providence Journal*, June 17, 2021, https://www.providencejournal.com/story/news/politics/2021/06/17/ri-house-approves-bill-allow-remote-electronic-voting/7729059002/; "Investigation: Unknown Number of Emailed Ballots Counted by RI Board of Elections," GoLocalProv, July 7, 2021, https://www.golocalprov.com/news/investigation-an-unknown-number-of-emailed-ballots-were-counted-by-ri-1.
28. "Electronic Transmission of Ballots," National Conference of State Legislatures, September 5, 2019, https://www.ncsl.org/research/elections-and-campaigns/internet-voting.aspx.
29. For a full set of groups that are associated with the Let RI Vote campaign, see

https://letrivote.org/. HR6003 and its companion bill in the Senate, S516, would have changed requirements for voter registration, voter rights, mail ballots, and early day voting. Also, S569 and companion HJR5983 focused on voting reform.
30. Like other states across the country, election law reform became a priority for Rhode Island legislators in 2021. Although this type of legislation gained traction due to the pandemic, some bills had already been introduced in previous sessions. Many of these election bills emphasized accessibility while others focused on election security.
31. "Elections in Rhode Island," Rhode Island Department of State, accessed January 9, 2023, https://vote.sos.ri.gov/Elections/Administration.
32. Several duties of the secretary of state are mentioned the state Constitution, including matters related to campaign finance, certification of statewide referendums related to gambling, and retaining copies of certified charters. The governor reports a pocket veto to the secretary of state. The Board of Canvassers is mentioned in the Constitution as responsible for certifying the results of local referendums about gambling and applying for and certifying a local charter. Although oversight of recall elections is the only duty of the Board of Elections that is explicitly stated in the constitution, they play a significant role in the election process.
33. "Rhode Island. State Board of Elections (1941–)," Rhode Island Department of State, accessed December 20, 2021, https://catalog.sos.ri.gov/agents/corporate_entities/17.
34. "Voter Turnout in Rhode Island," Rhode Island Department of State, accessed December 20, 2021, https://storymaps.arcgis.com/stories/6645c173c1f343e0a2411034e4594402.
35. "2020 November General Election Turnout Rates," United States Election Project, December 7, 2020, http://www.electproject.org/2020g. Rhode Island's voter turnout (65.3 percent) on the United States Election Project website is slightly higher than Rhode Island's Department of State data referenced in the chapter.
36. "Number of Voters as a Share of the Voter Population, by Sex," KFF, accessed December 20, 2021, https://www.kff.org/other/state-indicator/number-of-individuals-who-voted-in-thousands-and-individuals-who-voted-as-a-share-of-the-voter-population-by-sex/currentTimeframe=0&sortModel=%7B%22colId%22:%22Location%22,%22sort%22:%22asc%22%7D.
37. "Voting and Voter Registration as a Share of the Voter Population, by Race/Ethnicity," KFF, accessed December 20, 2021, https://www.kff.org/other/state-indicator/voting-and-voter-registration-as-a-share-of-the-voter-population-by-raceethnicity/?currentTimeframe=0&sortModel=%7B%22colId%22:%22Location%22,%22sort%22:%22asc%22%7D.
38. Angela Underwood, "Voter Demographics of Every State," *Stacker*, October 26, 2021, https://stacker.com/stories/4884/voter-demographics-every-state.
39. "Voter Turnout in Rhode Island."
40. Ibid.
41. Katherine Gregg, "Deputy Speaker Lima Says Voters Should Choose RI's Next Lt. Governor," *Providence Journal*, January 13, 2021, https://www.providencejournal.com/story/news/politics/2021/01/12/deputy-speaker-lima-calls-special-election-lieutenant-governor/6637521002/.
42. According to the RI Constitution, a recall cannot occur during the first six months or last year of an individual's term in office.

43. Shanna Pearson-Merkowitz, "RI News Survey Highlights and Analysis," Social Science Institute for Research, Education, and Policy, accessed December 20, 2021, https://web.uri.edu/ssirep/ri-news-survey-highlights-and-analysis/.
44. "Youth Voting and Civic Engagement in America," Center for Information and Research on Civic Learning and Engagement, Tufts University, accessed December 20, 2021, https://circle.tufts.edu/explore-our-data/youth-voting-and-civic-engagement-america#data-sources.
45. These indicators include registered voters, voters, political contributions, civic education engagement, voting accessibility, preparedness to vote in a pandemic, preregistration for young voter policies, volunteer political campaign opportunities, and participation in local groups or organizations.
46. Ben Geier, "Most Politically Engaged States – 2020 Edition," *smartasset*, January 27, 2020, https://smartasset.com/checking-account/most-politically-engaged-states-2020.
47. "Volunteering in America: States," *AmeriCorps.gov*, accessed December 20, 2021, https://americorps.gov/sites/default/files/document/Volunteering_in_America_States_508.pdf. 28.7% of the respondents in the survey stated they participate in local groups or organizations.
48. Survey question: "Compared with your involvement before the Coronavirus crisis, will you be more or less likely to engage in the following political activity in the future?"; "Rhode Island Leadership Survey for the Hassenfeld Institute for Public Leadership," Hassenfeld Institute for Public Leadership, April 2020, accessed December 20, 2021, https://hassenfeld.bryant.edu/wp-content/uploads/2020/04/Hassenfeld-Survey-Report-April-2020.pdf.
49. "Declaration of Candidacy," Rhode Island Department of State, accessed December 20, 2021, https://vote.sos.ri.gov/Content/Pdfs/Calendar/Declaration%20of%20Candidacy-SenateD3web.pdf. The declaration of candidacy form states that if a candidate declares "other" for party affiliation, then the organization or political principle represented must be three words or less and the title must not include the word "Republican" nor "Democrat."
50. "Information for Independent, Minor Party, and Indigent Candidates," Montana Secretary of State, accessed December 20, 2021, https://sosmt.gov/Portals/142/Elections/Documents/Officials/Independent-Minor-Party-Indigent-Candidate-Info.pdf.
51. In the 2020 primaries, there were a total of 102 Democratic primary elections, and 25 Democratic candidates won without the endorsement of the Democratic Party. On the Republican side, out of 31 Republican primary elections, 3 Republican candidates for the General Assembly won their primary without the endorsement of the Republican Party. The 28 unendorsed winners in 2020 General Assembly elections consisted of 9 Democratic Senate candidates, 16 Democratic House candidates, 2 Republican Senate candidates, and 1 Republican House candidate.
52. Thad Kousser, Scott Lucas, Seth Masket, and Eric McGhee. "Kingmakers or Cheerleaders? Party Power and the Causal Effects of Endorsements," *Political Research Quarterly* 68, no.3 (2015): 443–56, doi: http://jstor.org/stable/24637786.
53. "State of Rhode Island Board of Elections Campaign Finance Division Annual Report to the General Assembly 2018," State of Rhode Island Board of Elections, accessed December 20, 2021, https://elections.ri.gov/publications/Campaign_Finance/2018_Annual_GA_Report.pdf.

54. "Public Financing of Campaigns: An Overview," National Conference of State Legislatures, February 8, 2019, https://www.ncsl.org/research/elections-and-campaigns/public-financing-of-campaigns-overview.aspx.
55. Title 17: Elections, http://webserver.rilin.state.ri.us/Statutes/TITLE17/17-25/17-25-20.HTM.
56. Data provided by Board of Elections via email on June 10, 2021.
57. Candidates are prohibited from accepting cash contributions that exceed $25.
58. "State of Rhode Island Board of Elections Campaign Finance Division."
59. "Aging Fines," Rhode Island Board of Elections, September 30, 2021, https://elections.ri.gov/fines/index.php.
60. "Electoral Competitiveness in Rhode Island," accessed November 15, 2021, https://ballotpedia.org/Electoral_competitiveness_in_Rhode_Island.
61. Philip Cozzolino, "Bills Would Make Pandemic Voting Methods Permanent," *Narragansett Times*, May 26, 2021, accessed December 20, 2021, https://www.ricentral.com/narragansett_times/bills-would-make-pandemic-voting-methods-permanent/article_e3b4fcba-be81-11eb-8490-0f323445a50f.html.
62. See Patrick Anderson, "New Push to Expand Early Voting Meets GOP Pushback, April 6, 2021, https://www.providencejournal.com/story/news/politics/2021/04/06/new-push-expand-early-voting-meets-gop-pushback/7107330002.

5 / Political Parties

EMILY K. LYNCH[1]

In 2019 the Rhode Island Democratic Party suffered a major loss when the women's caucus split from the state organization. Liz Gledhill, the chair of the newly formed Rhode Island Democratic Women's Caucus, criticized Democratic leaders for adopting new bylaws requiring all party caucuses to support the same candidates. Democratic Party leaders defended the new requirements to unify the party. The disagreement was highly visible, as hostile and sexist remarks about party members were exchanged at meetings and posted online. The sharp differences between the Rhode Island Democratic Party and the women's caucus serve as an example of the coordination problems that can arise due to the nature of the American two-party system, in which power rests on broad and loose coalitions, and dissenting voices can emerge. A one-party state like Rhode Island can exacerbate the in-party fighting, since one party has control of state politics.

Rhode Island is a Democratic stronghold, like most other New England states. A closer examination of the parties represents a richer story, where Democrats dominate all elections in Rhode Island, yet partisan identification is weak, since there are just as many unaffiliated registered voters as Democrats. Furthermore, it is common knowledge among Rhode Islanders that some of their Democratic Assembly members would be considered Republicans in many other states based on their ideological views. The independent nature of the state is a critical factor to consider when examining political parties in the Ocean State. Rhode Islanders, with their independent and unsorted political identity, offer insights into the practices of political parties in Rhode Island. This may be one of the main underlying reasons why there is such a lack of party competition in the state.

This chapter examines the current state of political parties in Rhode Island. The first section is a brief historical overview of the political parties. The Rhode Island political party system consists of three interacting components, including the *party in the electorate*—the individuals who support the party, the *party in government*—the party candidates and members who hold public office, and the *party organization*—party leaders and activists. Each of these political party components in Rhode Island are examined throughout this chapter.

Development of the Rhode Island Party System

Political parties are meant to be vehicles of democracy and serve as intermediaries between citizens and political leaders. The strength of and support for the major political parties—the Democrats and Republicans—have shifted throughout Rhode Island history. Although Rhode Island has been a one-party state since the 1800s, Democrats have not been the only party in control. Wealthy Yankee Protestants, affiliated with the Republican Party in Rhode Island, initially controlled politics in the state. Similar to other states, early political cleavages in Rhode Island were along ethnic, class, and religious lines. Republicans used these divisions to their advantage to remain in power. Over time, the size of the electorate increased when the Bourne Amendment, legislation abolishing property qualifications, passed in 1888, and when women gained the right to vote in 1920. Even as enfranchisement expanded, Republicans remained in charge at the State House. It was rare for Democrats to win executive positions at the state level, although Democratic governors won in 1906 and 1922. Rhode Islanders put their support behind Democrat Woodrow Wilson in 1912 in a close race, with third-party candidate Theodore Roosevelt taking nearly 22 percent of the votes in the state.[2]

It wasn't until 1928 that another Democratic presidential candidate, Al Smith, won Rhode Island. New Democratic voters were mobilized in Rhode Island due to shifts in class, religion, and the labor movement.[3] The dire state of the economy led to a substantial shift to support the Democratic Party presidential candidate, Franklin Delano Roosevelt, in 1932. At the same time, Democratic gubernatorial candidate Theodore Francis Green was elected, which ultimately led to one of the most remarkable events that forever changed the landscape of Rhode Island politics—the Bloodless Revolution in 1935. The "well-planned coup" led by Democratic Lieutenant Governor Robert Quinn turned the red state blue within weeks by vacating the Supreme Court and replacing them with a Democratic majority court and reorganizing the administration to give the governor more authority over boards and commissions; this was accompanied by the recount of two disputed Senate elections, which Democrats won.[4]

Republicans continued to hold the majority of Senate seats in the General Assembly because of jurisdictional representation required in the state Constitution, since a larger proportion of Republicans lived in the rural towns.[5] Yet, Republican power, with deep roots in industrial and financial industries, was diminishing due to growing working-class support for the Democrats.[6] After the Supreme Court ruled in a series of cases about state reapportionment that both houses of a state legislature must have representation based on population, malapportionment was corrected in the state. Republicans all but vanished from the Senate as more Democratic representatives came from urban areas. The number of Republican General Assembly members shrunk considerably after new district maps were approved in 1966, which led to a Democratic majority reaching at least 70 percent in both chambers.[7]

Although Democrats gained control of Rhode Island politics in the decades following the Bloodless Revolution, patronage that had existed under Republican control remained a big part of RI political culture, albeit shifting from a more rural to urban machine.[8] There was a noticeable shift in the 1970s when professionalization of RI government greatly weakened the political machine. Reforms extended into every branch of government during this time due to exposure to state inefficiencies and national scandals along with the growth in a large suburban middle class that supported professional politics.[9] The General Assembly adopted reforms related to lobbying, the constitutional amendment process, the committee system, and scheduling practices. Governor Philip Noel established professional policy staff in the governor's office. Chief Justice Anthony Bevilacqua implemented a more efficient court system. Support for professionalization ushered in changes to the electoral system as well.

Rhode Island political parties have always controlled the nominating process in elections. Since 1948, direct primaries have been used to elect state and municipal candidates. The 1948 law included a "novel" feature: the primary ballot indicated the party committee endorsed candidate on the ballot with an asterisk and placed them at the top of the list.[10] The initial primary system was closed to allow only registered party voters to participate in their respective party's primary. In 1972, closed primary restrictions loosened due to *Yale v. Curvin*, in which US District Court judges struck down an "unreasonable and excessive" state statute prohibiting an individual from voting in a primary or signing nomination papers if they had voted in a primary or signed nomination papers for candidates from another party in the past 26 months.[11] This decision led to a short-lived period during which Rhode Island had an open primary system that allowed voters to freely choose if they wanted to vote in the Democratic or Republican primary, no matter which party they registered for.

There were immediate concerns about the open system in which voters could "raid" the primaries and strategically cast a vote in their opposing party's primaries to adopt the weaker candidate. A governor's commission to study the election process recommended changing the open primary to a semi-open primary in which voters could affiliate with the party before the election and then vote in their respective party's primary.[12] In 1978, the General Assembly passed legislation to adopt a semi-open primary system. This may have been a factor in the increase in registered independent voters, since voters had the flexibility to change their party affiliation before the primary. As discussed in the elections chapter, now unaffiliated voters may choose which party to vote for in the primaries and then can immediately fill out forms to disaffiliate from the party once they vote. This allows independent voters a choice of which party to support in each election.

Changes to the electoral system, political scandals, and population shifts certainly had an impact on party loyalties at this time. Although political campaigns across the nation were becoming more candidate centered, it was strongly apparent in Rhode Island. From the mid-1970s through the 1980s, Rhode Island held the top spot for the state with the highest percentage of independent voters.[13] Most Rhode Islanders were registered as independents or Democrats, even though the Republican Party attracted new voters under the Reagan presidency in the 1980s. Additional political scandals exposed in the 1990s led to further voter disapproval and distrust in the parties (e.g., Governor Edward DiPrete's corruption convictions, the Rhode Island banking crisis). Despite these scandals, the party composition of the state has largely remained the same, with a shift back in the direction of the Democratic Party, as seen by recent party registration data.

Party in the Electorate

Rhode Island is considered a one-party state since most state elected officials and a supermajority of the General Assembly are Democrats, and the electorate somewhat reflects this Democratic dominance. The Democratic Party's strength in the electorate is subdued based on the large size of unaffiliated voters; there is roughly the same percentage of registered unaffiliated voters as Democrats. The combined number of those who are registered Democrats and unaffiliated voters is six times the size of registered Republicans in the state. Independents are a key factor in understanding partisan strength in the Rhode Island electorate.

Voter registration data in 2021 indicates that 42 percent of voters are registered as Democrats and 14 percent registered Republicans (see Table 5.1). The largest group of registered voters are unaffiliated (44 percent). One noticeable trend in Table 5.1 is the significant drop in the number of active voters from 2016 through 2021. Secretary Nelly Gorbea focused on voter roll maintenance through the enrollment in the Electronic Registration Information Center in 2015 and removed over 180,000 voter records during her tenure as secretary of state.[14]

Rhode Island's independent citizenry is notable among other states. As one of ten states with more registered independents than registered Democrats or Republicans, the Ocean State is considered one of the least politically competitive states due to the relative size of registered Democrats and Republicans.[15] Political analysts have labeled Rhode Island as one of the most elastic states, with a high sensitivity to political shifts because of the large size of unaffiliated voters.[16]

Table 5.1. Registered voters in Rhode Island

Year	Democrats	%	Republicans	%	Moderate	%	Unaffiliated	%	Total
2008	296,283	43	76,345	11	N/A	–	322,099	46	694,727
2010	295,376	42	73,793	11	354	0	332,960	47	702,483
2012*	300,965	41	77,338	11	1,082	0	354,294	48	733,781
2014	315,455	42	83,177	11	1,935	0	354,298	47	754,865
2016	309,112	40	92,713	12	2,544	0	365,845	47	770,214
2018	320,700	44	100,401	14	3,352	0	307,465	42	731,918
2020	324,892	45	104,279	15	N/A	–	288,566	40	717,737
2021	298,694	42	99,131	14	N/A	–	311,452	44	709,277

Data retrieved from Department of State and https://datahub.sos.ri.gov/RegisteredVoter.aspx. Registration data are from August, October, or November of each year.* In 2012, 102 voters were registered under the "Americans Elect" party.

National survey data indicate that many independents lean toward one of the major parties. In 2017, survey data showed a Democratic advantage in Rhode Island where Democrats and leaners were estimated to be at 48 percent and Republicans and leaners made up 27 percent.[17] A large portion of Rhode Islanders neither identify as Democrat or Republican nor lean one way or the other. Comparatively speaking, Rhode Island had the largest percentage of non-identifiers of all the states, with a quarter of the respondents who did not identify or lean with either party. Similarly, state survey data show a large percentage of independents (see Table 5.2). Over 80 percent of Rhode Islanders consistently self-identify as Democrat or Independent.

Table 5.2. Party Identification in Rhode Island, 2010–2018

Year	Rep	Dem	Ind	Refused
2010	17	42	39	2
2012	17	40	40	3
2014	15	40	42	4
2016	*	*	*	*
2018	14	38	46	2

Source: Fleming & Associates, Providence, RI   No survey data available in 2016

While party identification survey questions measure an individual's attachment to a political party, political ideology questions can offer insights into their belief system about the scope of government. We must also rely on national surveys to assess the ideological spectrum of Rhode Islanders. In 2014, the breakdown of Rhode Island respondents in a national survey identified 26 percent conservative, 35 percent moderate, 30 percent liberal, and 8 percent don't know.[18] Another national poll shows a similar pattern: Rhode Island tends to have less self-identified conservatives and more liberals than other states.[19]

Examining primary election turnout is another way to assess the level of political party participation and competition in the state. Table 5.3 displays information about Democratic and Republican gubernatorial elections from 1990 through 2018. The average primary turnout as a percent of the general election turnout is 38 percent. The data indicate that in recent primaries, nearly four times more voters participated in the Democratic primaries than in the Republican primaries.

Table 5.3. Primary and General Gubernatorial Election Turnout

Year	Democratic Primary Turnout	Republican Primary Turnout	Primary Turnout Total	General Election Total
1990	167,916	10,801	178,717	356,588
1992	150,746	14,460	165,206	424,818
1994	99,132	45,023	144,155	361,377
1998	64,616	5,510	70,126	306,445
2002	119,524	25,745	145,269	332,056
2006	69,595	51,650	121,245	386,928
2010	73,142	18,817	91,959	342,290
2014	128,095	31,929	160,024	324,055
2018	117,875	33,087	150,962	376,401

Source: State of Rhode Island Board of Elections

Party in Government

Federal Elections: Presidency

If one takes a drive through rural Rhode Island, an outsider might be surprised to see Donald Trump signs and "Don't Tread on Me" flags flying in this Democratic stronghold. It is clear there is support for Republicans in the western rural part of the state, but the populations are not large enough for the state to swing Republican.

Rhode Islanders have supported almost every Democratic presidential candidate since 1928. Exceptions include support for New York's Dwight D. Eisenhower in 1952 and 1956, Nixon in 1972, and Reagan in 1984, all of whom gained an overwhelmingly majority of electoral college votes throughout the country. Since 2000, support for the Democratic presidential candidate has remained between 54 and 63 percent. With the exception of 2016, three-fifths of Rhode Islanders consistently support the Democratic presidential candidate.

Rhode Island stands out among the rest of the states as one of the most supportive states for Barack Obama in 2008 and 2012 (63 percent support in both election years). Rhode Island was in the top ten for most support of the Democratic presidential candidate in 2016 (tenth) and 2020 (seventh). In comparison to the other New England states, Rhode Island and Connecticut had the same split in the 2020 presidential election (59 percent for Biden; 39 percent for Trump).

Table 5.4 indicates that most votes go to the major party candidates in presidential elections. Two election years stand out as anomalies: a larger than normal portion of the electorate voted for independent candidates (or write-ins) in the 2000 and 2016 presidential elections. In 2000, popular Green Party candidate Ralph Nader secured a solid 25,000 votes in Rhode Island. Although Democratic candidate Hillary Clinton won in Rhode Island in 2016, third-party voting and write-ins consisted of nearly 7 percent of the vote total. Additionally, Republican candidate Donald Trump enjoyed an increase in overall support compared to support for the Republican candidate Mitt Romney in the previous presidential election. Future research should parse out the reasons why Rhode Islanders strayed from their usual 2 percent support for independents or write-ins and jumped to over 6 percent in these elections.

Table 5.4. Rhode Island Presidential Vote

Year	Democrat	Republican
2000	61%	32 %
2004	59 %	39 %
2008	63 %	35 %
2012	63 %	35 %
2016	54 %	39 %
2020	59 %	39 %

Data retrieved from State of Rhode Island Board of Elections

The most visible trend in Rhode Island politics at the presidential level over the past two decades is the strong urban–rural divide. Here, we see a clear Trump effect in the state. Trump won 11 of the 39 municipalities in Rhode Island in 2020, although he won more municipalities (14) in 2016. In 2000, rural Scituate and wealthy East Greenwich were the only towns that supported the Republican presidential candidate (see Figure 5.1). Scituate has been the only municipality that has supported the Republican candidate in every presidential election since 2000. This dramatically changed in 2016 where unconventional Republican presidential candidate Donald Trump carried 14 of the 39 towns in the state, which were all in the western, more rural part of the state. According to political scientist Adam Myers, Republicans missed a big opportunity at this time to translate presidential candidate support into support at the state level in part due to the lack of Republican state legislative candidates.[20] Further discussion of uncontested legislative seats is in the General Assembly section below.

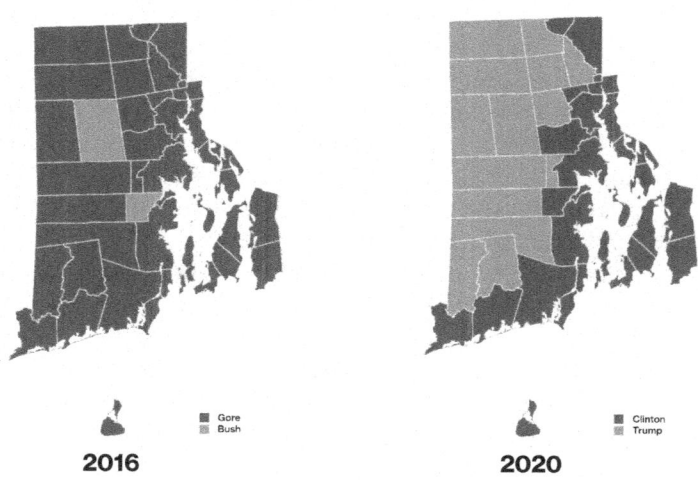

Figure 5.1. Presidential Election Results by Municipality

2016   2020

Source: Eli Sherman, "Here's how RI cities and towns have voted in every presidential race since Reagan," Target 12, October 28, 2020, https://www.wpri.com/target-12/heres-how-ri-cities-and-towns-have-voted-in-every-presidential-race-since-reagan/.

Federal Elections: US Congress

Four characteristics are shared by most of the Rhode Island federal delegation for decades: they are incumbents, Democrats, white, and men. A short review of federal election results highlights these common characteristics in this section.

US Senate

A quick peek at the late twentieth-century Senate delegation shows that the incumbency benefit has been a historical trend. Each Senate seat has been held by the same senators for decades. Senator Claiborne Pell, without the endorsement of the Democratic party in the primary, won a Senate seat in 1960. Pell's primary win against two former governors highlights the candidate-centered campaign, where Pell could use his personal wealth in his campaign and control his image, presenting himself as the same mold as the young and liberal John F. Kennedy.[21] US Representative Jack Reed ran for Pell's seat once he announced his retirement in 1996. Reed has been re-elected four times in 2002, 2008, 2014, and 2020 with between 66 and 78 percent of the vote (see Table 5.4). Reed serves as the chair of the Committee on Armed Services, and he is a member of the Committee on Appropriations, Committee on Banking, Housing, and Urban Affairs, and the Select Committee on Intelligence. Reed is respected by both parties in the Senate and has a reputation for supporting legislation that has a direct impact on Rhode Islanders, such as infrastructure programs that funded bridge repairs and an airport extension in the state.[22]

John Chafee, a former US secretary of the navy and popular governor, served alongside Pell as the junior senator from 1976 until he died in office in 1999. When Chafee passed away, his son Lincoln was appointed by Republican Governor Lincoln Almond to fill his seat, and then Chafee won the seat in 2000. John and Lincoln Chafee were the only Republicans elected to the US Senate from Rhode Island since voters re-elected Jesse Metcalf in 1930. Chafee, considered the most liberal Republican in the Senate, was ousted by former US and Rhode Island Attorney General Sheldon Whitehouse in 2006 (see Table 5.5). With the election of Whitehouse, the Democrats briefly regained majority of the Senate. Whitehouse kept his seat in the 2012 and 2018 elections with over 60 percent of the vote. In 2022, Whitehouse has served as a member of the powerful Budget, Judiciary, and Finance Committees, and he serves on the Environment and Public Works Committee. He has been a vocal advocate for campaign finance reform and a staunch supporter of climate action. In 2022, he delivered his 280th "Time to Wake Up" speech about climate change.

Table 5.5 Senate Vote

Year	Democrat %	Republican %	Winner
2000	41.1	56.9	Chafee
2002	78.4	21.6	Reed
2006	53.5	46.5	Whitehouse
2008	73.4	26.6	Reed
2012	64.8	35	Whitehouse
2014	70.6	29.2	Reed
2018	61.4	38.3	Whitehouse
2020	66.5	33.4	Reed

Data retrieved from State of Rhode Island Board of Elections

US House of Representatives

Since 1940, there have been only two Republican US Representatives from Rhode Island: Claudine Schneider (1981–91) and Ronald Machtley (1989–95).

Not only was Schneider one of two Republicans serving in the House from Rhode Island, but she is the only woman ever to hold this office. Both candidates won at a time when Republican support had strengthened in Rhode Island and nationwide. The Rhode Island Republicans overlapped in the House for just one term (1988). Democrat Jack Reed defeated Schneider in 1990 for Congressional District 2 seat. In 1994, Democrat Patrick Kennedy unseated Machtley in District 1.

Patrick Kennedy decided not to run for reelection in 2010, which was the first time since 1947 that someone from the Kennedy family had not been in politics.[23] David Cicilline, a former mayor of Providence, was elected to the US House in 2010 after defeating his opponents with 37 percent of the vote in a four-way race for the Democratic nomination. Cicilline's margin of victories have widened since 2010 (see Table 5.6), with some attribution paid to redistricting after the 2010 census where a Democratic section of Providence with a sizeable Latino population shifted to Cicilline's district and Burrillville, a conservative town in the northwest corner of the state, was moved to the second district.[24] Cicilline serves on the Judiciary Committee and Foreign Affairs Committee. Although Cicilline's time in office is relatively short, Cicilline has taken various leadership positions including serving as the chair of the LGBTQ+ Equality Caucus and the vice-chair of the Congressional Progressive Caucus.

Table 5.6: RI Partisan Vote for U.S. House of Representatives, 2000–2020

	District 1			District 2		
Year	Democrat %	Republican %	Winner	Democrat %	Republican %	Winner
2000	66.7	33.2	Kennedy	62.2	14	Langevin
2002	59.9	37.3	Kennedy	76.3	22.3	Langevin
2004	64.1	35.8	Kennedy	74.5	20.8	Langevin
2006	69.2	23.2	Kennedy	72.7	27.3*	Langevin
2008	68.6	24.3	Kennedy	70.1	29.2	Langevin
2010	50.6	44.6	Cicilline	59.9	31.8	Langevin
2012	53.0	40.8	Cicilline	55.7	35.1	Langevin
2014	59.5	40.2	Cicilline	62.2	37.6	Langevin
2016	64.5	35.1	Cicilline	58.1	30.7	Langevin
2018	66.7	33.1	Cicilline	63.5	36.3	Langevin
2020	70.8	27.1**	Cicilline	58.2	41.5	Langevin

*In 2006, no Republican candidate ran in District 2. 27.3 percent represents the percentage of votes for an independent candidate.
**In 2020, no Republican candidate ran in District 1. 27.1 percent represents the total percentage of votes for two independent candidates and write-ins.
Data retrieved from State of Rhode Island Board of Elections.

When Reed decided to run for the open US Senate seat due to Senator Pell's retirement, Lieutenant Governor Robert Weygand had the opportunity to run for the open District 2 seat. Weygand held the seat until he stepped down to run for Senate in 2000. The Rhode Island secretary of state, James Langevin, was elected to the open House seat in 2000. Langevin held this seat until he announced that he would not seek reelection in 2022. Langevin was the first quadriplegic to serve in Congress. In 2022, Langevin served on the House Armed Services Committee and the Committee on Homeland Security and has been recognized as a leader on cybersecurity issues.

General State Offices

Since 1935, Democrats have largely dominated the governor's office in the state. The handful of exceptions to this long era of Democratic dominance in the governor's seat include four Republican governors from the late 1930s through 1990s. More recently, Republicans Lincoln Almond and Donald Carcieri were elected in 1994 and 2002, respectively. It is apparent that gender dynamics played a role in recent elections when Myrth York, the first woman Democratic gubernatorial candidate, lost to Almond and Carcieri. Twelve years after York's final gubernatorial loss, Democrat Gina Raimondo proved a woman could win the state's highest leadership position.

Over the years the Democratic party has recruited viable candidates with past political experience for the other state offices—lieutenant governor, general treasurer, secretary of state, and attorney general. Three important trends stand out from the most recent data on the statewide elections (see Table 5.7). First, apart from Almond and Carcieri's terms as governor, Democrats have held every statewide office since 1998. Second, it has become more common for Democratic women to win statewide offices. Finally, it's clear that the winner has not always received the majority of votes. In fact, the Rhode Island constitution states that the candidate only needs a plurality of votes to win. Recently, legislation has been introduced to amend the constitution to require a candidate to win a majority of the votes. In 2010, Lincoln Chafee, the former US Senator, won as an Independent with only 36 percent of the vote. Most recently, in 2014, Gina Raimondo did not earn a majority of votes in the general election (40 percent). In a state with many independents, it is clear that if a third party runs for office, it can affect the major party candidates' chance to earn a majority vote.

Table 5.7: Party Control of Statewide Offices, 1994–2018

Election Year	Governor (% total votes)	Lt. Gov.	Gen. Treasurer	Sec. of State	Att. Gen.
1994	R – Almond (47.4 %)	D	R#	D	R
1998	R – Almond (51 %)	D	D	D	D
2002	R – Carcieri (54 %)	D	D	D	D
2006	R – Carcieri (51 %)	D#	D	D	D
2010	I/D* – Chafee (36.1 %)	D#	D#	D	D
2014	D# – Raimondo (40.7 %)	D	D	D#	D
2018	D# – Raimondo (52.6 %)	D**	D	D#	D

*Lincoln Chafee switched from Independent to Democrat in 2013.
# Indicates a woman winner.
**In 2018 voters elected Dan McKee, a Democrat, to the office of lieutenant governor, who vacated the seat in 2001 to become Governor when Gina Raimondo was appointed U.S. Commerce Secretary. Governor McKee appointed Sabina Matos, who became the first Latina lieutenant governor in Rhode Island.
Data retrieved from State of Rhode Island Board of Elections.

General Assembly

Democrats have had unmatched power in the Rhode Island General Assembly for decades. Democratic control solidified in the House in the late 1930s after the Bloodless Revolution. It wasn't until rural malapportionment was fixed in the 1960s that Democratic control of state Senate became the norm.[25] Contemporary politics indicate most states are similar to Rhode Island, where both houses in all state legislatures are controlled by one party (with the exception of Minnesota, which has the sole divided legislature, and Nebraska's unicameral and nonpartisan legislature), a trend that, until recently, had not occurred since 1914.[26] One-party control goes beyond the state legislature for most states. Taking into account the governor's party in 2020, Rhode Island was one of 15 Democratic trifectas (where the governor and state legislatures are the same party), with another 23 Republican trifectas, for a total of 38 party trifectas, the largest number of trifectas since 1952.[27] Many states are passing one-sided legislation, which underscores the polarized nature of American politics at this time.[28]

Despite Rhode Island's long-lasting run as a one-party state, Rhode Island is not passing what may be considered extremely liberal legislation and is not considered the most liberal state. Take, for example, Rhode Island's 2019 abortion legislation that codified *Roe* v. *Wade*. It took 25 years for the RI House Speaker to vote on an abortion-rights bill.[29] The main reason for this lack of a strongly progressive agenda is that RI Republicans and Democrats have fewer ideological differences than any other state.[30] Yet Republicans have carved a small space within state politics. Rhode Island is only behind Hawaii as having the smallest percentage of Republicans in the state legislature.[31] Currently, during the 2021–22 session, there are ten Republican representatives and five Republican senators, making up about 13 percent of each of the chambers.

The RI General Assembly continues to be considered one of the least competitive legislatures in the country, based on percentage of open seats, number of incumbents in contested primaries, and seats with major party competition.[32] The lack of competition in General Assembly elections is widespread and consistent throughout the past several decades. In 2014, competition, measured by winners by wide margins and number of uncontested seats, was the lowest it has been over the last 40 years.[33] The average percentages of uncontested seats in the RI Senate and House are 43 percent and 46 percent, respectively (see Table 5.8). The least number of uncontested seats over the past couple decades was in the 2010 election (21 percent in the RI House and Senate), perhaps due to national factors such as the Great Recession and overall discontent with the government. In addition, intra-party competition in elections is low, where the majority of primary elections tend to be uncontested. In 2020, 48 of 75 Democratic House primary seats were unopposed, and in 2018, there were 54 uncontested seats. For the Senate, 21 of the 38 seats were uncontested in 2020 and 20 in 2018. There were only a handful of primary elections for general assembly seats that included three or more candidates (5 Democratic primary races in 2020 and 3 in 2018). On the Republican side, the lack of competition is even more concerning, where only a few races each year include two candidates.

Table 5.8. Partisan Division of Rhode Island General Assembly, 1999–2022

Session	House Dem-Rep	Uncontested % in General Election	Senate Dem-Rep	Uncontested % in General Election
1999–2000	86–13*	57	42–8	56
2001–2002	85–15	54	44–6	54
2003–2004	63–11*	48	32–6	34
2005–2006	60–15	27	33–5	26
2007–2008	62–13	47	33–5	45
2009–2010	65–10	40	33–4*	39
2011–2012	65–10	21	29–8*	21
2013–2014	69–6	44	32–5*	39
2015–2016	63–11*	60	32–5*	53
2017–2018	64–10*	45	33–5	53
2019–2020	66–9	52	33–5	45
2021–2022	65–10	59	33–5	55

Source: State of Rhode Island Board of Elections   *Third party or independent elected

Party Organizations

The primary purpose of state party organizations is to support the parties within the state during and in-between elections. State party committees will recruit candidates, support candidates in campaigns, mobilize voters, and shape the party platform. Recently, there have been signs that the Democratic Party, aware of growing intra-party pressures, is motivated to strengthen its resources to support establishment candidates, such as through candidate training. Candidate training resources are available through both major parties, and other organizations like RI Political Co-op and Working Families Party train candidates.

The Democratic State Committee calendar includes dates of fundraisers at various venues for General Assembly members, beginning with leadership at the beginning of March and running through June. About 50 fundraisers are strategically held for Democrats during the legislative session. There have been few fundraisers scheduled for Republicans, with little incentive for the national or state Republican party organizations to increase its efforts to recruit and support local candidates because of the dominance of the Rhode Island Democratic Party.

Although state committees can help with endorsement or fundraising, the local feel of state races lead candidates to request support of party committees at the town or city level. Also, Rhode Islanders see more personalized campaigns in which candidates still use door-to-door campaigning as well as television ads and social media to reach out to constituents and voters. State politicians maintain their own Facebook, Instagram, and Twitter pages. Candidates tend to share campaign managers, or their family or friends take on the role due to the nature of the part-time legislature.

Party organizations are critical to promoting the party agenda. The party activists, committees, and leaders all work to elect party candidates and unify the party message. Despite the Democratic Party's dominance in the state, the Democratic state organization has recently faced resistance within their party. As noted in the introduction, a notable shift in the Democratic Party occurred when a group of women split from the Democratic State Committee in 2019. These Democratic State Committee members were upset that the Democratic State Committee supported a Trump supporter over a female Democratic incumbent in the General Assembly, and the state committee's bylaws restricted them from supporting candidates without the chair's approval. The Democratic State Committee's reasoning for the bylaw was to be unified in their messaging from the party.[34] In 2020, the newly formed Democratic Women's caucus endorsed 29 general assembly candidates, and 90 percent of them went on to win, exemplifying Democratic candidates' ability to be elected without the Democratic establishment's blessing. This put pressure on the Democratic State Committee to adjust their leadership to reflect the representation of women and minorities, so the Democratic party created a new Women, Children and Families Caucus, increased the number of at-large committee members by almost double, and helped to increase members of the minority community.[35]

The fissure in the Democratic State Committee is indicative of the weakening of the party system in the state. Twenty years ago, Rhode Island's party organizations were described as "waning vestiges of the past."[36] Party organizations are less influential within the state given today's candidate-centered campaigns, the expansive group of unaffiliated voters, and expanding and diverse coalitions. Both parties consist of multiple coalitions, and some have organized as caucuses. The Republican Party includes the RI Federation of Republican Women, the Conservative Caucus, the Young Republicans, the College Republicans, and the Liberty Caucus. The Democratic Party caucuses include the women's caucus, the LGBT community, and the veterans' caucus.

Third Parties

Third parties are not an anomaly in Rhode Island. Since the 1970s, third parties, such as the Cool Moose Party, the Constitution Party, the Citizens Party, and the Reform Party, among others, have had candidates run for governor or lieutenant governor. Few minor party candidates have won at the state level; there have been four legislative sessions, with one independent in the Senate over the past two decades. The most successful candidate running outside of the major parties was Lincoln Chafee, who won the 2010 gubernatorial election as an independent candidate.

In 2007, Ken Block, with support from Former Attorney General Arlene Violet, began to build a new third party in Rhode Island, the Moderate Party. The Great Recession in Rhode Island contributed to discontent with government at that time. The negative state of politics served as an opportunity for the Moderate Party leaders to advocate for ridding the electoral system of the master lever (the ability to check one box to vote for all the party candidates on the ballot), especially given the large number of independents in the state. Indeed, the General Assembly voted to end the master lever in 2014.

Attracting viable candidates to run as a third party (or even a Republican in Rhode Island!) is difficult without the resources and recognition that the RI Democratic party enjoys. Simply going through the arduous petition process to become and remain an officially recognized party makes it difficult for third parties. The Moderate Party quickly lost steam and was no longer recognized after the 2018 election, when the gubernatorial candidate William Gilbert failed to earn 5 percent of the vote. The short-lived third party highlights the difficulties in third-party viability, even in a state where a popular third party could have a chance at becoming influential since the largest group of registered voters are unaffiliated. In 2022, the chair of the Libertarian Party (an unrecognized party in the state) complained of "the overall unfairness of the state's ballot access laws" when their gubernatorial candidate failed to secure enough signatures to make it on the ballot, underscoring the obstacles that third parties face in Rhode Island.[37] As the Moderate Party faded from the Rhode Island political stage, other independent organizations and caucuses emerged to confront the Democratic establishment.

Intra-Party Competition

Intra-party divisions have been clear in the Democratic Party over the last several years. One example was the formation of the Reform Caucus in the RI House in 2018, which was a group of nineteen progressives who advocated for rules changes that would limit the power of the Speaker.[38] Other groups have recently formed to compete with the Democratic Party establishment.

The concern over the Trump presidency was an important factor in creating new progressive groups in the state. Matt Brown has become a leader among the progressives in the state. Brown, a former Democratic secretary of state, lost his race for governor in the Democratic primary in 2018 (although he took 33.5 percent of the vote). Brown organized a new progressive group called RI Political Cooperative (Co-op) with Senator Jeanine Calkin and former Senate candidate Jennifer Rourke. The Co-op was created to challenge conservative Democrats with the goal to elect enough progressive legislators to elect new leadership and provide working-class people the resources to run for office. Of the 24 Co-op candidates in 2020, five were elected to the Senate, three to the House, and two to the Central Falls City Council. The Co-op is not a third party. Instead, candidates pay for the organization's services, which are similar to those a political party typically provides, including training, recruitment, and research. The candidates pledge to use only grassroots donations. Their platform centers on raising the minimum wage, supporting the Green New Deal, and universal healthcare.

The Political Cooperative has quickly become a recognized political entity that is challenging the Democratic establishment. The Co-op is not alone in their push for more progressive candidates and policies. The Working Families Party (WFP), another progressive organization focused on the minimum wage and criminal justice reform, organized a chapter in Rhode Island in 2016. Shortly after they organized, they advocated for the Healthy and Safe Families and Workplaces Act, which passed in 2017. In Rhode Island, the WFP is similar to the Political Co-op in that it works outside the major political parties, endorses candidates, and helps with campaigns. The WFP has trained potential candidates, supported others, and become a competitor of the Co-op. In 2020, WFP supported eleven candidates, and all but one were elected to the General Assembly. These WFP and Co-op members have been credited with pressuring the General Assembly to support more progressive bills.

Other progressive groups in the state are engaged in elections. In a highly scrutinized special election for an open Senate seat in 2021, the primary included candidates endorsed by several groups: Co-op, Working Families Party, Democratic Party, Reclaim RI, RI Sunrise movement, Black Lives Matter PAC in RI, RI Black PAC, Climate Action RI, and the RI Democratic Women's Caucus, as well as unions and local politicians.[39] The winner, Sam Zurier, did not have the Democratic Senatorial District Committee's endorsement, but was supported by a few current state and local politicians from Providence. What's remarkable about this special election was the strong participation of groups outside of traditional parties, the extent of progressive in-fighting, and the observation that in a crowded race, the elected primary winner tends to win with about one-third of support from their party. This special election also suggests that although party and union endorsements can serve as cues to voters, they may be less critical when there are multiple groups with similar platforms that can use various social media outlets to reach voters. Despite the competitive nature of this special election, it is important to keep in mind that most General Assembly elections throughout the past four decades were uncontested.

The Future of Party Politics in Rhode Island

Rhode Island has been a one-party state for most of the past century, and the state looks like it will remain that way for years to come. There are clear concerns about transparency and accountability when a state has one party in power at all levels of government. The most recent and significant changes in party politics are within presidential voting patterns and intra-party competition. First, there has been a clear shift to support the Republican presidential candidate in the 2016 and 2020 election in the rural parts of the state, but not enough support to change the presidential election outcomes. This urban–rural divide mirrors trends in many states across the country. At the state level, this Republican wave has failed to make an impact, largely due to the way the district lines are drawn to benefit Democrats. It is unlikely that Republican candidates will become more competitive with Democrats since none of the state offices has been held by a Republican in over a decade, but there is always a possibility that untraditional forces within the Republican party might alter this trend. Second, the growth of progressive groups has placed new pressure on the Democratic establishment to reconsider their party platform and how they support party candidates. What is clear is that both parties must focus on creating diverse coalitions since Rhode Islanders are challenging the party establishments in the state.

Notes

1. The author thanks Adam S. Myers, Associate Professor of Political Science at Providence College, for his thoughtful review of this chapter.
2. Before Wilson, the last Democrat to win in Rhode Island was for Franklin Pierce in 1852.
3. Maureen Moakley and Elmer Cornwell, *Rhode Island Politics and Government* (Lincoln: University of Nebraska Press, 2000), chapter 8.
4. Russell DeSimone, *"Fighting Bob" Quinn: Political Reformer and People's Advocate* (Providence: The Rhode Island Publications Society, 2020).
5. Adam Myers, "The Reapportionment Revolution and the Decline of Contested State Legislative Elections: The Case of Rhode Island," *New England Journal of Political Science* 6, no. 2 (2019): 129–59.
6. Moakley and Cornwell, *Rhode Island Politics and Government*, chapter 5.
7. Myers, "Reapportionment."
8. Moakley and Cornwell, *Rhode Island Politics and Government*, chapter 8.
9. See Moakley and Cornwell, *Rhode Island Politics and Government*.
10. Richard S. Childs, "Rhode Island Tries Primary," *National Municipal Review* 38, no. 3 (March 1949): 126–29.
11. *Yale v. Curvin*, 345 F. Supp. 447 (D.R.I. 1972), Justia US Law, https://law.justia.com/cases/federal/district-courts/FSupp/345/447/1891732/.
12. "Report of the Special Governor's Commission to Study the Entire Election Process," Rhode Island Department of State, State of Rhode Island and Providence Plantations, January 31, 1978, https://catalog.sos.ri.gov/repositories/2/archival_objects/1598.
13. Moakley and Cornwell, *Rhode Island Politics and Government*, chapter 8.
14. Associated Press, "State Removes More Than 180,000 Records from Voter Rolls," *US News*, December 12, 2021. https://www.usnews.com/news/best-states/rhode-island/articles/2021-12-12/state-removes-more-than-180-000-records-from-voter-rolls.
15. Wyoming, Idaho, and Utah are less competitive based on registration numbers. Maryland is the same as Rhode Island. See Rhodes Cook, "Registering by Party: Where the Democrats and Republicans are Ahead," *Sabato's Crystal Ball*, July 12, 2018, https://centerforpolitics.org/crystalball/articles/registering-by-party-where-the-democrats-and-republicans-are-ahead/.
16. Micah Cohen, "Rhode Island: The Most Elastic State," *FiveThirtyEight*, October 8, 2021. https://fivethirtyeight.com/features/rhode-island-the-most-elastic-state/.
17. "2017 U.S. Party Affiliation by State," *Gallup*, n.d., https://news.gallup.com/poll/226643/2017-party-affiliation-state.aspx.
18. Pew Research Center, "Political Ideology by State," n.d., https://www.pewforum.org/religious-landscape-study/compare/political-ideology/by/state/.
19. Jeffrey M. Jones, "Conservatives Greatly Outnumber Liberals in 19 U.S. States," *Gallup*, February 22, 2019, https://news.gallup.com/poll/247016/conservatives-greatly-outnumber-liberals-states.aspx.
20. Adam S. Myers, "R.I. Republicans Miss a Big Opportunity," *Providence Journal*, November 19, 2016, https://www.providencejournal.com/story/opinion/2016/11/19/adam-s-myers-ri-republicans-miss-big-opportunity/24511078007.
21. Associated Press, "Newcomer Wins Senate Primary," *New York Times*, September

29, 1960, https://timesmachine.nytimes.com/timesmachine/1960/09/29/99955245.html?pageNumber=22.
22. Alex Kuffner, "Sen. Jack Reed Takes Nothing for Granted in Election Campaign against GOP's Allen Waters," *Providence Journal*, October 9, 2020. https://www.providencejournal.com/story/news/environment/2020/10/09/sen-jack-reed-takes-nothing-for-granted-in-election-campaign-against-goprsquos-allen-waters/114251908/.
23. Michael Levenson, "Pondering a Congress without Kennedys," *Boston.com*, February 13, 2010, http://archive.boston.com/news/local/rhode_island/articles/2010/02/13/pondering_a_congress_without_kennedys/.
24. Edward Fitzpatrick, "Decade-Old Gerrymandering Might Backfire on R.I. Democrats," *Boston Globe*, January 25, 2022, https://www.bostonglobe.com/2022/01/25/metro/decade-old-gerrymandering-might-backfire-ri-democrats/.
25. Moakley and Cornwell, *Rhode Island Politics and Government,* chapter 8.
26. National Council of State Legislatures, "NCSL State Vote," n.d., https://www.ncsl.org/research/elections-and-campaigns/statevote-2018-state-legislative-races-and-ballot-measures.aspx.
27. National Council of State Legislatures, "NCSL State Elections 2020: Postelection Partisan Legislative Control," n.d. https://www.ncsl.org/research/elections-and-campaigns/ncsl-state-elections-2020.aspx.
28. Williams, Timothy. "With Most States Under One Party's Control, America Grows More Divided," *New York Times*, June 11, 2019, https://www.nytimes.com/2019/06/11/us/state-legislatures-partisan-polarized.html.
29. Katherine Gregg and Patrick Anderson, "R.I. Lawmakers Appear Poised to Guarantee Right to Abortion," *Providence Journal*, June 19, 2019, https://www.providencejournal.com/story/news/politics/2019/06/19/governor-signs-abortion-rights-bill-into-law-following-house-senate-approval/4871588007/.
30. Borris Shor and Nolan McCarty, "The Ideological Mapping of American Legislatures," *American Political Science Review* 105, no. 3 (2011): 530–51.
31. National Council of State Legislatures, "State Partisan Composition," n.d. https://www.ncsl.org/research/about-state-legislatures/partisan-composition.aspx.
32. "Annual State Legislative Competitiveness Report: Vol. 10, 2020," *Ballotpedia*, 2020, https://ballotpedia.org/Annual_State_Legislative_Competitiveness_Report:_Vol._10,_2020.
33. Reid Wilson, "Study: State Elections Becoming Less Competitive," *Washington Post*, May 17, 2015, https://www.washingtonpost.com/blogs/govbeat/wp/2015/05/07/study-state-elections-becoming-less-competitive/.
34. Katherine Gregg, "Shunned by Their Party, Democratic Women's Caucus Votes to Go It Alone," *Providence Journal*, November 19, 2019, https://www.providencejournal.com/story/news/politics/2019/11/19/shunned-by-their-party-democratic-womens-caucus-votes-to-go-it-alone/2255171007/.
35. Katherine Gregg, "Is the RI Democratic Party Seeking to Woo Back the Women Who Rebelled in 2019?" *Providence Journal*, May 20, 2021, https://www.providencejournal.com/story/news/politics/2021/05/20/ri-democratic-party-seeking-woo-back-women-who-rebelled-2019/5186963001/.
36. Moakley and Cornwell, *Rhode Island Politics and Government,* chapter 8.
37. Katherine Gregg, "Libertarian Party of RI Fights to Get Its Candidate for Governor on Ballot," *Providence Journal*, July 25, 2022, https://www.providencejournal.

com/story/news/politics/2022/07/25/ri-libertarian-party-candidate-disqualified-over-ballot-signatures/10143697002/.

38. Ted Nesi, "'Reform Caucus' Calls on Mattiello to Publish Bills 48 Hours before a Vote," *WPRI*, accessed January 2, 2019, https://www.wpri.com/news/reform-caucus-calls-on-mattiello-to-publish-bills-48-hours-before-a-vote/.

39. Edward Fitzpatrick, "Endorsements Helping Voters Pick a Democrat in R.I. Senate Special Election," *Boston Globe*, September 21, 2021, https://www.bostonglobe.com/2021/09/21/metro/endorsements-helping-voters-pick-democrat-ri-senate-special-election/

6 / Interest Groups

Matthew Ulricksen

> More than a decade of special interest bills promoted by the Auto Body Association of Rhode Island have resulted in Rhode Island's 700,000 licensed drivers paying some of the highest auto-insurance premiums in the nation. This has absolutely nothing to do with safety and everything to do with increasing auto body shops' profits at the expense of Rhode Island drivers who could end up paying THE highest auto insurance premiums in the nation.
> Frank O'Brien, Vice President of State Government Relations,
> Property Casualty Insurers of America, *Providence Journal*, 16 May 2018

> As a result of the ABARI'S efforts, every Rhode Islander also has the right to choose a rental vehicle agency; the right to an independent appraisal to be certain all damage is considered in the loss; the right to decide if your vehicle will be deemed a total loss when it meets a certain threshold; the right to use the National Automobile Dealers Association's retail value, not a deflated insurer-based valuation for your totaled vehicle; and the right to choose to have a new vehicle repaired with manufacturer parts, not with imitation parts that diminish its value . . . In truth, ABARI protects consumers, the motoring public and small businesses that employ thousands in Rhode Island. If we don't, who will?
> Jina Petrarca, Auto Body Association of Rhode Island,
> *Providence Journal*, 3 June 2018

> I give the auto body shop membership a lot of credit. They are small businesses and they are spread throughout the state and they've all worked the entire summer contacting their legislators. It resonated.
> Speaker of the House K. Joseph Shekarchi,
> *Providence Journal*, 29 December 2021

Between 2003 and 2019, the Rhode Island General Assembly passed 22 bills benefitting the state's auto body shops, and presumably the state's car owners, though not their insurers. These bills addressed everything from parts to due process in appraisal appeals to how appraisals may be conducted. The General Assembly extended from 30 months to 48 months from a vehicle's manufacture a prohibition against insurers requiring auto body shops to use after-market parts, as opposed to original equipment manufacturers (OEM) parts, without the written consent of vehicle owners; it authorized a "private cause of action" for vehicle owners claiming insurers violated their rights in disputes over what constitutes a "major repair' versus a "total loss" declaration; and, it banned insurers from conducting photo-based appraisals of vehicle damage.

"Rhode Island," lamented Property Casualty Insurers of America's chief lobbyist Frank O'Brien," has passed more auto body legislation than any other state. Period. It costs upwards of 40 percent more to repair a car here."[1] O'Brien's lament followed the General Assembly's 2019 spring fundraising season, conveniently scheduled to precede the end of the legislative session, when dozens, if not hundreds, of bills would be left to the "vagaries" of the legislative process. In the first quarter of that year, members of Rhode Island's auto body industry made $65,550 in political donations, mostly to legislators, with Providence Auto Body's Petrarca family alone accounting for $22,550 of those contributions.[2]

This decades-long political power struggle between Rhode Island's small but feisty auto body shops and the insurance industry culminated with high drama in 2021 over the Unfair Claims Practices Act. The act declared insurers guilty of an "unfair claims practice" for refusing to compensate auto body shops for standard industry mark-ups—e.g., paint, body work, refinishing, etc. The General Assembly passed the auto body industry-backed legislation. Governor Dan McKee vetoed the bill, citing Rhode Island's seventh highest in the nation auto insurance premiums, arguing the provision would "add costs without adding commensurate benefits to consumers."[3] In response to McKee's veto, the auto body shop owners launched a full-court press to persuade legislators to override the veto when the Assembly convened for its 2022 session. Over the ensuing months, both sides energetically lobbied legislators directly and labored to influence public opinion. Writing in the *Providence Journal* on the eve of the 2022 legislative session, Thomas Casale, owner of Casale's Auto Body Inc., framed the issue in David versus Goliath terms, "The Unfair Claims Practices Act levels the playing field somewhat for small family-owned businesses who fight against giant insurance companies on behalf of their customers."[4] Echoing two decades of failed appeals in an op-ed to the *Valley Breeze*, O'Brien, seemingly resigned to the General Assembly's impending override, despaired of the Unfair Claims Practices Act as, "the latest in a long line of special interest bills passed by the General Assembly that have benefited the auto body industry at the expense of Rhode Island drivers."[5] On the first day of the 2022 legislative session, the House of Representatives overrode the Governor's veto of the Unfair Claims Practices Act by 44 to 17, and the Senate sustained the House's action.[6] The outcome was unsurprising. Between January 1, 2021, and September 30, 2021, auto body shop owners made over $99,000 in campaign contributions, mostly to legislators.[7]

Pluralist Democracy

The crack-up on Smith Hill between Rhode Island's auto body shops and the insurance industry epitomizes pluralist democracy. The pluralist theory of democracy holds that political power is dispersed among a variety of interest groups, and that it need not be equally distributed for the system to be competitive and beneficial.[8] Buttressed by the First Amendment's guarantees of freedom of speech and freedom of assembly to petition the government for redress of grievances, these autonomous interest groups foster civil society by integrating individuals and groups into the community, promoting a diversity of interests, and necessitating political negotiations and compromises ultimately beneficial to society.

Interest Groups and Pluralist Democracy

Motivation

Interest groups are the lifeblood of pluralist democracy. As organizations engaged in collective action to influence public policy, interest groups seek new public policies beneficial to their members' interests and defend existing benefits to protect their members' interests. While the benefits interest groups seek to gain and preserve serve the narrow interests of their memberships, occasionally those narrow self-interests complement society's wants and needs, too. Who is to say that what is good for Rhode Island's auto body shops is not also good for Rhode Island's auto owners, or that what is good for insurers is not also good for drivers? Perhaps, the truth is somewhere in between. The benefits interest groups seek vary. Selective benefits are tangible goods and services—e.g., the right of a consumer to pursue a "private cause of action" against an auto insurer in a claims dispute.[9] Solidary benefits are intangible and difficult to quantify—e.g., the benefits to be derived from socialization and camaraderie.[10] Purposive benefits—e.g., the personal satisfaction we derive from pursuit of a "worthy cause"—are also intangible and difficult to quantify, though perhaps most significant for establishing an emotional connection between citizens and the democratic process.[11]

Formation

The *why* of interest groups is clear. *How* interest groups actually coalesce is debatable. The pluralist theory of interest group formation posits that interest groups form in reaction to events or circumstances, and in that regard are simply natural extensions of an open political system that guarantees freedom of speech and association. Black Lives Matter, formed by activists for racial justice in response to the murder of Trayvon Martin in 2012, raises awareness of centuries of racism institutionalized by law, policy, and practice. The exchange theory of interest group formation emphasizes entrepreneurial motivation.[12] A self-annointed leader offers selective benefits to those who join their group and contribute to achieving the group's—or perhaps, more precisely, the leader's—objectives. For example, a one-time state officeholder and multi-timed failed aspirant for higher political office creates an entity that offers campaign services to paying members who share the politico's ideological proclivities, but simultaneously promotes the politico's electoral aspirations—more on that later. The niche theory of interest group formation points to the "carrying capacity" of the political system, specifically the system's ability to accommodate more interest groups as groups carve out narrow policy interests, or policy niches.[13] The partitioning of the policy environment into niches is facilitated by technologies—e.g., social media—that make it easier to identify and reach relevant constituencies; have Twitter, will travel. On its face, the partitioning of the policy environment into niches suggests a hyper-particularization of interest group activity, but in reality groups with narrow but related policy interests will find common cause in broader issue networks that share policy expertise and collaborate on an ad hoc basis to influence public policies of mutual concern.[14] For example, the Environmental Council of Rhode, Let RI Vote, and the Rhode Island Coalition for Reproductive Freedom are issue networks comprised of dozens of interest groups that have lobbied the General Assembly on the Act on Climate, the Let RI Vote Act, and the Reproductive Privacy Act, respectively.

Categories

Interest groups fall into three categories. Economic and occupational interest groups represent business, labor, and professional organizations, and typically pursue selective benefits. The Auto Body Association of Rhode Island, the Rhode Island AFL-CIO, and the Rhode Island Medical Society are examples. Public interest or citizen groups pursue a wide range of solidary and purposive benefits spanning an array of policy and ideological interests from conservation to environmental justice to social justice and civil rights to government reform and beyond. Save the Bay, the American Civil Liberties Union of Rhode Island, Black Lives Matter PAC, Common Cause Rhode Island, Planned Parenthood of Southern New England, and the Rhode Island Second Amendment Coalition are examples. Intergovernmental interest groups represent the policy interests of local governments. The Rhode Island League of Cities and Towns, the Rhode Island Association of School Committees, and the Rhode Island Land Trust Council are examples.

Resources and Tactics

The failure or success of any interest group is ultimately a function of the political resources it musters and the political tactics it employs. Political resources include the size and scope of the group's membership, the geographical distribution of its members, the group's status, its financial capacity—i.e., its capacity to employ lobbyists and make political contributions—and the status and expertise of its leadership. Political tactics employed by interest groups include lobbying, grassroots mobilization, coalition-building, public information campaigns, and electioneering—e.g., voter contact and political action committee (PAC) contributions. By these metrics, the Auto Body Association of Rhode Island is the gold standard of Rhode Island interest groups. Its members are few, but they enjoy status in their communities by virtue of being established businesses that provide essential services. They are dispersed across the state, and able to maintain a presence across General Assembly districts. They have committed large sums of money to employing lobbyists and making political contributions, especially to legislators. At the end of the day, the Property Casualty Insurers of America simply could not compete with the size, scope, status, resources, and energy of the Auto Body Association of Rhode Island.

Rhode Island's Pluralist Landscape

Rhode Island is fertile ground for interest group activity. The nature and scope of public goods and services provided by state and local governments here have expanded since the 1970s into many aspects of daily life. Interest group growth has mirrored this expansion and been responsible for it.[15] The political environments at the state and local levels, where barriers are fewer and lower, are more conducive to interest group formation and activity. These barriers are even less so, given Rhode Island's small size. The constitutional framework of Rhode Island state government is amenable to interest group activity, too. Interest groups tend to be stronger in fragmented political systems—i.e., those systems characterized by plural executive branches with numerous boards, commissions, quasi-public corporations and agencies. In Rhode Island, executive power and administrative and regulatory functions are distributed among four general officers—governor, secretary of state, attorney general, and general treasurer—and an extensive ecosystem of boards, commissions, and agencies—e.g., the Narragansett Bay Commission, the Coastal Resources Management Council, the Resource Recovery Corporation, and the Turnpike and Bridge Authority. Interest groups tend to be more influential in states with "citizen" legislatures, such as Rhode Island's, in which part-time legislators without staffs are dependent on interest groups for reliable information. Interest groups also tend to be stronger in political environments with weak political parties. Despite the Rhode Island Democratic Party's commanding lead in voter registration and dominance of federal and state offices, the party's endorsement does not carry nearly the weight it once carried in the state's primaries. Indeed, Rhode Island's semi-open primaries, in which unaffiliated voters can participate in choosing a party's general election nominee, provide an opening for interest groups willing and able to engage in electioneering to influence the policymaking process by influencing who ultimately is chosen to make policy. The perennial weakness and, frankly, electoral irrelevance of Rhode Island's Republicans, and their lack of any meaningful presence in state government, enable interest groups to harness their political resources more efficiently by focusing their electioneering efforts on Democratic primaries.

Rhode Island's pluralist landscape is indeed fertile. What follows is a "10,000-foot" exploration of this landscape, the issues animating it, and the interest groups occupying it. This exploration offers merely a sampling of the issues and interest groups driving Rhode Island's politics and policy, and is not meant to be an exhaustive analysis.

The Economy

Economic concerns historically top the most salient issues to the American people, and Rhode Islanders are no different. State government's capacity to promote economic growth and regulate economic activity mean that economic and occupational interest groups are among the most active—and influential—in shaping public policy. Hospital mergers, minimum wages and pay equity, minimum staffing levels in nursing homes, pandemic relief funding, affordable housing, collective bargaining rights, pension obligations, insurance regulation, and consumer protection have kept a myriad of professional, trade and industry, and labor groups busy. In 2021, after a protracted legislative battle against the nursing home industry, Service Employees International Union District 1199 New England won passage of the Nursing Home Staffing and Quality Care Act, requiring nursing homes to implement minimum staffing levels. That same year, organized labor and economic justice groups successfully advocated for legislation increasing Rhode Island's minimum wage from $11.50 per hour to $15 per hour by 2025. These groups also negotiated compromise pay equity legislation with the Greater Providence Chamber of Commerce and other business groups that prohibits prospective employers from requesting job candidates' salary histories and extends prohibitions on wage differentials for comparable work beyond sex to include race, sexual orientation, gender identity, age, and disability. In 2019, public sector unions lead by the Council 94 of the American Federation of County, State, and Municipal Employees and the National Education Association Rhode Island secured passage of legislation allowing for "evergreen contracts," which automatically extend all provisions of expired collective bargaining agreements for municipal employees, pending approval of new collective bargaining agreements. This policy achievement was notable given public sector unions' acrimonious relationship with then-Governor Gina Raimondo, who as General Treasurer from 2011 to 2015, promoted public pension reforms anathema to the unions' memberships. In 2018, trade unions secured passage of a $250 million bond to repair, renovate, and build public schools across Rhode Island, and are pushing for another $300 million school construction bond.

Reproductive Rights

Reproductive rights dominated the 2019 General Assembly session, driven by national and local political trends. Nationally, the prospect of President Donald Trump filling one or more Supreme Court vacancies, raised alarm bells among reproductive rights advocates that *Roe* v. *Wade* (1973), the seminal Supreme Court decision affirming a woman's right to an abortion, was at risk of being overturned. Reproductive rights advocates sought legislation in the General Assembly to codify *Roe* in state law. Rhode Island was never friendly terrain for reproductive rights. It is the most Roman Catholic state, as a percentage of population in the United States. The state's 1986 constitution banned abortion—if only symbolically. And, a male-dominated General Assembly leadership, historically conservative on social and cultural issues, had long stymied legislative efforts to expand reproductive rights under state law. Speaker of the House Nicholas Mattiello and Senate President Dominick Ruggerio were no exceptions. Both legislators espoused "right-to-life" bona fides, having consistently secured the endorsements of the Rhode Island Right-to-Life Committee, and worked assiduously behind the scenes to suppress reproductive rights legislation. Then, politics happened. The 2018 Democratic primaries saw several progressive, pro-reproductive-rights candidates unseat or win the open seats of the leadership's moderate and right-of-center colleagues. With support for reproductive rights legislation, and discontent with their leadership, among rank-and-file Democratic legislators growing, Mattiello and Ruggerio capitulated and allowed the Reproductive Privacy Act of 2019 to come to the House and Senate floors. An effort to codify the provisions of *Roe* v. *Wade* (1973) into Rhode Island law, the bill permitted abortions up to the point of fetal viability outside of the womb, and allowed late-term abortions when necessary to preserve the life and health of the woman.

Though the number of avowedly pro-reproductive rights legislators had increased and the speaker and president had opened the door for its consideration, passage of the bill was hardly assured. The Rhode Island Coalition for Reproductive Freedom, an issue network including Planned Parenthood Votes! Rhode Island, American Civil Liberties Union Rhode Island, League of

Women Voters Rhode Island, the Rhode Island Coalition Against Domestic Violence, National Organization for Women Rhode Island, the Rhode Island National Association of Social Workers, and the American College of Obstetricians and Gynecologists Rhode Island Chapter, among others, mounted an aggressive lobbying and public information campaign for the bill. The Rhode Island Right to Life Committee, Servants of Christ for Life, and the Roman Catholic Diocese of Rhode Island labored to defeat the bill, with the Servants of Christ for Life resorting to a "Hail Mary" play for a judicial restraining order blocking the General Assembly from passing the bill. Their efforts were to no avail. The Reproductive Privacy Act passed the House of Representatives 45 to 29 and the Senate 21 to 17, prompting Rhode Island Right to Life to lash out at Mattiello and Ruggerio for their "stubborn, treacherous, nasty, deceitful, and thoroughly self-serving" betrayal.[16] Ultimately, Rhode Island Right to Life claimed partial vengeance. Mattiello, denied the group's endorsement at the 2020 election, lost re-election—though Mattiello's betrayal of the right to life movement was hardly the sole cause of his electoral demise. Perhaps more significant were the implications of the Reproductive Privacy Act's passage for the Roman Catholic Diocese of Providence and its strident shepherd, Bishop Thomas J. Tobin. In the aftermath of the Diocese's legislative rout over the Reproductive Privacy Act, to say that Rhode Island is the most Roman Catholic state in the country is technically correct demographically, but effectively meaningless politically. Despite, or perhaps because of, Bishop Tobin's penchant for lobbing pastoral Twitter bombs into the culture wars, his flock appeared unmoved.

Guns

Gun legislation is a consistent foray into the culture wars for Rhode Island legislators. Dozens of bills are introduced each session seeking to expand or restrict gun rights. In past years, these bills have sought to: ban assault weapons; ban high capacity magazines; prohibit carrying concealed weapons on school grounds; ban ghost guns and 3-D printed guns; categorize tasers as firearms; increase the age for possession, sale, or transfer of firearms from 18 to 21 years old; require gun dealers to notify the hometown police chiefs of prospective buyers; prohibit "straw" purchases, transfers, or sales of firearms on behalf of those legally prohibited from possessing them; and, create a statewide records management system to ensure that law enforcement agencies across the state can access pertinent information regarding the records of prospective gun buyers. The Rhode Island Second Amendment Coalition, a gun rights group for "anyone . . . who values their God-given, Constitutionally-protected right to defend themselves," an alliance of sportsman's clubs and gun dealers, allied with the Rhode Island Rifle and Revolver Association and Rhode Island

Firearms Owners League, has waged aggressive campaigns against gun control legislation, even employing the lobbying services of former Speaker of the House William J. Murphy. Despite the pro-gun community's strenuous efforts to stop gun control legislation, the Rhode Island Coalition Against Gun Violence, working with national anti-gun groups, has been modestly successful. In the 2021 and 2022 General Assembly sessions, gun control advocates secured passage of legislation prohibiting gun possession on school grounds, banning "straw" purchases, limiting magazine capacity, raising the age to buy guns and ammunition to 21, and prohibiting open carry of loaded rifles and shotguns in public.

The Environment

Conservation and environmental justice groups coalesced in recent years to coordinate state-level public policy responses to climate change. In 2021, the Environmental Council of Rhode Island, an issue network of 70 groups, including Save the Bay, the Audubon Society of Rhode Island, Climate Action Rhode Island, the Rhode Island Bicycle Coalition, the Rhode Island Food Policy Council, the Rhode Island State Anglers Association, the American Lung Association, the Rhode Island Land Trust Council, and others, joined with legislative champions lead by Senator Dawn Euer of Newport to pass the Act on Climate. The Act on Climate is an example of Rhode Island "thinking globally, and acting locally" to reduce carbon emissions. The act mandates that Rhode Island incrementally reduce its carbon emissions to net-zero by 2050, with target reductions of 45 percent below 1990 levels by 2030, and 80 percent below 1990 levels by 2040. It requires the Executive Climate Change Coordinating Council to develop a comprehensive plan for meeting those reduction goals, makes the goals enforceable by authorizing legal action against the state if it fails to meet them, and addresses the problems of food insecurity and environmental and public health inequities.

Another green conflict unique to Rhode Island, involves the state's natural resources and Rhode Islanders' constitutional rights to enjoy them. Article I, Section 17 of the Rhode Island Constitution guarantees Rhode Islanders "all the rights of fishery, and the privileges of the shore." Those privileges, however, frequently clash with the rights of private property owners against trespassing. In *State* v. *Ibbison* (1982), the Rhode Island Supreme Court attempted to resolve the shoreline access dispute by setting the boundary between private property and public access at the "mean high tide line," a position calculated by using an average of 18.6 years of data derived from tidal gauges. This standard is problematic, as the mean high tide line is difficult to identify without proper equipment and scientific knowledge, and is typically underwater after 18.6 years anyway. Prodded by the Rhode Island Shoreline Access Coalition and shoreline community lawmakers, in 2022 the House of Representatives voted unanimously to guarantee public access up to six feet above the "recognizable high tide line."[18] The bill languished in the Senate.

Ideology

Ideology is a potent conduit of solidary and purposive benefits, and a stimulant of interest group formation. In Rhode Island, the network of ideologically motivated public interest and citizens groups, especially on the left, has exploded in recent years. Progressive interest groups are the tribbles of Rhode Island's pluralist ecosystem and a testament to how quickly interest groups can form and multiply in state and local politics. On any given day, a Rhode Islander can login to their Twitter account and confront Tweets by the newest denizens of Rhode Island's left, inveighing against Rhode Island's Democratic establishment or issuing the latest clarion calls against injustice. Vermont Senator Bernie Sanders's erstwhile campaigns for the Democratic presidential nomination in 2016 and 2020 were ideological catnip for Rhode Island's progressives. Inspired by the Sanders phenomenon and the ascendant chorus of progressive voices in the Democratic Party nationally, multiple progressive groups have formed in Rhode Island, at times sharing members and policy objectives, at times working at cross-purposes with each other, but by and large committed to purging the Rhode Island Democratic Party and, more precisely, the ranks of its General Assembly leadership, of the moderates and conservatives who have historically dominated the party in the state.[19]

Reclaim Rhode Island is an outgrowth of Sanders's 2020 campaign. A group of Sanders 2020 volunteers formed the organization to train progressive activists in the arts of political organizing, and to craft model legislation for progressive legislators to sponsor.[20] Sunrise Rhode Island is a subsidiary of the national Sunrise Movement, with regional and campus chapters throughout the state, is committed to the Green New Deal, and promotes policies to combat climate change and environmental justice. Black Lives Matter PAC raises money to support candidates of color for the General Assembly and Providence City Council, and advocates for repeal of the Law Enforcement Officers Bill of Rights and for equity in marijuana legalization policies. The Rhode Island Political Cooperative (the Co-op) is a unique organization formed by Matt Brown, a former Secretary of State and failed candidate for US Senate and governor. The Co-op is not a traditional interest group. It occupies a netherworld between political party and political action committee. The Co-op is a vendor of political consulting and campaign services, but it vends only to dues paying members. It is effectively a progressive price club, akin to BJs or Costco, offering discounted solidary benefits, including: candidate training; campaign manager recruitment, training, and oversight; campaign plan development; communications support; and canvassing support. In exchange for these benefits, Co-op candidates for the General Assembly must commit to opposing the Assembly's Democratic leadership if elected.[21] While Co-op candidates won eight General Assembly seats at the 2020 election, it remains to be seen whether the Co-op is here to stay, or is simply vehicle for Brown's political aspirations. The Rhode Working Families Party (RIWFP) is a progressive work horse. Unlike its fellow travelers, the RIWFP can boast real policy chops. With financial ties to organized labor, it actively supports progressive candidates through its Rhode Island Working Families PAC and lobbies for progressive policy priorities. In 2021, the RIWFP was instrumental in negotiating a legislative compromise with the Greater Providence Chamber of Commerce and other business groups to end wage discrimination in Rhode Island, and in enacting legislation to incrementally raise Rhode Island's minimum wage to $15.00 by 2025.[22]

Interest Group Political Tactics

Lobbying

Lobbying is the most common interest group tactic. It is about providing expert information to policymakers to influence the development of public policy, and, occasionally, offering an implicit *quid pro quo* exchange of political support for policy support, though it must be noted that not all lobbyists or interest groups engage in electioneering.[23] Interest groups lobby to realize their policy interests and for societal benefit.[24] Monitoring, or keeping track of what policymakers and other interest groups are doing, is the most common lobbying activity, and is difficult to quantify, as only a fraction of the bills of interest to lobbyists are acted upon in any given legislative session.[25] Classic lobbying tactics include testifying, drafting legislation, and alerting policymakers to the effects of proposed legislation or regulations.[26] As a result of these efforts over time, "lobbying enterprises" might form. These groups of lobbyists and their legislative allies coordinate lobbying and legislative efforts.[27] Lobbying enterprises can "grease the skids" of the legislative process by reducing uncertainties, ensuring ready access to legislators, and enabling lobbyists to reach uncommitted legislators through their legislative allies.[28] The Auto Body Association of Rhode Island, its lobbyists, and its General Assembly allies are a textbook example of a lobbying enterprise.

Grassroots lobbying is another common lobbying tactic. Harnessing the power of modern communications technology and mass marketing techniques, interest groups might urge their members to contact policymakers directly. It is important to note that grassroots lobbying is distinct from "advocacy," which is activism in support of an idea or cause intended to raise awareness, influence public opinion, direct decision-makers towards a solution, and change public policy.[29] In Rhode Island, advocacy is subject to different legal standards and regulations than lobbying.

Though protected by the First Amendment's guarantees of freedom of speech and freedom of assembly to petition the government for redress of grievances, lobbying has long been regulated to insure the transparency and integrity of the policymaking process. The Rhode Island General Assembly enacted the state's first lobbying law in 1912. It required those lobbying the Assembly to secure written authorization of employment from the entities for which they lobbied, and present that written authorization to and register their name, address, and subject legislation with the secretary of state. Any lobbyist who failed to do so was guilty of a misdemeanor and subject to a fine between $5 and $500, approximately $280 and $14,000 today.[30]

In 2016, the General Assembly was at it again. Secretary of State Nellie Gorbea introduced the Rhode Island Lobbying Reform Act of 2016 for the "preservation of responsible government" and "public confidence in the integrity of our government."[31] It defines "lobbying" as:

> acting directly or soliciting others to act for the purpose of promoting, opposing, amending, or influencing any action or inaction by any member of the executive or legislative branch of state government or any public corporation.[32]

Furthermore, it defines "lobbyist" in multiple contexts.[33] A "contract lobbyist" is "any person who lobbies as the appointed or engaged representative of another person." An "in-house lobbyist" is "any employee, officer, director, or agent of a corporation, partnership, or other business entity or organization whose job responsibilities include lobbying." A "governmental lobbyist" is "any employee, of any federal, state, or local government office or agency or any public corporation who engages in lobbying." The act excludes from the designation "lobbyist" qualified expert witnesses, elected or appointed officials, persons appearing on behalf of a business entity or organization employing them if their regular duties do not include lobbying, persons appearing on their own behalf, and persons attending rallies, protests or assemblies.[34] The law expressly prohibits "contingent lobbying," which it defines as "compensation relative to the degree to which lobbying was successful."[35] All lobbyists are subject to the same requirements regardless of whether they are lobbying the legislative or executive branches.[36]

Rhode Island's lobbying industry appears to be thriving despite these efforts to regulate it. In 2011, there were 585 lobbyists, 436 lobbying entities, and 40 lobbying firms registered with the secretary of state.[37] Ten years later, these had more than doubled. By 2021, there were 1,317 lobbyists, 973 lobbying entities, and 96 lobbying firms registered with the secretary of state.[38] It is difficult to account for a 44 percent increase in lobbyists, a 49 percent increase in lobbying entities, and a 42 percent increase in lobbying firms in ten years. It could be that the interest group ecosystem is expanding as the nature and scope of state government's power and the public goods and services it provides expands. It could be that the Rhode Island Lobbying Reform Act of 2016 simply forced more lobbyists, lobbying entities, and lobbying firms into the sunlight. Most likely, the answer is both.

Not only has Rhode Island's lobbying sector grown, it has become a multi-million-dollar industry. In 2020, over $12.4 million in lobbying fees were reported to the secretary of state.[39] Star-crossed lovers Lifespan and Care New England spent $343,000 and $170,000, respectively, on their attempted merger.[40] Frenemies International Gaming Technology (IGT) and Twin River spent $470,750 and $313,500, respectively, competing over a 20-year extension of the state's lottery contract.[41] This, is on top of the $4.4 million they spent in 2019 lobbying on the same issue.[42]

Lobbying is especially lucrative for former officials. Former legislators, former executive officers, and former legislative and executive aids are top lobbyist recruits. Their "connections" offer them ready access to legislative and/or executive branch officials. They have a knowledge of process, which enables them to provide the right information to the right decision-makers at the right time. Since legislatures are the primary targets of lobbying activities, hiring former legislators is simply common sense.[43] Rhode Island's three highest paid lobbyists in 2021 were former legislators. Former Senate Minority Leader Robert Goldberg, whose clients included FedEx, Lifespan, CVS Health, and the Humane Society, reported $875,499.92 in lobbying fees.[44] Former Speaker of the House William J. Murphy, whose clients included Amica Insurance, Care New England, Walmart, Anheuser-Busch, Bally's Corporation, and the Rhode Island Hospitality Association, reported $662,495.92 in lobbying fees.[45] Former Senate Finance Committee Chair Stephen D. Alves, whose clients included the Auto Body Association of Rhode Island, Care New England, VISA U.S.A., Inc, the Rhode Island Pawnbrokers Association, Inc., and the Rhode Island Library Association, reported $505,000 in lobbying fees.[46] Other former legislators turned lobbyists included former House Majority Leader George Caruolo and former House Majority Whip Christopher Boyle. A notable entrant into the ranks of Rhode Island's lobbyists was former Speaker of the House Nicholas Mattiello. After his defeat in 2020, Mattiello joined Westminster Consulting, representing Lifespan in its attempted merger with Care New England.[47]

Political Action Committees (PACs)

Electioneering is the most common interest group activity next to lobbying, though not all interest groups engage in electioneering. The most common type of electioneering undertaken by interest groups is making campaign contributions to officeholders and candidates through political action committees. A political action committee (PAC) is an entity formed to raise and spend money for the election or defeat of candidates. PAC donation strategies suggest interest group contributions are intended to gain access to officeholders.[48] PAC contributions are more common among economic and occupational interest groups.[49] PAC contributions typically favor incumbents, which suggests interest groups prefer access and the status quo.[50] Indeed, legislators' behavior frequently reflect the interests behind the PAC contributions they receive.[51]

In Rhode Island, a PAC is defined as "any group of two or more persons who accepts any contributions to be used for advocating the election or defeat of any candidate or candidates."[52] A "contribution" is defined as "anything of value given to influence an election."[53] Aggregate contributions by PACs to candidates may not exceed $1,000 in a calendar year. This limit is significant, as it suggests that Rhode Island's campaign finance system is not wholly designed to protect the status quo. Higher PAC contribution limits tend to moderate legislators' behavior.[54] Compared nationally, Rhode Island's PAC contribution limits are in the middle.[55] Rhode Island's PAC regulations also emphasize transparency. All PACs must file a Notice of Organization that states the goals and purposes of the committee.[56] If the PAC derives more than 50 percent of its contributions from employees, officers, or directors of a corporation, then the PAC must incorporate the entity's name into the PAC's name — e.g., Delta Dental of RI PAC, Hinckley, Allen & Snyder PAC, CVS Rhode Island State PAC, etc., or if a PAC derives more than 50 percent of its contributions from persons in one industry, trade, profession, or union, then the PAC's name must identify the industry, trade, profession, or union—e.g., Defense Counsel PAC, Independent Insurance Agents RI PAC, Realtors PAC RI, RI Carpenters PAC, Providence Firefighters Public Safety PAC, etc.[57]

Approximately half of all PACS in Rhode Island are affiliated with economic and occupational interest groups. Four out of every five of those are aligned with organized labor.[58] This would explain, in part, the power labor unions wield in Rhode Island politics and public policy. Take firefighters unions, for example. In the first six months of 2021, PACs affiliated with firefighters' unions contributed over $97,000 to candidates, all but $4,300 of that going to incumbent legislators.[59] In that year's legislative session, firefighters' unions secured passage of legislation allowing municipal police officers and firefighters to receive accidental disability pensions—two-thirds of which are tax-free for life—regardless of their age. Paul Valletta, of the Rhode Island State Association of Fire Fighters, acknowledged the costs of doing business on Smith Hill. "I don't want to say a necessary evil," Valletta said, "but everybody knows the cost of campaigns now is expensive."[60]

Think Tanks

A less common interest group tactic is the *think tank*. Think tanks are organizations of experts that study public policy problems, and offer advice and ideas for public policies to resolve those problems to policymakers. Think tanks are financially dependent on the individuals and entities funding them, frequently calling into question just how "independent" the policy analyses and solutions think tanks offer actually are. Rhode Island's think tank ecosystem is small, but worth noting.

The Rhode Island Public Expenditure Council (RIPEC) and the Economic Progress Institute are Rhode Island's preeminent think tanks. Though their analyses and recommendations are framed from different ideological perspectives and reflect divergent economic interests, each makes clear that its work is nonpartisan. RIPEC, founded in 1932 to advance "fiscally responsible government, competitive tax policies, and economic opportunities for all Rhode Islanders," focuses its public policy analysis on state and municipal finance, taxation, education, and economic development.[61] RIPEC's leadership represents a "Who's Who" of corporate Rhode Island, with its officers and trustees representing the likes of Citizens Financial Group, Lifespan, Textron, Amgen, and Electric Boat.[62] The Economic Progress Institute is dedicated to improving economic security and opportunity for low- and moderate-income Rhode Islanders. Its public policy analysis focuses on issues of economic security and justice, including tax fairness, healthcare, equity, and immigration.[63] The Institute draws its leadership from academia, social and human services, law, and business.[64] Despite their divergent policy interests, RIPEC and the Economic Progress Institute occasionally find common cause and collaborate to develop public policies in the public interest. In 2021, they collaborated with The Rhode Island Foundation to recommend how to spend over $1 billion of Rhode Island's American Rescue Plan funding. Their recommendations included using the federal government's COVID-19 pandemic recovery funds to address the affordable housing crisis, reform the state's mental healthcare system, and job training.[65]

The Rhode Island Center for Freedom & Prosperity, which bills itself as a "pro-family, pro-growth research and advocacy organization," is Rhode Island's subsidiary of the State Policy Network, a national cabal of deep-pocketed, rightwing and corporate interests.[66] The Center has weighed in on issues ranging from easing occupational licensing regulations, to eliminating the state's minimum corporate tax. Complementing the Center on Rhode Island's right wing is the Gaspee Project, a 501c4 dark money political nonprofit corporation.[67] The Gaspee Project pushed legislation in 2017 allowing parents to opt their children out of the state's human papillomavirus (HPV) vaccine mandate.[68] The package of bills, sponsored mainly by Republican legislators, and opposed by the Rhode Island Department of Health, the Rhode Island

Medical Society, the American Medical Association, and the Rhode Island Chapter of the American Academy of Pediatrics, went nowhere.[69] In 2019, the Gaspee Project turned to litigation in an effort to create a "safe space" for its dark money machinations. The Supreme Court's 2010 ruling in *Citizens United v. Federal Election Commission* allowed corporate entities, for-profit and nonprofit, to make independent expenditures to support or defeat candidates.[70] Though federal law does not require political nonprofits, such as the Gaspee Project, to disclose their donors, Rhode Island law requires independent expenditure groups to disclose all donors contributing at least $1,000, and identify the group and its top five donors in its advertisements.[71] The Gaspee Project challenged Rhode Island's disclosure requirement in federal court in an effort to shield its donors' identities and create a "'safe space' for their anonymous political advocacy."[72] Buttressed by amicus briefs submitted by Common Cause Rhode Island and the League of Women Voters of Rhode Island supporting the disclosure requirement, federal courts rejected the Gaspee Project's claim. Besides filling column inches on the *Providence Journal*'s opinion pages and offering rightwing talking points for talk radio, the Rhode Island Center for Freedom & Prosperity and the Gaspee Project have made no discernible impact either on politics or public policy in the state.

Conclusion

Rhode Island's pluralist ecosystem is vibrant, dynamic, and reflects national trends. Interest group growth in Rhode Island has been driven by advances in media technology that facilitate identification, contact, and exchange; left wing and right wing, national political movements that energize people to seek solidary and purposive benefits; and the largely unimpeded flow of financial resources from deep-pocketed individuals and entities to state- and locally based organizations to boost their efforts to compete for political power and influence over public policy.

That being said, this is Rhode Island after all, and the more things change, the more they stay the same. Despite the surge in public interest and citizen groups in recent years, economic and occupational interest groups consistently outpace them in political resources and political efforts. Lobbying has grown, PAC-giving remains robust, and think tanks well-connected financially and socially to the corporate and professional establishments continue to analyze policy problems and develop policy solutions. While more diverse voices will rise and be heard across Rhode Island's pluralist landscape, the voice that says "I know a guy" is unlikely to be drowned out. Just ask Frank O'Brien of the Property Casualty Insurers of America.

NOTES

1. Katherine Gregg, "Few Industries Are More Generous to Rhode Island Political Leaders," *Providence Journal*, June 18, 2019.
2. Ibid.
3. Dan McKee, 2021-H6324 Unfair Claims Settlement Practices § (2021), https://governor.ri.gov/newsroom/legislative-transmittal-messages.
4. Thomas Casale, "Assembly Should Override Veto of Auto Bill," *Providence Journal*, January 3, 2022.[AU: Is URL available?]
5. Frank O'Brien, "Opinion/O'Brien: Veto Override of Auto-Body Bills Would Cost Drivers," *Providence Journal*, December 29, 2021. https://www.providencejournal.com/story/opinion/2021/12/29/opinion-obrien-veto-override-auto-body-bills-would-cost-drivers/8975396002/.
6. "Floor Votes," State of Rhode Island General Assembly, January 4, 2022, http://webserver.rilegislature.gov/votes.
7. Katherine Gregg, "Will Lawmakers Override Mckee's 'Auto Body Shop' Veto?" *Providence Journal*, December 29, 2021. https://infoweb-newsbank-com.ccriezp.idm.oclc.org/apps/news/openurl?ctx_ver=z39.88-2004&rft_id=info%3Asid/infoweb.newsbank.com&svc_dat=WORLDNEWS&req_dat=F992EE99E2204C5881A1606717EF4BB6&rft_val_format=info%3Aofi/.
8. Robert Dahl, *Who Governs? Democracy and Power in an American City*, 2nd ed (New Haven, CT: Yale University Press, 2005). For a thoughtful counterclaim to Dahlian orthodoxy see Christine Hebden, "Unequal Political Engagement and the Possible Risks to Democracy." *Theoria: A Journal of Social and Political Theory* 65, no. 3 (September 2018): 1–26.
9. Mancur Olson Jr., The Logic of Collective Action (Cambridge, MA: Harvard University Press, 1965).
10. Peter B. Clark and James Q Wilson, "Incentive Systems: A Theory of Organizations," *Administrative Science Quarterly* 6, no. 2 (September 1961): 129–66.
11. James Q. Wilson, *Political Organizations* (New York: Basic Books, 1973).
12. Robert H. Salisbury, "An Exchange Theory of Interest Groups," *Midwest Journal of Political Science* 13, no. 1 (February 1969): 1–32.
13. Virginia Gray and David Lowery, "A Niche Theory of Representation," *Journal of Politics* 58, no. 1 (February 1996): 91-111.
14. Jeffrey M. Berry, "Citizen Groups and the Changing Nature of Interest Group Politics in America," *The Annals of the American Academy of Political and Social Science* 528 (July 1993): 30–41.
15. Clive S. Thomas and Ronald J. Hrebenar, "Interest Groups in the American States," in Politics in the American States, edited by Virginia Gray, Russel L, Hanson, and Herbert Jacob, 7th ed. (Washington D.C.: Congressional Quarterly Press, 1999), 118
16. Katherine Gregg, "Anti-abortion Lobby to Punish 'Betrayers,'" *Providence Journal*, November 17, 2019. https://infoweb-newsbank-com.ccriezp.idm.oclc.org/apps/news/openurl?ctx_ver=z39.88-2004&rft_id=info%3Asid/infoweb.newsbank.com&svc_dat=WORLDNEWS&req_dat=F992EE99E2204C5881A1606717EF4B-B6&rft_val_format=info%3Aofi/fmt%3Akev%3Amtx%3Actx&rft_dat=document_id%3Anews%252F1775113FDEC94D48.
17. Rhode Island Constitution.

18. Antonia Noori Fazan, "Shoreline Access Bill Unanimously Passes RI House; Awaits Senate Action," *Providence Journal*, June 2, 2022. https://infoweb-newsbank-com.ccriezp.idm.oclc.org/apps/news/openurl?ctx_ver=z39.88-2004&rft_id=info%3Asid/infoweb.newsbank.com&svc_dat=WORLDNEWS&req_dat=F992EE99E2204C5881A1606717EF4BB6&rft_val_format=info%3Aofi/fmt%3Akev%3Amtx%3Actx&rft_dat=document_id%3Anews%252F18A6564643C93148.
19. Antonia Noori Fazan, "Robust Ecosystem of Left-Wing Groups Aims to Take on the Democratic Party," *Providence Journal*, November 1, 2021. https://infoweb-newsbank-com.ccriezp.idm.oclc.org/apps/news/openurl?ctx_ver=z39.88-2004&rft_id=info%3Asid/infoweb.newsbank.com&svc_dat=WORLDNEWS&req_dat=F992EE99E2204C5881A1606717EF4BB6&rft_val_format=info%3Aofi/fmt%3Akev%3Amtx%3Actx&rft_dat=document_id%3Anews%252F185FF6ACoB4A1360.
20. Ibid.
21. Ibid.
22. Katherine Gregg, "Compromise Reached in Long-Running Standoff over RI Pay-Equity Legislation," *Providence Journal*, June 23, 2021. https://infoweb-newsbank-com.ccriezp.idm.oclc.org/apps/news/openurl?ctx_ver=z39.88-2004&rft_id=info%3Asid/infoweb.newsbank.com&svc_dat=WORLDNEWS&req_dat=F992EE99E2204C5881A1606717EF4BB6&rft_val_format=info%3Aofi/fmt%3Akev%3Amtx%3Actx&rft_dat=document_id%3Anews%252F1834F59792257648.
23. Lee Drutman, "The Complexities of Lobbying: Toward a Deeper Understanding of the Profession," *PS: Political Science and Politics* 43, no. 4 (October 2010): 834–37.
24. Christopher R. Prentice and Jeffrey L. Brudney, "Nonprofit Lobbying Strategy: Challenging or Championing the Conventional Wisdom?," *Voluntas: International Journal of Voluntary and Nonprofit Organizations* 28, no. 3 (June 2017): 935–57.
25. Anthony J. Nownes and Patricia Freeman, "Interest Group Activity in the States," *Journal of Politics* 60, no. 1 (February 1998): 87.
26. Ibid.
27. Scott Ainsworth, "The Role of Legislators in the Determination of Interest Group Influence," *Legislative Studies Quarterly* 22, no. 4 (November 1997): 517–33.
28. Ibid.
29. Prentice and Brudney, "Lobbying."
30. "Republicans Plan Anti-lobbying Law," *Providence Journal*, February 21, 1912. https://infoweb-newsbank-com.ccriezp.idm.oclc.org/apps/news/openurl?ctx_ver=z39.88-2004&rft_id=info%3Asid/infoweb.newsbank.com&svc_dat=WORLDNEWS&req_dat=F992EE99E2204C5881A1606717EF4BB6&rft_val_format=info%3Aofi/fmt%3Akev%3Amtx%3Actx&rft_dat=document_id%3Aimage%252Fv2%253A14728889532D3B69%2540EANX-NB-162BCF7BAD128E47%25402419454-162ABBCED312F201%25400-162ABBCED312F201%2540/hlterms%3ARepublicans.
31. Rhode Island General Laws, §42-139.1-2.
32. Rhode Island General Laws, §42-139.1-3(3).
33. Rhode Island General Laws, §42-139.1-3(5).
34. Rhode Island General Laws, §42-139.1-3.
35. Rhode Island General Laws, §42-139.1-8.
36. "Lobbying in Rhode Island," Rhode Island Department of State, 2017, p. 5, https://www.sos.ri.gov/assets/downloads/documents/Lobbying-Entities-Guide.pdf.

37. "Lobby Tracker," Rhode Island Department of State, https://lobbytracker2016.sos.ri.gov/Public/LobbyingReports.aspx.
38. Katherine Gregg, "Making Lobbyists Play By the Rules: A Peek at Nellie Gorbea's Efforts," *Providence Journal*, June 7, 2021. https://infoweb-newsbank-com.ccriezp.idm.oclc.org/apps/news/openurl?ctx_ver=z39.88-2004&rft_id=info%3Asid/infoweb.newsbank.com&svc_dat=WORLDNEWS&req_dat=F992EE99E2204C5881A1606717EF4BB6&rft_val_format=info%3Aofi/fmt%3Akev%3Amtx%3Actx&rft_dat=document_id%3Anews%252F182F79DAABFC9308.
39. Patrick Anderson. "No Legislating? No Problem for RI lobbyists," *Providence Journal*, February 7, 2021. https://infoweb-newsbank-com.ccriezp.idm.oclc.org/apps/news/openurl?ctx_ver=z39.88-2004&rft_id=info%3Asid/infoweb.newsbank.com&svc_dat=WORLDNEWS&req_dat=F992EE99E2204C5881A1606717EF4BB6&rft_val_format=info%3Aofi/fmt%3Akev%3Amtx%3Actx&rft_dat=document_id%3Anews%252F18082815AE9070D0.
40. Ibid.
41. Ibid.
42. Ibid.
43. Nownes and Freeman. "Interest Group," 96.
44. "2021 Lobby Tracker Search," Rhode Island Department of State, https://apps.sos.ri.gov/lobbytracker/.
45. "2021 Lobby Tracker," Rhode Island Department of State."
46. Ibid.
47. Patrick Anderson, "Lifespan Hires Former Rhode Island House Speaker Nicholas Mattiello as a Lobbyist," *Providence Journal*, November 19, 2021. https://infoweb-newsbank-com.ccriezp.idm.oclc.org/apps/news/openurl?ctx_ver=z39.88-2004&rft_id=info%3Asid/infoweb.newsbank.com&svc_dat=WORLDNEWS&req_dat=F992EE99E2204C5881A1606717EF4BB6&rft_val_format=info%3Aofi/fmt%3Akev%3Amtx%3Actx&rft_dat=document_id%3Anews%252F186615046F1F7618.
48. Michael Barber and Mandi Eatough, "Industry Politicization and Interest Group Campaign Contribution Strategies," *Journal of Politics* 82, no. 3 (May 7, 2020): 1008–25. 5
49. Robert E. Hogan, "State Campaign Finance Laws and Interest Group Electioneering Activities." *Journal of Politics* 67, no. 3 (August 2005): 898..
50. Michael J. Barber, "Ideological Donors, Contribution Limits, and the Polarization of American Legislatures." *Journal of Politics* 78, no. 1 (October 2015): 297.
51. Ibid.
52. Rhode Island General Laws, §17-25-3(10).
53. Rhode Island General Laws, §17-25-3(3).
54. Barber, "Ideological Donors," 308.
55. "State Limits on Contributions to Candidates 2021-2022 Election Cycle," National Conference of State Legislatures, September 2021. https://www.ncsl.org/Portals/1/Documents/Elections/Contribution_Limits_to_Candidates_2020_2021.pdf.
56. Rhode Island General Laws, §17-25-15(a).
57. Rhode Island General Laws, §17-25-15(e).
58. Patrick Anderson, "Wide Array of PACs Helped Finance RI Campaigns," *Providence Journal*, December 10, 2018. https://infoweb-newsbank-com.ccriezp.idm.oclc.org/apps/news/openurl?ctx_ver=z39.88-2004&rft_id=info%3Asid/infoweb.newsbank.com&svc_dat=WORLDNEWS&req_dat=F992EE99E2204C5881A1606717EF4BB6&rft_val_format=info%3Aofi/fmt%3Akev%3Amtx%3Actx&rft_dat=document_id%3Anews%252F1703CF79463C8308.

59. Katherine Gregg, "Top Legislative Donors Win Some, Lose Some," *Providence Journal*, August 23, 2021. https://infoweb-newsbank-com.ccriezp.idm.oclc.org/apps/news/openurl?ctx_ver=z39.88-2004&rft_id=info%3Asid/infoweb.newsbank.com&svc_dat=WORLDNEWS&req_dat=F992EE99E2204C5881A1606717EF4BB6&rft_val_format=info%3Aofi/fmt%3Akev%3Amtx%3Actx&rft_dat=document_id%3Anews%252F1848E6C048BCDCB8.
60. Ibid.
61. "About RIPEC," Rhode Island Public Expenditure Council, https://ripec.org/about-ripec/.
62. "About Us," Rhode Island Public Expenditure Council, https://ripec.org/about-ripec/directors-officers-trustees/.
63. "Issues We Work On," The Economic Progress Institute, http://www.economicprogressri.org/index.php/issues-we-work-on/.
64. "Meet Our Board," The Economic Progress Institute, http://www.economicprogressri.org/index.php/meet-our-board-2/.
65. Patrick Anderson, "RI Foundation: Use Federal COVID Aid to Build Homes, Not to Fix Superman Building," *Providence Journal*, October 19, 2021. [AU: Is URL available?]
66. About Us," Rhode Island Center for Freedom & Prosperity, https://rifreedom.org/about-us/.
67. The Brennan Center for Justice defines "dark money" as campaign funds from groups—including nonprofit corporations—that do not disclose their donors. (See "Dark Money," Brennan Center, https://www.brennancenter.org/issues/reform-money- politics/influence-big-money/dark-money).
68. Lynn Arditi, "Opponents Make R.I. HPV Vaccination Mandate a Legislative Target," *Providence Journal*, April 11, 2017. https://infoweb-newsbank-com.ccriezp.idm.oclc.org/apps/news/openurl?ctx_ver=z39.88-2004&rft_id=info%3Asid/infoweb.newsbank.com&svc_dat=WORLDNEWS&req_dat=F992EE99E2204C5881A1606717EF4BB6&rft_val_format=info%3Aofi/fmt%3Akev%3Amtx%3Actx&rft_dat=document_id%3Anews%252F163CED54188AC6A0.
69. "Legislative Status Reports," Rhode Island General Assembly, https://status.rilegislature.gov/.
70. The Federal Election Commission defines "independent expenditure" as "an expenditure for a communication, such as a website, newspaper, TV or direct mail advertisement that: expressly advocates the election or defeat of a clearly identified candidate; and is not made in consultation or cooperation with, or at the request or suggestion of any candidate, or his or her authorized committees or agents, or a political party committee or its agents." (See "Making Independent Expenditures, Federal Election Commission, https://www.fec.gov/help-candidates-and-committees/making-independent-expenditures/).
71. Rhode Island General Laws, §17-25.3-1(h).
72. Patrick Anderson, "RI Donor-Disclosure Laws Upheld Again; Conservative Group Says It Will Appeal To High Court," *Providence Journal*, September 16, 2021. https://infoweb-newsbank-com.ccriezp.idm.oclc.org/apps/news/openurl?ctx_ver=z39.88-2004&rft_id=info%3Asid/infoweb.newsbank.com&svc_dat=-WORLDNEWS&req_dat=F992EE99E2204C5881A1606717EF4BB6&rft_val_format=info%3Aofi/fmt%3Akev%3Amtx%3Actx&rft_dat=document_id%3Anews%252F1850FD0B6C882D50.

7 / Media

Rob Horowitz

Over the past 20 years or so, Rhode Island has experienced the same sweeping changes in the structure of media as the rest of the nation, with corresponding major impacts on its politics and government. Generally speaking, the rise of the internet, with its seemingly endless online options for news and information and the multiplication of cable channels, has resulted in a still unfolding transition from a mass media system, in which most of us read the same newspaper and watched the same news and television programs, to a niche media structure, in which the audience chooses to view or click on the sites that tend to confirm its preexisting opinions. Here in Rhode Island, this major transition is not as pronounced as it is nationally, where the audience for Fox News is comprised of mainly Trump supporters, and MSNBC and CNN attract mainly Biden supporters, and where a voter's ideology and party identification can pretty much predict which news and opinion sites they regularly go to. However, it still has fundamentally changed how Rhode Islanders consume news and information.

This chapter will detail and discuss the impact of these changes, which Josh Fenton of *GoLocalProv* calls "the most seismic transition in a shorter period of time than media has faced in any other time."[1] First, it considers the decline of *The Providence Journal*, leading to a decision by *The Boston Globe* to fully enter the Rhode Island market, but to do so only by competing online, and it then examines the impact of the transition on local television news, which has mainly adapted and thrived. It then explores the online alternative sources of news and information about Rhode Island politics and government that are also seeking to fill the vacuum created by the *Journal*'s downward spiral, zeroing in on the expanding role of social media in the Rhode Island political conversation. It then turns to the role of talk radio, a stubborn perennial that plays an outsized role well beyond the size of its audience in our politics and evaluates the pronounced negative effect on coverage of Rhode Island cities and towns, due to these still-unfolding changes in media. Finally, it explores how policy makers have adapted to these changes in media and some of the implications of this change.

The Decline of *The Providence Journal* and *The Boston Globe* Drive to Fill the Vacuum

The single most consequential change in the Rhode Island media market over the past 20 years or so has been the precipitous decline of *The Providence Journal*. While most daily newspapers have experienced a large drop in circulation, revenue and corresponding influence as news and information moved online, with advertising dollars following, the *Journal*'s fall—perhaps because it was so dominant at one point—has been especially pronounced. The print circulation has fallen from more than 200,000 in the 1990s to about 30,000 today, and while there has been some growth online, it doesn't come close to making up for this nearly sevenfold decrease. This drop in circulation is matched by a marked shrinkage in the breadth of the newspaper's coverage of politics and government. *The Providence Journal* in its heyday was the paper of record in Rhode Island, with regional bureaus throughout the state and exhaustive coverage of local government meetings and political developments. If you wanted to know what would lead the local news in the evening, nine nights out of ten you just had to look at the *Journal*'s front page.

Today, all the bureaus have been closed and, a staff that at one point was more than 500 and filled a four-floor building on Fountain Street can now squeeze onto one floor.[2] While the remaining skeleton crew of reporters and editors do a yeoman's job of still putting out a relatively good paper, the *Journal* is now merely one source of news and information in Rhode Island among many. As with most independently owned newspapers, it was sold by its local owners, initially to the Belo Corporation. It is now part of Gatehouse/Gannett, which continues to engage in severe cost-cutting initiatives across pretty much all its newspapers, the *Journal* included. And in 2020, in another cost-cutting move, the paper unloaded their Editorial Page editor and discontinued publishing editorials, removing a still strong editorial voice from the market and further reducing the paper's influence among elected officials, other opinion leaders, and elites who pay close intention to editorials.

Sensing the market vacuum created by the decline of the *Journal*, *The Boston Globe* made a full-fledged entry into the market in the spring 2019, hiring three established and well-respected Rhode Island based journalists: Ed Fitzpatrick, a former *Journal* political reporter and columnist; Dan McGowan, a Channel 12 correspondent known for his granular knowledge of Providence politics; and Amanda Milkovitz, another veteran *Journal* reporter. It added three more reporters in 2021.

This was not a reprise of an old-fashioned newspaper war. The *Globe* is not attempting to boost its print circulation in Providence. Its strategy is completely online, seeking to sign up Rhode Islanders to subscribe to its web publication for $27 a month, using email blasts and social media as the main drivers of those new online subscriptions. They are also not attempting to match the breadth of the *Journal*'s state coverage, even with its diminished news footprint. As Dan McGowan puts it, "We don't think we need to be the paper of record. We focus on stories we believe that readers will find interesting."[3] The *Globe* does pay special attention to state and Providence politics and government as well as education, healthcare, and crime, but doesn't view its role as covering the whole landscape.

Before the *Globe* added its local Rhode Island reporters, as its own editors have noted, "it had a strong brand identity, but no local equity." It has now established that local equity and gained a solid foothold in the Rhode Island market, adding a credible and valuable source of coverage of politics and government. It is a perhaps the number one source of news about Providence city government. Dan McGowan's local email list alone has grown to 75,000 or so mainly Rhode Islanders to whom he daily sends out free tidbits and references articles from the *Globe* that only subscribers can then access. Ed Fitzpatrick has nearly 10,000 local Twitter followers and is the main host of a weekly podcast, launched in 2021 with former governor and current US Secretary of Commerce Gina Raimondo as its first guest. The *Globe*'s online Rhode Island subscriptions already total more than 10,000.

A limiting factor in the *Globe*'s Rhode Island growth may be the strength of its paywall—one of the tightest in the nation, which limits new people from exposure to the articles without subscribing. This paywall undergirds one of the highest monthly charges for online subscriptions in the nation. The *Globe*'s $27 monthly charge is about 3 times the cost of *The New York Times*, for example. This combination may limit the *Globe*'s growth to a boutique product—still highly profitable—but without broad reach. Still, in a media environment where venues mainly establish a niche, the *Globe* is well on its way to establishing an important one and is already a must-read for the politically active and involved as well as elected and appointed officials.

Local Television News Adapts and Mainly Thrives

Throughout the nation, local television news has retained most of its market share and its foothold. As a still-reliable deliverer of the local weather, sports, and top local news developments, local television news has largely escaped the targeting of the audience based on ideology and the corresponding division of the audience along those lines. National surveys show there is generally more trust in local news than national news, and this was also the case for news about COVID-19, which provided a short-term boost in the ratings for local news.[4] Identifiable local anchors and local personalities are still the predominant drivers of audience loyalty. While as Les Moonves, the former Chair of CBS famously and accurately said, in discussing the national broadcast news, "There are no more voice of God anchors," on the local level the voice of your neighbors' anchors are still highly trusted and transcend politics.

But over time, as ratings have fallen markedly for the national broadcast networks, local stations including in this market have experienced ratings drops for their local news broadcasts. This is particularly the case for the 11:00 p.m. news, as Channel 12's Ted Nesi noted, because the lead-ins from the network primetime programming that used to provide at least some of the audience are dramatically reduced.[5]

As a result, local news has had to adapt to the new emerging media structure, building robust websites with strong video and print components. In Rhode Island, Channel 12 has led the way, making an innovative decision—if one looks across the nation at the local news landscape—to invest more in original investigative reporting and in coverage of politics and government. Channel 12 also moved to robust online reporting earlier than its two competitors in the market; generally speaking, Channel 10 and Channel 6 stayed with a more traditional approach to their news operations.

Recognizing that they could no longer rely on a diminished *Providence Journal* to do most of the original reporting that would fuel their newscast, and sensing an opportunity in much the same way the *Globe* did later, Channel 12 hired reporters like Ted Nesi, who, when he began, wrote mainly for their website, which became an important source of understandable information about the state budget and other major political and governmental topics. *Nesi's Notes*, a Friday political and governmental news "bites" column that is distributed via email and is also posted on the Channel 12 website, is a regular read for the politically involved. Channel 12 also significantly expanded its hosting of candidate debates.

As Nesi noted, the website is central to Channel 12's news operation, and websites are becoming central to all local news operations, including those of its competitors, Channel 10 and Channel 6. For certain stories, more people in total view them online than during the newscasts themselves. And local websites are becoming a significant and growing source of Channel 12's news advertising revenues generated online in 2020.[6] As more people de-bundle from cable packages, the audience for online local news viewing will continue to expand as well.

Another reason Channel 12 took the innovative approach it did was because it has traditionally lagged significantly behind Channel 10 in the ratings. In part due to these investments, while Channel 10 remains the ratings leader,

Channel 12 has narrowed the gap as of 2021. Following Channel 12's example, all three local television news operations recognize that today building and keeping an audience requires a multi-media approach that integrates and promotes online viewing options along with traditional local news broadcasts.

New Online Outlets Filling the Void

In addition to *The Boston Globe*, a broad array of online outlets with varying business models are working to fill the void created by the decline of the *Journal*. Examples of several that have broken though, built an audience, and established themselves as credible sources of news about politics and government are provided below.

Capitalizing on the decline of the *Journal* and the move of news and information from print to online, *GoLocalProv* has experienced dramatic growth since it launched around 2010. (Full disclosure: The author, Rob Horowitz, writes a weekly column for *GoLocalProv*.) It is one of the few freestanding local online news outlets that is profitable, and it now has at least 190,000 people who visit the site regularly.[7] Politicians and other decision-makers, many of whom initially avoided responding to questions from *GoLocalProv* because of what some felt was over-the-top negative coverage now realize that its audience is too sizable to ignore.

GoLocalProv built its audience in four major ways, according to Josh Fenton, its founder: 1) they focused on "big stories" of interest to a significant percentage of Rhode Islanders and at least initially put heavy emphasis on being first to break these stories; 2) they publicized and drew visitors to the site through heavy use of email and social media—daily email blasts with featured articles, for example, go out to 50,000 people; 3) they used big names in the market as contributors, including a popular former Channel 10 weatherman, and 4) they added *GoLocal Live*, which livestreams video interviews and, during the pandemic, went live to the governor's daily briefings. Video interviews stay on the *GoLocalProv* site and as a result can be viewed at the visitors' convenience.

Without an instantly recognizable brand like *The Boston Globe*, *GoLocalProv* has foregone a paywall, building its business model mainly on selling online advertising. Without a paywall, it is easier to draw people in, in part because they can read individual stories that come up in Google searches without subscribing first. Also, the cost of the product overall doesn't serve as a barrier for entry as it may for the *Globe*. Recently, *GoLocalProv* has boosted its readership by carrying obituaries online and for free, driving new readers to the site. Signing up an overwhelming majority of the funeral homes in Rhode Island, *GoLocalProv* provides a cost-free option, in contrast to *The Providence Journal*, which charges to print or post obituaries.

Founded by Jim Hummel in 2009, *The Hummel Report* is similar in many ways to outlets such as *Texas Tribune* and *ProPublica*. Organized as a 501C3 non-profit, it took the brand of investigative reporting Jim Hummel was known for at Channel 6, the ABC affiliate—where he did many "You Paid for It" segments exposing corruption and wasteful government spending—to the internet, where one is not limited to two minutes or so, as with local broadcast news. As a result, the *Report* can do expansive stories. It was one of the first online ventures in the nation to make extensive use of video—particularly long-form nine-to-ten-minute videos that were transcribed, so if people preferred, they could read the reports instead of viewing them.

From the beginning, the *Report* broke major stories, such as mayor of Central Falls Chuck Moreau giving a contractor city business boarding up homes at excessive costs in return for free work and furnishings for one of his homes, which resulted in the mayor losing his post and serving jail time. As Jim Hummel said, "Our goal is to do stories that nobody else is doing."[8]

Hummel also does stories celebrating community heroes, people making a positive difference in their communities and the state as a whole. These kinds of positive features that can serve as example for other citizens to step forward are all too rare in media, both locally and nationally. In this way, Hummel is also achieving his goal of providing unique content.

The Hummel Report has expanded its audience for its reports over the years by partnering with other news outlets. These include previewing its reports in weekly segments on WPRO, having its videos air on RI PBS, and recently and most prominently, collaborating with *The Providence Journal*, where Jim Hummel's long-form articles often are placed on page one on Sunday, in old-fashioned newspaper parlance above the fold, as well as featured on the *Journal*'s website. Among the investigative pieces that have run in the *Journal* is a series of articles chronicling the controversial closed-door mediation agreement reached between the RI Coastal Resources Management Council (CRMC) and Champlin's to expand its Marina on Block Island—one conducted without the participation of the opponents, including the Town of Block Island—and its aftermath. At one point, the *Report* calculated that through all its partnerships at least some of its content reached 322,000 "readers, listeners or viewers" per week.[9]

Since 2016, Jim Hummel has served as the host of *A Lively Experiment*, a long-running weekly public affairs program that airs on Rhode Island Public Television. This prominent hosting role helps him stay visible in the market and undoubtedly brings new eyeballs to the *Report*.

The Hummel Report relies mainly on the support of large individual donors and grants to fund its operations. It supplements these revenues by soliciting some advertising. This non-profit model has been postulated as one possible alternative to the decline of newspapers like the *Journal*. For *The Hummel Report*, it has certainly worked, but non-profit media successes are rare as foundations, and other funders usually only supply money for a few years before moving on to other interests. The non-profit model also does raise questions about whether stories are selected to reflect the interests of the donors, who would then have outsized influence on media content if this model was to become widespread. While this general concern is certainly well taken, the *Report*'s adherence to its professed mission over the years and its willingness to break stories without regard to who may face consequences shows that such concerns do not apply at least in any discernible way to this outlet. As a go-to source for investigative reporting—an area which the *Journal* no longer has the resources to robustly pursue—the *Report* is a strong positive addition to the market and is helping to fill some of the void.

During the 2018 election season, Bill Bartholomew launched the first and still one of the only Rhode Island podcasts dedicated to politics and government. As he recounts, his first guest was then Lt. Governor Dan McKee, whom he invited because he figured that, given the limited duties of the office, McKee would have time in his schedule.[10] Relatively rapidly, *The Bartholomewtown Podcast* succeeded in securing most of the 2018 statewide candidates as guests and began to build an audience, starting with the candidates and their staffs who monitored it regularly. He seized on a format that has been steadily growing in popularity nationally. In general, the audience for podcasts has increased about fourfold over the past decade or so. "As of 2021, 41% of Americans ages 12 or older have listened to a podcast in the past month," according to *The Infinite Dial* report by Edison Research and Triton Digital, "up from 37% in 2020 and just 9% in 2008."[11]

Now, Batholomew produces two separate weekly podcasts listeners can access on Apple, Spotify, and Google, among other podcast apps. Along with a continued focus on elected officials, candidates, and campaigns, he also features interviews with local issue experts and advocates.

To expand his audience, Bartholomew has built a robust social media presence, forming a Facebook group of 1,200 or so members who often share his podcasts with their individual social media networks, creating a viral effect. During the pandemic he produced a Facebook Live show that combined the governor's daily briefing with a real time reaction from other politicians or public health practitioners, such as Meagan Ranney, Associate Dean of the Brown University School of Public Health and a recognized national expert during the COVID crisis. Similarly, he employed Facebook Live to cover the local protest in the wake of the cold-blooded killing of George Floyd, attracting 13,000 viewers. He also contributes to *Motif Magazine,* an alternative publication that still produces a free print edition and is a regular guest host on WPRO AM. Bartholomew believes that the importance of amplifying the content you provide over several platforms will become only more essential over the next decade as the move of media online will—if anything—accelerate.[12]

The Rise of Social Media

Social media sites are outsized new distributors of news and information, with Facebook still ruling the social media roost. So far, the interrelated and vexing problems facing social media, including but not limited to how to grapple with the spread of falsehoods and disinformation, how to prevent sites from being used to organized domestic terrorism, and the belief of many conservatives that the "liberal media" selectively enforce their policies in a way that discriminates against people on the right have not been solved. Taken together, this has led to overwhelmingly negative media coverage but has not reduced their use. Social media remain a pervasive source of news and information for the American public as a whole and for Rhode Islanders.

A little under half (48 percent) of US adults say they get news from social media "often or sometimes," according to a 2021 Pew Research Center poll. Facebook continues to rule the roost with 36 percent of American adults getting news from the site on a regular basis. Nearly seven in ten American adults are Facebook users. Twitter comes next with 22 percent of adults getting news from the site at least some of the time. A high percentage of Twitter users consume news on the site, but Twitter has much smaller reach overall than Facebook does.[13]

Realizing the importance of social media, reporters, activists, elected officials, and other leaders are active users of these sites to sometimes break news, convey information, persuade voters, drive social media users to their websites, and make the case for their point of view. Rhode Island journalists such as Kathy Gregg and Dan McGowan use Twitter and Facebook to give takes on the news and call attention to their articles, and this occasionally leads to engagement with readers or other journalists who react in real time. Ed Fitzpatrick also uses Twitter to share bite-sized news items that may not fit into or be sufficiently germane to the stories he is working on at the time. His colleague, Amanda Milkovitz, employs Facebook and Twitter as a research tool, using the search functions, for example, to track down people who were present at crime scenes and posted their observations or reactions.[14] As mentioned above, social media and email are prime marketing vehicles used to attract new readers/visitors to outlets ranging from *The Boston Globe* to *GoLocalProv*.

Elected officials and candidates are also robust users of social media. Nearly all Rhode Island elected officials have Facebook pages, for example, and most post items relatively often. They often give responses to breaking news on social media, enabling them to get their messages out to voters directly, bypassing the sometimes-critical filter of reporters. These tweets and Facebook posts are now often quoted by reporters in news stories.

Additionally, given the nearly universal reach of Facebook, voters are more likely to see a candidate's social media post than to go to a candidate's website.

And now in most statewide races candidates devote some of their advertising budget to Facebook ads, which can be precisely targeted to the demographic and ideological groups a candidate is seeking to reach and as a result are highly cost-effective. In a state like Rhode Island, where you have an older electorate, and television advertising is relatively inexpensive, it remains the number one way in a statewide race candidates use advertising dollars. However, social media is taking an increasing share every election cycle. Gina Raimondo's 2018 gubernatorial re-election campaign, for example, spent heavily on Facebook and did so smartly.[15]

Social media provides an enhanced role for so-called influencers—the one-out-of-ten of us who tell the rest of us where to shop, whom to vote for, and what issues to be concerned about—and as a result people who fit this category have even greater importance to the public discussion of issues and election campaigns than they have had traditionally.[16] Most of the posts containing news stories that people read on Facebook come from family and friends—not as a result of 'liking' and then receiving posts from news outlets or individual journalists. Research shows that people by and large are interested in the news they receive from family and friends, and curious enough about it to seek out more details. In other words, the traditional agenda-setting role played by the news media, signaling what is important to know about, is now in some measure being played by the rest of us as we share what we believe is important on social media.

The rise of social media enables politically active people who want to reach beyond their close acquaintances a way to influence a broader number of people. Research shows that in a world in which choices have multiplied and the average person receives thousands of marketing messages each week, paradoxically the persuasive power of old-fashioned word of mouth has actually grown. "At a time when the number of media is exploding and marketing is becoming pervasive throughout life, the channel with the greatest influence is neither the traditional media world of television nor the new medium of the World Wide Web but the human channel of individual, person-to-person word of mouth communication," wrote Ed Keller and John Berry in *The Influentials*, so "the challenge then for society's institutions—businesses and government and the people who run them—is to adjust to this new reality in which word of mouth rules and to the learn the word-of-mouth rules."[17] Rhode Island election and issue campaigns, as well as those in the rest of the nation, recognize that the reality the authors describe is even more the case today than in 2003, when their famous book was published, and now devote more time and energy into recruiting these influencers and encouraging and facilitating their social media outreach.

The force multiplying power for influencers and, to a lesser degree, the rest of us to make our voices heard on social media is a mainly positive development. But the dream that the interactive features of social media would facilitate a constructive dialogue and enable political conversations across geographic boundaries, in which people with differing views could grow to understand one another and at least occasionally reach common ground, remains elusive here in Rhode Island, as it does across the nation. For Rhode Island journalists, for example, social media is primarily a way to reach a broader audience for the content they produce. There are the occasional constructive exchanges between readers or viewers and journalists about a specific article, post, or television segment; however, that remains the exception, not the rule. The dominant mode of online discourse engaged in by the small slice of the public that engages directly with journalists are nasty personal attacks or simply posts promoting one's political or issue agenda. The potential for using the technology for the kind of dialogue that brings us together instead of further polarizing us still exists. And in terms of media, the opportunity to move beyond the old print paradigm, which pretty much left readers with the option of submitting a "letter-to-the-editor" to respond to an article—but without the possibility of an ongoing conversation, is tantalizingly present. But has yet to be realized.

Talk Radio: A Stubborn Perennial

Where, paradoxically, there is genuine conversation between the public and media, is in the old-fashioned format of talk radio, in which hosts take calls from members of their audience, usually on topics in the news. Despite cost-cutting by Cumulus, the national media company that owns WPRO, the leader in local talk radio in Rhode Island, this format is holding on to its audience of about 5 percent of Rhode Island adults during its highest rated hours and about 15 percent of Rhode Island adults as cumulative weekly listeners, and it continues to play a more substantial role in the political conversation than the size of its audience alone would merit.[18]

Reflecting the audience for talk radio, which skews old, male, white, and conservative, the local hosts tend to tilt more to the right, but mainly generate callers and interest through opposition to whomever happens to occupy the governor's seat and to the General Assembly leadership. With a notable exception or two, they are not the kind of doctrinaire hard-core conservatives, such as Glenn Beck and Sean Hannity, nationally syndicated in hundreds of markets around the nation. In fact, the Rhode Island market stands out for the vibrancy and reach of its local talk. "If you look at the big picture of how talk radio works in medium to large markets, Rhode Island is one of the special ones in that WPRO is very, very live, and local," said Michael Harrison, publisher of *Talkers* magazine, a national trade publication based in Springfield, Massachusetts.[19]

The state's political class and elected officials, with state legislators tending to be the most habitual listeners, pay close attention to what Gene Valicenti, Dan Yorke, Tara Granahan, and Matt Allen on WPRO are discussing, or what Jim Polito, who does the morning drive on WHJJ, is talking about. (After Polito's show, WHJJ runs mainly national syndicated conservative talk shows.) Regionally host John DePetro, who was heard on WNRI, a Woonsocket-based radio station, makes the occasional waves. Since the politicians and other people who influence politics listen, talk radio plays a significant role in setting the public agenda and in generating reactions from elected officials.

Another perennial in most markets are National Public Radio (NPR) affiliates, which generally still garner ratings that most commercial radio stations can only dream about. But until relatively recently, Rhode Islanders who wanted to listen to public radio had to rely on Boston stations that carried national favorites like *All Things Considered* and *Morning Edition*, whose local news and public affairs programming only occasionally touched on Rhode Island. In fact, before 1998, when Rhode Island public radio—now known as "The Public's Radio"—went on the air as an NPR member radio station/network, Rhode Island was one of only two states not to have its own public radio signal.

While the lingering audience attraction to the Boston NPR affiliates have so far resulted in "The Public's Radio" failing to match the ratings performance of other NPR member stations, it has emerged as a vital addition to local coverage and discussion of politics and government. Its focus on more long-form news stories—four to seven minutes or so—enables it to provide listeners with depth and context beyond the headlines or the breaking news of the day, or as The Public Radio's political reporter Ian Donnis puts it, "do a deeper dive and take a closer look." Along with state politics and government, the station focuses heavily on healthcare developments with its own reporter, Lynn Arditi, dedicated full time to that beat. It also concentrates on coverage of the environment and provides features on the various ethnic groups and communities that comprise the Ocean State. It is beginning to do more original investigative reporting and is beefing up its staff to do so. Its Friday morning local political roundtable show that generally features interviews with political newsmakers is a must-listen for the politically active and for elected officials and staffers.

The Public's Radio also works to expand on, amplify, and increase its reach for its journalism through a robust website that includes stand-alone features, such as Ian Donnis's weekly *TGIF* political tidbits/roundup column, comprised of twenty or so bite-sized political news items, which he also distributes via email. Similarly, Donnis and other NPR reporters are active on social media, calling attention to their stories on Twitter in particular. The Public Radio's on-air reporters, like other journalists in Rhode Island and across the nation, recognize that with the readers, viewers, and listeners fragmenting with so many news and information options to choose from, building an audience requires a multi-media approach.

City and Town News Takes a Big Hit

When it comes to coverage of Rhode Island's 39 cities and towns, the advent of online options has not come close yet to offsetting the dramatic decline in the *Journal*'s coverage of municipal government, politics, and civic affairs, best illustrated by the closing of all the *Journal*'s regional bureaus around the state and the corresponding elimination of separate regional editions of the newspaper. As M. Charles Bakst—who, as a young reporter, worked in the *Journal*'s Warren Bureau—noted, the paper used to cover every local government meeting, not just the City Council meetings, along with all other city and town events, ranging from weddings to deaths. The paper now only fitfully covers city and municipal news, and that is even the case for coverage of Providence itself, the state's largest city—where about one in five Rhode Islanders reside.

Compounding the coverage gaps created by *The Providence Journal*'s retreat is the decline of the state's other daily papers. *The Pawtucket Times* and *The Woonsocket Call* are shadows of their former selves and have experienced steep circulation reductions and *The Kent County Daily Times* no longer exists. *The Newport Daily News*, which is now also owned by Gatehouse, the parent company of the *Journal*, has experienced a less pronounced decline—but a decline nonetheless.

To be sure, most of Rhode Island's cities and towns still have weekly papers, and they do at least cursorily cover local politics and government. They are limited, however, by their usually small staffs and the plain fact that they publish only once a week and often update their websites mainly on that same weekly cycle. When they were a supplement to *The Providence Journal*'s robust daily coverage, the public was served well. But as a substitute, they do not suffice.

There is some excellent reporting done by weeklies, however, and some have stepped up their coverage of local government and politics. For example, *The Valley Breeze* occasionally breaks important local government stories. In 2021, it broke the news of Governor McKee's chief of staff's personal lobbying of the Cumberland mayor on removing local objections to building on a property his family owned in an area that is prone to flooding. As this story developed and was advanced by other outlets, it resulted in the chief of staff's resignation. *The Valley Breeze*'s total weekly print circulation has grown to nearly 60,000, and its website attracts about 100,000 monthly visitors. The print edition is free and available for pick-up at supermarkets, convenience stores, and other locations.²⁰ It publishes separate editions for most of the 11 Northern Rhode Island communities it serves.

There are now several so-called hyperlocal news websites established in Rhode Island dedicated to covering municipalities. The *Patch* network, which has unique websites for most Rhode Island towns that are also connected statewide and nationally, is the most prominent. *Patch* does provide a useful platform for citizens to post their own local news items, but it is limited in the news it produces by the fact that usually one reporter is responsible for several towns. *Patch* was initially relatively well funded by *Huffington Post* and then by AOL when it acquired *Huffington Post*. The envisioned path to major profitability, which was never able to achieve sufficient fruition, was that if you could attract enough eyeballs in cities and towns through the United States by providing hyperlocal coverage, national advertisers would come on board in big numbers. That dream, unfortunately, fell short, and AOL as a result decided to cut their losses. *Patch* is now owned by Hale Global, an investment firm, which is not supplying the resources required to produce robust local coverage. Still, it does provide an additional source of credible local coverage in a market that needs all it can get.

The decline of local news coverage in Rhode Island, which is part of a national trend, has negative implications for civic engagement in the state. "Numerous studies have explored the impact of local news coverage on core qualities of a healthy democracy such as people's political knowledge, voting rates and number of people running for office," wrote Josh Stearns, program director of the Public Square Program at the Democracy Fund. "While there are nuances between them, the studies are fairly unanimous in finding that erosions in local news are tied to drops in civic engagement.²¹ In fact, as a Pew Research Group study found, "overall, the civically engaged are indeed more likely than the less engaged to use and value local news." A strong connection to one's community and always voting in local elections are particularly "closely associated with local news habits," noted Pew.²²

Additionally, the core media function of holding elected and appointed officials accountable by providing critical scrutiny of their actions is not performed as well today in Rhode Island than it was 20 years ago or so. The bottom line is that the Rhode Island public is provided with less useful information about government and politics in their own communities via media than they were in the not too distant past.

Rhode Island Policy Makers Adapt to the New Media Environment

The closest observers of these changes in RI media, because they have the most at stake, are the state's elected officials, political consultants, lobbyists, leaders in interest groups, businesses, and the non-profit world—often called the state's political class.

Elected officials—whose re-elections depend in part on media coverage—are among the keenest observers and among the quickest to adapt to the changes still unfolding. They know the importance of media to setting the public agenda. Research shows that issues that receive saturation coverage in the news tend to be viewed as the most important by the public as measured in polls. Favorable media coverage helps elected officials gain and maintain popularity, while negative coverage can lead to declines in popularity and put re-elections at risk. Additionally, for elected officials seeking to win adoption of their policy objectives or specific legislation, even if favorable coverage does not penetrate to the broader public, it can influence other elected officials and elites. For example, a well-placed opinion piece making the case for an initiative will be read by only a small percentage of the general public, but it will be seen by most fellow elected officials and/or their staffs.

Generally speaking, the changes in media in Rhode Island have given elected officials and policy makers more leverage because the diffusion of the audience to outlets with varying standards for the information they use leaves no powerful media gatekeepers who can demand a certain level of credible information before they will publish an item. The market power to enact a big price for politicians that don't comply simply no longer exists. Similarly, requests for information from media that may be embarrassing for a politician or at least may reflect somewhat negatively are more easily deflected or postponed, despite the state's open records law requiring government documents in most cases to be made public when a specific written request is submitted.

As a Rhode Island media veteran recounted, when *The Providence Journal* dominated the market, elected officials, candidates, and interest groups would more often provide the information the reporter was looking for, knowing that if they didn't, they risked negative coverage that would penetrate the whole state and likely also be picked up by the local broadcast news. One could argue that Governor Raimondo's frequent strategy of fighting against or at least postponing the release of government information that would not reflect well on her administration during her tenure as governor from 2015 until early 2021, when she resigned to assume the post of US Secretary of Commerce, demonstrated that she and her team well understood this new reality.

Another example is that in the *Journal*'s heyday, when a candidate wanted to release their own poll showing better electoral prospects than other recently released media polls, the whole questionnaire and results would be shared with the *Journal* so the reporters could make sure it was credibly done. Now, campaigns can pick or choose to which outlet to release selective results from their poll—and count on a good percentage of the rest of the media to then pick up the results as the campaign chooses to frame them.

Elected officials and candidates also have more ways to get their message out directly to the public, unfiltered or unmediated by reporters. Social media and email distribution are powerful ways to reach voters, and nearly all Rhode Island elected officials and candidates make major use of these vehicles that allow bypassing of reporters. The fact that none of the four Democrats who announced their candidacies for the 2022 governor's race in 2021 chose to hold a traditional media conference is telling. Helena Foulkes, for example, when she announced her candidacy for governor in the fall of 2021, did it by posting an announcement video and letter online rather than having a media conference or campaign kick-off event and making herself available for press questions. Nellie Gorbea and Matt Brown employed a similar approach. Seth Magaziner did have an event to announce his candidacy, but took no press questions, knowing his announcement would receive wide coverage anyway and making sure that the message he wanted to deliver would not be muddied by any of his answers to questions from reporters who may have raised topics he preferred to avoid.

For issue groups, elected officials, and candidates in less prominent races, press conferences to get proposals covered are not used as much as previously, for a far different reason. With the cuts in newsrooms, there are simply fewer reporters to cover them. There are few things more depressing for a politician or press secretary than holding a media conference that no one attends. In most cases, people simply send out media releases via email and then do follow-up emails and calls to help generate coverage.

Similarly, to reach the largest possible audience through media today requires doing interviews and appearances or generating coverage of media releases over a broad range of outlets and venues. As the audience has fragmented and dispersed to many different outlets and publications, far greater effort is required to reach even a remotely comparable number of people as was possible 20 years ago with a well-placed *Providence Journal* article and coverage at 6:00 p.m. on Channel 10, the top-rated local broadcast television news station in the market.

Conclusion

Fueled by the sweeping and still unfolding transition from print to online methods of delivering news and information, the decline of *The Providence Journal,* leaving Rhode Island with no widely read paper of record, has had a markedly negative impact on the quality of news and information available to the Rhode Island public. The largely successful adaptation of local broadcast news, coupled with the advent of new online alternatives filling the vacuum, however, have left the Ocean State with a still relatively robust local news market, especially as compared to most of the local media markets in the rest of the nation.

Rhode Island and other local media markets are not immune to national trends in news and information toward a more nakedly ideological and partisan approach, best illustrated by the national cable news networks, where outlets deliberately appeal to a slice of the electorate by catering to their political views, and the audience then selects their information options mainly by choosing to watch or click on outlets that share their political opinions and provide confirmation of their existing views. All in all, however, local news still provides a counter to these polarizing national trends. In fact, a 2018 study shows that as local news contracts, people rely more on national news, and that in itself contributes to increased polarization, as measured by a decline in split-ticket voting: "Shifts in news consumption to national media seem likely to increase (or at least not diminish) the effect of partisan heuristics, given the prevalence of high-intensity messages about national party politics in the national news during elections.... A relative reduction of local news in the media marketplace may result in less exposure to local news and more regular exposure to national media, with significant effects on engagement and partisan voting."[23]

As Ed Fitzpatrick asserted, "Local news brings us together. Everyone wants to know the local governor and what is happening in their own community and state."[24] While he may somewhat overstate the case, here in Rhode Island, local news still does provide the kind of common corps of information and basic facts upon which most of us can agree, which does contribute to a more constructive political dialogue than we often see on the national level, where often the basic facts are in dispute and subject to rampant disinformation efforts.

We are probably only in the middle of an ongoing transformation in how we receive news and information. This will undoubtedly provide new challenges to Rhode Island media outlets, elected officials, and other policy makers to whom they are so essential, and to the public at large.

So far, however, with the notable exception of coverage of our cities and towns, Rhode Island is still being served relatively well by its local media, and an interested citizen can stay well informed.

Notes

1. Interview with Josh Fenton by the author, September 22, 2021.
2. M. Charles Bakst, former *Providence Journal* editor, reporter, and columnist. Interview by the author, September 22,2021.
3. Interview with Dan McGowan by the author, September 13, 2021.
4. Pew Research Center, "Trends and Facts on Local News: State of the News Media," *Pew Research Center's Journalism Project*, July 13, 2021. https://www.pewresearch.org/journalism/fact-sheet/local-tv-news/.
5. Interview with Ted Nesi by the author, September 23, 2021.
6. Ibid.
7. *GoLocalProv* Package for Advertisers, 2021.
8. Interview with Jim Hummel by the author, September 7, 2021.
9. Hummel Media Guide, 2013.
10. Interview with Bill Bartholomew by the author, October 13, 2021.
11. Pew Research Center, Audio and Fact Sheet, 2019. https://www.pewresearch.org/journalism/fact-sheet/audio-and-podcasting/.
12. Interview with Bill Bartholomew by the author, October 13, 2021.
13. M. Walker and K. E. Matsa, "News Consumption Across Social Media in 2021," *Pew Research Center's Journalism Project*, September 31, 2021, https://www.pewresearch.org/journalism/2021/09/20/news-consumption-across-social-media-in-2021/.
14. Interview with Amanda Milkovitz by the author, October 19, 2021.
15. Raimondo 2018/2014 campaign finance reports. https://www.ricampaignfinance.com/RIPublic/Filings.aspx.
16. E. B. Keller and J. L. Berry, *The Influentials: One American in Ten Tells the Other Nine How to Vote, Where to Eat, and What to Buy* (Free Press, 2003). New York, NY.
17. Ibid.
18. Neilson Radio Ratings, 2021. [AU: Is full publication information, print or online, available? If so, please provide it.]
19. E. Fitzpatrick, "In Rhode Island, Talk (and Talk and Talk) Radio Is Long Tradition In State Politics," *The Boston Globe*, June 24, 2019, https://www.bostonglobe.com/metro/rhode-island/2019/06/24/rhode-island-talk-and-talk-and-talk-radio-holds-outsized-influence-state-politics/e0JSyD7HnxnNzfmhPtS0DO/story.html
20. *The Valley Breeze*, Package for Advertisers, 2021.
21. J. Stearns, "How We Know Journalism Is Good for Democracy," *Medium*, December 1, 2020, https://medium.com/office-of-citizen/how-we-know-journalism-is-good-for-democracy-9125e5c995fb.
22. M. Barthel, J. Holcomb, J. Mahone, and A. Mitchell, "Civic Engagement Strongly Tied to Local News Habits," *Pew Research Center's Journalism Project*, May 30, 2020, https://www.pewresearch.org/journalism/2016/11/03/civic-engagement-strongly-tied-to-local-news-habits?.
23. J. P. Darr, M. P. Hitt, and J. L. Dunaway, "Newspaper Closures Polarize Voting Behavior," *Journal of Communication* 68, no. 6 (2018): 1007–28, https://doi.org/10.1093/joc/jqy051
24. Fitzpatrick, Ed. Interview. By Rob Horowitz. October 15, 2021.

8 / The General Assembly

Adam S. Myers

The most closely watched 2020 general election race in Rhode Island was not the one for the state's presidential electors, for US senator, or for either of the state's two US House seats. It was not even the referendum on whether to strike the words "Providence Plantations" from the state's 357-year-old name. Instead, as polls closed across the state on November 3, observers of Rhode Island politics focused the bulk of their attention on a single state House race in the western neighborhoods of Cranston. It was there that Democrat Nicholas Mattiello, the controversial speaker of the state House of Representatives, was fighting for his political life against Republican challenger Barbara Ann Fenton-Fung.

When election-day returns finally came in, it became clear that Fenton-Fung had amassed an insurmountable lead and thus that Mattiello's time as a member of the House—and, more importantly, as its presiding officer—would soon be coming to a close. The implications for Rhode Island were enormous. Mattiello's six-year tenure in what many consider to be the most powerful position in state government was anything but peaceful. His top-down leadership style, support for pro-business policies, and concerted efforts to scuttle progressive legislation on hot-button cultural issues led to acrimonious fights with the growing cadre of left-wing legislators in his own party. On top of that, a series of scandals involving Mattiello and his lieutenants fed a longstanding public perception (well deserved or not) that Rhode Island state government is deeply corrupt. Mattiello's loss was thus viewed by many as potentially harkening the dawn of a gentler, more consensus-oriented, and more respectable era of Rhode Island government. While it is still too early to tell, the signs thus far suggest that this may indeed be the case: upon being chosen as Mattiello's replacement, newly elected House Speaker Joseph Shekarchi promised "collaboration and consensus," and his selection of an ideologically diverse leadership team suggested to many that he was backing up his words with deeds. State House politicians and observers have largely concurred that the 2021 and 2022 legislative sessions were significantly more harmonious than the sessions of the Mattiello years.

The intense focus on Mattiello's re-election race in 2020, and the substantial shift in Rhode Island government that occurred in the aftermath of his defeat, is a testament to the centrality of the General Assembly (and particularly its leadership) in the state's political system. Indeed, the outsized power of the General Assembly vis-à-vis the other branches of state government is just one of its many distinctive features, most of which are products of the legislature's long and colorful history. This chapter begins by providing a brief overview of that history, with a focus on the structural feature that most affected the legislature's character until the early 1960s: the apportionment of seats in its two chambers. The chapter then describes key aspects of the modern, post-1960s General Assembly and examines how the absence of a competitive two-party system in late-twentieth-/early-twenty-first-century Rhode Island has affected the legislature's inner workings. It ends with a consideration of the legislature's performance during the COVID-19 pandemic vis-à-vis that of the governor and considers whether the unusually large influence of the governor during this period might signal the end of over 350 years of legislative dominance in Rhode Island politics.

The Development of the Rhode Island General Assembly, 1663–1965

The history of Rhode Island's legislative branch can be traced back to 1663, when the British Crown issued the Royal Charter of Rhode Island and Providence Plantations. Like the originating charters of the other American colonies, Rhode Island's charter stipulated that representation in the colonial assembly would be based on town boundaries rather than according to an equal-population standard. Thus began a centuries-long struggle over apportionment of legislative seats that would consume Rhode Island politics until the mid-twentieth century.

According to the 1663 Charter, the unicameral (single-chambered) colonial assembly would be composed of six representatives from Newport, four each from Providence, Warwick, and Portsmouth, and two from "each other place, towne or city" in the colony.[2] In 1696, the assembly formally divided into two chambers: a lower chamber called the House of Deputies and an upper chamber called the House of Magistrates.[3] Representation in the House of Deputies continued to be based on the system of town representation laid out in the charter, while membership in the House of Magistrates was determined via statewide elections. This bicameral structure was in place throughout the remainder of the colonial period and beyond: the House of Deputies periodically expanded as new towns were incorporated, while the size of the House of Magistrates stayed the same.[4]

Following American independence from the British crown, Rhode Island maintained the Royal Charter as its primary governing document in lieu of adopting a state constitution. Thus, the structure of the colonial assembly (now the state legislature) continued to be in place into the early nineteenth century. By then, the town-based system of representation in the General Assembly had become a focal point of discontent for those living in the state's industrializing and rapidly growing areas, including Providence and the Blackstone River Valley. Residents of these areas felt that the town-based system gave disproportionate influence to residents of the sparsely populated, economically stagnant towns in the southern and western parts of the state.[2] Displeasure with the composition of the legislature was an important factor leading to the most famous incident in Rhode Island history—the Dorr Rebellion, which began when a group of political dissidents attempted to bypass the Assembly and propose a new state constitution featuring, among other things, a fairly apportioned legislature.[6]

The dramatic events that followed need not detain us here. What is important for our purposes is that, in the aftermath of the Rebellion, the state's political establishment finally agreed to the drafting of a written state constitution. But while this new constitution (adopted in 1843) did address some of the sources of disenchantment that led to the Rebellion, it fell well short of creating a system of equal representation in the legislature. Under the 1843 Constitution, representation in both chambers of the General Assembly (now called the House of Representatives and Senate) would continue to be based on town boundaries. In the House, every town would be guaranteed at least one representative, with more populous towns gaining a larger number, but the substantial population differences between the state's largest and smallest jurisdictions meant that citizens from the former would be somewhat underrepresented. In the Senate, the inequalities in representation were far worse: every town would be represented by exactly one senator regardless of population, an even more inequitable arrangement than what existed under the Charter.[7] Moreover, through a variety of provisions, the new Constitution made the legislature the most powerful branch of state government, allowing it to run roughshod over a governor selected via substantially more democratic procedures. As Patrick Conley and Robert Flanders point out, this system of government, with a malapportioned legislature at its center, was intentionally designed by the Constitution's framers (generally members of the conservative old guard who opposed the Dorr Rebellion) to prevent the political ascendancy of the state's foreign-born, often-Catholic "urban proletariat" and the concomitant decline in political power of the industrialists and rural Yankee farmers who predominated in the state's small towns.[8]

The persistence of a highly malapportioned General Assembly under the 1843 Constitution determined important elements of the legislature's trajectory in the late nineteenth and early twentieth centuries. Between the 1860s and the 1920s, it facilitated the dominance of Rhode Island's Republican Party, which became the political home of the Yankee Protestants in the state's overrepresented small towns following the Civil War. Indeed, between the 1880s and 1910s, the most powerful force in Rhode Island politics was a political machine that, unlike machines in other states, was run by rural Republicans rather than big-city Democrats. Between 1884 and 1907, the machine's boss was the infamous General Charles Brayton, a Yankee of small-town origins who controlled the legislature from his office next to the senate chamber in the state house.[9] Under Brayton's direction, the legislature passed a law in 1901 (known as the Brayton Act) giving the Senate control of the state budget and most state government appointments, thereby further weakening the governor and centralizing power in the state's rural-dominated upper legislative chamber.[10]

Meanwhile, in the century that followed the adoption of the 1843 Constitution, population growth in Rhode Island continued to be overwhelmingly concentrated in the cities and towns of the state's industrialized northeastern quadrant, exacerbating malapportionment even further. By 1920, the inequalities had become obscene: Providence (population: 237,595) had the same representation in the state Senate as West Greenwich (population: 367).[11] Despite minor changes in 1928 that gave the state's cities additional senate seats, the disparities continued to be pronounced into the mid-twentieth century: according to one study from that period, the General Assembly was the most malapportioned state legislature (and the state Senate the second-most malapportioned state legislative chamber) in the entire country.[12] The resulting pro-rural bias allowed the Rhode Island GOP to maintain control of the legislature until the 1930s when, following nationwide Democratic landslides in the 1932 and 1934 elections, Democrats gained a majority in the House and a near-majority in the Senate. Taking advantage of an opportunity to end Republican hegemony in state government, Senate Democrats then executed what became known as the "Bloodless Revolution" of 1935: refusing to seat two Republican senators, they collaborated with Lieutenant Governor Robert Quinn (the Senate's presiding officer and tie-breaking voter) to take control of the chamber, after which the legislature quickly passed a series of laws reorganizing state government and effectively demolishing the state's rural-based, Republican political machine (needless to say, the ultimate outcome was its replacement by an urban-based, Democratic machine). Among these laws was a repeal of the Brayton Act, which ended the Senate's outsized role in the General Assembly and in Rhode Island politics more generally.[13]

Despite the dominance of Democrats in statewide elections after 1932 and the effects of the Bloodless Revolution, the Senate continued to be very malapportioned, allowing Republicans to maintain control of the chamber throughout much of the 1940s and parts of the 1950s, even as Democrats controlled the House and governorship during most of this period. Thus, the three decades between the early 1930s and early 1960s constitute an unusual period in Rhode Island history in which neither political party thoroughly dominated the state government (though the bulk of the power generally lay with the Democrats).

This unique era abruptly ended in the early 1960s thanks to the intervention of the US Supreme Court. In a series of decisions often referred to as "the reapportionment revolution," the court adopted the precedent that the equal representation of individuals, regardless of geography, must be "the highest . . . priority" in the drawing of districts for both upper and lower state legislative chambers.[14] In chambers composed of single-member districts like the Rhode Island House and Senate, this meant that ensuring that districts have nearly equal populations must take precedence over the representation of local jurisdictions. After an extended period of political intrigue and gamesmanship, the Democrat-controlled General Assembly finally responded to the Supreme Court's new mandate in 1965 by drawing equal-population districts for the House and Senate—the first time in the state's history in which its legislative districts were not primarily based on town boundaries.[15] The Assembly would go on to redraw its districts at the beginning of every subsequent decade, following the decennial Census, to comply with the Supreme Court's equal-population standard.

It is hard to overstate the impact of the reapportionment revolution on the General Assembly (and Rhode Island politics more broadly) in the late twentieth century. First and foremost, by vastly diminishing the political influence of the state's small-town voters, the reapportionment revolution directly led to a major decline in the percentage of Republican legislators, particularly in the Senate. This can be seen in Figure 8.1 (below), which presents the percentage of Democrats in the House and Senate from 1926 to 2006. As the figure shows, a major shift occurred around 1966, when state legislative elections were held using districts drawn according to an equal-population standard for the first time. Prior to 1966, a significant gap existed between the (less malapportioned) House and the (more malapportioned) Senate, with the percentage of Democrats consistently higher in the former. After 1966, Democratic representation in both chambers rose but more so in the Senate, and the gap between the two chambers largely disappeared. Indeed, both chambers in the post-1966 period exhibited Democratic representation rates consistently above 70 percent and often above 80 percent. Thus, in the post-1966 period, the Democrats became the overwhelmingly dominant party in both sides of the Rhode Island State House, with the Republicans reduced to a tiny minority.

The steep decline of the Rhode Island GOP in the aftermath of the reapportionment revolution manifested itself not just in reduced numbers in each legislative chamber, but also in a vastly reduced ability to compete in General Assembly elections. Soon after the requirement of equal-population districts was implemented, the percentage of Rhode Island state legislative races featuring a Republican candidate plummeted substantially, leading to a rate of uncontested legislative seats that, by the late twentieth century, was among the highest in the country.[16] This happened for three reasons. First, the GOP's dimin-

Figure 8-1: Percentage of Democratic Members of the Rhode Island House and Senate, 1926–2006

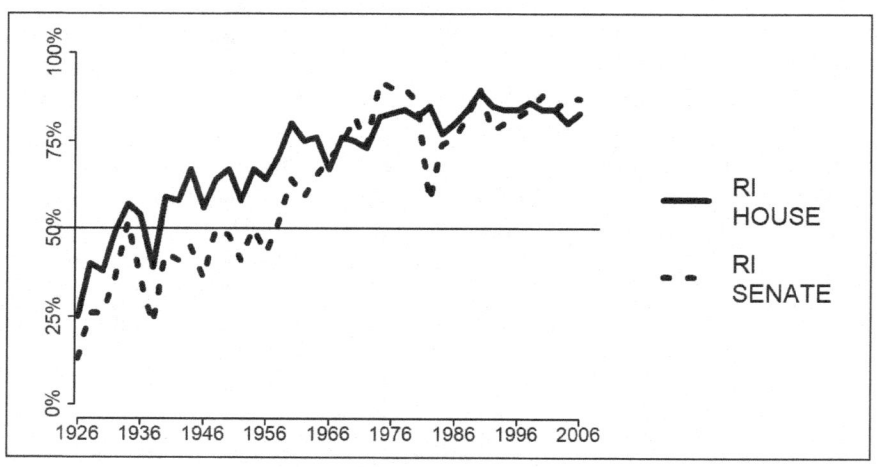

Sources: Walter Dean Burnham, "Partisan Division of American State Governments, 1834–1985," Inter-university Consortium for Political and Social Research, https://doi.org/10.3886/ICPSR00016.v1; Carl Klarner, William Berry, Thomas Carsey, Malcolm Jewell, Richard Niemi, Lynda Powell, and James Snyder, "State Legislative Election Results (1967–2010)," Inter-university Consortium for Political and Social Research, 2013, https://doi.org/10.3886/ICPSR34297.v1.

ished status in the redistricted General Assembly made the prospect of serving in it unattractive for would-be Republican aspirants, thereby discouraging many of them from running for office. Potential GOP candidates were further dissuaded from running by the fact that the demise of town-based apportionment made it easier for Democratic majorities to pass gerrymandered redistricting plans, which created an even larger number of districts effectively impossible for Republicans to win. Lastly, the emergence of districts unaligned with town boundaries made it more difficult for the traditional, town-based Republican party organizations to recruit state house candidates.[17] The combination of these three factors created a situation in which over two-thirds of Rhode Island House and Senate races in the late twentieth and early twenty-first centuries regularly featured only Democratic candidates.

The post-1960s General Assembly has therefore been distinctive not just in terms of the dominance of the Democratic Party within it, but also in the absence of a competitive electoral system from which Republicans might conceivably challenge Democratic hegemony. This reality has been fundamental to shaping politics in the modern General Assembly, the subject to which I now turn.

The Modern General Assembly: Key Aspects

Describing the modern, post-1960s General Assembly requires separately delving into several of its key facets, including legislative powers and legislative-executive relations, bicameralism, low interparty conflict, and high intraparty factionalism.

A Strong Legislature (But Less So Than Before)

Scholarly research and conventional wisdom concur: the Rhode Island General Assembly is among the most powerful of the 50 state legislatures.[18] In terms of formal powers, the General Assembly exceeds most state legislatures in a number of areas, including its significant role in confirming gubernatorial appointments and the ease with which it can override a gubernatorial veto (the state constitution requires only a three-fifths majority of those present in each chamber, a lower threshold than in most states). However, the area in which the constitutional advantages of the General Assembly over the governor are most regularly apparent is the state budget. Unlike all but five other states, the Rhode Island Constitution does not give the governor the power to strike out individual appropriation items from the legislature's budget bill.[19] In the vast bulk of states in which governors enjoy this power (known as the "line-item veto"), they use it to assert themselves as co-equal partners in the budget-making process. Unlike governors in these states, Rhode Island's governor must either sign the legislature's budget or reject it as a whole. Aware of budgetary time constraints and generally not eager for a showdown with the General Assembly, recent governors have almost always opted to sign the budget the Assembly has submitted to them. The infrequency with which governors have vetoed budget bills is a sign of the fact that, in Rhode Island, the spending power is primarily in the legislature's hands.

As we have seen, the extensive powers of the General Assembly have deep historical roots: the legislature has been at the center of Rhode Island government since 1663, and the framers of the 1843 Constitution (which was in effect for 143 years) deliberately made it more powerful than the other branches. Within this institutional context, a political culture arose in which legislative leaders routinely sidelined the state's governors. To be sure, politically astute governors were occasionally able to assert themselves, and the powers of the governor were strengthened following the Bloodless Revolution of 1935 and the adoption of a new Constitution in 1986. Nonetheless, in large measure, Rhode Island state government continued to be centered on the legislature into the modern, post-1960s era.

However, the last 30 years have witnessed an important new trend in Rhode Island politics: on three separate occasions, the General Assembly has agreed to give up some of its most unusual and expansive constitutional powers. In each of these instances, the legislature's actions were a reluctant response to public anger over multiple scandals and an extensive grassroots campaign organized by reform groups. Bowing to incessant pressure, the legislature proposed constitutional amendments curtailing its authority, each of which were subsequently ratified by voters. The first such instance occurred in 1994, when the legislature proposed and voters passed an amendment shifting control of the judicial nomination process from the General Assembly to the governor.[20] Ten years later, a series of amendments were passed declaring that the legislative, executive, and judicial powers of Rhode Island government were "separate and distinct," prohibiting legislators from serving on executive boards, and repealing a controversial constitutional clause previously interpreted to give the legislature a wide array of implied powers. Most recently, in 2016, an amendment was passed that placed the legislature under the jurisdiction of the State Ethics Commission.

The cumulative effect of these amendments (especially the transformational 2004 separation of powers amendments) has been to move Rhode Island closer to the mainstream of states in terms of the status of the legislature and legislative-executive relations. Whereas Rhode Island was previously a major outlier in its system of "quintessential parliamentary supremacy" (to borrow from a landmark 1999 state supreme court decision), it is now not so distinct, even if its legislature continues to hold various constitutional advantages over the governor. Of course, formal powers (i.e., rules inscribed in constitutional provisions or statutes) are only one component of political power. Informal powers (i.e., longstanding norms reinforced by the actions of contemporary political leaders) are another, and the continued dominance of the legislature (in particular, the Speaker of the House) during much of the Chafee (2011–15) and Raimondo (2015–21) governorships suggests that the General Assembly has retained its informal powers even as it has given up some of its formal ones. On the other hand, the legislature's lackadaisical response during the COVID-19 crisis between 2020 and 2022 suggests that it may be prepared to give up some of its informal powers to the executive as well. I return to this important topic at the end of the chapter.

A Citizen Legislature (But Less So Than One Might Expect)

In addition to varying in their constitutional powers, American legislatures differ in their degree of *professionalization*, i.e., the extent to which they have the institutional capacity to "perform [their] role... with an expertise, seriousness, and effort comparable to other actors in the [policymaking] process."[21] In highly professionalized legislatures, being a legislator is a full-time, year-round job for which extensive compensation and personal staff are provided. In highly un-professionalized (or "citizen") legislatures, on the other hand, being a legislator is a part-time position with little compensation (meaning most legislators have additional sources of income while serving), and a pool of legislators often shares a single staff member. Thus, in the California state legislature (the country's most professionalized), legislators are in session throughout much of any year, they receive an annual salary of $114,877, and they are collectively assisted by over 2,100 permanent staff. Conversely, in the North Dakota Legislative Assembly (among the nation's least professionalized legislatures), legislators meet for 80 days every two years, have an annual salary of $6,180, and are assisted by only 37 permanent staff.[22]

Among the 50 state legislatures, the Rhode Island General Assembly is on the "citizen" side of the spectrum, though nowhere near its end. Members of the General Assembly have an annual salary of $15,959 as of 2020, higher than that of legislators in other small states but requiring additional sources of income for all but the independently wealthy. The Assembly generally meets in regular session every year from January to June, ostensibly a longer stretch of time than the regular sessions of other small-state legislatures. However, during regular-session periods, the Assembly usually only meets on Tuesdays through Thursdays and during the late-afternoons and evenings. This unique arrangement is made possible by Rhode Island's small physical size. Because the state house is no more than an hour away from every corner of the state, the General Assembly is able to function as the nation's only "commuting legislature": representatives and senators stay in their permanent residences and work their regular jobs during the legislative session, arriving at the state house after their regular workday ends. In terms of human resources, there were a total of 259 staff members working for the General Assembly as of 2015.[23] Rank-and-file members of the House and Senate (i.e., those who are not in leadership positions or serving as committee chairs) do not have paid personal staff, instead sharing staff members with their colleagues.

As suggested above, state legislative professionalization is highly correlated with state population: generally speaking, more populous states have more professionalized legislatures. The Rhode Island General Assembly is a bit of an outlier here, with the General Assembly being somewhat more professionalized than one would predict based on Rhode Island's small population size. This is likely related to the state's long tradition of having a strong legislative branch.

A Bicameral Legislature

Like 48 of the 49 other state legislatures, the Rhode Island General Assembly is a bicameral (i.e., double-chambered) body. Since 2003 (when it was downsized following a constitutional amendment passed in 1994), the Assembly has consisted of a 75-member House and a 38-member Senate. In sharp contrast to previous eras of Rhode Island history (when the Senate had far greater formal powers than the House), there are few differences between the two chambers in terms of their formal roles today. As in the US Congress, the two chambers are essentially equal in the lawmaking process: no bill can become law unless it is passed by both. One fairly important difference between the chambers is that (also like in Congress) only the Senate exercises "advice and consent" over executive branch appointments. However, unlike at the federal level, both chambers of the legislature get to weigh in on the governor's judicial picks of State Supreme Court nominees. Another important difference is that, under state law, the House gets the first crack at revising the governor's annual budget proposal; as a result, it is generally the House that creates the framework for the budget bill that the legislature ultimately sends to the governor's desk.[24]

But as we saw in the sub-section on legislative-executive relations, assessing institutional strength requires considering informal norms and practices in addition to formal, constitutional powers. Regarding the relationship between the legislature's two chambers, it is clear that, in the modern era, informal practices have developed that favor the House over the Senate. This is most evident when considering the respective powers of House and Senate leaders: while the Senate presidency is surely a position of much importance in Rhode Island government, most observers see the House speakership as more powerful. Indeed, many consider the speakership to be the most powerful position in all of state government. The Speaker's outsized role appears to be related to his (and it has thus far always been a "he") control of two important institutions: the state Democratic Party organization, and the Joint Committee on Legislative Services (the five-member committee in charge of the legislature's budget and personnel decisions).[25] Because of the unique position of the Speaker, observers of the Rhode Island State House have often focused the bulk of their attention on happenings in the House (much to the chagrin of senators).

Power structures can be changed, however, and there is some recent evidence that a jealous Senate may be seeking greater influence in various affairs of the state. For example, in the 2021 legislative session, the Senate jumped in front of the House to pass a bill legalizing and regulating recreational marijuana. In contrast to Governor McKee's preferred approach of keeping marijuana regulation within the Department of Business Regulation (DBR), the Senate-passed bill would have created an independent commission for oversight and regulation purposes.[26] From a power perspective, this was significant because members of the commission, though appointed by the governor, would have needed to be confirmed by the Senate (as mentioned above, confirming executive branch appointments is one of the few legislative powers vested exclusively in the Senate). After much back-and-forth spanning two legislative sessions, legislative leaders and Governor McKee ultimately agreed on a compromise regulatory framework in which an independent Cannabis

Control Commission would operate alongside a new marijuana office established within the DBR, thus paving the way for passage of a bill legalizing recreational cannabis in Rhode Island in 2022.[27] The Senate's approach to the marijuana issue in 2021–2022 could be a preview of how the chamber will use one of its only constitutional trump cards (i.e., the "advice and consent" power) to assert itself on other hotly contested state issues in the future.

Low Party Competition Leads to Low Party Polarization

Ever since the reapportionment revolution ended the overrepresentation of Rhode Island's small-town voters, both chambers of the General Assembly have regularly featured very large Democratic majorities. In the first two decades of the twenty-first century, the percentage of Democrats in the House and Senate never fell below 80 percent and 90 percent, respectively. Moreover, as in the late twentieth century, Rhode Island Republicans in the early twenty-first century have consistently failed to field candidates for the majority of House and Senate seats (in many instances, they have not even run candidates in districts whose partisan compositions favor the GOP!).[27] As a result, Democrats have continued to dominate the legislature with essentially no threat to their power coming from the state's minority party.

This fundamental reality helps to explain what has until recently been a puzzling feature of the modern General Assembly: its exceptionally low rates of party polarization. Perhaps the most well-known fact about American national politics in the twenty-first century is that it has become highly polarized by party. To greatly oversimplify, this means that, whereas previously America's two main parties were ideologically diverse and close to the center of the political spectrum, over the last several decades they have become more uniform and moved toward the extremes (to the left in the case of Democrats, and to the right in the case of Republicans). While a debate endures among political scientists regarding the extent of polarization among ordinary voters, there is widespread agreement that party polarization has risen substantially among politicians, not just in Congress but in most state legislatures as well.[28] The Rhode Island General Assembly, however, has resisted this national trend in a truly remarkable way. According to recent data from the political scientists Boris Shor and Nolan McCarty (who have developed a technique for placing all American state and federal legislators on the same ideological scale), Rhode Island's legislature is the *least polarized* state or federal legislature in the country.[29] Unlike in most American legislatures, the median Democrat and median Republican in the Rhode Island General Assembly have not been ideologically very far apart. This is because, on average, Democrat legislators in Rhode Island have been more conservative—and Republicans more liberal—than their counterparts in other states. Importantly, in recent years, the House and

Senate GOP caucuses have shed their more moderate members and have thus become more uniformly conservative. It thus appears that party polarization is gradually finding its way into the General Assembly, though its polarization levels are likely to remain lower than those of most other state legislatures given the still high amount of ideological heterogeneity within the Democratic caucuses.

As alluded to above, there is a clear link between Democratic dominance in (and overall lack of party competition for control of) the General Assembly and the fact that the legislature features such low rates of party polarization. Scholars of state politics have long theorized that higher levels of interparty competition cause state parties to become more internally united and ideologically distinct. The logic behind this relationship is simple: within a context of significant party competition, parties have an electoral incentive to sharpen the differences between themselves and their opponents. This is especially important for the minority party, which seeks to convey to voters how its approach contrasts with the majority party's most unpopular positions, but it is also important for the majority party, which cannot ignore the minority party if it constitutes a genuine electoral threat. Within the context of low party competition such as exists in Rhode Island, on the other hand, the parties have little incentive to emphasize interparty differences, causing ideological divisions between them to be minimal. A recent study of the relationship between party competition and party polarization across the 50 state legislatures provides significant empirical support for this theory: no matter how party polarization is measured, it is highly correlated with high rates of party competition.[30]

Low Party Competition Also Leads to High Intra-Party Factionalism

In the absence of a competitive party system featuring internally cohesive and ideologically distinct parties, legislative politics tends to be defined by factional struggles inside the dominant party. As any observer of Rhode Island politics knows, this has been the case in the Ocean State. In the modern era, the struggle for power within the Rhode Island House and Senate has been a struggle between factions inside the Democratic caucuses (with the tiny Republican minorities occasionally playing the role of kingmaker).

Factional struggles within the Democratic Party have not always revolved around differences in substantive policy. During the war over separation of powers that consumed Rhode Island politics from 1997 to 2004, Democrats in the legislature were divided over issues involving the political process and government reform, with Republicans shrewdly exploiting these divisions in their efforts to strengthen the state's governorship (which, not coincidentally, was held by Republicans during these years).[31]

In the past decade or so, however, factionalism among Democrats in the legislature has more clearly broken down along ideological lines, with moderate-to-conservative legislators affiliated with the longstanding party establishment increasingly squaring off against a growing cadre of progressive insurgents. This schism has emerged due to a combination of long-term trends and contingent events in state and national politics. From a zoomed-out, historical perspective, the emergence of the conflict seems inevitable: the national Democratic party's leftward drift over the past two decades has made the contrast between its priorities (particularly regarding hot-button social issues like abortion, LGBT rights, and so forth) and those of the Rhode Island Democratic party establishment more profound. At the same time, the growing nationalization of American politics in the twenty-first century has made it more difficult for state parties to maintain ideological identities distinct from the national party brand.[32] These overarching trends suggest that conservative control of the Rhode Island Democratic Party (and therefore of the General Assembly) could not be sustained in the long term, and that an extended fight between the party's ideological factions inside the legislature would likely have occurred regardless of the personalities involved or the results of particular elections.

At the same time, it also seems likely that the ascension to the speakership of Nick Mattiello in 2014 hastened the arrival of the intra-Democratic schism and made it more pronounced than it otherwise would have been. In stark contrast to his predecessor Gordon Fox (a progressive, albeit a consensus-oriented one), Mattiello was a prototypical conservative Rhode Island Democrat: pro-life, pro-gun, and pro-business to boot.[33] Unlike Fox, Mattiello's attitude toward progressives in the House was often dismissive and sometimes confrontational. In response to his rise, Rhode Island progressives began organizing themselves into campaign groups (like the Rhode Island Progressive Democrats) and fielding primary challengers to conservative Democratic incumbents. They had considerable success in the 2016 primaries, when six longstanding conservative Democratic lawmakers (including Representative John DeSimone, the House majority leader) were dislodged. Later that year, Donald Trump was unexpectedly elected to the US presidency, a titanic political event that triggered a dramatic increase in progressive grassroots energy nationwide. Trump's election had an especially galvanizing effect on the progressive activist community in Rhode Island, where a small network of activists mushroomed into a complex panoply of newly formed political organizations (including the Rhode Island Political Cooperative, the Providence chapter of the Democratic Socialists of America, Reclaim RI, and others). These organizations created an extensive new progressive infrastructure for the purposes of candidate recruitment, campaign planning, and volunteer assistance. The work of these organizations bore fruit in the 2018 and especially the 2020 primary elections, when numerous incumbent Democratic state legislators were defeated by progressive challengers.

The growing presence of progressive legislators restless for major policy change and eager to confront Mattiello and Senate President Dominic Ruggerio (as well as the conservative Democratic old guard in the legislature more generally) led to frequent ideological battles inside the General Assembly during the latter half of the 2010s. Perhaps the most prominent of these battles concerned the Reproductive Privacy Act (RPA), which (when eventually passed) codified into state law the right to an abortion as established in the seminal Supreme Court decision *Roe* v. *Wade*.[34] In most state legislatures, conflict over abortion policy pits Democrats against Republicans, but in the modern Rhode Island General Assembly—with its still-substantial contingent of pro-life Catholic Democrats alongside the growing progressive bloc—abortion bills spark internal divisions among Democrats as much as they spark interparty conflict. Eager to avoid squabbles within their ranks, Mattiello and Ruggerio blocked the Reproductive Privacy Act from advancing to a final vote in their respective chambers during the 2017 and 2018 legislative sessions. In interviews explaining his position, Mattiello argued that abortion was a "a very divisive issue" that was distracting the legislature from more pressing challenges, and that the RPA was "irrelevant" given the low likelihood that the US Supreme Court would overturn *Roe* v. *Wade*.[35] In 2019, however, increased progressive strength within the legislature as well as intense grassroots activism on the abortion issue caused both leaders to change their minds. Allowing the bill to be voted on by the full House and Senate, the leaders watched the bill pass their chambers even as both voted against it.[36]

The story of the RPA demonstrates how the growing clout of progressives has caused the Assembly's Democratic leadership to cautiously move in a leftward direction. This was especially evident following progressive gains and Mattiello's defeat in the 2020 elections. In their successful post-election efforts to keep their leadership positions, Senate President Ruggiero and Majority Leader Mike McCaffrey (themselves targets of progressive primary challengers in 2020) promised to advance left-wing agenda items like marijuana legalization, raising the minimum wage, climate legislation, and tax hikes on the wealthy.[37] Likewise, and as mentioned earlier, incoming House Speaker Joseph Shekarchi offered an olive branch by bringing progressive lawmakers into his leadership team. Moreover, the 2021 legislative session delivered some important progressive legislative priorities (such as the minimum wage increase and passage of the Act on Climate), even if some on the left were disappointed with its results.

These developments notwithstanding, prospects for a full-fledged progressive takeover of the General Assembly are highly uncertain. While progressives have clearly made much recent headway, a large cadre of more conservative Democrats with significant political resources and substantial local support remains within both the House and Senate. These longstanding incumbents demonstrated their resilience in 2022, when the vast majority of them (including the House Speaker and Senate President) defeated energetic left-wing challengers in Democratic primaries. Finally, there is always the possibility (even if it seems remote at this point) that the state's long-suffering Republican Party will be able to take advantage of voter backlash over the leftward swing of the Democrats to increase its power on Smith Hill. The next few years should provide important clues regarding the long-term trajectory of party politics in the General Assembly.

Is the General Assembly's Power Waning? The COVID-19 Crisis as a (Possible) Harbinger of Things to Come

To reiterate one of the central messages of this chapter: since the inception of the 1663 Royal Charter, Rhode Island's political system has been defined by the dominance of the legislative branch. Under the 1843 Constitution, the General Assembly had vastly greater powers than the governor, who was a fairly marginal figure in state politics until the 1930s. The tradition of a strong legislature largely carried over into the modern, post-1960s era, even as the adoption of a new state Constitution in 1986, and the ratification of several constitutional amendments since then have weakened the General Assembly to some extent.

The performance of Rhode Island state government during the COVID-19 pandemic, however, makes one wonder if the long tradition of legislature-centered government in Rhode Island may be on the verge of ending. In response to the pandemic's arrival in the state in early 2020, the legislature suspended its session on March 16 of that year. Apart from two brief meetings in June and July, it did not reconvene again until the end of the year, when it finally passed a state budget and approved several judicial nominees. In the interim, the responsibility for running the state largely fell to the executive branch, with Governor Raimondo issuing a flurry of pandemic-related executive orders over the course of the summer and fall. Many of these orders related to issues such as election administration, unemployment insurance, and education, over which the legislature has traditionally held sway. But apart from some complaints by Republicans, few members of the legislature publicly expressed concerns about executive overreach or legislative deference (though there may have been greater discussions about these matters in private). Most notable of all was the silence of the General Assembly leadership, which seemed completely unperturbed by the governor's vastly increased role.[38]

When considered in the context of Rhode Island's centuries-long history of legislative dominance, the outsized role of the governor during the coronavirus pandemic represents a truly striking turn of events, one that raises serious questions about the future of legislative–executive relations in the state. To be sure, there is no doubt that the circumstances of 2020 were both highly unique and unusually conducive to increased executive power: in addition to being a veritable emergency (a condition that generally leads to a larger executive role), the pandemic required social-distancing measures that made it difficult for the legislature to meet and thereby fulfill its constitutional duties. For these reasons, governors took the front seat in managing the affairs of government in nearly all states during the pandemic; Rhode Island was certainly not alone in this regard. On the other hand, there is some evidence that, compared to other states, the extent of COVID-era gubernatorial dominance has been particularly large in Rhode Island. For example, an analysis by WPRI showed that Governors Raimondo and McKee collectively issued more coronavirus-related executive orders between the beginning of the pandemic and July 2021 than the governors of all but two states.[39] Additionally, in other states, unilateral executive action during the pandemic eventually prompted significant legislative oversight and occasional rebuke; both legislative responses have been mostly absent in Rhode Island.[40]

These outcomes, combined with the curtailment of the Assembly's constitutional powers over the last several decades, raise the possibility that Rhode Island government may be transitioning to a new era in legislative–executive relations, one defined by the dominance of the executive. Interbranch relations in the modern federal government—which arguably experienced a similar transition during the mid-twentieth century—may well provide an indication of where Rhode Island is headed. In the twenty-first-century federal government, it is generally the president who sets the policy agenda, while much standard policymaking occurs within executive agencies rather than the US House and Senate. Congress has not been reduced to complete irrelevance, but its role is far more reactive than the one it enjoyed in earlier times. The acclaimed legal scholars Eric Posner and Adrian Vermeule argue that this sort of arrangement is a natural consequence of modernity: because legislatures are ill equipped to deal with the complex issues of the modern administrative state, power inside modern regimes inevitably concentrates within the executive.[41] If Posner and Vermeule are right, Rhode Island may be belatedly embarking on a path upon which all governments must proceed if they are to remain functional in the twenty-first century.

Not all observers are so pessimistic about the capacities of modern legislatures, however, and it is too early to know how far the growth of executive power (and the concomitant decline of legislative power) in Rhode Island will extend. Despite recent trends, the General Assembly continues to enjoy significant constitutional advantages over the governor, as well as the benefits of tradition. Moreover, the dramatic increase in legislators and legislative candidates campaigning on highly ambitious policy programs in recent years may portend a renewal of legislative productivity, potentially shifting the center of gravity in state government back to the General Assembly in the near future. Much will depend on the approach taken by the leaders of the House and Senate, particularly regarding their relationship with whoever occupies the governor's office. More than the rank-and-file, it is the actions of the General Assembly's leadership that will play a decisive role in shaping the institution and its place in Rhode Island government in the decades to come.

Notes

1. Patrick Anderson and Katherine Gregg, "Shekarchi Takes Reins as House Speaker as Assembly Convenes," *Providence Journal*, January 5, 2021. https://www.providencejournal.com/story/news/politics/2021/01/05/shekarchi-takes-reins-ri-house-speaker-assembly-reconvenes/4125480001/.
2. "Charter of Rhode Island and Providence Plantations—July 15, 1663," Yale University Law School, accessed October 12, 2021, https://avalon.law.yale.edu/17th_century/ri04.asp.
3. Patrick T. Conley and Robert G. Flanders, Jr., *The Rhode Island State Constitution: A Reference Guide* (Westport, CT: Praeger, 2007), 8.
4. Michael J. Dubin, *Party Affiliations in the State Legislatures: A Year by Year Summary, 1796–2006* (Jefferson, NC: McFarland, 2007), 162–63.
5. Conley and Flanders, *The Rhode Island State Constitution*, 16–18; Patrick T. Conley, *Democracy in Decline: Rhode Island's Constitutional Development, 1776–1841* (Providence: Rhode Island Historical Society, 1977), 150–61.
6. Conley and Flanders, *The Rhode Island State Constitution*, 21.
7. Robert B. McKay, Reapportionment: *The Law and Politics of Equal Representation* (New York: Simon and Shuster, 1965), 416–17.
8. Conley and Flanders, *The Rhode Island State Constitution*, 25.
9. John D. Buenker, "The Politics of Resistance: The Rural-Based Yankee Republican Machines of Connecticut and Rhode Island," *New England Quarterly* 47, no. 2 (June 1974): 212–37.
10. Conley and Flanders, *The Rhode Island State Constitution*, 27.
11. Ibid.
12. Gus Tyler, "The Majority Don't Count," *New Republic*, August 22, 1955, 13–15.
13. Conley and Flanders, *The Rhode Island State Constitution*, 213.
14. Bruce E. Cain, Karin MacDonald, and Michael McDonald, "From Equality to Fariness: The Path of Political Reform Since *Baker* v. *Carr*," in *Party Lines: Competition, Partisanship, and Congressional Redistricting*, edited by Thomas E. Mann and Bruce E. Cain (Washington, DC: Brookings Institution Press, 2005), 8.
15. Adam S. Myers, "The Reapportionment Revolution and the Decline of Contested State Legislative Elections: The Case of Rhode Island," *New England Journal of Political Science* 11, no. 2 (2019): 130–59.
16. Keith E. Hamm and Nancy Martorano Miller, "Legislative Politics in the States." in *Politics in the American States: A Comparative Analysis*, 11th edition, edited by Virginia Gray, Russell L. Hanson, and Thad Kousser (Thousand Oaks, CA: CQ Press, 2018), 199.
17. Myers, "The Reapportionment Revolution and the Decline of Contested State Legislative Elections."
18. Katie Mulvaney, "Gov. Lincoln Chafee Says R.I. Legislature is Strongest in U.S.," *Politifact*, November 30, 2014, https://www.politifact.com/factchecks/2014/nov/30/lincoln-chafee/gov-lincoln-chafee-says-ri-legislature-strongest-u/; Margaret Ferguson, "Governors and the Executive Branch," in *Politics in the American States: A Comparative Analysis*, 11th edition, edited by Virginia Gray, Russell L. Hanson, and Thad Kousser (Thousand Oaks, CA: CQ Press, 2018), 252.
19. "Separation of Powers: Executive Veto Powers," National Conference of State Legislatures, accessed October 12, 2021, https://www.ncsl.org/research/about-state-legislatures/separation-of-powers-executive-veto-powers.aspx.

20. John Marion, "Judging How We Pick Judges: Fifteen Years of Merit Selection in Rhode Island," *Rogers Williams University Law Review* 15, no. 3 (2010), 735–54.
21. Christopher Z. Mooney, "Citizens, Structures, and Sister States: Influences on State Legislative Professionalism," *Legislative Studies Quarterly* 20, no. 1 (February 1995), 48.
22. Data are from the website of the National Conference of State Legislatures. Session length data are found here: https://www.ncsl.org/research/about-state-legislatures/legislative-session-length.aspx; staff data found here: https://www.ncsl.org/research/about-state-legislatures/staff-change-chart-1979-1988-1996-2003-2009.aspx; compensation data from: https://www.ncsl.org/research/about-state-legislatures/2020-legislator-compensation.aspx; websites accessed August 10, 2021.
23. Ibid.
24. Because of the larger role of the House in the budget process, the House Finance Committee—the House committee in charge of crafting the budget—is arguably the most consequential committee in the General Assembly.
25. Dan McGowan, "Is Rhode Island's Speaker of the House Too Powerful?," *Boston Globe*, November 6, 2020, https://www.bostonglobe.com/2020/11/06/metro/is-rhode-islands-speaker-house-too-powerful/.
26. Steph Machado, "RI Senate Approves Recreational Marijuana Bill," *wpri.com*, June 22, 2021, https://www.wpri.com/news/politics/ri-senate-approves-recreational-marijuana-bill/.
27. Adam S. Myers, "R.I. Republicans Miss a Big Opportunity," *Providence Journal*, November 19, 2016, https://www.providencejournal.com/opinion/20161119/adam-s-myers-ri-republicans-miss-big-opportunity.
28. The scholarly literature on polarization in American politics is enormous; indeed, it may be the most studied topic in contemporary political science. For a good synthesis of the discipline's findings regarding polarization at both the mass and elite levels, see Nolan McCarty, *Polarization: What Everyone Needs to Know* (New York: Oxford, 2019).
29. Their technique is described in: Boris Shor and Nolan McCarty, "The Ideological Mapping of American Legislature," *American Political Science Review* 105, no. 3 (2011): 530–51. Their most recent data were downloaded from https://dataverse.harvard.edu/dataset.xhtml?persistentId=doi:10.7910/DVN/AP54NE on August 8, 2021.
30. Kelsey L. Hinchliffe and Frances E. Lee, "Party Competition and Conflict in State Legislatures," *State Politics and Policy Quarterly* 16, no. 2 (2016), 172–97.
31. Indeed, Republicans in the legislature were some of the most stalwart supporters of the "Separation of Powers" amendments that transformed legislative–executive relations in Rhode Island.
32. Daniel J. Hopkins, *The Increasingly United States: How and Why American Political Behavior Nationalized* (Chicago: University of Chicago Press, 2018).
33. Mike Stanton, "Who Is Rhode Island House Speaker Nick Mattiello?," *Rhode Island Monthly*, September 29, 2014, https://www.rimonthly.com/who-is-rhode-island-house-speaker-nick-mattiello/.
34. The law (as well as similar laws in states across the country) was motivated by the prescient fear among abortion rights advocates that an increasingly conservative US Supreme Court would overturn *Roe* v. *Wade* in the future.

35. Katherine Gregg, "Women's Groups Push Back at Mattiello on Abortion," *Providence Journal*, May 4, 2018. https://www.providencejournal.com/story/news/politics/2018/05/05/womens-groups-push-back-at-mattiello-on-abortion/12305095007/.
36. Edward Fitzpatrick, "Rhode Island latest State to Pass a Bill Protecting Abortion Rights," *Boston Globe*, June 19, 2019. www.bostonglobe.com/metro/rhode-island/2019/06/19/governor-raimondo-signs-rhode-island-abortion-rights-bill/Ipl9e1MjmSHIdfzkMDXWVL/story.html.
37. Edward Fitzpatrick, "RI State senate Leaders Withstand Challenge, Outline Progressive Agenda," *Boston Globe*, November 6, 2020. https://www.bostonglobe.com/2020/11/06/metro/senate-leaders-withstand-challenge-outline-progressive-agenda/.
38. This may have been because most of the leaders were facing stiff re-election challenges and preferred not to be mired in official legislative business while campaigning to keep their jobs.
39. Tolly Taylor, "RI's Third-Most Executive Orders Nationwide not the Whole Story," *wpri.com*, June 4, 2021, https://www.wpri.com/target-12/ris-third-most-executive-orders-nationwide-not-the-whole-story/, accessed October 12, 2021.
40. As John Marion of Common Cause Rhode Island has pointed out, these divergent outcomes are likely related to differences in party control of state government. For example, in Kansas—where the legislature curtailed the governor's authority to issue executive orders during the pandemic—the legislature is Republican-controlled, while the governor is a Democrat. The fact that Democrats control both the legislative and executive branches in Rhode Island makes it less likely that the legislature will assert itself against gubernatorial overreach. Tolly Taylor, "RI's Third-Most Executive Orders Nationwide Not the Whole Story," *wpri.com*, May 27, 2020, https://www.wpri.com/target-12/ris-third-most-executive-orders-nationwide-not-the-whole-story/.
41. Eric A. Posner and Adrian Vermeule, *The Executive Unbound: After the Madisonian Republic* (New York: Oxford, 2010).

9 / The Executive Branch

GARY SASSE

Rhode Island did not have a consequential executive branch of state government until the so-called "Bloodless Revolution" of 1935. The Ocean State was not placed on a constitutional foundation until 1843, half a century after the American Revolution. Prior to that, the fundamental law of the state resided in the Royal Charter of 1663. Under this Charter, Kenneth F. Payne writes, "the General Assembly's power to shape Rhode Island governance was broad."[1] The legislature had plenary powers and could establish the form of government it believed the state should have.

The Evolution of the Executive Branch

The framers of Rhode Island's first Constitution provided that the chief executive powers of the state be vested in a governor who shall take care that the laws be faithfully executed, be commander-in-chief of the state military forces, have powers to grant reprieves after conviction, and fill vacancies until the Assembly acts. Payne explains that "The governor's powers were few and limited, there was no extensive governmental apparatus for the governor to oversee."[2]

The Constitution did not provide for the separation of powers between the branches of government and assigned specific executive duties to other constitutional officers such as the secretary of state, attorney general, and general treasurer. For example, the state's general treasurer was responsible for revenue receipts and disbursements, managing state indebtedness, and serving as a member of boards that dealt with investments and pensions. The attorney general functioned as the state's chief legal officer, giving advice to executive agencies and issuing written legal opinions. These constitutional officers plus a separately elected lieutenant governor could propose their own initiatives that may or may not be supportive of the governor's agenda.[3]

The 1843 Constitution did not give the state's chief executive the ability to veto legislation. Veto power was not constitutionally granted to the governor until 1909, and today Rhode Island's governor still does not have a line-item veto of legislative appropriation, as governors do in 44 states. Rhode Island historian Patrick Conley opined that the framers of the 1843 Constitution "gave Rhode Island's governor no veto, no appointive power and no budgetary powers."[4] In 1856, Samuel Ames, the chief justice of the Rhode Island Supreme Court, in *Taylor v. Place*, said the following about Rhode Island's governor: "However great the personal influence of him who, from time to time may fill the executive chair, of the state, may be, from his character and his standing, his official power amounts to nothing."[5]

While the 1843 Constitution said little about specific governmental functions, Article XII established education as a governmental responsibility. However, it did not make education an enforceable constitutional right and said it was the duty of the General Assembly, not the chief executive, to promote public education. The issue of whether the Rhode Island Constitution requires all students be given access to equal educational opportunities is still being debated in Rhode Island.

After adoption of the Constitution of 1843, modifications to the state's fundamental law were scant and sparse. Into the third decade of the twentieth century, Rhode Island's executive branch of government had "no system of management, just a welter of boards, commissions, commissioners, departments and agencies, not really constituting an executive branch, and certainly not accountable to the governor," Payne relates.[6]

A research report prepared for the Connecticut General Assembly in 2000 found that compared to most states today, Rhode Island's chief executive still has relatively limited institutional powers.

The Bloodless Revolution

The creation of a modern executive branch of government in Rhode Island was in reaction to legislative dominance of the levers of power, political corruption, and changes in federalism resulting from Franklin Delano Roosevelt's New Deal.

In 1901, the General Assembly enacted the Brayton Act. The architect of this law was Charles R. Brayton, who served as chairman of the Republican state steering committee. In the age of political machines, Ocean State Republicans had one, and Brayton was the boss. The Brayton Act permitted the state Senate to control most executive appointments to agencies, boards, and commissions. If the Senate choose not to confirm the governor's nominees, the Senate could fill the positions with whomever it proposed.[8] According to Payne, "If the Governor was of the same party as the Senate, and he often was, then the Senate might decide to accept his appointment, if the Governor was of a different party, as some of the Governors of the first decade of the century were, then the Senate could put its own people into the position."[9]

In 1932, at the height of the Great Depression, there was a national Democratic landslide. In Rhode Island, Democrat Theodore Francis Green (1933–1937) was elected to be governor. After taking office, Governor Green called a special session of the General Assembly for the purposes of piggybacking on the New Deal's economic relief initiatives and enhancing state government efficiency. In justifying the need for state government reorganization, Green argued, "Undoubtedly large sums, no one knows how much, may be saved to the State by a reorganization of the State departments and commissions."[10] The General Assembly approved legislation for Rhode Island to participate in the New Deal, but largely ignored the Governor's call for a commission to study reorganization of the executive branch.

In 1934, Governor Green was reelected, and the Democrats also gained control of the House of Representatives. The Senate appeared to still be controlled by the Republicans. However, the Democrats claimed fraud, and the vote counts remained disputed in two districts, with the secretary of state unwilling to certify the results in those districts. The result was a Senate with 20 Republicans and 20 Democrats. In this situation, the Democratic lieutenant governor was able to break any tie vote, which gave the Democrats control of both the legislative and executive branches of state government.

On New Year's Day, 1935, the Democrats executed a bloodless revolution. To ensure the state Supreme Court would not overturn their actions, the General Assembly approved a resolution declaring vacant the positions of the chief justice and associate justices. The justices were allowed to keep their pensions if they agreed to retire.[11]

Once the Democrats had gained control of both legislative houses and sidelined the state Supreme Court, they enacted legislation providing that "all of the powers and duties now vested in the several state boards, bureaus, commissions and other administrative agencies shall be vested in eleven departments."[12] Seven of these would be headed by a director appointed by the governor with the advice and consent of the Senate. These were the departments of Public Works, Public Welfare, Taxation and Regulations, Education, Labor, Agriculture and Conservation, and Public Health. The remaining departments were led by elected constitutional officers, such as the attorney general, secretary of state, general treasurer, and the governor, who headed the executive department, which included the budget director, controller, purchasing agent, state police, adjutant general, and the division of parole.[13]

The transition to a well-organized executive branch would take about 15 years to fully complete. The basic structure was established in 1935, the assignment of function was finished in 1939, and operational efficiency was maximized in 1951.[14]

In one day the "Bloodless Revolution of 1935" totally restructured state government and the relationship between the executive and legislative branches. As Payne explains, "The General Assembly gave up an enormous amount of power, in at least two senses and perhaps three. First, it lost whatever direct influence it had exerted through the various boards and commissions now superseded by administrative departments. Second, it lost much of the control it may well have had over staff and other appointments, that is, over state patronage. Third it participated in the creation of a gubernatorial office that was certain to become a powerful rival and alternative source of authority in the governing system — an influence that had no counterpart in the old assembly-centered system."[15]

Reorganizing the executive branch was continued in 1939 by William H. Vanderbilt, a reform-minded Republican governor. Two major administrative reforms were enacted during his tenure. The first was the Administrative Act of 1939, which placed budget management responsibilities along with taxation functions in a new Department of Coordination and Finance, the precursor of the Department of Administration. This act also centralized responsibilities for the regulation and oversight of businesses in Department of Business Regulations.[16] The second and the more profound reform was the State Civil Service Act, which created a merit system for hiring, and institutionalized professionalism in the state service. This act was aimed at insulating most state jobs from patronage. It provided for both a classified and unclassified service. Classified employment was based on the candidate's qualifications.[17]

Some have speculated that Vanderbilt served only one term "because rural Republicans resented his legislative blow to the patronage pool they had lived on for years."[18] However, the civil service initiative limited the patronage of the Democrat governors as well who soon regained power.

The Halcyon Years of the Executive

In the decade following the reforms of the 1930s, the roles and responsibilities of the executive branch were expanded. State government programs were administered by departments who reported to the state's chief executive, state employment was merit-based, and the expansion of federal programs caused states to be more responsive to economic and social needs.

In 1941, the General Assembly authorized Governor J. Howard McGrath (1941–1945) to appoint a Commission to Study the Financial Problems of the State and Municipalities. One issue the Commission examined was the financing of unemployment relief and assistance to the needy. The result was comprehensive legislation to support state financing of unemployment relief.[19]

In his budget address to the General Assembly, Governor Pastore (1945–1950) requested a Commission to "Re-Examine the Field of Government Operations, the Cost of Government Services and the Tax Structure of the State." The Commission made important findings in the areas of budgeting, federal relations, public assistance, and, most significantly, education, where it recommended a new system of school aid. In 1947, a sales tax of 1 percent was levied, which was described as necessary to "assure the maintenance of proper educational standards in the public schools" and to provide "for additional aid to several cities and towns now confronted with financial crisis."[20]

These examples demonstrate how the role of the executive branch was expanding as the state become more engaged in intergovernmental fiscal relations.

The evolution of the executive branch, to what essentially it is today, was completed in 1951 when Governor Dennis Roberts (1951–1959) proposed the establishment of the Department of Administration.

This Department become the command center of state government management and administration. According to Payne, "It collected the state's revenues, taxes, fees, and other income, and managed the state's budget. It provided central purchasing for state agencies. And it oversaw the personnel system, taking over the duties of the independent Department of Civil Service, which had been established in 1939."[21] Subsequently, it assumed responsibility for the planning, information processing, and general services functions.

During Governor Roberts's tenure, an economic development agency, the Rhode Island Development Council, was established, the Board of Education was reorganized and given oversight over the Department of Education, and the constitutional home rule amendment gave municipalities the authority to determine their government structure.

Over the next 20 years, executive agencies were reorganized and created in response to emerging environmental, social, and economic challenges. Some notable examples include the following:

- Raising environmental concerns led to the enactment of a myriad of federal laws and regulations. In response, the Department of Natural Resources was retooled as the Department of Environmental Management. This department manages and regulates air, water, and land resources to protect public health and ecological integrity.
- Administering a myriad of federally supported health and human service programs has proven challenging. In 1970, the cumbersome Department of Welfare was divided into two agencies: the Department of Social and Rehabilitative Services and the Department of Mental Health, Retardation, and Hospitals.
- Funding Medicaid is a shared federal–state responsibility that requires states to administer medical insurance programs. Since several Rhode Island human service agencies provided medical assistance to their clients, an Executive Office of Health and Human Services was

established in 2005 to coordinate this program. The secretary was given responsibility to coordinate all Health and Human Services agencies. However, the directors of those agencies still reported directly to the governor. This organizational arrangement has not been without problems.

The growth of these agencies reflects the influence federal policies has had on the structure of the state's executive branch. Policies determined by Congress and federal regulations are often administered by state departments and agencies. Similar to the New Deal and Great Society, future transformational federal policies may continue to trigger changes to the executive machinery of state governments.

Federal policy is not the only driver of state organizational changes. Efforts to improve effectiveness and efficiency has also motivated the General Assembly and Governors to establish or consolidate operating departments. In 2006, the Department of Revenue was established to enhance revenue collections and focus on matters of tax and revenue policy. Previously, these revenue responsibilities were embedded in the Department of Administration. In 2012, the Office of Budget and Management was established within the Department of Administration to coordinate budget and management policy.

The need to remain economically competitive has also influenced the organization and roles of departments and agencies. The Economic Development Corporation (now Rhode Island Commerce Corporation) was transformed to respond to changes in how states compete for jobs and investments. The secretary is charged with managing a cohesive direction of both economic and community development.

The following table (Table 9.1) sets forth the evolution of the administrative structure of state government since the Bloodless Revolution. While the foundation established in 1935 as been enduring, modifications have been made to respond to demographic, economic, and technological challenges as well as changes in the federal system.

Separation of Powers

Around 1970, Rhode Island entered a period that saw the expansion of quasi-independent agencies. These boards and commissions were established to undertake essential public purposes. Between the early 1970s and 2000, "power and capacity in state government would disperse, and administrative state would fragment and decline on coherence."[22]

The quasi-independent agencies are not departments of state government. However, they have the authority to enter into contracts, own property, assume debt that is a moral obligation of the state, and sue and be sued.

Table 9.1 Administrative Departments, 1935–2020	
Departments Set up in 1935 Reorganization	Current Departments (2020)
Executive	Executive Administration
State	State
Justice	Attorney General
Treasury	Treasury
Public Welfare	Health and Human Services
	Health
	Human Services
	Children, Youth, and Families
	Behavioral Healthcare, Developmental Disabilities and Hospitals
	Corrections
Public Works	Transportation
Taxation & Regulation	Business Regulation
Revenue	Revenue
Education	Education
Labor	Labor & Training
Agriculture & Conservation	Environmental Management
	Economic Development
	Executive Office of Commerce
	RI Commerce Corporation

A partial list of quasi-independent agencies created during this time included the Rhode Island Port Authority and Economic Development Corporation, the Rhode Island Mortgage Finance Corporation, the Solid Waste Management Corporation (now the Resource Recovery Corporation), the Lottery Commission, the Higher Education Assistance Authority, the Health and Education Building Authority, the Public Transit Authority, the Rhode Island Airport Corporation, the Rhode Island Depositors Economic Protection Corporation, the Clean Water Finance Agency, the Convention Center Authority, the RI Partnership for Science and Technology, the Rhode Island Commerce Corporation, the Coastal Resource Management Council, the Narragansett Bay Water Quality Management Commission, and others.

In some instances, the use of quasi-independent agencies is justified to finance public activities, regulate private activities, and operate public utilities. However, they may limit public accountability and transparency, and potentially be in conflict with executive departments and agencies.

In Rhode Island, the growth of quasi-independent agencies was causing governance issues because the state constitution did not provide for the separation of powers between the executive and legislative branches of government. Senator Sheldon Whitehouse, who was then Governor Bruce Sundlun's legal counsel (1991–1995), said of legislative membership on quasi-independent boards and commissions, "It's about dispensing jobs from economic development to the landfill. Pots of public money, heaps of patronage, conflicts up the kazoo."[23]

Until 2004, quasi-independent boards, authorities, and commissions included members of the General Assembly or persons appointed by legislative leaders. No distinction was being made between legislators both writing the laws and then exercising executive prerogatives to administer the very same laws. Reformers argue this represented a violation of the principle of separation of powers that fostered cronyism or worse. Proponents of legislative appointments to quasi-independent agencies argued that Rhode Island's part-time legislature was disadvantaged in overseeing executive departments. Membership on the boards of quasi-independent agencies made up for this limitation.

In 1997, Governor Lincoln Almond (1995–2003) asked the state Supreme Court if limits could be imposed on legislators serving on quasi-independent boards and commissions. The Supreme Court advised that the Rhode Island Constitution did not include a separation of powers requirement. The only solution was to secure passage of a constitutional amendment. Reformers promoted an amendment, which was overwhelmingly approved by the voters in 2004, thus enhancing gubernatorial powers.

The adoption of the separation of powers amendment coupled with changes initiated by the Bloodless Revolution suggests that Rhode Island governors have the constitutional and statutory authority to be effective chief executives.

Governors as Policy Leaders

Legislators and interest groups all have their own policy agendas. Alan Rosenthal writes, "Yet not all agendas are created equal. The governor's agenda is far and away the most equal of all."[24] The governor is best positioned to assess the problem, design a solution, secure enactment of the solution, and oversee its implementation. What a governor can do, that no other state leader can do as well, is tell the people where the state is, where it needs to be, and when it gets there.[25] The chief executive's agenda receives predominant media attention and shapes major policy initiatives during most legislative sessions.

Rhode Island governors who have succeeded as policy leaders heeded the advice of the National Governors Association and recognized the importance of focusing on a limited number of major challenges. A national survey of governors who were in office between 1980–2010 found that almost 50 percent said their legislative agendas encompassed one to five items.[26]

To be effective policy-makers, governors need professional staff to identify, analyze, and assess policy options and then monitor implementation. To both carry through on campaign promises as well as respond to unanticipated problems, governors do not rely solely on the judgement and recommendations of agency heads whose political perspectives might not coincide with theirs.

It is hard to pinpoint precisely when governors began to focus on long-term policy goals. However, the governor's policy leadership seems to have been institutionalized by Governor Philip Noel (1973–1977) when President Nixon withdrew the Navy from Rhode Island. The relocation of the Atlantic destroyer fleet from the Ocean State to the South had a draconian impact on the state's economy. Rhode Island lost thousands of civilian jobs as well as naval personnel and their dependents.

In response, Governor Noel established a professional team in his office to develop policy options to cope with the economic crisis. This was a departure from the traditional method of staffing the governor's office with former campaign aides and other political appointees. As a result, the governor secured legislation to establish a Department of Economic Development and a Port Authority and Economic Development Corporation. This team was the forerunner of the governor's policy office, which for decades has been invaluable in developing and monitoring policy solutions to the state's challenges.

The policy model established by the Noel Administration changed only marginally between the 1974 and 2015. Policy staffs have played key roles in developing policy options to implement campaign promises, deal with statewide crises such as the credit union crisis in 1991, manage projects, and coordinate policy and budget decisions during periods of fiscal stress.

While policy staffs have coordinated policy development and attempted to act as a traffic cop to assure department proposals were based on accurate information and consistent with administration goals, they did not always have the resources to develop operational polices and systematically evaluate all departmental initiatives. Lack of resources in the policy office has become more important as the operations of government have become more complex.

Based on their experience and management style, governors have used the policy office somewhat differently. Governor Sundlun trusted his senior policy staff and they played key roles in proposing solutions to the credit union crisis, reforming the dysfunctional workers compensation system, and in planning for the construction of a modern airport. In contrast, during the Carcieri Administration (2003–2011), transformational proposals to modernize the tax structure and address the bankruptcy of the Twin River Casino emanated from the governor directing members of the cabinet.

In 2015, Governor Raimondo (2015–2021) modified the policy process. The governor assigned portfolios to deputy chiefs of staff who were responsible for working with selected departments and agencies. One deputy chief of staff was primarily responsible for education and workforce matters, another for health and human services, and a third for transportation and the environment. Two cabinet members, the director of administration, and the secretary of commerce, did not report to a deputy chief of staff. Furthermore, Governor Raimondo took a proactive role initiating policies regarding her priorities, namely education and economic development.

Each governor has managed the policy process based on their experience and management style. Often, a key organizational decision was the allocation of responsibility between line departments and the policy staff. Consistently effective governors have recognized that good policy is good politics.

The Governor and the General Assembly

A governor's effectiveness is dependent in part on the goodwill and responsiveness of the General Assembly. The executive and legislative branches cannot be expected to forego their institutional prerogatives and agree on every issue. Conflicts are both healthy and inevitable in a partisan political system built on checks and balances. How a governor manages these potential conflicts goes a long way in determining whether their tenure will be effective.

In establishing a working relationship with the legislature, governors should discuss their priorities, solicit ideas, and identify common ground before one branch or the other becomes locked into a position. This is important, because governors are new to the office every four or eight years, while a legislature consisting of 113 members is a continuing body. This is particularly the case in Rhode Island, where legislative leaders have substantial authority over their chambers.

Governors, of course, have numerous opportunities to inject themselves into the legislative process through budget proposals, the veto, command of technical experts who administer complex programs, and the use of the bully pulpit. Even with the General Assembly's growing professionalism, "[w]hen the two partners in state governance stand up to dance, it is typically the governor who leads and the legislature that follows."[27]

Since the advent of the modern executive branch in 1935, Rhode Island history is replete with examples of governors who skillfully created win-win situations in dealing with the General Assembly and those who failed miserably. Much of the history of the relationship between the executive and legislative branches "has been a quest for an agreed-upon and stable balance between the two roles of the institutions."[28] Achieving this balance has been dependent upon the chief executive's leadership ability and the prevailing political and economic climate during a governor's term.

In addition to Governor Theodore Francis Green (1933–1937), several governors played an assertive role in dealing with the General Assembly when it came to the budget and overall state direction. William Vanderbilt (1939–1941) created a merit-based civil service, which was a fatal blow to political patronage. John O. Pastore (1947–1951), secured the adoption of the direct primary and the statewide sales tax. Dennis Roberts (1951–1959), who had served as Providence mayor, modernized the state's administrative structure with passage of legislation establishing the Department of Administration. Republican John Chafee (1963–1969) had excellent relations with the General Assembly and was able to usher in a new era of land conservation."[29] In 1974, when the Navy left, Governor Noel championed important changes to the state's economic development organizational infrastructure.

The accomplishments of these governors underscore the tradition of strong gubernatorial leadership set in motion by the Bloodless Revolution and Governor Green. However, by the end of the 1960s, the General Assembly became restless about its secondary position to the executive branch. However, fiscal realities forced governors from both parties, who were elected opposing the state income tax, to change their positions. The income tax episode began to weaken executive dominance in its dealing with the General Assembly.

The process was completed in 1996 when Governor Lincoln Almond vetoed the budget sent to him by the General Assembly. The General Assembly flexed their muscles by overriding the Governor's veto and understood that budget adoption was their show. In subsequent years there were instances when the legislature enacted the state's budget without having meaningful negotiations with the state's chief executive.

Over the last 20 years, the governor's leverage and influence with the General Assembly has depended on his or her leadership style and ability to communicate with the legislature and voters alike, as well as the underlying economic and challenges facing the state.

When Governor Sundlun took office in 1991, the credit union crisis and unprecedented budget deficit created conditions that demanded bold leadership. While keeping the legislature informed, Sundlun put recovery plans in place and enjoyed considerable leverage when dealing with legislative leadership. It helped that both the governor and legislative majority were from the same political party. Fifteen years later, the state faced a similar fiscal crisis caused by the Great Recession of 2008. Finding common ground was more difficult because the governor and legislature were from different political parties.

In the twenty-first century, the General Assembly has become increasingly assertive about its policy-making prerogatives. Several important initiatives have originated in the General Assembly, such as the phase-out of the property tax on motor vehicles.

In the future, the balance of power between the executive and legislative branches is likely to become more competitive and situational. Changes in retail politics, fostered by progressives in Rhode Island, control of the "purse strings" during a period of exponential growth in federal financial support, and increasing institutional professionalism may enhance the General Assembly's policy-making role.

On the other hand, governors have resources that a legislature cannot match. As programs become more complex, an executive branch has the technical resources needed to assess problems and provide solutions to complex matters. Also, the governor is best positioned to make effective use of the bully pulpit to mold public opinion needed to garner support for tough choices.

However, the General Assembly's power and influence should not be underestimated. It has the unrealized potential to play a pivotal role providing quality oversight over the executive branch. How the legislature chooses to exercise its oversight and appropriating responsibilities may define executive-legislative relations going forward.

State Employees and Unions

Rhode Island's personnel system can be characterized as a hybrid civil service/collective bargaining arrangement. The state's personnel system has evolved from one that was based solely on a civil service system to a one largely driven by collective bargaining.

In 1939, the Ocean State adopted the Civil Service Act, which established merit as the basis for hiring most state workers. Prior state employment was subject to political decision-making characterized by battles over patronage.

The Civil Service Act's stated objective was "to guarantee to all citizens a fair and equal opportunity for public service, to establish conditions for service which will attract officers and employees of character and capacity and to increase the efficiency of the governmental departments and agencies by the improvement of methods of personnel administration."[30]

A three-member civil service commission was also established. Its primary responsibility was to appoint a three-member examining committee and recommend to the governor three candidates for the position of director of civil service. This director would have civil service protection, but would not serve at the pleasure of the governor.[31]

The law also required that all positions in state government be placed in either classified or unclassified service. Classified employees were supposed to be hired based on merit and had the protections of the civil service system. The civil service director was also charged with the task of preparing a classification plan based on "the duties and responsibilities of each position."[32]

In 1951, the functions and responsibilities of the independent Department of Civil Service were absorbed into the new Department of Administration.

Currently, a Division of Human Resources reports to the Director of Administration and is responsible for personnel administration, labor relations, employee benefit management, and training.

Numerous modifications have been made to Rhode Island's civil service law since its inception over 80 years ago. According to Maureen Moakley and Elmer Cornwell, "These amendments can be interpreted either as desirable injections of flexibility or as making it more permeable to political or other 'non-merit' kinds of appointments."[33] The number of candidates the personnel administrator may certify to an appointing authority was increased from one in the original law to six. Temporary appointments may be made if a list of qualified candidates does not exist. Originally, a temporary appointment was limited to 60 days and the temporary appointee could not be reappointed. Today a temporary appointment can be made for one year, and if a certified list of candidates is not available, the temporary appointee can receive provisional status.

Over the years, good government groups have recommended ways to reform Rhode Island's personnel system to achieve the fairness and thoroughgoing professionalism envisioned in the merit system, but to little avail. However, while the basic structure of the civil service law remains, it has less relevance to the modern workforce due to increasingly technical positions and collective bargaining.

In the 1960s and 70s, Rhode Island's public employees won the right to bargain collectively regarding wages, hours, and other working conditions. According to the Rhode Island AFL/CIO Labor History Society, "In 1961, Rhode Island Firefighters obtained collective bargaining rights. Following the Firefighters, State Police (1963). Teachers (1966), municipal workers (1967), and state workers (1972) won passage of bargaining laws governing union recognition and dispute resolution."[34]

The rules of the road regarding state–employee relations have been largely determined by the General Assembly, not the executive branch of state government. In granting state employees the right to bargain collectively, among other provisions, the legislature defined the duty and scope of bargaining and the rights and obligations of both labor and management.

Given past practices, if unions believe any changes to the state's personnel system or collective bargaining laws are not in their interest, they are not likely to be made. With the influence state and local employee unions have with the General Assembly, the odds of enacting modifications to personnel practice without their support is problematic. According to Moakley and Cornwell, "Union-secured and protected worker benefits and the de facto, if not de jure tenure in many cases have meant the surrender or modifications of traditional management prerogatives."[35]

In a practical sense, modifying personnel rules and laws is a shared function between the governor, legislature, and the public employee unions. This poses both opportunities and challenges for the executive and employee organizations to work cooperatively to achieve efficiency and effectiveness in providing necessary state services.

Future Executive Leadership

Future Rhode Island executive leadership will have to deal with the disruptions caused by COVID-19 and possibly future pandemics. The *transactional* approach to governing, characterized by a give-and-take system between traditional organizations, will still be evident but it may not be adequate for the uncertain future.

Abraham Lincoln remarked, "The dogmas of the quiet past are inadequate to the stormy present, as our case is new, so we must think anew and act anew." In the post-pandemic period, leaders will need to confront pandemic disruptions that have affected our economic and governmental infrastructure. These include student learning losses, changing sectorial needs for workers, mental health, and social equity challenges.

Lincoln's advice to think and act anew especially applies to executive leadership. As opposed to "business as usual" leaders, the state's future may require *transformational* leaders who are long-term problem-solvers.

Governors cannot always be expected to anticipate all crises that emerge. The quality of executive leadership is sometimes defined by how governors react to such contingencies. Governor Raimondo's initial reaction to COVID-19 is an example of a governor effectively managing a crisis. However, if decisions are driven primarily by a reaction to political pressure, the quality of executive leadership can be both shortsighted and reactionary. In Rhode Island, examples of *reactionary* leadership include Governor DiPrete's 1991 response to the credit union crisis and Governor McKee's handling of school masking in 2021.

Transformational chief executives will govern by aligning authority with responsibility and organizing departments and agencies to think and act like a system. The difficulties encountered in implementing Rhode Island's United Health Infrastructure Project—an effort to integrate eight federal and state benefit programs into a seamless unified system—may have been exacerbated by state government not acting as an interdisciplinary organization.

A governor probably cannot be a transformational leader unless departments provide management, policy development, and communication skills as well as the resources needed to implement change. This may present challenges because all governors do not have the same approach to leading and managing. According to the National Governors Association, "Some governors view themselves as having a mission and concentrate on the big picture, leaving most policy development and management to appointees and staff. Other governors look at the governorship with the primary purpose of becoming the chief manager of the state government. Still other governors are concerned with a limited number of high-priority issues and are content to delegate policy considerations to others in the administration."[36]

Regardless of their management style, a transformational governor's success starts first and foremost with the ability to focus. For example, Governor Bruce Sundlun focused on solving the state's banking and fiscal crises as well as building a modern airport. Governor Carcieri (2003–11) focused on making Rhode Island taxes more economically competitive and pursuing the nation's first commercial offshore wind farm. Governor Raimondo's attention to education and economic development resulted in free tuition at the state's community college and the retooling of economic development programs. Earlier, Governor J. Joseph Garrahy (1977–85) took the first necessary steps to clean up Narraganset Bay.

Governors committed to making one major policy reform have had a transformational influence on the nation. Examples include James Hunt's (D-NC) leadership in education and Governor Tommy Thompson's (R-WI) role in welfare reform.

In response to COVID-19, effective governors needed to rethink how bureaucracies functioned to address the challenges of student learning losses, helping small businesses survive, linking labor force training and participation, and providing affordable health care and housing. An early indication of transformational leadership were decisions made to allocate and monitor over $1 billion in federal rescue funds.

A transformational chief executive will need extraordinary professional support and buy-in from the departments and agencies they oversee. Transformational executive leaders are focused, get the right people onboard, use the bully pulpit, and recognize that success depends on the goodwill and actions of others—most critically the General Assembly.

Notes

1. Kenneth F. Payne, Kenneth F. "An Essay Concerning Rhode Island Government," *Systems Aesthetics LLC*, December 2010, 11. Mr. Payne's essay is a comprehensive summary of the development and evolution of executive government in Rhode Island. It was invaluable to this chapter.
2. Ibid., 31.
3. Maureen Moakley and Elmer, Maureen, and Cornwell,. *Rhode Island Politics and Government*. (Lincoln: University of Nebraska Press, 2001), 85.
4. Patrick T. Conley, *Neither Separate nor Equal: Legislature and Executive in Rhode Island Constitutional History*. (Providence, RI: Rhode Island Publication Society, 1999), 74.
5. Payne, "An Essay Concerning Rhode Island Government," 33.
6. Ibid., 47.
7. Connecticut General Assembly, Office of Legislative Research, *Gubernatorial Powers*, 2000.
8. Payne, "An Essay Concerning Rhode Island Government," 57.
9. Ibid.
10. Ibid., 70.
11. Ibid., 73.
12. Ibid., 73–74.
13. Ibid., 74.
14. Ibid.
15. Ibid., 88.
16. Ibid., 81.
17. Ibid., 83.
18. Moakley and Cornwell, *Rhode Island Politics and Government*, 90.
19. Payne, "An Essay Concerning Rhode Island Government," 85.
20. Ibid., 86.
21. Ibid., 88.
22. Ibid., 97.
23. West, Philip West, Jr., *Secrets and Scandals: Reforming Rhode Island, 1986–2006*. (Providence. Rhode Island: Rhode Island Publication Society, 2014), 306.
24. Alan Rosenthal, *The Best Jobs in Politics: Exploring How Governors Succeed as Policy Leaders*, 1st ed, (Los Angeles: CQ Press, 2012), 87.
25. Gary Sasse, "How Republican Governors Are Turning New England Red," *Ripon Society*, February 14, 2017, https://riponsociety.org/article/how-republican-governors-are-turning-new-england-red/.
26. Rosenthal, 94.
27. Ibid., 89.
28. Moakley and Cornwell, *Rhode Island Politics and Government*, 89.
29. Payne, "An Essay Concerning Rhode Island Government," 94.
30. Chapter 661, Public Laws, 1939.
31. Payne, "An Essay Concerning Rhode Island Government," 83.
32. Ibid.
33. Moakley and Cornwell, *Rhode Island Politics and Government*, 100.
34. RI AFL/CIO, *Rhode Island Labor History Society*, 2018.
35. Moakley and Cornwell, *Rhode Island Politics and Government*, 103.
36. National Governors Association, *Transition and the New Governor* (Washington, DC: National Governors Association, 1998), 62.

10 / The Rhode Island Judiciary

Maureen Moakley[1]

An opening on the State Supreme Court occurred in 2020 that allowed the Governor Gina Raimondo to appoint a candidate, State Senator Erin Lynch Prata, to that bench. Lynch Prada had deep roots in Rhode Island. She was elected to the State Senate in 2009 and served as chair of the Senate Judiciary Committee. She shouldered through legislation that was a critical part of the governor's agenda as well as policies relating to women's rights.

The selection involved a reformed process whereby the governor could choose a candidate from a short list of five individuals vetted by a judicial nominating committee. This reform was part of a prior merit selection process for choosing judges adopted in 1994. The appointment however, appeared to many to run afoul of a revolving door statute, instated in 1992, mandating all elected officials to wait a year before taking state positions that are financially remunerated. Lynch Prata, however, argued that the state Supreme Court was a constitutional position akin to the statewide general officers and therefore the revolving door restriction did not apply. Others noted the restriction did apply as statewide constitutional officers are all elected, and this was an appointed position.

The issue was then taken up by the Ethics Commission, where the legal staff recommended denying the appointment due to the revolving door statute. In turn, the Commission's chair and one other committee member voted against the appointment, but the final vote of the commissioners was 5–2 in favor of Lynch Prata's position. She was appointed to the court in 2020. Reform groups like Common Cause were "sickened" by what they argued was a pass through the revolving door restriction;[2] others demurred that this was probably an example of enlightened patronage.

There was also another opening to the Supreme Court at that time. Governor Raimondo's second appointment was Superior Court Justice Melissa Long, the first woman of color appointed to the high court. These nominations resulted in women being a majority on a five-member court bench—a composition that would have been unthinkable a decade earlier.

The Rhode Island Judiciary

The Rhode Island court system has evolved from a political institution inextricably linked to the legislature and the executive branch through constitutional design, budget authority, and traditional patronage to a more professional and independent judiciary.[3] It was a long time coming.

Since the creation of the colony, the court system in Rhode Island was a highly political institution. The original Rhode Island charter gave authority to the General Assembly to annually elect judges and set their rate of compensation. The character of the judiciary changed little after statehood, since the charter was essentially grafted onto the Constitution. Before statehood, the court took on distinctly partisan patterns as many factions, tied to the court, attempted to shape the post-colonial system. One of the results of this struggle was the delayed entry of Rhode Island into the Union; it was the last state to ratify the Constitution in 1790.[4]

Attempts to create a more independent judiciary in the Constitution of 1843 failed. While it provided a separation of powers provision, the legislature retained broad authority over the courts through salaries and appointments to the bench. It continued to be a rich source of patronage for leaders of the legislature and powerful elites. After the Civil War, the courts routinely supported the ascendent Republican Party, which used the courts to sustain its power.

The constitutional link to the judiciary also played a critical factor of the Democrats takeover of state politics, referred to as the" Bloodless Revolution" or "Green Revolution" in 1935. Having taken over the three branches of government, the Democrats, via some curious machinations in the state Senate, invoked a provision that during the annual reorganization meeting, any sitting judge's seat could be declared vacant by a resolution of the General Assembly. The new Democrat majority was able to vacate all seats of the existing Supreme Court, capturing one of the Republicans' bastions of power and preventing the sitting judges from striking down sweeping changes in government the Democrats proceeded to enact.

The Democrats initiated many positive administrative and structural reforms but continued to use the courts as their own patronage system. Although excellent appointments were not uncommon, appointees were often supporters or members of the legislature or both. Governors would also routinely nominate members of their staff to the bench before leaving office. While the quality of the court's decisions usually maintained reputable judicial standards, a bloated and parochial judiciary remained a source of patronage and inefficiency in a changing environment. This, and some highly visible scandals, prompted reform legislation that created structural and administrative changes.

Many of the recent reforms occurred in the 1990s. A constitutional amendment establishing a merit selection protocol for the selection of judges for all state judicial openings was approved by the voters in 1994. Previously, selection to the bench was done by members of both houses of the legislature sitting in the Grand Committee. All members were free to nominate candidates, and many members would use this opportunity as a perk to nominate political associates or constituents, whether qualified or not. The process, however, was controlled by the legislative leaders, particularly the speaker of the House who, by virtue of the numbers in that chamber, controlled the vote.

The new system created a nine-member Judicial Nominating Commission drawn from nominations by the governor and the legislature, thus allowing a political dimension to the process. It is a more open process, however, in that the Commission issues an open call for applications, and after reviewing all candidates, makes recommendations by nominating a list of from three to five potential candidates from which the governor appoints a candidate. That appointment is then confirmed by the state Senate or, in the case of a Supreme Court nominee, the state Senate and House acting separately. While this represents a marked improvement in the selection process, in that it is regarded as the most insulated from political influence, reformers reluctantly note the impossibility of eliminating all politics from an inherently political process.[5]

Another reform that involved the judiciary was a revolving door statute adopted by the legislature in 1992.[6] The statute mandated a one-year waiting period between elected service and political appointment for any position in state government involving financial renumeration. This is generally considered a positive change, especially for some elected officials who viewed appointment to a judgeship as a final next step in public service. As one federal official noted, "The state court system is still Valhalla for a lot of pols in this state."

Changes were also initiated to rectify a bloated bureaucracy and excessive incentive policies for court employees. One telling example was rescinding an incentive provision that allowed court clerks to receive a yearly bonus for having college degrees! Depending on the rank and degree, clerks received a 10 to 16 percent yearly bonus; in some cases, administrators with salaries of at or about $80,000 got bonuses of more than $12,000 a year. A program such as this might have been appropriate in the post-war period, when advanced degrees were much less common, but it was initiated in 1976 and enhanced in 1987, suggesting a culture of excess reminiscent of the nineteenth century. Legislative leaders finally acknowledged that this was not an incentive program but an example of "planned greed" and amended the legislation in 1994 to a flat stipend for those in the system and eliminating it for new hires.[7]

A back-door patronage system that remains is the appointment of magistrates to the court system.[8] Magistrates are appointed directly by the chief judge of each court, thus circumventing the open judicial nomination process. Magistrates perform many the same duties as judges but cannot preside over a trial. There were a few magistrates in the court system before the creation of merit selection, but the ranks subsequently increased thereafter, as appointees are not subject to merit selection. They are appointed for ten-year renewable terms, subject to Senate confirmation, with salaries somewhat comparable to full judges. While these appointments usually go to qualified applicants, most of whom do conscientious work, they are still able to avoid the scrutiny of a public hearing. Those with ties to the governor and legislative leaders as well as prominent public figures get access to these appointments, as do high-level staff of a governor or the legislative leadership. It is not unusual for these magistrates to then go on to get an appointment to full judge through the judicial nominating process. These appointees, however, are generally qualified persons who perform well on the bench. This process, however, gives fits to reform groups, who call out the inside loophole in the system as a remanent of the "I know a guy" culture in the state, but it is obliquely tolerated in a vastly improved professional court system.

These early reforms came in the 1990s as the judiciary began to evolve into a more autonomous and independent system. Progress continued in subsequent years.

The Judiciary of the Twenty-first Century

The courts continued to modernize in the 2000s; key factors, as one practicing lawyer noted, were "leadership, technology and space." Many of the changes enacted by judicial leaders reflected a changing ethos of professionalism, openness, and responsibility to the public. Technology has also had a profound effect on the efficiency of the system. In response to the COVID-19 health crisis of the 2020s, other technological accommodations, initially implemented to control the spread of the virus, further improved efficiency and some were retained.

An electronic filing system for court case documents was first introduced in Workers' Compensation Court in 2014, and then initiated for the courts in 2015. It is mandatory for appellate cases in the Supreme Court, civil and criminal cases in Superior and District courts, domestic relation cases in Family Court, Workers' Compensation Court, and the Traffic Tribunal.[9] Documents can be filed 24/7 by registered users. Filings are mandatory for all parties except self-represented litigants, incarcerated persons, or those granted a waiver. The documents are openly held for 30 days and then are available through courthouse or remote access. This is boon to all parties involved, especially for lawyers; although it cuts down on billable hours, it vastly improves the filing process so that lawyers no longer need to trek to the courthouse to file a single document and documents are, with a few confidential filing exceptions, generally viewable to all parties.

Additional technological improvements, including streaming of all court proceedings, was initiated under the leadership of Chief Justice Paul Suttell. Originally prompted by the COVID crisis, it proved to be more efficient and was adjusted to promote transparency and convenience yet protect privacy.[10] During this period, all trail proceedings were available to all parties, the press, and the public via live streaming. This originally posed concerns about privacy in some contentious cases, especially Family Court proceedings involving minor children with, for example, medical records. Sensitive parts of court proceedings are usually held privately in the judge's chambers.

Getting on the court calendar was also streamlined. Lawyers now file online to get on the docket and receive a time to appear with their clients. Previously, lawyers and their clients would all congregate at the court and await a docket time. This could take hours, given the number of participants who might show up. This change, instituted during COVID, has been retained, creating a timelier system. Most lawyers are positive about the changes, and judges attempt to provide accommodation to inevitable glitches that are a result of the digital changes.

The court established an Ethics Advisory Panel in 1986, which was updated in 2018. It created a professional evaluation program that codified professional standards for lawyers and mandated standards for court personnel. It also updated the Code of Judicial Conduct with standards for judges, including individual evaluations of judges and court personnel and a process of review for judicial conduct. Although state judges are constitutionally subject to impeachment by the House and trial by the Senate, this is an unusual and rare occurrence. Judges who were considered for impeachment were former State Supreme Chief Justice Joseph Bevilacqua in 1984 and Chief Justice Thomas Fay in 1993. Both opted to resign.

The judiciary is now more diverse, but some groups indicate more is to be done. A survey by members of the Rhode Island Bar Association indicated there have been inequities and discrimination in the system, but a majority of respondents did agree that both the Bar Association and the Supreme Court were committed to diversity and inclusion.[11] Allowing for ongoing vacancies that skew estimates, in 1998 women were approximately 20 percent of judicial officers and minority representation was at 3 percent. By 2021, women represented 38 percent of judicial officers, and minorities were at 8 percent.[12] Women made steady progress under various governors. During his tenure, Republican Governor Donald Carcieri (2003–11) appointed women as chief judge in three of the five courts, and Governor Gina Raimondo increased women and minority representation, including appointments that resulted in women being a majority on the state Supreme Court.

The Court System

Rhode Island has a unified state court system of six statewide courts.[13] The Supreme Court is the court of last review or the "court of last resort." The Superior Court is the general trial court. The district, family, and worker's compensation courts are trial courts of limited jurisdiction. The administrative adjudication court—the traffic tribunal—hears all non-criminal traffic cases and reviews decisions of municipal courts and the Department of Motor Vehicles.

Figure 10-1

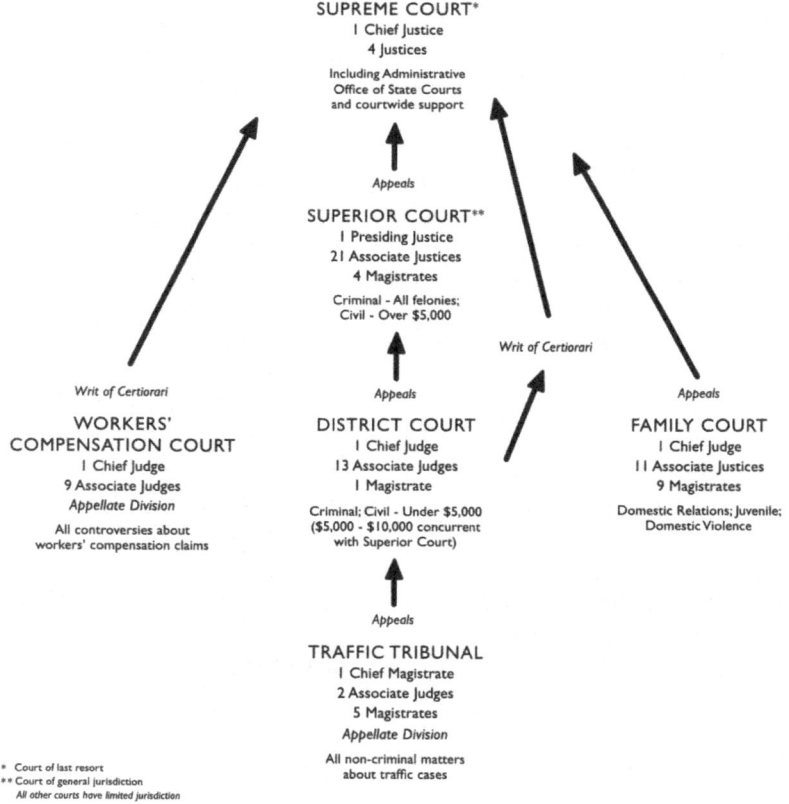

State of Rhode Island, *2020 Report on the Judiciary*

These courts are all state funded; probate and municipal courts are of limited jurisdiction and are the responsibility of local cities and towns.

Supreme Court

The state Supreme Court was established in the Rhode Island Constitution of 1843 and redefined by statute in 1905. It is the only court established in the Constitution; the others were established by statute. This court, which hears appeals and rules on points of law only, is the court of last resort. It has final jurisdiction for all civil and criminal appellate cases in the state. There are five justices who preside over an extensive array of cases since some district and Superior Court rulings can be appealed directly to the Supreme Court. Most cases are expedited fairly routinely; some cases, especially with political overtones, can take longer to settle.

In addition to the adjudicative responsibilities, the court oversees multiple boards and commissions, many of which were established to increase professionalism, transparency, and ethical standards in the entire court system.

Another important role of the Supreme Court is as part of a constitutionally mandated advisory opinion process whereby the court issues, on request, a non-binding opinion on the constitutionality of proposed legislative and executive actions. It is a general option designed to give a judicial perspective to state leaders, particularly on highly contentious issues. During the reform period of the 1990s, it was frequently solicited, but less so in the 2020s, as it has the potential to tip the debate in highly visible issues with political ramifications.

Superior Court

The Superior Court was established by statute in 1905 as the court of general jurisdiction. It hears all felony criminal cases and civil cases in which the amount in controversy exceeds $10,000. The Superior Court hears appeals, *de novo*, or a new trial, on cases from the district court. Any appeal from a decision given in Superior Court can be taken directly to the Supreme Court. The court also has jurisdiction over decisions from municipal and probate courts. It hears appeals from various boards and commissions, including zoning boards. It also hears appeals from the Ethics Commission and reviews disciplinary actions against local or state police officers.

The court has four jurisdictions, analogous to county jurisdictions in Kent, Washington, and Newport counties, with Providence and Bristol being one jurisdiction. In 1994, the legislature established a gun court—the first in the nation. The court expedites filing and disposition of gun-related cases in about a third of the time it would have required these to go through the Superior Court process.

Another initiative is a court administered arbitration program that expedites the resolution of certain civil cases involving $100,000 or less. Contract disputes, personal injury claims, and property damage suits can be remanded to this dispute resolution process. Arbitration hearings allow evidence to be presented to a court-trained attorney/arbitrator who then makes an award. This process speeds case resolution and saves litigants and taxpayers the costs associated with lengthy, formal trials. Other cases, administrated through the court arbitration office, allows cases to be resolved through mediation. Successful settlements through mediation account for a growing number of disposed civil cases.

A business calendar was established in 2011 for the Superior Court, and under the leadership of Judge Michael Silverstein, provided a coherent alternative to the general calendar. This innovation greatly expedited complex commercial issues involving cases related to business disputes. The court created a separate case calendar for civil cases involving an extensive array of civil cases, including motion practice, discovery disputes, injunctive relief, and hearing on merits of a case. Three judges with expertise on business affairs are assigned to the calendar, expediting cases and providing more informed and timely adjudication.

District Court

District courts, in four geographical locations, are usually the initial venue for most court proceedings; district court has jurisdiction over all civil actions involving disputes under $5,000 and concurrent jurisdiction with Superior Court on controversies between $5000 and 10,000. The court handles criminal arraignments for felony and misdemeanor case. There are no jury trials in District Court, but appeals can be made to Superior Court and in some cases, to the Supreme Court. Small claims involving damages of $5,000 or less are handled in this court; the process is designed to achieve a quick and final resolution, often without the necessity of lawyers.

The General Assembly also initiated reforms that mandated more efficient procedures and a sixty-day case disposition requirement. The court has made considerable progress in meeting these requirements, making the system more efficient and respected. Technological changes in the court system have also made for faster resolutions. Online payments and court fees are filed online using the courts electronic filing system. Civil cases can be scanned and filed into the judiciary case management system, eliminating cumbersome duplication. One key challenge for the district court was to reconfigure traffic court into a workable system and hear appeals from the traffic tribunal.

Family Court

Family Court hears all petitions for divorce and related proceeding such as property distribution, alimony, as well as child support and custody issues. The court has jurisdiction over all matters related to children including adoption and paternity proceedings. Appeals from the court are heard in the Supreme Court. The number of divorce and alimony cases has been reduced, but juvenile custody and parental rights caseloads have increased due to various and contested definitions of appropriate standards for and solutions to child neglect, child abuse, and parental neglect. Given the increase of violent juvenile incidents, some cases, after an initial hearing in Family Court, can be shifted to other courts as a result of demands that these offenders be tried as adults.

Workers' Compensation Court

Worker's compensation court was formally established by the legislature in 1990. It adjudicates disputes and claims between employees and employers on matters related to occupational issues and disabilities, hospital and medical billings, and the extent and conditions of disability. The integration of this court into the unified court system and reforms passed by the legislature provide a true success story.

A Workers' Compensation Commission was created in 1954 to resolve labor disputes. Over the years, the system became bogged down by a bloated and inefficient administration that perpetuated a huge backlog. Existing law and union contracts encouraged large numbers of complaints, expensive insurance settlements, and escalating insurance rates. In an ill-fated attempt to depoliticize the system, a two-tiered structure was implemented that split litigation from administration by creating a new department with additional procedures, hearing officers, and staff. These new positions provided an ideal source of patronage in the state system where patronage appointments in other branches of government were drying up. By the late 1980s, this "reformed" system was on the verge of collapse. The backlog of cases was over eighteen months, and insurance rates were so high that that several insurers announced they were withdrawing from the state system.[14]

The governor and the legislature responded with legislation that created new court framework mandating a 21-day limit for petitions to be heard. Under the direction of a new chief judge, Robert Arrigan, the system was transformed within a year. The backlog was eliminated, and, in conjunction with reforms in workers' compensation law, complaints began to steadily decline. Judge Arrigan, with the assistance of three new judicial appointees, transformed a lax working culture of late morning starts, long lunches, and brief hearing hours that set a tone of indifference and inefficiency. He held 8:30 a.m. pretrial hearings for judges and staff, increased judicial caseloads, and demanded scrutiny of legal and case resolutions, setting a higher standard of accountability and professionalism. It was so successful that lawyers in the state who practiced workers' compensation law often had to supplement their practice with other legal endeavors.[15] Claims dramatically declined, lump-sum settlements decreased by over half, and as of 1997, annual fees paid to lawyers declined dramatically. These reforms represented a "reinventing government" example that has been cited as a national model.[16]

Traffic Tribunal

The Traffic Tribunal is the court of original jurisdiction over civil traffic offenses and concurrent jurisdiction with municipal courts over lesser traffic offenses. This court is where most Rhode Islanders interact with the judiciary. For years its tattered history and inefficient standards frustrated citizens, lawyers, and observers. One elected official, after visiting the court noted, "It's like Baghdad down there."

As part of an effort to improve a disjointed system, the administrative adjudication court, where traffic cases were heard, became part of the state judicial system in 1993. To professionalize the process, hearing officers were made full-time administrative judges with salaried lifetime appointments and benefits. Unfortunately, over the subsequent years, while budgets and staffs expanded, productivity and service to plaintiffs remained abysmal.

Instances of malfeasance emerged in the late 1990s. In 1997, a lawyer and other staff were fined for doing private client work in court facilities and on state time. In that same year, a misdirecting of traffic ticket fines cost the state millions in uncollected revenue. This suggested a working culture reminiscent of "old style" features. An excellent investigative series by the *Providence Journal* revealed a system where judges put in only a few hours daily on the bench, computer records were in shambles, millions were lost in uncollected fines, and citizens were subject to maddening inefficiencies in dilapidated surroundings.[17] Moreover, judges were criticized for denying due process by issuing "boilerplate" decisions without considering both sides of a case review.[18]

The result was that in 2008, a revamped court, named the traffic tribunal, was placed under the authority of the Supreme Court. The chief justice, after a review process, appoints all magistrates to the tribunal. The first chief magistrate of the court was given the responsibility for operating a revamped traffic court system.[19] The enabling legislation ran into some pushback in that it expanded the number of magistrates, but the ultimate results were transformative.

An online filing system was implemented in 2015. With electronic filing of documents and a massive transfer of older data online, the court has a database that allows an enhanced collection system whereby millions of dollars in fines go into the general fund. User-friendly changes included allowing walk-in clients to have access to a judge or magistrate during working hours, providing for an online payment process, initiating integrated data application process, and allowing for case entry using scanned copies of summonses.

The court also instituted an E-Citation program that validates details of the initial stop and eliminates redundancy in data-entry efforts.[20] This central database provides an integrated record of a motorist's history whereby all violations are available to the court. The program also includes an open online traffic record site, initiated in 2021, where traffic records, ticket history, and speeding records of individuals are available to the public.

From 1947 to 2007, traffic court was located in an old, retrofitted factory, across from a strip club in a downtrodden section of Providence. Dingy and ill lit, it was where Rhode Islanders often endured long waits and indifferent service. A new state-owned building with ample space, parking, and lighting was built in Cranston.[21] The spacious surroundings and efficiencies related to a revamped online system and more scrutiny of court personnel have resulted in a more cooperative climate where plaintiffs and lawyers engage with the system. There was some debate about moving the court out of Providence, where many immigrants and low-income people reside, to a suburban neighborhood, but the improvements in the system and online services have mitigated many of these concerns. Moreover, due to lobbying by then–Chief Justice Frank Williams, a bus stop at the traffic tribunal was established.

Municipal Courts

Municipal courts are established and funded by local cities and towns. Many of these courts began as local police courts but developed into courts with judges and clerks. The number of courts increased significantly from the 1980s through the 2000s. As of the early 2000s, about half of all municipalities have established municipal courts. These courts deal mostly with local traffic violations, town and harbor ordinances, zoning, and minimum housing violations. However, appeals can be heard in District Court, Superior Court, or in rare cases, the Supreme Court.

Probate Courts

Probate is the court-supervised procedure where affairs of a deceased person are handled.[22] Each town or city in Rhode Island has its own probate court with its own probate judges; they are appointed by the town or city council, although the laws governing this process are state laws. Variations in procedures may vary slightly by municipality but the general process consists of collating probate property of the deceased; protecting their assets; paying all debts and claims; and determining who is entitled to a share of the estate. If administrated correctly, the court establishes an orderly legal record and protects the interest of all persons connected with probating an estate and adjudicating claims and conflicts related to the estate.

The reforms of the 1990s and 2000s have had a pronounced effect on the character of the state judiciary in Rhode Island; an emerging ethos of professionalism and responsibility have resulted in a more positive environment where citizens, for the most part, receive fair and informed adjudication. While there are remnants of the "I know a guy" or an insider track, and patronage remains on the margins, these changes have earned the respect of most entities that engage with the courts; most lawyers are more positive; advocates have better access; and all parties generally get a fairer hearing in the process. After generations of political manipulation and inefficient administration, the state courts have evolved into a vastly improved branch of Rhode Island government.

The Attorney General

In an ongoing debate about the role and restrictions of for-profit hospitals in Rhode Island, the General Assembly in 1997 enacted the Hospital Conversions Act, giving addition oversight and regulatory power over for-profit hospitals and all hospital mergers and conversations in the state to the attorney general and the Department of Health. These entities strictly oversee and police hospital transactions and can impose conditions for their implementation. The Private Equity Stakeholder's Project, which monitors such state's provisions across the country, notes that Rhode Island is an outlier from other states in how strictly it polices hospital transactions.

In 2021, a proposed reconfiguration of for-profit stakeholders of Prospect Medical Holdings, a national company that owns two hospitals in the state— Roger Williams Medical Center and Fatima Hospital—came under the scrutiny of the Office of the Attorney General, which is charged with reviewing such transactions. The attorney general, Peter Neronha, ultimately allowed the transaction to go through after some private equity stakeholders dropped out, but imposed strict conditions related to the quality of care in these hospitals as well as demanding 80 million dollars in escrow accounts to prevent other private owners from walking away with impunity. He noted these demands had never been made before in Rhode Island and that other states were looking into this strategy.

In a scathing report[23] and a subsequent interview, Neronha noted that the previous stakeholders involved were greedy and irresponsible: "Let's be clear;

what happened is that they took on debt, took out loans and put the proceeds of these loans in their pockets." To remedy such transactions, he went on to note that his office should use the tools given to them. "It's great to have the tools but they're only effective if you're prepared to use them, if you're prepared to stand up when you think you need to . . . I think regulators in this state, my office and regulators elsewhere need to be prepared to take those tough stands and withstand the criticism . . . I feel limited only by my imagination in terms of what this office can do."[24]

* * *

The Office of the Attorney General was originally established in 1650 and grafted onto the state Constitution in 1843. The attorney general is one of the five general officers subject to statewide election by voters. In 1842, county government was abolished, and unlike most other states, Rhode Island has no district attorneys or county prosecutors. The attorney general is the top legal official in Rhode Island, and the office has broad authority over all criminal and civil issues statewide.

The office has been generally respected, and with few exceptions, has had strong leadership that protected the public in terms of cases or defenses related to criminal issues. During the 2020s, there were more robust efforts to improve the organization of the office, reducing a backlog of intake cases, and expanded initiatives related to criminal issues.

As the central legal agency in the state, the office is responsible for prosecution of all felony criminal cases and misdemeanor appeals, as well as prosecution of misdemeanor cases brought by state law enforcement agencies. Additionally, as chief legal officer of the state, the office represents all agencies, departments, and commissions in litigation and initiates legal action to protect the interests of Rhode Island citizens. The office is also charged with operating and maintaining the Bureau of Criminal Identification, which is the central repository for all criminal records in the state.[25]

The office investigates and prosecutes violent crimes, white collar crimes, and criminal drug offences, among others. It expanded its activities by creating a Special Victims' Unit to handle domestic violence, sexual assault, and child and elder abuse. It is active in pursuing offences related to narcotics, organized crime, and Medicaid fraud. The attorney general has been particularly active and vocal in prosecuting public officials for crimes related to violations of election and finance laws. More emphasis on these activities, some of which heretofore might have been considered lesser infractions, have resulted in extensive fines and some jail time for offenders. The office indicated that these prosecutions are intended to send the message that such infractions will no longer be tolerated in the hope that public confidence in the process and in state and elected officials will improve.

The legal facets related to criminal activity are the expected responsibilities that most people associate with this office. Less known and appreciated are the responsibilities and power of the office over myriad civil matters. The standard responsibilities include Antitrust, Charitable Trust, and Government Litigation Units as well regulatory units covering public utilities and contractors' registration and licensing. More recently, emphasis and activity have been focused on advocacy units such as issues on civil rights, environmental regulation, and healthcare. The office has taken on a prominent role in such cases and deems its mission to act as an advocate for the broader public, using latent powers that existed but are now used to expand the reach of the office.

One telling example was the participation of the attorney general in a controversial case involving a marina expansion proposal on Block Island, a case that had been in litigation for almost two decades.[26] It involved the proposed expansion of large marina on the central pond on the island that was objected to by the Town of New Shoreham and several land trust and conservation organizations on the island. The expansion plan was rejected in 2006 by the Coastal Resource Management Council, a state organization that oversees such petitions, and that decision was consistently affirmed in over a decade of litigation. Eventually, a mediation process was initiated that allowed the expansion to go forward on a limited basis. The case was then appealed to the Supreme Court and remanded back to Superior Court. The fact that the settlement was reached without opposing parties present, over zoom, between Christmas and New Years of 2020–21, created a huge controversy and accusations of "inside backroom dealings."

Enter the attorney general, who claimed intervenor status as a party for the town in the capacity as environmental advocate. This move enraged the defense, who ultimately lost. The attorney general took issue with the courts finding[27] for the marina, noting that ". . . the decision is a win for deals constructed behind closed doors while doing the people' s business when the law demands precisely the opposite." He noted he would continue to pursue the case, noting that this "was not the last battle."[28]

In another decision in 2022 that stunned the establishment, Neronha denied the proposed merger application between Lifespan and Care New England—the two largest hospitals groups in the state, whose merger would have controlled 80 percent of inpatient services in the state.[29] The proposed merger took over two years to craft; it included the heft of the two hospitals and Brown University. The players had access to money, influential lobbyists, and union support as well as the claim that, without the merger, the hospital could close. Neronha expressed multiple reservations about costs and quality of care and took issue with the fact that the hospitals had failed to answer key questions. As reporter Dan McGowan noted, "The two health care groups have arrogantly taken the approach that everyone—regulators, state lawmakers, the public—should trust implicitly that this proposal was good for Rhode Island, and Neronha called their bluff."[30] The office then filed a joint lawsuit with the Federal Trade Commission, and the merger failed.

As the attorney general continues to affirm the state's role in a more expansive capacity, one can anticipate that the office will be involved in other policy cases. "As the people's lawyer, I want to expand our lane, not narrow it. I want this Office to be in places people don't expect, because I believe there are more places where we can make a real difference. The phrase 'we've never done that before' holds no meaning for me."[31]

This emphasis to redefine the office with expanded authority over an array of civil matters has broad ramifications for the future shape and tenor of cases involving public policy, the office's interactions with the judiciary, and the other branches of government in Rhode Island.

The Federal Courts in Rhode Island

Cases heard in US federal courts involve violations of the Constitution or federal law, bankruptcy cases, and cases based on state law involving parties from different states. US district courts are the only courts that have jurisdiction over federal criminal cases, hearing cases involving public corruption as well as cases related to other criminal behavior. It also adjudicates trials related to bribery, extortion, fraud, and embezzlement, under the auspices of violations of civil rights and interstate criminal actions.

In the federal system there are 94 federal district courts, 13 circuit courts, and one Supreme Court. The District Court for Rhode Island is one of the 94 district courts. US district court decisions can be appealed to the US Court of Appeals in Circuit 1, which includes Rhode Island, Massachusetts, Maine, New Hampshire, and Puerto Rico. There are six active judges and four active senior judges in the US First Circuit. Appeals to the circuit court are generally heard by a panel of three court judges who affirm or reverse the decision of the District Court. In some unusual instances, appeals may go on to be heard *en banc*, meaning they are heard by all the judges of the First Circuit. Decisions can then be appealed to the US Supreme Court, which, in rare cases, accepts the case.

Federal judges are lifetime appointments made by the sitting president and confirmed by the US Senate. It is a political process in that such appointments tend to reflect the views of the president's party, and the confirmation is influenced by senators from the nominee's state or other senators, from either party, who might have an interest in or objection to a nominee.

It has become increasingly common for nominations to the federal bench to be stalled over political considerations. Federal District Court Chief Judge John J. McConnell was first nominated to the bench in Rhode Island by President Barack Obama due to recommendations from Rhode Island Democratic Senators Sheldon Whitehouse and Jack Reed in March 2010, but was denied a confirmation hearing; he was again nominated in September 2010, but again did not receive a hearing due to partisan wrangling of the Senate Nominating

Committee. He was finally confirmed by the Senate in May 2011, and in 2021 presided as the chief judge of US District Court.[32]

US attorneys for the federal district in Rhode Island are also appointed by the president, approved by the Senate, and subject to change with successive administrations. Their purview is to bring charges of violations of federal statutes. In some cases, the US attorney might coordinate their efforts with the state attorney general to assure the most effective way to bring cases that also might involve violations of both state and federal law.

The office of the US attorney works with federal law enforcement agencies such as the FBI, the Drug Enforcement Administration, and Immigration and Customs Enforcement. Given the nature of many of these cases, as well as the US district courts' charge over federal criminal cases, these tend to be high-visibility cases. Unfortunately, given the sensationalism and resulting extensive media coverage of many such trials, the public's as well as the media's perception of extent of crime in Rhode Island is off the mark, in that Rhode Island usually ranks in the middle or the lower half of 50 states when it comes to federal criminal convictions.[33]

The US district court system has also implemented a Next Generation Case Management Electric filing system in 2021 that allows attorneys to electronically file and maintain one account for appellate, bankruptcy and district courts, creating a centralized access to all court US district court attorney filings.[34]

When one considers the history and current context, the judicial system in Rhode Island in the main provides citizens with professional, efficient, and fair adjudication. It represents a success story in that after centuries of political linkages to the legislative and executive, inefficient administration, and patronage, it now more closely fulfills the ideal stated by Montesquieu that "... there can be no liberty... if the power of judging be not separated from legislative and executive power."[35] While remnants of the past remain, the judiciary has evolved into a modern and accountable system.

Notes

1. The author thanks Attorney William Lynch for his thoughtful review of this chapter.
2. "GOP Criticize Lynch Prata for Trying to Circumvent Revolving Door Law for Supreme Court Seat," *GoLocalProv*, October 1, 2020, https://www.golocalprov.com/news/gop-criticize-senator-lynch-prata-for-trying-to-circumvent-revolving-door-l.
3. Some examples in this chapter are drawn from previous work of the author in Maureen Moakley and Elmer Cornwell in *Rhode Island Politics and Government* (Lincoln: University of Nebraska Press, 2001).
4. Andrew Glass, "Rhode Island Ratifies Constitution, May 29, 1790," *Politico*, May 29, 2014, https://www.politico.com/story/2014/05/this-day-in-politics-107177.
5. Editorial Board, "Mulling Pension Reform," *Providence Journal*, November 3, 1997.
6. Ethan Shorey, "House Passes Corvese's Controversial Revolving Door Bill," *Valley Breeze*, May 27, 2014, https://www.valleybreeze.com/news/house-passes-corveses-controversial-revolving-door-bill/article_e1cdc0a9-a043-56b5-a65a-b1fb976c36ac.html.
7. Moakley and Cornwell, *Politics*, 114.
8. Editorial Board, "A Bad Way to Pick Magistrates," *Providence Journal*, May 14, 2018, https://www.providencejournal.com/story/opinion/editorials/2018/05/14/editorial-bad-way-to-pick-magistrates/12239547007/block-island/5570642001/.
9. "Electronic Filing," Rhode Island Judiciary, https://www.courts.ri.gov/efiling/Pages/default.aspx.
10. "YouTube Court Live Streaming," United States Bankruptcy Court, District of Rhode Island, https://www.rib.uscourts.gov/youtube-court-live-streaming.
11. Katie Mulvaney, "Survey Finds Inequities, Discrimination in Rhode Island Courts, Legal Profession," *Providence Journal*, November 14, 2021, https://www.providencejournal.com/story/news/courts/2021/11/14/bar-association-survey-finds-inequities-discrimination-ri-courts-legal-profession/8586140002/.
12. The author would like to thank Craig Berke of Superior Court for these data.
13. "Home," Rhode Island Judiciary, https://www.courts.ri.gov/Pages/default.aspx. Descriptions of the functions of the various state courts were taken from this website.
14. Moakley and Cornwell, *Politics*, 118.
15. William Donovan, "Workers Comp Law: A Dying Profession," *Providence Journal*, February 22, 1998.
16. "Chief Judge Robert F. Arrigan Rehabilitation Center," Department of Labor and Training, State of Rhode Island, n.d., https://dlt.ri.gov/workers-compensation/arrigan-rehabilitation-center.
17. Christopher Rowland and Jonathan Saltzman, "Disorder in the Court," *Providence Journal*, February 8-9, 1998, https://providencejournal.newsbank.com/search?text=traffic%20court%20opens%20in%20Cranston&content_added=&date_from=&date_to=&pub%5B0%5D=PJRI.
18. Katie Mulvaney, "Chief Justice Names Disandro to Lead Traffic Tribunal," *Providence Journal*, March 22, 2018, https://www.providencejournal.com/news/20180321/ri-supreme-court-chief-justice-picks-disandro-to-lead-traffic-tribunal.

19. Public Resources, 2007 Annual Report (2007), Rhode Island Judiciary, https://www.courts.ri.gov/PublicResources/annualreports/PDF/2007.pdf.
20. Rhode Island Courts, Electronic Filing Updates and Notices, 2015.
21. Steve Peoples, "New Traffic Tribunal Opens Tomorrow in Cranston" *Providence Journal*, January 16, 2007.
22. "Probate—What To Do About It," Rhode Island Bar Association, https://ribar.com/page.aspx?id-123.
23. "Give Some Money Back," Private Equity Stakeholder Project, June 7, 2021, https://pestakeholder.org/rhode-island-ag-slams-leonard-green-partners-for-raiding-hospitals-and-requires-that-firm-gives-some-money-back/.
24. Ted Nesi, "Nesi's Notes: June 5," *WPRI*, June 5, 2021, https://www.wpri.com/news/local-news/ted-nesi/nesis-notes-june-5/
25. Descriptions of the functions of the Office of the Attorney General are drawn from its website at https://riag.ri.gov/
26. Jim Hummel, "Sept. 9 Deadline Looms for Ruling on Controversial Block Island Marina Deal," *Providence Journal*, August 26, 2021, https://www.providencejournal.com/story/news/local/2021/08/26/sept-9-deadline-looms-court-ruling-on-settlement-champlins-marina-expansion-
27. Jim Hummel, "Judge: Settlement Allowing Champlin's Marina Expansion Was Properly Reached," *Providence Journal*, September 9, 2021, https://www.providencejournal.com/story/news/local/2021/09/09/judge-says-settlement-block-island-marina-case-reached-properly/8259040002/.
28. Mary Serreze, "AG Neronha Opposes Block Island Marina Expansion Pact," *Patch*, March 5, 2021. https://patch.com/rhode-island/newshoreham/ag-neronha-opposes-block-island-marina-expansion-pact.
29. Dan McGowan, "The Arrogance of Lifespan and Care New England Leaders Doomed Their Merger," *Boston Globe*, February 18, 2022, https://www.bostonglobe.com/2022/02/17/metro/arrogance-lifespan-care-new-england-leaders-doomed-merger/.
30. McGowan, "Arrogance."
31. Office of the Attorney General, Annual Report, 2019.
32. Bill Mears, "Controversial Judicial Nominee Clears Key Senate Confirmation Hurdle," *CNN*, May 4, 2011, http://www.cnn.com/2011/POLITICS/05/04/senate.judicial.nominee/index.html.
33. Harry Enten, "Ranking the States from Most to Least Corrupt," *FiveThirtyEight*, January 23, 2015, htpps://fivethirtyeight.com/features/ranking-the-states-from-most-to-least-corrupt/.
34. "Next Generation of CM/ECF Information & Resources," United States District Court, District of Rhode Island, accessed January 4, 2022.
35. *Taylor Co. v. Place* (Supreme Court of Rhode Island September 1, 1856).

11 / Local Government

June Speakman

In Rhode Island, as in most New England states, local governments formed governing structures, political identities, and popular allegiances long before the creation of the states in which they now exist. We can see the imprint of these pre-Revolutionary structures, identities, and allegiances to this day, as they create a situation in which governors and state legislatures are in ongoing struggle with municipalities for the control of public policy. And municipal governments continue to tap into this sense of local pride and preference for local control as they assert their independence and autonomy.

Consequently, the one million Rhode Islanders, living together on 1,545 square miles, hold tightly to their hometown identities, local traditions, and local control of policy. Over the years, there have been calls for consolidation and regionalization, and even for the elimination of local governments to create instead a "city-state" that would realize efficiencies and equity. The depth of localism is revealed with a look at the results of these calls: of the thirty-nine cities and towns, only nine have chosen to regionalize their schools into four districts. The preference for hyperlocal control is further manifested in the proliferation of dozens of other units of government within the state that pull power away from the State House—from fire districts to water authorities and housing authorities.

There is also, in the tradition of New England self-governance, a wide array of volunteer boards and commissions—including school committees, and planning and zoning boards—that assist, guide, and sometimes impede municipal government, and certainly foster significant diversity in the approaches to public policy across this tiny state.

In terms of the structure of local government, Rhode Island municipalities also offer an array of flavors. There are strong mayor forms of local government, professional administrator forms, town meetings, at-large councils, councilmanic districts, and partisan and non-partisan elections and offices. In terms of politics, there are decidedly Democratic cities and towns, and clearly Republican ones, and several that are moving in one direction or the other.

This chapter will examine the origins and development of local governments in Rhode Island and their evolving relationship with state government. A close look at the capital city will reveal whether the truism "as Providence goes, so goes Rhode Island" has any truth to it.

A look at the various forms of local government will be followed by an analysis of electoral trends in local government.

What Came Before

On July 13, 2021, the Town Council of the town of Warren, in the area of Rhode Island knows as the East Bay, unanimously adopted a statement acknowledging that, for thousands of years before the British settlers arrived in 1632, the land on which the town sits had been the home of the Pokanoket people.[1] This first-in-the-state land acknowledgment honors the people and governing structures that preceded the first English settlements in Rhode Island and Roger Williams's founding of the city of Providence in 1636.

When white settlers arrived from Europe in the early seventeenth century, they encountered many tribes that were part of several nations, organized into farm and fishing villages. The stories of disease and displacement are told elsewhere, but we do know that the colonial villages of Rhode Island would not have survived but for what they learned from these native peoples about living along the northeast coast.

The memories of those peoples and their settlements can be seen throughout Rhode Island's cities and towns today in the names of roads, rivers and villages: Massasoit, Sowams, Conimicut, Narragansett, Pascaog, Pawtucket, Apponaug, Chepachet, Weekapaug, Moshassuck.

Early Nineteenth and Beyond

What kinds of local governments existed prior to the founding of Providence and the state of Rhode Island? Historians tells us that there were farming and fishing villages, clusters of teepees on the shore in the summer and longhouses with communal living in the winter. We know a bit about hierarchies of power in these communities: sachems were the leaders and handed their power to their sons and sometimes their daughters. And we have Roger Williams's observations on their self-government. According to one historian, Williams "admired their internal self-government, and their tolerance of others, including, one imagines, of him. In many ways, their successful society seemed to be a model for the kind of new community he wanted to create. . . . Their society worked communally, much as Roger wanted Rhode Island to work."[2]

Throughout the seventeenth century, the area that is now Rhode Island began to fill with white settlers who founded what we know now as some of Rhode Island's most significant cities and towns. Roger Williams established Providence in 1636 and helped Anne Hutchinson found Portsmouth (then Pocasset) two years later. In 1639, William Coddington split with the Hutchinson community and founded Newport. In 1643, Samuel Gorton and his supporters seceded from Providence to establish Shawomet (now Warwick). These four towns became the basis for the first royal patent for Rhode Island granted by the British Parliament in 1644, which created the colony but granted it little authority over the towns. According to historian Sidney James, "At every occasion the towns kept asserting their importance ... [and] were left to handle their own affairs with little interference from above."[3]

Given the designs of the colonies to the east and west, and internal dissension among the four towns, this weak state government would not survive. It was replaced by a new charter in 1663, which remained in place until 1842. This document created a governor, deputy governor, and ten "assistants" who were granted the authority to "take care for the best disposing and ordering of the general business and affairs of and concerning the lands, and hereditaments hereinafter mentioned to be granted, and the plantation thereof, and the government of the people." The charter also authorized a General Assembly composed of six representatives from Newport; four each from Providence, Warwick, and Portsmouth; and two each from such other communities that may exist. The Assembly was granted several powers, including the appointment of officials, the establishment of a judicial system, the setting of city and town borders, the regulation of trade with the local tribes, and the making of laws.[5]

Still, as James notes, even with the creation of this state government, the situation was more a "federal structure" than a centralized one because "[t]he towns had come first ... Obviously ... they cherished localism and ... insisted that it be further honored by the central government."[6]

The Evolution of State Power

The 1663 Charter remained in place until 1842, long after independence was gained by the colonies. In 1842, in the wake of the Dorr Rebellion, a constitutional convention was called to create a proper state constitution. As with the charter, the 1842 document contained few specifics regarding the relationship between state and local governments. The key features of this new document were the prohibition of slavery and the expansion of the franchise, dropping the native-born requirement but setting a property qualification at $134 for naturalized voters. The property requirement remained in place until 1888, when the voters approved the Bourn Amendment that removed it from the Constitution.

The 1842 document did establish a Senate and allocated one senator to each community regardless of the size of the population, thus cementing the power of rural communities in the general assembly for decades to come. By 1928, the 20 smallest towns of Rhode Island's 39 could dominate the Senate even though they contained only 7 percent of the population.[7] This malapportionment stood, with some minor adjustments in between, until the 1962 *Baker v. Carr* "one man-one vote" Supreme Court decision. For the most part, though, the 1842 constitution left local governments on the own to do their own thing in their own way, and the nominally stronger General Assembly left them alone.

Throughout the late nineteenth and early twentieth centuries, Rhode Island's cities and towns grew, the economy industrialized, and the population became more diverse as waves of immigrants found their way to the Ocean State. At the same time, a legal theory of state-local relations was promulgated and widely accepted by legal scholar John Dillon. Dillon's Rule, as it is commonly known, asserts that local governments are the "creature" of state government and can exercise only those powers expressly granted by the state or indispensable to the operation of the local government.[8]

Several decisions by the Rhode Island Supreme Court in the first half of the twentieth century, including *Horton v. Newport* (1900) and *Providence v. Moulton* (1932), reveal that the courts "embraced a view which was entirely consistent with Dillon's Rule."[9] In the Newport case, the city challenged the state's authority to appoint the city's chief of policy; the Court concluded that Newport did not retain authority over its police force. In the Providence case, the capital city challenged a state law that created a state-appointed Board of Public Safety to replace the local police department. Here, too, the Court said, "cities and towns have no inherent right of local government."[10]

Home Rule in Rhode Island

At the turn of the twentieth century, a movement developed to push back on the loss of local autonomy in American cities and towns. As the cities grew in population, diversity, and economic complexity, the argument goes, state governments, often located far from urban centers, were ill equipped to meet the needs of these population and industrial centers. This Home Rule movement led to the renegotiation of the relationship between state and local governments across the country by encouraging broad delegation of powers by the state to the localities, the adoption of individual municipal charters, and clarification of situations in which state governments could overrule local laws and policies.[11]

Rhode Island jumped on the Home Rule bandwagon in 1951 when a Constitutional Convention recommended, and the voters adopted, an amendment to the Constitution that began: "It is the intention of this article to grant and confirm to the people of every city and town in this state the right to self-government in all local matters." The amendment laid out the procedures by which local governments could become home rule communities, establish their own charters, and exercise their own control over many areas of public policy.

In 1986, following another Constitutional Convention, the voters of Rhode Island had the opportunity to further expand home rule and further limit the ability of the state to interfere in local affairs. This provision to further expand the scope of municipal autonomy was rejected by the voters by a vote of 147,578 opposed to 126,542 in favor.[12]

The language from 1951 remains the law of the land today as Amendment XIII of the Rhode Island Constitution. Thirty-six Rhode Island cities and towns have adopted Home Rule charters. North Providence and Warwick have legislative charters and Scituate has no local charter.[13] So, for the most part, *the principle* of home rule is firmly established in Rhode Island.

What Amendment XIII means *in practice*, however, is that local governments cannot tax or borrow without authorization from the General Assembly. A review of state law over the years reveals the General Assembly's primacy in shaping local tax policy and property valuation. In 1981, the state passed a law requiring that municipalities have balanced budgets and be subject to increased state oversight over their finances. In 2006, the General Assembly prohibited local governments from raising property tax levies by more than 4 percent per year. Today, should a municipality find itself unable to balance its budget without going over the 4 percent limit, it must meet a number of conditions that are validated by one of several state agencies and have the increase approved by four-fifths of the town's governing body (RIGL 44-5-2). Between 2015 and 2020, eleven communities have used the process to exceed the 4 percent cap. One community, Central Falls, did not use the process, but did raise the tax levy to 8.95 percent in 2020 and had to issue refunds to taxpayers to restore the 4 percent cap.[14]

Amendment XIII also assigns to the General Assembly, not to local governments, responsibility for the "diffusion of knowledge" through the promotion of public schools and libraries. The administration of education at the local level is the responsibility of school committees, empowered and defined in state law (RIGL 16-2-9). These committees do not have taxing power but must rely on local city or town councils to fund the school budgets. Since 1995, with the passage of the Caruolo Act, state law has mandated that local councils meet this funding obligation and has established a process for state intervention and even lawsuits if the council refuses.

The General Assembly passes dozens of laws each session that seek to shape how education is delivered by local school districts. In its 2022 session alone, for example, the General Assembly enacted and the governor signed statutes requiring that school districts pay school lunch workers for a minimum of 180 days, that all public schools adopted trauma-informed practices, that all teachers demonstrate proficiency in the knowledge and practice of scientific reading by the 2025–26 school year, and that all public schools provide at least one unit of instruction in Asian American, Native Hawaiian, and Pacific Islander History and culture.

Clearly, home rule in Rhode Island remains an invitation for struggle between state and local governments about control of public policy and spending priorities. Over the 70 years of home rule in Rhode Island, many of these struggles have ended up in court. In 1960, for example, in *Newport Amusement v. Maher* (92 RI 51), the Court ruled that home rule does not vest municipalities with licensing power and the legislature is vested with plenary authority to license as part of its police power.[15] In 1984, *Xavier v. Cianci, Jr.* (479 A.2d 1179) clarifies that the city charter gives the city purchasing agent authority to sell street-sweeping equipment without approval of the city council. In 1992, in *Town of East Greenwich v. O'Neil* (617 A.2d 104), the Court ruled that a town ordinance regulating transmission of high-voltage electric power within its border exceeded the town's home rule authority because the action "has significant effect upon people outside of the home rule town." These cases, some wins for home rule, and some wins for state authority, are tracked by the Rhode Island Department of Revenue.[16] The list reveals several cases a year, across all policies areas, from communities across the state.

Still, even as the Rhode Island General Assembly flexes its legislative muscles annually, and Dillon's Rule leads the courts to tend to side with the state, localism persists into the twenty-first century as Rhode Island's 39 communities guard their autonomy, resist state mandates, use their voice, and vote to block state-sponsored projects opposed by the local residents. And, as the Rhode Island Public Expenditures Council notes, despite the power of the General Assembly to control the taxing and borrowing power of towns and to fund and deliver essential services, "there are striking differences between Rhode Island's municipalities in terms of family income, property wealth, home ownership, and demographic makeup.... For some municipalities, these differences, along with debt and pension obligations, have enormous impacts on the ability to raise revenues and provide adequate services, particularly for education, raising serious issues as to equitable educational funding."[17]

Burrillville: Second Amendment Sanctuary Town

In April of 2019, the Town Council of the Town of Burrillville passed a resolution declaring the town to be a "Second Amendment Sanctuary Town" in reaction to several pieces of gun control legislation introduced in the General Assembly that year. The resolution encouraged the local police department to use "sound discretion" when enforcing laws that "impact the rights of citizens under the Second Amendment," and asserted that the Town Council would not appropriate funds to store weapons seized pursuant to such legislation.[18]

In the summer of 2022, in the wake of the passage of a state ban on high-capacity magazines, Council President Donald Fox brought his own ammunition to the council meeting and declared that he had no intention of complying with the ban. He said, "Most of the stupid laws passed by Providence are usually unfunded mandates, but we have to follow them. But in this particular case the Burrillville Town Council took an oath to uphold the Constitution."[19]

The Capital City

On March 24, 1636, Roger Williams signed a formal agreement with Narragansett sachems Miantonomo and Canonicus that codified Williams's purchase of a tract of land from the tribe that would become the City of Providence. The spot along the Moshassuck River where Williams first set foot on this land is memorialized at a freshwater spring along North Main Street right down the hill from the State House in the capital city.

Providence, as one of the oldest of colonial American cities, played an important role in most of the significant events in seventeenth- and eighteenth-century American history. In 1676, the community was burnt to the ground by the Narragansetts in one of the battles of King Philip's War. Throughout the early 1700s, the port of Providence grew, as did the volume of maritime trade and associated industries. By the time of the Revolution, the town had a population of 4,000, several of whom played a role in the burning of the British ship the *Gaspee*, an event that Rhode Islanders claim as the start of the Revolutionary War, as it predated the Boston Tea Party by several months.

Unlike Newport, Providence was not occupied during the Revolution, and despite the blockade of Narragansett Bay by the British, continued its maritime trade through the ports of New London and New Bedford.

By 1830, the population of Providence had reached 16,832 people as the city led the state and the country into the Industrial Revolution, with manufacturing replacing maritime trade as the economic driver for the city. Providence became a national center for the metal, jewelry, textile, and silver industries, and also developed into a financial, banking, and transportation hub of the Northeast. The city's population peaked in 1940 at 253,504 people, making it the 37th largest city in the United States. In 2022, with a population of 179,472, its rank is 135.

As Providence grew, so did the diversity of its population. In 1830, descendants of colonial families and descendants of enslaved Blacks comprised almost all of the city's populace. In the 1840s, the first wave of Irish Catholic immigrants began arriving as the potato famine took hold in Ireland, filling up the tenements in Fox Point, the North End, Smith Hill, Olneyville, Manton, Wanskuck, and South Providence.[20] By 1885, one out of every three Rhode Islanders was Irish-born or of Irish descent.

In the first decade of the twentieth century, the wave of immigrants came from Italy, into neighborhoods in Providence and in West Warwick, Barrington, Westerly, and Cranston. In Providence, the newcomers displaced the Irish in Eagle Park, Charles Street, and Federal Hill.[21] By 1920, 19 percent of Rhode Island's foreign-born residents were Italian.

The Experience of Blacks in Providence

The social and economic integration of European immigrants to Providence, while not smooth, was not nearly as traumatic as the experience of Blacks in post-Revolutionary Providence and beyond. The history of Rhode Island's role in the slave trade is told elsewhere; Providence, Bristol, and Newport were leading slave ports throughout the eighteenth century. Less well known is the role of Rhode Island's textile mills in the production of so-called "Negro cloth." In the early nineteenth century, at least 84 textile mills in the state, two of which were in Providence, produced this rough, durable fabric sold to southern slave-owners, displacing the "more costly, less durable, and clumsy foreign fabric" produced in the mills of Europe.[22] Rhode Island businesses remained complicit. Stokes and Stokes write of an 1835 meeting of Providence business leaders in which several resolutions were passed indicating that "a majority of the city's leading citizens [were] united in endorsing economic prosperity over human bondage and suffering."[23]

This complicity occurred alongside the emergence of a new demographic group in Providence: what Stokes and Stokes call "African heritage residents." In 1790, they comprised about 7 percent of the population of the city and lived primarily on College Hill and at the northern edge of Providence between North Main Street and the Great Basin.[24] In the nineteenth century, as Providence grew and urbanized, "its Black residents faced new levels of prejudice."[25] In 1822, the General Assembly disenfranchised the state's Black residents. "Warning out" laws were passed in many towns that allowed for the removal of people who were not "from town."[26] A system of segregated schools was established by the state in 1828. Most houses of worship required Black congregants to sit separately. And economic opportunity was increasingly limited as immigrants from Europe arrived to compete for jobs in factories and as domestic workers.

In Providence, the tensions created by racism as well as rapid growth and development came to a head with race riots in 1824 and again in 1831. First, in a neighborhood then called Hardscrabble, now called Moshassuck Square, a mob of 50 white men destroyed 20 Black-owned homes and businesses.[27] Seven years later, on Olney's Lane in Snowtown (near the current day State House), a group of rock-throwing sailors rampaged through the neighborhood attacking people and structures. Five people, including one sailor, were killed.[28]

Throughout the nineteenth century, Providence's African heritage population built its own communities and established churches, schools, businesses, and civic groups. The National Association for the Advancement of Colored People established its Providence chapter in 1915, in part to organize against the proliferation of Ku Klux Klan activity in the state. Throughout the twentieth century, Black residents of Providence were subject to the same discrimination and segregation that occurred in many American cities.

In 1935, for example, five Black neighborhoods—Fox Point, South Providence, West Elmhurst, Lippitt Hill, and College Hill, were categorized by the Federal Housing Administration as "hazardous or declining," thus making potential buyers ineligible for federally-supported mortgages. In 1939, the Providence Housing Authority was created and implemented a policy of building racially segregated housing, a policy in place until 1956.[29]

In *A Matter of Truth*, Stokes and Stokes tell the stories of the displacement of hundreds of Black families and businesses in Lippitt Hill (now University Heights), Fox Point, and College Hill in the name of slum clearance, urban renewal, or the expansion of Brown University. As they point out, the planners of these projects gave little thought to what would happen to those families and businesses, but it is certain that vibrant, safe, thriving communities were destroyed. And the racist real estate policies of the time—redlining, steering, denial of mortgages—made their re-establishment impossible.

It was not until 1946, under pressure from the NAACP and the Urban League, that the Providence Police Department hired its first Black officer, and not until 1969, Philip Addison of the Third Ward, became the first Black elected to the Providence City Council.

In 2020, the median income for Black families in Providence was $41,093; for white families, $54,272. Statewide, the wealth gap and homeownership gap render these differences difficult to overcome. Nationally, the median net worth of white families was eight times higher than that of Black families, and in Rhode Island, the homeownership rates for whites, at 68 percent, was twice that for Black families.[30]

With the election of David Cicilline as Mayor in 2002, the policy focus began to change at least rhetorically, as he campaigned on promises to address police brutality, housing affordability, and the lack of diversity in the city workforce. His successor, Angel Taveras, the first Latino mayor of the city, focused on education, neighborhood revitalization, and environmental justice. The next mayor, Jorge Elorza, continued this policy focus and went a giant step further. On July 15, 2020, Elorza signed an executive order on truth, reconciliation and reparations that put into place a commitment to research the city's role in indigenous displacement and the enslavement of people of African heritage, and to develop processes for reconciliation and reparations that emanate from that research. The first output of this effort was the 2021 publication of *A Matter of Truth*, a 200-page study of the history of displacement and enslavement.[31] Any policy changes will be left to a new mayor, elected in November of 2022.

Still, it should be noted that Providence voters have yet to elect a Black mayor.

Providence Gets a New Form of Government

The race riots of the early nineteenth century and the growing tension of population growth and industrialization led for calls in the city for "law and order." Historians Howard Chudacoff and Theodore Hirt put it this way: "These events blended race and vice issues to produce heightened concern over public order, a concern made by acute urbanization. Thus, the disorder had a significant role in stimulating the reform of Providence's government and forcing citizens to acknowledge problems that a once small town never had faced."[32] That reform was the adoption of a city charter in 1832 that changed governance from a weak, town-meeting form to a strong, council-weak mayor form of city government. The city was divided into six wards, and the council had two chambers: a Board of Alderman and a Common Council. In 1940, the structure was changed again to the strong mayor model and a unicameral Council with 15 wards; it remains that way today.

Under the 1832 charter, the mayor with the most impact was Thomas Doyle, a Republican Irish Protestant, who served from 1864–86. During his tenure, referred to by some as the "Golden Age of Providence," the police and fire departments were modernized, modern public health and sanitation measures were implemented, public schools were built, a new City Hall was constructed, and Roger Williams Park was established. By 1900, Providence was considered one of the wealthiest cities in the country.

Both the 1832 and 1940 charter revisions fostered a municipal government that could provide the infrastructure, public safety, and social services to support the rapidly growing economy and the increasingly diverse population. Still, these changes alone do not reveal *who* is running the city. For many decades—from the founding of the city through the eighteenth and nineteenth centuries, wealthy white Republican men were elected mayors and councilmen in Providence because (1) the franchise was limited to native-born, and (2) it was limited to residents who paid property taxes. The nativist restriction was problematic in Providence, as waves of immigrants arrived to find themselves unable to participate in politics. In 1888, the foreign-born restriction was lifted, but the property restriction continued to suppress the vote as most immigrants—as renters—did not own the required $134 in real estate. That restriction was lifted in 1928, and immediately enfranchised 60 percent of Providence residents.

Unsurprisingly, this dramatic change in the size and composition of the electorate led to a major shift of political control away from the Yankee Republicans who had controlled the city since its founding, to Irish Catholic Democrats. Consequently, from 1913 to 1975, the mayor's office was occupied by one Irish Catholic Democrat after another.

The revision of the City Charter in 1940 and the adoption of Home Rule in 1951 strengthened the office of the mayor significantly and saw that executive power applied to bring significant change to the capital city. This newly empowered mayor's office came at a time when the city needed strong decision-makers. The textile factories had moved to the American South in search of cheaper, non-union labor, and the Great Depression pushed unemployment past 25 percent. The Hurricane of 1938 brought seven feet of water and devastation to downtown Providence, symbolizing the end of the golden era for the city.

All American cities were transforming in the post–World War II period as the decline of manufacturing, the rise of the automobile, the creation of the interstate highway system, and the mortgage program for returning soldiers fostered population shifts out of the old cities into the new suburbs. In the late 1950s, that highway system bisected Providence east to west with Route 195 and north to south with Route 95, cutting off neighborhoods to the west and south of the city center. As was the case in city after city around the United States, those areas cut off by the highways and inhabited primarily by poor families of color began to deteriorate physically, economically, and socially.

In addition to this physical undermining of the city's community and economy, between 1950 and 1970, Providence saw the largest outmigration of residents of any major American city, dropping from 248,674 to 179,116 residents in those two decades. Many of these families were Irish-Americans, relocating from South Providence, West Elmwood, and West River to Cranston, Warwick, and elsewhere.

A Shift in Power, and the Rebirth of Providence

Just as the enfranchisement of immigrants in 1928 had consequences for the distribution of power in the city, so too did this outmigration. In 1974, Vincent "Buddy" Cianci was elected as the first Italian American mayor of the city. Cianci, a Republican at first and then an independent, was in office from 1975 to 1984 and 1991 to 2002. His first stint as Mayor ended when he pleaded *nolo contendere* to conspiracy to commit assault on his wife's presumed lover; his second ended when he was convicted and jailed for racketeering. Despite these indiscretions, Cianci was a popular and effective mayor and presided over the city's "renaissance." Between his two terms, Joseph Paolino, now a major player in Providence downtown development, served as mayor and also played a major role in the city's transformation.

During these years, Providence underwent a transformation from a shrinking, tired, old industrial city to a vibrant, service industry–oriented, "comeback" city... at least for some of its residents. During Cianci's and Paolino's tenures, the downtown area, once characterized by parking lots, raised train tracks, and track siding, saw the tracks buried and the Woonasquatucket and Moshassuck Rivers uncovered and relocated. Among the amenities that emerged "downcity" were the Civic Center and adjacent hotel, a skating rink (twice as big as Rockefeller Center's!), the Providence Place mall, a renovated train station, the arrival of the Providence Bruins hockey team, and Waterfire, a night lighting of braziers in the rivers. Cianci, through the force of his personality and boosterism—including his ability to marshal millions of dollars of federal aid—crafted the image of a city that was focused on arts, culture, and entertainment, as well as education and healthcare.

This renaissance is largely the result of what urban sociologist Clarence Stone calls an urban development regime: "an informal arrangement by which public bodies and private interests function together in order to be able to make and carry out governing decisions."[33] In his 2000 study of the "new Providence," Wilbur Rich describes the arrangement as "[A] broad array of economic leaders [that] included some old wealth, as well as the nouveau riche white ethnics."[34] Rich continues his analysis of this development regime by pointing out that in the New Providence, "not a single minority individual was at the center of decision-making, and even after all the changes downcity, "there is still job and residential discrimination in Providence."[35] Finally, Rich points out that Cianci was "clever" about keeping minority neighborhoods in his coalition and avoiding opposition to downtown development by providing cosmetic changes to those areas—new sidewalks, community centers. But as Rich points out presciently, the state of the public schools in Providence is "the Achilles heel" for the sustainability of the New Providence.[36] That problem plagues Providence to this day, three mayors and three decades later.

Another Power Shift

In November of 2002, to open a new phase in Providence politics, David Cicilline was elected mayor, just months after Cianci was sentenced to five years in prison for racketeering. Cicilline ran on the promise to clean up corruption in the city and bring the Providence renaissance to the neighborhoods.[37] Cicilline rode a new electoral coalition to victory; his campaign headquarters were set up in South Providence, a community of color, and his base was made up of white East Side liberals, Latinos, African Americans, and Asian Americans. This coalition was large enough to elect a mayor, and another and another, because by 2000, Providence had become a majority-minority city. By 2020, according to the 2020 census, 33 percent of Providence residents were white, 43.5 percent Hispanic, 13.3 percent Black, and 5.5 percent Asian.[38] The days of white ethnic political dominance in Providence ended at the turn of the twenty-first century.

The most stunning element of this political transformation is the dramatic increase in the Latino population of Providence, which is, according to the Pew Hispanic Center, one of the fastest-growing "new destination" cities for Latinos coming to the United States. Between 1980 and 2020, the Latino population in the capital grew by a remarkable 906 percent, from 15,935 to 160,323.[39] This dramatic growth brought with it an increase in political involvement and influence. Within two decades of the first wave of immigration in the 1970s, Latinos were politically organized, running for office, and winning. In 1992, Anastasia Williams was elected to the House of Representatives from South Providence; in 1998, Luis Aponte was elected to the Providence City Council, and in 2010, Angel Taveras was elected as mayor.[40] And in 2014, Jorge Elorza was elected mayor in a contest against Buddy Cianci in which Elorza garnered 52 percent of the vote. In 2018, he was re-elected by a more comfortable margin of 63 percent of total. The 2022 Democratic primary was a contest between Brett Smiley, a white progressive, Nirva LaFortune, a Black female city council member, and Gonzalo Cuervo, Latino former Deputy Secretary of State. This contest epitomizes the shifting demographics of Providence and the increasing electoral significance of the Latino population. However, the result confounds the trend. Smiley—not Irish, not Italian, not Latino—with broad and deep experience in state and city government, carried the day with 41 percent of the vote. Does this signal the end of ethnic voting in Rhode Island?

Providence is a city rich in history with a story about success built on slavery and immigrant labor, decline based on deindustrialization and neglect, and resurgence based on collaborations between politicians and the captains of business. There is a saying in Rhode Island: "As Providence goes, so goes Rhode Island." Others say that, really, Rhode Island is so small, it should be a city-state, with one school system, one police department, one identity. As the next section reveals, the diversity of Rhode Island's other local governments, and the proud localism of their residents, makes that unlikely.

Rhode Island's Other 38 Communities, and More

The Ocean State is home to its "renaissance city," but also to 38 other municipalities and 90 special purpose governments. The latter include 32 municipal school districts, four regional school districts, thirty-nine fire districts and several water districts.

Fire Districts in Rhode Island: Sometimes Not What You Think They Are

Rhode Island is home to 39 fire districts in 16 towns. Many of these districts were created to handle fires in mill towns or shore communities away from large municipal fire departments. Today, 31 of them actually exist to provide fire service, three (two in Portsmouth and one in Tiverton) are actually water authorities, and six are part of beach communities and often serve as private beach clubs that provide access to members only. Five of these districts are in Westerly, Charlestown, and Narragansett, including Weekapaug in Westerly and Bonnet Shores in Narragansett, both of which have been the focus of recent discussions of shoreline access.[41] Altogether, these districts own 400 acres of property at the shore, for a value of $18 million.

The districts are separately incorporated public bodies, subject to state law, with the power to tax their members. Municipal governments in the towns in which these districts rest have limited control over them. Buttonwoods in Warwick—governed by a board of elected supervisors—levies a tax of $1.76 for every $1,000 of property for residents of the district. For that, residents get road maintenance, groundskeeping ,and upkeep of the tennis courts—and exclusive access to the beach. The city of Warwick provides trash collection, policing, and fire service![42]

These districts have generated controversy in recent years, as there has been a move to increase access to the shoreline. But the property they own, the taxes they collect, and the services they provide to property-owners living in these fire districts are the result of the actions taken by the General Assembly. Whether or not it's appropriate or legal for the districts to limit public access to the shoreline they encompass is an open question.[43]

There is great diversity from one Rhode Island community to another in size, population, form of government, and social and economic indicators. Central Falls, the smallest in area, is the highest in population density, with 16,000 residents per square mile. New Shoreham, by contrast, has 91 residents per square mile. Five communities—Central Falls, Providence, Pawtucket, Woonsocket, and North Providence, have a population density of 5,000 people per square mile, while eleven towns are under 300 per square mile.

Like people, wealth is unevenly distributed across the state. East Greenwich has a median family income of $153,475, compared to $34,623 in Central Falls. Homeownership—another indicator of the wealth of a community and the health of its tax base, also varies widely from community to community. In Barrington, 89 percent of families live in a home they own; in Woonsocket, the homeownership rate is 36 percent; in Central Fall, it's 20 percent.[44]

And, as we know, the wealth of a community is associated with many other outcomes. A local government's property tax base as measured by the value of the town's land that allows it to collect property taxes to fund services: healthcare, education, social services, public safety, and parks. Without that tax base, communities must rely on intergovernmental aid, which may come, or may not, and which diminishes the municipality's ability to control its own affairs. Barrington, Portsmouth, and East Greenwich each raise about 80 percent of their revenues from property tax: property values are high, and residents are willing to pay higher taxes for better services. At the other end of the spectrum, only 43 percent of Pawtucket's revenues come from property tax; for Woonsocket, 39.6 percent; and for Central Falls, 20.3 percent.[45]

The Rhode Island Public Expenditures Council's analysis of these discrepancies leads RIPEC's President Michael DiBiase to conclude: ". . . there are significant imbalances in our system that lead to serious consequences for some communities and the people who live and own businesses there. The imbalance in Rhode Island's property tax systems also has a negative impact on larger priorities such as housing and education."[46]

The data support this observation. Regarding education, for example, 70 percent of Barrington eighth graders meet expectations in 2021; in Central Falls, it was 6 percent. The four-year graduation rate for East Greenwich's class of 2021 was 94 percent; for Woonsocket, 64 percent.[47] While there are, of course, many reasons for differences in student success across communities, the amount of wealth is certainly one of them. Across the board, from healthcare to housing to safe neighborhoods, despite Rhode Island's small size and population density, there are major differences from one community to another in measures of economic and social well-being.

Rhode Island's communities also differ in the forms of government they use. Nine of the bigger cities are organized in the typical mayor–council form of government, a form modeled on the state and national governments and used in most large American cities. Twenty towns use a council–manager form of government with an elected council and an appointed city manager. Nine small towns use a town meeting system in which there is a town administrator running day-to-day operations, but voters gather once or more each year to approve the budget, authorize borrowing and other major decisions.

Local governments are required to examine their charter and consider revisions every ten years. Often these revisions are minor, such as adding a member to the cemetery commission or creating the position of town engineer, but they can involve major changes in how a community is governed. In 2017, for example, the voters of East Providence agreed to a charter change that created a strong-mayor form of government, dramatically decreasing the power and authority of the city council and transferring that authority to the mayor. Voters in the City of Providence considered ten changes to that charter in November of 2022, the most significant of which transferred from the mayor to the voters the power to select half the members of the Providence School Board.

The Division of Municipal Finance at the Rhode Island Department of Revenue has gathered these 38 charters (the town of Scituate does not have one) and analyzed key features and similarities and differences.[48] The analysis reveals 38 varieties of governance—from lengths of terms to duties of the harbormaster to qualifications for office to zoning and land use. Occasionally, the General Assembly will step in and provide a state-wide approach to a certain issue, as it has done over the years regarding residency requirements for municipal employment. Many communities had them, but the state has prohibited such requirements for teachers and school administrators, police and fire personnel, and municipal employees.[49] Still, the town-by-town differences in the structures and powers of municipal government is in keeping with the origin story—the communities preceded the creation of the state government and do their own thing.

And So Do the Voters

Since 1928, Rhode Island voters have appeared to be loyal Democrats, voting for a Republican for president only when everyone else did: twice for Eisenhower, once for Nixon, and once for Reagan (in 1984, when only Minnesota voted for Mondale). That pattern, however, masks significant partisan allegiance and voting behavior from community to community. About a dozen communities are predictable Republican strongholds—voting red for presidents and governors, but less so for state representatives, state senators, and local officials. These communities, listed in the table below, have a total population of approximately 170,685 people, while the "blue" communities are home to about 902,786 Rhode Islanders.[50]

The table below shows how loyal these "red" communities are to the national Republican ticket. There was very little change in support for Donald Trump between 2016 and 2020, nor was there much movement in the statewide vote.

Table 11.1 Republican voters in Rhode Island

Community	% for Trump 2016	% Trump 2020
Burrillville	56.9%	57.5%
Coventry	52.5%	52.3%
Exeter	50.8%	49.2%
Foster	54.2%	55.2%
Glocester	55.4%	54.8%
Hopkinton	50.5%	50.0%
Johnston	54.6%	53.9%
North Smithfield	51.9%	49.3%
Richmond	49.9%	48.7%
Scituate	58.9%	57.0%
Smithfield	50.6%	49.8%
West Greenwich	57.9%	56.0%
Statewide vote	38.9%	38.5%

Source: State of Rhode Island Board of Elections, https://elections.ri.65/elections/preresults/index.php.

Reporter Patrick Anderson notes the same pattern held in the 2018 gubernatorial election, with these communities bringing home majorities for challenger Allan Fung, while all others—with the exception of Fung's hometown of Cranston—strongly supported incumbent Democrat Gina Raimondo.[51] Again in 2022, as shown in Figure 11.1, these patterns held with incumbent Dan McKee defeating newcomer Republican Ashley Kalus, this time with Cranston returning to the Democratic fold.

At the other extreme are the communities in the urban core, the East Bay and Aquidneck Island. In Central Falls and Providence, voters supported candidate Biden by margins of 80 percent and 72 percent, respectively. Seventy-

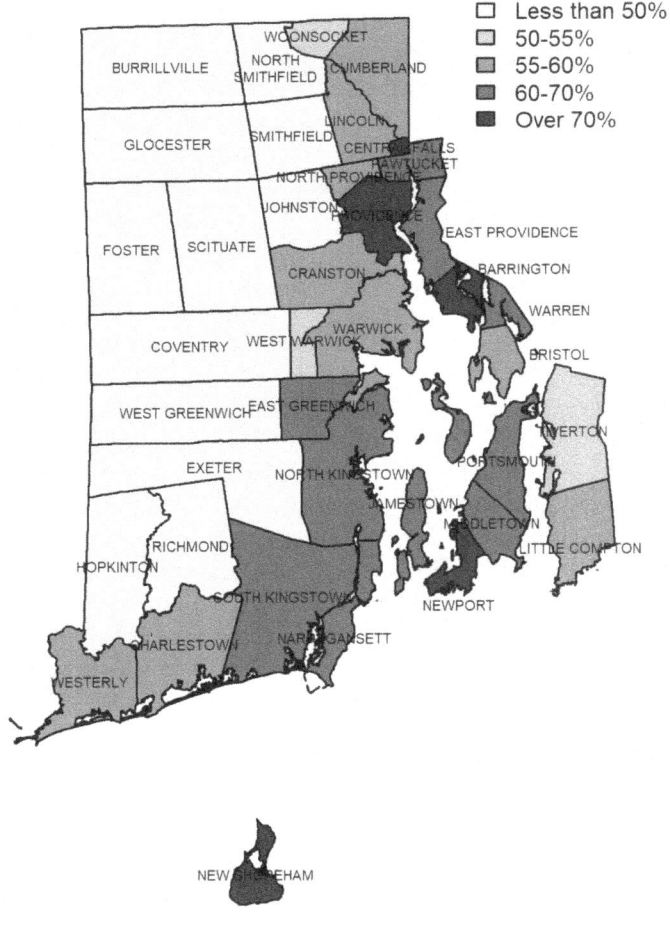

Fig. 11-1 Democratic Share of Two-Party Vote in 2022 Governor Race
Source: Adam Myers, Providence College. Town-level election returns were calculated using data provided by the Rhode Island Board of Elections (https://www.ri.gov/election/results/2022/general_election/). The shapefile used to create the map was provided by the Rhode Island Geographic Information System (https://www.rigis.org/).

one percent of Barrington voters chose Biden; 73 percent of Newport voters did so. And so it goes.

The pro-Trump communities are the inland and rural communities of the state; not one of them touches the coast in the Ocean State. This reflects the pattern in national politics—coastal communities lean left; inland communities lean right. But again, in Rhode Island, many of these Trump voters identify as Democratic and vote that way locally—one of the many idiosyncrasies of Rhode Island politics.

The strength of this Democratic identity, but not necessarily commitment to Democratic values and the party's platform, is on display in Johnston, a community just north and west of Providence, and home to many Italian American families who migrated from Providence and who have *always* identified as Democrats. In their study of "Trump Democrats," Muravchik and Shields note that in 2019, there were 10,507 Democrats registered in Johnston and 2,717 Republicans. They report that "local politicians struggle to remember a Republican winning a municipal office in Johnston."[51] And yet Donald Trump received 54 percent of the vote in both 2016 and 2020. The authors connect this attraction to Trump with the political culture of Johnston and the other two communities they study—a culture based on loyalty and transactions, not policy preferences and values.[52]

A similar ethnographic study could be done of all Rhode Island communities. Why did Barrington—a wealthy, bedroom community full of doctors and lawyers—flip from Republican dominance of local offices throughout the twentieth century—to Democratic dominance in the twenty-first? Why is support for Bernie Sanders so strong in South County (the informal name for Washington County, in the southwest of the state) where "huddles" continue to meet in 2022? The answer lies in history, population shifts, the strength of local political organizations, and the emergence of specific local issues at specific points on time. Just as there are 39 different flavors of history and forms of government, so too are there 39 flavors of partisanship and electoral dynamics.

Rhode Island's municipal governments—many established before the state itself—are remarkably diverse in their histories, how they look, their economic base, and their political behavior. Without county governments to bring some uniformity to law and policy, and with a constitutionally weak governor and a part-time General Assembly, these 39 communities, packed closely together this smallest state, can be engines of policy creativity or obstacles to change. They are certainly sources of local pride and fierce allegiance and will resist attempts at consolidation and centralization. Although the arguments of the policy analysts may be strong for a statewide school district, or countywide police and fire protection, it will be a long time before local governments and their residents will let that happen.

Notes

1. Ted Hayes, "Pokanokets, Warren Sign Historic Pact," July 21, 2021, https://www.eastbayri.com/stories/pokanokets-warren-sign-historic-pact,91809.
2. Ted Widmer, "Native Americans," *Finding Roger Williams*, Carter Roger Williams Institute, n.d., http://www.findingrogerwilliams.com/essays/native-americans.
3. Sidney James, Essay, in *Colonial Rhode Island* (New York: Scribners, 1975). As cited in Moakley and Cornwell.
4. Secretary of State "Rhode Island Royal Charter, 1663," Rhode Island State Archives, n.d., https://www.sos.ri.gov/assets/downloads/documents/RI-Charter-annotated.pdf.
5. Ibid.
6. James, *Colonial*, 72.
7. Maureen Moakley and Elmer E Cornwell. *Rhode Island Politics and Government* (Lincoln: University of Nebraska Press, 2001), 68.
8. Terrance P. Haas, "Constitutional Home Rule in Rhode Island," *Roger Williams University Law Review* 11, no. 3 (2006): 681, http://docs.rwu.edu/rwu_LR/vol11/iss3/.
9. Ibid., 691.
10. Ibid., 692.
11. Rick Su, "Have Cities Abandoned Home Rule?" *Fordham Urban Law Journal* 44, no. 1 (2017): 192, https://ir.lawnet.fordham.edu/ulj/vol44/iss1/6.
12. Inter-university Consortium for Political and Social Research, Referenda and Primary Election Materials, June 2002, "Referenda and Primary Election Materials," *Ballotpedia.org*, https://cdn.ballotpedia.org/images/0/07/Referenda_Elections_for_Rhode_Island_1968-1990.pdf.
13. John C. Caruso, Joseph E. Coduri, and Susan D. Moss, "Municipal Charters in Rhode Island," Rhode Island Division of Municipal Finance, Rhode Island Department of Revenue, 2013, https://municipalfinance.ri.gov/sites/g/files/xkgbur546/files/documents/resources/Home_Rule_Charter_Publication.pdf.
14. Dan McGowan, "R.I. Has a Law That Caps Property Taxes. Now One City Has to Issue Refunds," *Boston Globe*, February 4, 2020, https://www.bostonglobe.com/2020/02/04/metro/ri-has-law-that-caps-property-taxes-now-one-city-has-issue-refunds/.
15. State of Rhode Island General Assembly, https://status.rilegislature.gov/.
16. Caruso, Coduri, and Moss, "Municipal."
17. Ibid.
18. "An Introduction to Municipal Finance in Rhode Island," Rhode Island Public Expenditure Council, April 2021, https://ripec.org/wp-content/uploads/2021/04/2021_Intro_Municipal_Finance.pdf.
19. "Burillville Town Council Resolution Declaring the Town of Burrillville a 'Second Amendment Sanctuary Town,'" Town of Burillville, April 24, 2019, https://www.burrillville.org/sites/g/files/vyhlif2886/f/uploads/4-24-2019_sanctuary_town.pdf.
20. Amanda Milkovits, "A '2A Sanctuary Town' in Rhode Island Declares It Won't Comply with New Gun Law," *Boston Globe*, July 23, 2022, https://www.bostonglobe.com/2022/07/20/metro/2a-sanctuary-town-rhode-island-declares-it-wont-comply-with-new-gun-law/.
21. Patrick T. Conley, "The Irish in Rhode Island," Historical Preservation & Heritage Commission, The Rhode Island Heritage Commission and The Rhode Island

Publications Society, 1986, https://preservation.ri.gov/sites/g/files/xkgbur406/files/pdfs_zips_downloads/heritage_pdfs/pamphlets/irish.pdf.
22. Carmela E. Santoro, "The Italians in Rhode Island," Historical Preservation & Heritage Commission, The Rhode Island Heritage Commission and The Rhode Island Publications Society, 1990, https://preservation.ri.gov/sites/g/files/xkgbur406/files/pdfs_zips_downloads/heritage_pdfs/pamphlets/italian.pdf.
23. Keith Stokes and Theresa Guzman Stokes, "A Matter of Truth: The Struggle for African Heritage and Indigenous People Equal Rights in Providence, Rhode Island (1620–2020)," Rhode Island Black Heritage Society & 1696 Heritage Group, 2021.
24. Stokes and Stokes, "Heritage," 53.
25. Ibid., 36.
26. Ibid., 42.
27. Ibid., 46.
28. Ibid., 40.
29. Ibid., 41. For a more detailed description see William R. Staples, *Annals of the Town of Providence* (n.p.: Knowles and Lose, 1843), https://www.google.com/books/edition/Annals_of_the_Town_of_Providence/OP01UnWXBLUC?hl=en&gbpv=0.
30. Stokes and Stokes, "Heritage," 106.
31. "2021 Housing Fact Book," HousingWorksRI, Roger Williams University, 2021, https://www.housingworksri.org/Portals/0/Uploads/Documents/HWRI_HFB21.pdf?ver=5nrQwMVsMPHl5PtR9Uk6vA%3D%3D.
32. Stokes and Stokes, "Heritage."
33. Ibid.
34. Clarence N. Stone, *Regime Politics: Governing Atlanta, 1946–1988* (Lawrence: University of Kansas, 1989), 6.
35. Wilbur C. Rich, "Vincent Cianci and Boosterism in Providence, RI," *Governing Middle Sized Cities* (2000): 203.
36. Ibid., 208.
37. Marian Orr and Carrie Nordlund, "The Political Transformation of Providence: The Election of Angel Taveras," in Ravi K. Perry, editor. *21st Century Race Politics: Representing Minorities as Universal Interests* (2013: Emerald Group Publishing Limited), 6.
38. Ibid., 211.
39. Martinez, Marta. "Latino Political Empowerment in Rhode Island," *Providence Journal*, 6/21/22, https://www.providencejournal.com/story/opinion/columns/2021/06/12/our-hidden-history-martinez-latino-political-empowerment-rhode-island/7630395002/.
40. "Providence, RI." Data USA, 2020. https://datausa.io/profile/geo/providence-ri/#demographics.
41. Pew Research Center, "Hispanic Population Growth and Dispersion Across U.S. Counties, 1980–2020," Pew Research Center, February 3, 2022, https://www.pewresearch.org/hispanic/interactives/hispanic-population-by-county/. See Excel workbook of data.
42. Alex Nunes, "In Coastal South County, Fire Districts Fight Shoreline Access Instead of Fires," *The Public's Radio*, March 31, 2021, https://thepublicsradio.org/article/fire-districts.

43. Brian Amaral, "In Rhode Island, Some Fire Districts Are under Fire over Beach Access," *Boston Globe*, August 26, 2021, https://www.bostonglobe.com/2021/08/26/metro/rhode-island-some-fire-districts-are-under-fire-over-beach-access/.
44. Nunes, "Fire."
45. HousingWorksRI, "Fact Book."
46. "A System Out of Balance: Property Taxation Across Rhode Island," Rhode Island Public Expenditure Council, January 25, 2022, https://ripec.org/a-system-out-of-balance-property-taxation-across-rhode-island/.
47. Ibid.
48. Kids Count, "High School Graduation Rate," 2022 Rhode *Island KIDS COUNT Factbook*, 2022, https://www.rikidscount.org/Portals/0/Uploads/Documents/Factbook%202022/High%20School%20Graduation%20Rate%20FB2022.pdf?ver=2022-05-12-085928-010.
49. Caruso, Coduri, and Moss, "Municipal."
50. Ibid.
51. "Providence," *Data Commons*, n.d. https://datacommons.org/place/geoId/4459000?category=Equity.
52. Patrick Anderson, "Governor's Race Shows R.I. Turned Redder and Bluer" *Providence Journal*, November 7, 2018. https://www.providencejournal.com/story/news/politics/2018/11/08/governors-raceshows-ri-turnedredder-and-bluer/9067642007/.
53. Stephanie Muravchik and Jon A Shields, *Trump's Democrats* (Washington, DC: Brookings Institute Press, 2020), 20.
54. Muravchik and Shields, *Democrats*, 40–42.

Policy Essays

A The Legacy of Women in Rhode Island Politics: 225
   From the State House to Governor
   WENDY J. SCHILLER

B Taxing and SPENDING   235
   MICHAEL DIBIASE

C The Politics of Rhode Island Education   245
   DIANE E. KERN AND SHANNA PEARSON-MERKOWITZ

D Health Policy in Rhode Island   255
   ROBERT B. HACKEY, COLLEEN M. KENNEDY,
   MICHAELA C. SZYMCZAK

E Overview of Environmental Policy in Rhode Island   271
   AARON LEY

F Transportation Policy in Rhode Island   283
   BARRY SCHILLER

A / The Legacy of Women in Rhode Island Politics: From the State House to Governor

WENDY J. SCHILLER

"I'd knock on doors and people would tell me that women really don't belong in politics."
LILA SAPINSLEY, as quoted in the *Providence Journal*[1]

In 2023, Rhode Island ranked seventh in the country in the percentage of women who serve in the state legislature.[2] In 2003, when the number of members was downsized, women represented just over 19 percent of members in the General Assembly; by 2023, women were over 44 percent of the legislature. There are 17 out of 38 female state senators, and 33 out of 75 women in the House. Not only is that ratio one of the highest in the nation, but it also exceeds the percentage of women who serve in the US Senate and House, respectively.[3] While Rhode Island has elected women to statewide office since 1983, it was not until 2014 that a woman was elected to be governor of the state, and Rhode Island has not yet elected a female US Senator. By 2023, all of Rhode Island's surrounding New England states had already reached one or both of these milestones in women's politics, starting with Madeline Kuhn (governor) in Vermont, Jodi Rell (governor) in Connecticut, Jeanne Shaheen (governor and US Senator) and Maggie Hassan (governor and US Senator) in New Hampshire, Janet Mills (governor), Olympia Snowe (US Senator), Susan Collins (US Senator) in Maine, and Elizabeth Warren (US Senator) in Massachusetts.

Rhode Island did not get there by accident. Instead, the trajectory of power for women in politics nearly 50 years earlier, when Lila Sapinsley was elected to the state Senate as an Independent who opposed the machine-type politics that dominated the legislature at that time. She soon decided to affiliate as a Republican; at that time in American politics, a politician could be in favor of women's rights and reproductive choice and still win as a Republican, something that would be considerably more difficult today in Rhode Island, and nearly impossible anywhere outside New England.

The Long and Winding Path to Electing a Female Governor in Rhode Island

Lila Sapinsley was elected Senate minority leader in 1975 and joined very few women around the nation in that role.[4] It was a milestone for women in politics in the state, and it came at the cusp of the explosion of the women's rights movement across the nation. She tried to make the leap to statewide office and ran for lieutenant governor in 1984 but lost that election. However, by that time, a Republican woman, Claudine Schneider, had won a seat to the US House of Representatives from Rhode Island, and there were 12 women serving in the Rhode Island Senate and 14 women in the Rhode Island House. Just two years later, Rhode Island had both a female secretary of state in Susan Farmer and a female attorney general in Arlene Violet; it would not be until 1992 that a woman, Republican Nancy Mayer, would be elected state treasurer, and 2006 before a woman, Elizabeth Roberts, would be elected lieutenant governor. It would not be until 2008 that another woman was elected to a top legislative leadership post when Teresa Paiva-Weed, a Democrat, was elected as president of the RI state Senate after serving as majority leader. When Paiva-Weed was asked in an interview in 2021 about the high percentage of women now in the RI legislature, she said "It is important that chambers reflect the population, so it's good . . . and again, as an early woman leader, I'm happy to see it."[5]

Table A.1. Women who have held statewide office in Rhode Island, 1983–2021

Name	Office	Years
Sabina Matos (D)*	lieutenant governor	2021–present
Nellie Gorbea (D)	secretary of state	2015–present
Gina Raimondo (D)	governor	2015–21
Gina Raimondo (D)	state treasurer	2011–14
Elizabeth Roberts (D)	lieutenant governor	2007–14
Nancy J. Mayer (R)	state treasurer	1993–98
Barbara Leonard (R)	secretary of state	1993–94
Kathleen S. Connell (D)	secretary of state	1987–92
Arlene Violet (R)	attorney general	1985–1986
Susan L. Farmer (R)	secretary of state	1983–1986

*Matos was appointed to fill a vacancy.

Source: Adapted from the Center for American Women and Politics, Rutgers University, https://cawp.rutgers.edu/state_fact_sheets/ri

When Gina Raimondo was elected first to be state treasurer in 2010 and then to the top position of governor in 2014, it marked the culmination of a long succession of women who followed in Sapinsley's large footsteps. But it was no easy path for Raimondo, who had to defeat two other main party challengers with significant roots in Rhode Island politics in the Democratic Party gubernatorial primary election. Angel Taveras was the incumbent mayor of Providence, Rhode Island's largest city and he had attracted a base of support in that city. Clay Pell was the grandson of Senator Claiborne Pell, a much beloved and long serving US senator from Rhode Island.

The third man who ran in that primary was Todd Giroux, who was considered a spoiler candidate with little chance of winning the nomination. Unions played a key role in this primary in different ways. The Rhode Island teachers union was unhappy with Angel Taveras for his negotiations with teachers who worked in Providence and unhappy with Gina Raimondo for leading the successful effort to reform the state pension system. That pension reform required increased contributions from teachers, raised the age of retirement for certain personnel, and eliminated the automatic yearly 3 percent cost-of-living adjustment that had been given to retired state employees who received state pensions. Public unions did not favor either Taveras or Raimondo, so they actively recruited Clay Pell to run in the primary. Clay Pell's entry into the election split the "anti-Raimondo" votes between himself and Taveras, and while he had the state public employees in his electoral coalition, they did not comprise a big enough sector of the Democratic Party to win a plurality in the primary. Raimondo was able to forge a winning campaign by securing early endorsements from private unions, business leaders, elected officials, and prominent elected Latina women like Representative Grace Diaz, who had been serving in elected office for more than decade. Raimondo won the primary with 42.1 percent of the vote, compared to 29.1 percent for Taveras, 26.9 percent for Pell, and 1.8 percent for Giroux.[6] The outcome of that primary showed just how important it was that Raimondo faced two viable opponents rather than one; the combined vote for them exceeded her vote margin by more than 14 percent. In retrospect, Raimondo's public union opponents may have miscalculated in recruiting Clay Pell because doing so divided the opposition.

Winning the Democratic primary in the race for RI governor was not sufficient; Raimondo had to find a way to win the general election, where she was once again facing two main opponents who were men, out of a total of four other candidates on the ballot. The Republican candidate was Allan Fung, then-mayor of Cranston, who was generally well liked and respected in the state. Raimondo and Fung each raised and spent considerable money to run advertisements against each other. The other main opponent was Robert Healey, who was well known to RI voters as the head of a third party commonly known as the "Cool Moose" Party. Prior to 2014, Healey had been best known for running for the office of Lieutenant Governor and promising to abolish it if he won the election, but he lost.

Healey's candidacy turned out to be more important in the final results than political observers might have expected. For public union employees who identified as Democrats, voting for the Republican candidate was not an attractive option, as they did not expect to fare better in contract negotiations with a Republican governor than with a Democratic governor. On the other hand, they would not vote for Gina Raimondo because of her efforts on pension reform. Healey provided a viable "protest" vote for these voters, and without him in the race, it is very possible that Allan Fung would have peeled off enough anti-Raimondo votes from public union employees to win the general election. Again, as with the 2014 Democratic Party primary, Raimondo was elected because two men who ran against her split the vote. Because Fung was the better known and more experienced political opponent, it is quite likely he would have defeated Raimondo if Healey had not been on the ballot. Ultimately, Raimondo was elected the first female governor in Rhode Island history with only 40.7 percent of the vote, as compared to 36.2 percent for Fung and 21.4 percent for Healey.[7]

In 2018, Raimondo ran for reelection and again faced a primary challenge from a male opponent. This time the challenger was Matt Brown, who served one term from 2003–7 as secretary of state of Rhode Island and was then running from the Progressive wing of the Democratic Party. External conditions, particularly economic, were much different in 2018, with the Great Recession further in the rear-view mirror than in 2014 when the Rhode Island economy was more stagnant. That year was also a good year for women in the Democratic Party across the country, largely in response to the #MeToo movement and to the Trump presidency. Raimondo easily won the primary, defeating Matt Brown with 57.2 percent of the vote as compared with 33.5 percent for him; a third candidate, Spencer Dickinson, took 9.3 percent of the vote.[8] Unlike during her first run for governor, this time Raimondo was in no danger of losing the nomination, as the combined total of her opponents fell well short of her margin of victory.

Despite overcoming opponents in the gubernatorial primary for a second time, Raimondo faced a repeat challenge from Republican Allan Fung, who had been reelected as Cranston mayor in the intervening years. In his second attempt to run for governor, Fung faced two opponents for the Republican nomination, one of whom was a woman named Patricia Morgan, a member of the RI House of Representatives and minority leader from 2016 to 2018. But it is not clear that Lila Sapinsley would have recognized her as being a member of the same Republican Party. Patricia Morgan was considerably more conservative on social and fiscal issues, reflecting where the national and local party had moved in the three decades since Sapinsley had served in office. Morgan ran a far more competitive race than expected, but Fung won the contest by securing the nomination with 56.4 percent of the vote to 40.1 percent for Morgan; a third candidate businessman, Giovanni Feroce, took 3.5 percent of the vote.⁹ Although Morgan lost that contest, her presence in the primary pushed Allan Fung further right along the ideological spectrum than he had been in the 2014 gubernatorial contest, which did not align as well with the median voter in the state. Fung also had to walk the tightrope of the Trump presidency and run in a midterm election year when members of the president's party traditionally do not do as well.

To complicate matters more for Fung, Joe Trillo, a former Republican member of the state legislature, ran as an Independent. Trillo was a conservative and a strong supporter of Donald Trump. However, he had difficulty raising campaign funds, and despite the potential threat he posed to siphon off voters from Fung, his candidacy did not have a strong effect in the end. In addition to Trillo, three other minor party candidates ran in that election. Ultimately, Raimondo had a larger margin of victory in her reelection bid; she won 52.6 percent of the vote against 37.2 percent for Fung.¹⁰

Raimondo governed strictly from the middle of the ideological spectrum as a moderate Democrat, a reputation established while she was serving as state treasurer. Even then, Raimondo demonstrated that she was a firm leader who governed based on fiscal policy, not political pressure. Having survived the opposition of the public unions as a Democrat in a union-friendly state, she drew national attention as the pension reform effort proved to be successful in stabilizing the state employee pension system.

As governor, Raimondo maintained that reputation by working to keep corporate taxes low, recruiting businesses to Rhode Island with tax breaks, and supporting a gradual increase in the minimum wage spread out over a number of years. She was not particularly gregarious or the typical "back slapping" politician, but she was a born and bred Rhode Islander who relied on that identity to persuade Rhode Island voters she was acting in their interest, even if they did not warm to her on a personal level. While she could be described as heavily pro-business, Raimondo also strongly supported liberal positions such as codifying the right to abortion and allowing the temporary removal of weapons from individuals who might pose a danger to themselves or others (known as the "red flag" law). Her successes led her to be asked to chair the Democratic Governors Association, providing her with a national platform. During the COVID-19 pandemic, Raimondo's popularity in Rhode Island grew as she held daily press conferences to explain state policies and keep voters informed.¹¹ Her straightforward delivery and unvarnished description of the crisis again drew her national attention for leadership skills. and put her in contention for the vice-presidential slot on the Democratic ticket in 2020. Ultimately, she was not selected to run for vice president but was chosen by President Biden to be secretary of commerce; she officially resigned the RI governorship on March 2, 2021, after she won US Senate confirmation.¹²

The Rise of Latina Politicians in Rhode Island Politics

In the same year that Gina Raimondo was first elected as governor, Nellie Gorbea, a Latina politician, was elected to the office of secretary of state; she was the first statewide elected Latina in Rhode Island, as well as in New England more generally. Gorbea was reelected in 2018 without any major competition from within her own party or from opposition parties. By 2022, the landscape in Rhode Island had changed, and the growing power of Latinos, especially women, was on display. Overall, Latinos comprise 14 percent of adults over the voting age of 18 in Rhode Island, but in terms of eligible voters, they comprise closer to 11 percent of the voting eligible population over age 18.[13] Out of 113 members in the state House (75) and state Senate (38), there were 21 self-identified Latino and Black members, 14 in the House and 7 in the Senate, 11 of whom were women.[14] According to National Council of State Legislatures, Rhode Island was in the middle of New England on the percentage of Latino members of the state legislature (Massachusetts and Connecticut are above, Maine, New Hampshire, and Vermont are below).[15] Notably, Latina women appear to have outpaced their male counterparts at the state level; former Latino mayor of Providence, Angel Taveras (mentioned above) ran in a gubernatorial primary and lost, and former Latino mayor Jorge Elorza, who had given indications he would run for governor in 2022, ultimately chose not to run when support for his candidacy did not materialize.

Raimondo's resignation set off a chain reaction in Rhode Island politics. The positions of governor, lieutenant governor, and secretary of state in Rhode Island are limited to two terms. Under normal circumstances then, if Raimondo had stayed on to complete her term, the governor's race would have been an open seat race with no incumbent official standing for reelection. The same would have been true of the lieutenant governor's position where Dan McKee (D) would have completed his two terms in that position. Instead, Dan McKee (D), a white male, was sworn into the position of governor, and he subsequently appointed Sabina Matos (D), a Latina and then-president of the Providence City Council, to be lieutenant governor. Consequently, instead of having open seat elections, now both the governor and lieutenant governor were incumbents who were free to seek re-election.

With Sabina Matos's appointment to lieutenant governor, Nellie Gorbea was no longer the only Latina in Rhode Island (or in New England) holding statewide office. As she was also term limited, Gorbea had already been making plans to run for governor before McKee took over the top spot in RI government. McKee's appointment did not dissuade her from running, and she was one of the earliest to declare her candidacy. On what was a celebratory day for women and Latinos in Rhode Island, their Latina secretary of state swore in the Latina lieutenant governor. But the appointment of Sabina Matos complicated the electoral landscape for Gorbea as a Latina in statewide politics.

Although the governor and the lieutenant governor are elected separately for their respective positions, McKee and Matos quickly positioned themselves as an electoral team.

In addition, another "pair" of contenders entered the races for governor and lieutenant governor, respectively: Matt Brown, a white Progressive Democrat who had challenged Gina Raimondo in 2018 declared his candidacy for governor and formed a team with Cynthia Mendes, a Latina RI state senator elected in 2020 who declared her candidacy for lieutenant governor. Luis Daniel Munoz was also in the race for governor, as was a former executive at the RI-based drugstore chain CVS, Helena Foulkes; neither of these candidates had ever won statewide office. In a crowded and competitive field, Nellie Gorbea found herself running against McKee, Brown, Munoz, and Foulkes in the Democratic primary for governor. While she could say she was the only Latina in that contest, with the additions of Matos and Mendes running for lieutenant governor, she could no longer lay claim to being the only Latina statewide candidate who could promise to represent the interests of Latino and Latina voters.

Latinos are not a monolithic cultural, ideological, or a partisan voting bloc, either in Rhode Island or nationwide; and they are a diverse population with different origins. As Latina politicians, Gorbea, Matos, and Mendes differ in terms of their backgrounds, style, and ideology. Nellie Gorbea was born in Puerto Rico, Matos was born in the Dominican Republic, and Mendes was born in Rhode Island and has both Black and Latina heritage. Gorbea was educated at two Ivy League universities (Princeton and Columbia), while Matos came to the United States in her early 20s and graduated from Rhode Island College with a bachelor's degree, and Mendes graduated from a Rhode Island community college with a two-year associates degree and was a dental assistant and technician in the early part of her career. They each also lived in different parts of the state reflecting different levels of economic affluence and racial diversity: Gorbea lived in North Kingstown, which tends to be less diverse and more affluent; Matos lived in Olneyville, which is more diverse and less affluent, and Mendes lived in East Providence, which lies between the other two communities in terms of diversity and affluence.

In terms of governing style and ideology, both Gorbea and Matos had higher profiles than Mendes, but all three of them tried to connect with RI voters, and the Latino voting community specifically. Gorbea promoted her election reforms, outreach to Spanish-speaking voters, and improving state services that fall under her jurisdiction; Matos maintained her focus on small business owners and the importance of local community; Mendes was much newer to RI politics and tried to merge her progressive liberal ideology to her background in the Latino and African American community. While Gorbea and Mendes were consistent in most of their policy positions, Mendes has had to adapt her views on issues such as abortion, moving from an anti-abortion policy stance to a pro-choice stance in her evolution within the Progressive movement. Latinas career trajectories demonstrate the continued progress of Latinas in RI politics.

Conclusion

From Lila Sapinsley to Cynthia Mendes, women in Rhode Island have consistently challenged the white male-dominated sphere of elected politics and have had to overcome an entrenched political patriarchy. Compared to its New England neighbors, Rhode Island voters were slower to elect a female governor and have yet to elect a female US Senator, but were first to elect a Latina to statewide office. Whether these female candidates were born in the state, or arrived 10 or 20 years ago, there is constant pressure to prove themselves to be as capable as their male opponents and to establish that they are "true Rhode Islanders."

Each of the women in this essay forged ahead with her own style and appeal, and in doing so, laid the groundwork for the women who followed. Today, as opposed to when Lila Sapinsley first ran for office, women from all backgrounds are more active in politics and hold more elected offices than ever before in the state's history. In some ways then, the ascendance of women, especially Latina politicians, in Rhode Island reflect trends in US politics that continue to produce a broader and more diverse set of elected officials with every election.

Notes

1. Paul Edward Parker, "Lila Sapinsley, a Trailblazer for Women in R.I. Politics, Dies at 92," December 9, 2014, *Providence Journal*, https://www.providencejournal.com/article/20141209/News/312099992.
2. "State by State Information," Center for American Women and Politics, Rutgers University, https://cawp.rutgers.edu/state-by-state.
3. "State Fact Sheets," Center for American Women and Politics, Rutgers University, https://cawp.rutgers.edu/state_fact_sheets/ri.
4. Nellie Gorbea, "A Guide to Rhode Island Government & History," Office of the Secretary of State, 2021, https://www.sos.ri.gov/assets/downloads/documents/RI_Activity_Book.pdf.
5. Alex Maim. "This Week's Conversation with Teresa Paiva-Weed," *Newport ThisWeek.com*, June 3, 2021, https://www.newportthisweek.com/articles/this-weeks-conversation-with-teresa-paiva-weed/.
6. "Gina Raimondo," *Ballotpedia*, https://ballotpedia.org/Gina_Raimondo.
7. Ibid.
8. Ibid.
9. Ibid.
10. Ibid.
11. A study that was conducted in the first year of the pandemic found that women governors were more successful in reducing overall deaths from COVID in their states than their male counterparts. See Kayla Sergent and Alexander D. Stajkovic. Sergent, Kayla., & Alexander D. Stajkovic, (2020). Women's leadership is associated with fewer deaths during the COVID-19 crisis: Quantitative and qualitative analyses of United States governors. *Journal of Applied Psychology*, 105(8), 771–783. https://doi.org/10.1037/apl0000577.
12. Katherine Gregg and Patrick Anderson, "Raimondo Resigns after Winning Senate Confirmation as U.S. Commerce Secretary; McKee sworn in as RI governor," *Providence Journal*, March 2, 2021. https://www.providencejournal.com/story/news/politics/2021/03/02/ri-may-have-new-governor-today-heres-how-would-happen/6883302002/.
13. US Census Bureau, "Decennial Census: Hispanic or Latino, and Not Hispanic or Latino by race for the population 18 years and over," Census.gov, https://data.census.gov/cedsci/table?q=voting%20population&tid=DECENNIALPL2020.P4; Angela Underwood. "Voter Demographics of Every State," Stacker.com, https://stacker.com/stories/4884/voter-demographics-every-state.
14. "Rhode Island Black and Latin Caucus," Rhode Island Legislature, https://www.rilegislature.gov/commissions/blackandlatincaucus/Pages/welcome.aspx.
15. "State Legislator Demographics," National Council of State Legislatures, https://www.ncsl.org/research/about-state-legislatures/state-legislator-demographics.aspx.

B / Taxing and Spending

Michael DiBiase

"Every decision we make must pass the test of whether or not it will create opportunity for Rhode Island families. In everything we do, we must ask ourselves 'how will this create good middle-class jobs?' and then have the fortitude to act accordingly."
Governor Gina Raimondo, Inaugural Address, January 6, 2015[1]

A state's taxing and spending policies reflect its history, demographics, culture, values, interests, and political climate. Beginning with the Bloodless Revolution in 1935, Rhode Island's taxing and spending policies have been aligned with the controlling Democratic coalition of working-class interests and organized labor, resulting in relatively high spending for public employment and for government services, and, by necessity, relatively high taxes imposed on Rhode Island residents and businesses. While taxes and spending in Rhode Island remain above the national average, the last few decades have seen a shift toward a more fiscally conservative approach, focused on resisting broad-based tax increases and reducing taxes for business. While state policymakers generally have continued to support government programs and to disfavor cutting government services, revenue constraints have limited major new programs and large program expansions. When there have been major shortfalls in revenues, particularly during the Great Recession, significant cutbacks in expenditures have resulted.

Taxes

In Rhode Island, the personal income tax and the sales and use tax are the dominant sources of state revenues, together comprising two-thirds of all general revenues at the state level, as depicted in Figure B.1.[2] Rhode Island has a relatively progressive personal income tax, ranging from 3.75 percent up to 5.99 percent based on income. The Ocean State also has a comparatively high sales

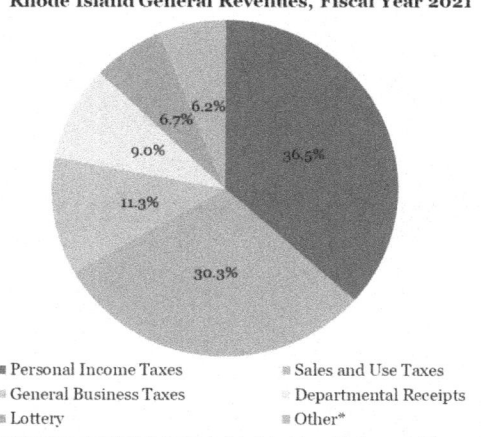

Figure 1
Rhode Island General Revenues, Fiscal Year 2021

- Personal Income Taxes
- Sales and Use Taxes
- General Business Taxes
- Departmental Receipts
- Lottery
- Other*

* Other includes motor vehicle, cigarette, alcohol, and controlled substances taxes, inheritance and gift taxes, racing and athletics taxes, realty transfer taxes, unclaimed property and other miscellaneous
Source: November 2021 Revenue Estimating Conference Report

and use tax rate, at 7 percent, but a relatively narrow base of goods and services subject to tax (food, clothing, and prescription medicine are excluded).

Over the past two decades, the personal income tax and the sales and use tax have been remarkably stable in terms of policy. While Rhode Island in 2019 joined nearly every state in extending the sales and use tax to online sales,[3] the General Assembly has rejected efforts to significantly alter the tax. The Assembly rejected Governor Lincoln Chafee's 2011 proposal to lower the sales and use tax rate to 6 percent and expand the base of goods and services to be taxed,[4] and, more recently, largely resisted efforts by Governor Gina Raimondo to expand the sales and use tax to certain business services.[5] Under Governor Donald Carcieri, the General Assembly in 2010 restructured the top personal income tax rate from 9.9 percent to 5.99 percent, but this change was revenue neutral as certain exemptions and deductions were eliminated.[6] The Assembly has resisted efforts to increase the personal income tax for high earners in recent legislative sessions.[7]

Instead, the focus of state tax policy since at least the 1990s has been to reduce the tax burden for Rhode Island businesses, motivated by a consistent political consensus to improve the tax climate and make the state more economically competitive. Pro-business initiatives along these lines include the enactment of the historic tax credit program in 2013,[8] the adoption in 2014 of combined reporting and single sales apportionment of corporate income,[9] and, in 2015, a reduction of the corporate income tax rate from 9 percent to 7 percent, and the phase-out of the sales tax on energy for commercial users.[10] At the urging of Governor Raimondo, the General Assembly adopted a robust set of new economic development tax incentives in 2016, including tax credits for generating new jobs and for real estate investment.[11] As a result of these tax policy changes, as well as tax increases in other states, Rhode Island's ranking on the Tax Foundation's Business Tax Climate Index improved from 44th best in 2015 to 37th best in 2021, while still remaining in the bottom one-third of states.[12]

Rhode Island's overall state and local tax burden remains high relative to the United States. As depicted in Figures B.2 and B.3, the Ocean State's tax revenues for fiscal year (FY) 2019 were slightly higher than the national average on a per capita basis and based on $1,000 of personal income, which gauges a state's ability to pay.[13] Compared to the New England region, Rhode Island's tax revenues were higher in terms of personal income, but lower on a per capita basis.

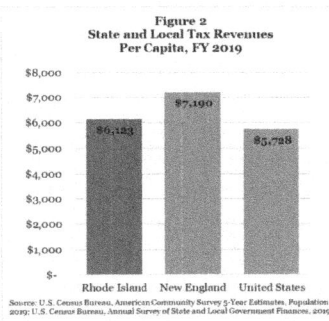

Figure 2
State and Local Tax Revenues
Per Capita, FY 2019

Source: U.S. Census Bureau, American Community Survey 5-Year Estimates, Population for 2019; U.S. Census Bureau, Annual Survey of State and Local Government Finances, 2019

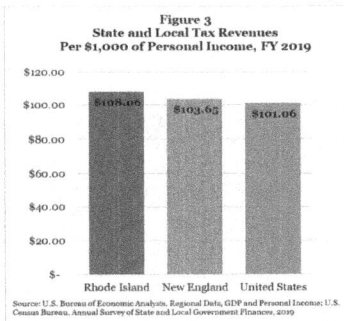

Figure 3
State and Local Tax Revenues
Per $1,000 of Personal Income, FY 2019

Source: U.S. Bureau of Economic Analysis, Regional Data, GDP and Personal Income; U.S. Census Bureau, Annual Survey of State and Local Government Finances, 2019

Municipal Taxes

The property tax is the dominant source of revenue for Rhode Island's cities and towns. Like other New England states, Rhode Island relies more heavily on property taxes than US states overall.[14] Since K–12 education is the largest municipal expense, and property wealth is unevenly distributed among Rhode Island's cities and towns, this reliance on property taxes creates inequity with respect to school funding. While the adoption of a school funding formula by the General Assembly in 2010 has reduced overall reliance on the property tax for education,[15] and resulted in more generous funding for less affluent communities, serious equity issues remain, as discussed more fully below.

The most significant tax policy change at the municipal level in recent years is the phase-out of the motor vehicle excise tax, a class of property tax. Initiated by then House Speaker Nicholas Mattiello, the General Assembly in 2017 decided to restart the phase-out of car taxes that was first adopted in 1998 but largely dismantled in 2010 in response to revenue shortfalls during the Great Recession. The most recent phase-out, implemented over seven years, incrementally reduces the minimum tax rate levied and percentage of assessed value subject to taxation, while increasing the minimum exemption. Cities and towns are paid by the state for the lost taxes resulting from the levy reductions. For FY 2022, the phase-out program transferred $139.7 million to cities and towns. Under current law, the tax will be eliminated by FY 2024.[16]

Perhaps the most concerning feature of Rhode Island's property tax structure is the imbalance of tax rates imposed among types of property subject to taxation, particularly in urban communities. Many cities and towns impose relatively high taxes on commercial real estate and tangible commercial property, creating a potential disincentive for investment, and resulting in a proliferation of tax stabilization agreements to provide tax relief to developers—an inherently political process that favors new investment over existing businesses. Also significant is the use of homestead exemptions in many communities, with the most extreme example employed in the City of Providence, where resident homeowners enjoy an exemption of 40 percent of the assessed value of their residence. Left without the benefit of these homestead exemptions, landlords (and indirectly renters) face relatively high residential rates, or even higher commercial rates in the case of larger apartment buildings.[17]

In 2006, the General Assembly tightened the cap on property tax increases, requiring that no city or town increase taxes by more than 4 percent as of FY 2013. The tax cap law however has several exceptions that allow the cap to be exceeded through a super-majority vote by the municipality's governing body.[18] It is unclear to what extent the law has restrained the growth in property taxes, particularly given that large increases in school funding were provided to urban communities over the past several years under the new school funding formula, which has relieved the pressure for these communities to raise taxes to fund district schools.

State and Local Spending

As with tax revenues, state and local spending in Rhode Island is somewhat high when compared to the region and nation. As depicted in Figures 4 and 5, the Ocean State's expenditures were higher than the United States and New England in both per capita and personal income terms in FY 2019.

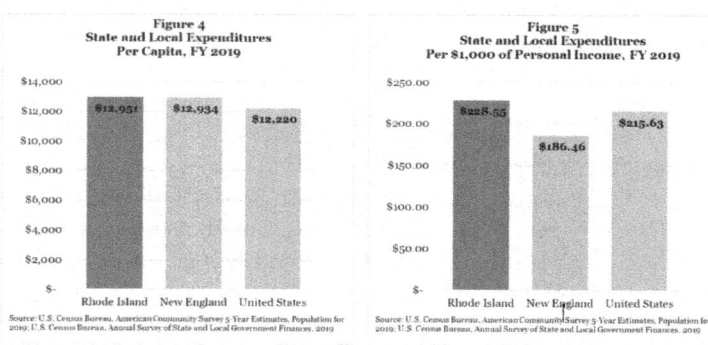

The Great Recession brought drastic cuts to state spending, particularly with respect to state aid to cities and towns. General state aid to municipalities, exclusive of education, totaled $189.7 million in FY 2005. Such aid for cities and towns was cut to $65.5 million by FY 2015, and only recently returned to FY 2005 levels, largely due to funding connected with the motor vehicle tax phase-out. State education aid also was reduced in FY 2009, and again in FY 2010, not returning to FY 2008 levels until FY 2012.[19]

The Great Recession also brought passage of one of the most far-reaching reforms of state public pension plans in the country. At the urging of then General Treasurer Gina Raimondo, and facing severe underfunding of the state pension system, the General Assembly in 2011 enacted changes to pensions for both active and retired state employees and teachers. The pension reform law suspended cost-of-living adjustments for retirees, increased the retirement age for active employees, and introduced a hybrid defined benefit/defined contribution plan.[20] Importantly, the Assembly did not address pensions for other municipal employees. Certain municipal pension plans are critically underfunded, most notably the Providence pension system, which has unfunded pension liabilities of over $1.2 billion.[21]

State and local spending on social services and income maintenance constitutes the largest spending category in Rhode Island (26.7 percent of all expenditures in FY 2019). Expenditures in this category increased dramatically at a rate far exceeding total expenditure growth (28.1 percent vs. 16.1 percent) between FY 2014 and FY 2019, in large part due to the expansion of Medicaid under the 2010 Affordable Care Act (ACA), with the federal government funding nearly all of the increased expenditures.[22] Since ACA expansion, Medicaid enrollment in Rhode Island increased by 63 percent, such that nearly one-third of all Rhode Islanders (334,500 enrollees) are now covered by Medicaid.[23]

Education expenditures make up the second largest portion of Rhode Island's total expenditures—only slightly less than social services and income maintenance and essentially the same proportion (26.7 percent in FY 2019). Like the New England region generally, in FY 2019, Rhode Island overspent compared to the United States on K–12 education (12.5 percent higher on a per capita basis) but underspent on higher education (32.5 percent lower on a per capita basis).[24] As depicted in Figure B.6, Rhode Island spends significantly more than the nation for K–12 education on a per pupil basis, although less than New England. Despite investing more in K–12 education than most states, Ocean State student proficiency scores are on par with or below the nation overall, with particularly poor outcomes for students in urban schools. These outcomes raise serious questions as to the state's return on its investment. Rhode Island's relative under investment in higher education also raises concerns, since economic development and growth are tied closely with education levels.[25]

In 2010, Rhode Island adopted a K–12 school funding formula based on the

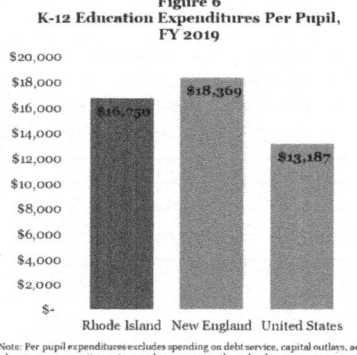

Figure 6
K-12 Education Expenditures Per Pupil, FY 2019

Note: Per pupil expenditures excludes spending on debt service, capital outlays, adult education, community services, and payments to other school systems
Source: U.S. Census Bureau, 2019 Annual Survey of School System Finances

principle that the money follows the student. The formula is based on a core instructional amount, a poverty weight as a proxy for student supports, and a state share ratio that considers a district's ability to generate revenues and its poverty concentration. The funding formula, phased in over ten years, redistributes funding such that less affluent school districts receive a greater allocation of state funding, while more affluent districts receive a proportionally lesser share. State education aid provided through the formula grew from $5,393 per pupil in FY 2012—the first year the formula went into effect—to $7,395 per pupil in FY 2022. However, local funding in some communities did not grow at the same pace, such that some urban districts remain among the lowest in per pupil expenditures.[26] This funding inequity, together with poor student outcomes in urban districts, likely will soon require reassessment of the current funding scheme.

While the school funding formula provided greater state aid to education, targeting more funding to less affluent communities, the capital needs of school districts in Rhode Island had long been neglected. The state historically has supported school construction through reimbursement of a share of completed project costs according to a share ratio based on a community's property wealth. Following a four-year moratorium on most new school construction projects beginning in 2011, the General Assembly enacted comprehensive legislation temporarily expanding incentives to enhance the aid share ratio for school construction projects meeting certain criteria. This increase in state support was funded through a $250 million bond approved by voters in November 2018, with a second $250 million bond planned to be submitted to voters in November 2022. Since the school construction aid expansion was adopted, approximately $1.8 million in school building projects have been approved or are expected to be approved.[27]

State and local spending on public safety made up only 8.2 percent of Rhode Island's total expenditures in FY 2019, but the Ocean State spent more in this category on a per capita and per income basis than any other New England state. Compared to the United States, Rhode Island spent 23.1 percent more in per capita terms. Spending in this category was driven largely by Rhode Island's high police and fire protection expenditures (fire protection expenditures were the highest per capita in the nation in FY 2019).[28]

In contrast, Rhode Island's transportation expenditures, consisting of 5.1 percent of all state and local spending in FY 2019, were low for the nation but typical for New England.[29] The condition of Rhode Island's roads and bridges has been reported recently as among the worst in the nation.[30] In response, the state in 2016 embarked on an ambitious RhodeWorks program, which included new truck-only tolls, to invest more in roads and bridges. The program's impact on transportation spending is already evident as spending in this category grew at a higher rate than total expenditures (27.0 percent vs. 16.1 percent) between FY 2014 and FY 2019.[31]

Consistent with the general political consensus for fiscal conservatism, Rhode Island has taken steps to improve its financial position and spending practices over the past two decades. In 2006, the General Assembly and voters approved a constitutional amendment to further limit spending to 97 percent (from 98 percent) of estimated revenues, to increase the rainy-day fund from 3 percent to 5 percent of revenues, and to dedicate 3 percent of current revenues each year to fund capital projects. The Ocean State also has dramatically reduced the state's debt level over time. After reaching a peak debt ratio of 8.4 percent of personal income in FY 1994, the state reduced its overall debt level significantly over time, such that the projected debt ratio for FY 2022 is only 3 percent, below the guideline recommended by the state's Public Finance Management Board.[32]

Outlook for the Future

Since the turn of this century, taxing and spending policies in Rhode Island have been marked by stability and a generally conservative approach by policymakers. Dramatic changes have been few and have typically resulted from disruptive events, like the Great Recession, federal program expansions (as in the case of Obamacare), or urgent situations (like the severely underfunded state pension plan). At the state level, tax changes generally have aimed toward reducing taxes on business. At the municipal level, the phase-out of the motor vehicle tax is the most noteworthy development. Besides Medicaid expansion, funded almost entirely with federal funding, major state spending initiatives largely have been limited to a new school funding formula, and an expansion of school construction aid.

Rhode Island is potentially entering a period of change, however. In response to the COVID-19 pandemic, the federal government had transferred unprecedented levels of funding to state and local governments. As of FY 2022, federal COVID relief to Rhode Island is expected to total approximately $6.7 billion, including $1.25 million to the state under the Coronavirus Aid, Relief, and Economic Security Act, nearly $1.8 billion to state and local governments under the American Rescue Plan Act, and over $600 million to K–12 education under various COVID relief measures. While this one-time funding presents tremendous opportunities to address long-standing needs and bring transformative changes, it also could lead to unsustainable spending commitments. Regardless, this massive infusion of federal funding undoubtedly will alter spending priorities and expenditure patterns for years to come.

Perhaps as significant is the political change taking place in the General Assembly, as progressive legislators have gained greater influence in both chambers, particularly as a result of electoral wins beginning in 2020.[24] While this political shift has resulted in the enactment of more progressive legislation in areas such as climate change, reproductive rights, and pay equity, it has not yet been reflected in a significant shift in taxing and spending policies, perhaps because of the abundance of federal resources available to increase spending on government programs in the short term.

Looking ahead, it is uncertain whether these progressive political advances manifest themselves in more progressive tax policies and more generous spending initiatives, consistent with the current Democratic agenda at the national level. Alternatively, as Rhode Island's economy continues to lag the region and the country,[35] more conservative political forces may continue to hold sway in keeping Rhode Island's economic competitiveness and fiscal conservatism at the forefront of policy considerations.

> ". . . there was a lot of pressure from many, many members of the caucus who wanted to raise taxes on the rich. But when you dig into that and find out what it is, it's really raising taxes on small business."
>
> House Speaker JOSEPH SHEKARCHI explaining the Assembly's rejection of a proposed income tax hike on higher earners in 2021.[36]

Notes

1. Office of the Governor, State of Rhode Island, Press Releases, http://www.governor.ri.gov.
2. House Fiscal Advisory Staff, FY 2022 Budget as Enacted, at 36.
3. Rhode Island Department of Revenue, "New Law Requires Remote Sellers to Collect and Remit Sales and Use Tax," May 24, 2019. [AU: Is URL available?]
4. House Fiscal Advisory Staff, *FY 2012 Budget at a Glance*, at 3.
5. House Fiscal Advisory Staff, *FY 2020 Budget at a Glance*, at 2–3.
6. R. Forster, "Rhode Island Approves Tax Reform Package," Tax Foundation, June 9, 2010.
7. P. Anderson and K. Gregg, "RI House Democrats Shun Most Tax Hikes in State Budget Proposal," *Providence Journal*, June 17, 2021.
8. House Fiscal Advisory Staff, *FY 2014 Budget at a Glance*, at 8.
9. House Fiscal Advisory Staff, *FY 2015 Budget as Enacted, Special Reports*, at 69.
10. Senate Fiscal Office, *FY 2015 Budget as Enacted*, at 8; House Fiscal Advisory Staff, *FY 2016 Budget at a Glance*, at 4.
11. House Fiscal Advisory Staff, *FY 2017 Budget at a Glance*, at 36.
12. Rhode Island Public Expenditure Council, "RIPEC Analyzes Rhode Island's Improved Business Tax Climate Index Ranking of 37th Among States," December 2020.
13. Rhode Island's fiscal year runs from July 1 through June 30 of the following year; FY 2019 began on July 1, 2018, and ended on June 30, 2019.
14. In FY 2018, property taxes made up 42.3 percent of all state and local revenues in Rhode Island, compared to 32.8 percent of all state and local revenues in the United States. RHODE ISLAND Public Expenditure Council, "How Rhode Island Compares," March 2021.
15. Rhode Island Public Expenditure Council, "How Rhode Island Compares," March 2021.
16. House Fiscal Advisory Staff, *FY 2022 Budget as Enacted*, at 74950.
17. Rhode Island Public Expenditure Council, "[Property Tax Report]," to be published.
18. Rhode Island Public Expenditure Council, "An Introduction to Municipal Finance in Rhode Island," April 2021.
19. House Fiscal Advisory Staff, *FY 2022 Budget as Enacted*, at 746, 775.
20. Rhode Island Retirement Security Act of 2011, *P.L. 2011, ch. 408*.
21. Rhode Island Public Expenditure Council, "An Introduction to Municipal Finance in Rhode Island," April 2021.
22. US Census Bureau, Annual Survey of State and Local Government Finances; US Census Bureau, American Community Survey 5-Year Estimates.
23. L. Norris, "Rhode Island and the ACA's Medicaid expansion," Healthinsurance.org, November 18, 2021.
24. US Census Bureau, Annual Survey of State and Local Government Finances; US Census Bureau, American Community Survey 5-Year Estimates.
25. Rhode Island Public Expenditure Council, "How Rhode Island Compares," March 2021.
26. House Fiscal Advisory Staff, *FY 2022 Budget as Enacted*, at 77576; Rhode Island Public Expenditure Council, "An Introduction to Municipal Finance in Rhode Island," April 2021.

17. House Fiscal Advisory Staff, *FY 2022 Budget as Enacted*, at 78386. US Census Bureau, Annual Survey of State and Local Government Finances; US Census Bureau, American Community Survey 5-Year Estimates.
18. Ibid.
19. S. Stebbins, M. Sauter, and E. Comen, "Infrastructure: Unsafe roads, bridge, railways across the US, conditions by state," *USA Today*, August 18, 2020.
20. US Census Bureau, Annual Survey of State and Local Government Finances; US Census Bureau, American Community Survey 5-Year Estimates.
21. House Fiscal Advisory Staff, *FY 2022 Budget as Enacted*, at 404–7; Rhode Island Public Finance Management Board, "Debt Affordability Study," July 25, 2019.
22. House Fiscal Advisory Staff, *FY 2022 Budget as Enacted*, at 883–85.
23. J. Rock and H. August, "Progressive Democrats Sweep Rhode Island," *Nation*, October 26, 2020.
24 Rhode Island Public Expenditure Council, "Rhode Island Economic Indicator Briefing," Spring 2021.
25. J. Howell, "Shekarchi: Staving off tax hikes a success for Assembly," *Warwick Beacon*, July 22, 2021.

C / The Politics of Rhode Island Education

Diane E. Kern and Shanna Pearson Merkowitz

> "[It is the] Duty of the General Assembly to promote schools and libraries. — The diffusion of knowledge, as well as of virtue among the people, being essential to the preservation of their rights and liberties, it shall be the duty of the general assembly to promote public schools and public libraries, and to adopt all means which it may deem necessary and proper to secure to the people the advantages and opportunities of education and public library services."
>
> Rhode Island State Constitution

While the Rhode Island constitution calls on the state legislature to "promote" schools in the state, education is not a constitutional right in Rhode Island. Rhode Island is not alone in this, about half of US states have formalized a right to education for its residents.[1] As a result, in Rhode Island, all state education policy and state education funding decisions are the exclusive purview of the legislature. The court has repeatedly held they have no jurisdiction and as a result, several high-profile lawsuits alleging the state is failing at its responsibility to provide an equal and equitable education to all Rhode Island residents have failed. The legislature grants almost all education decisions, school administration, and historically, school funding, to each of the 39 municipalities, many of which have only a few schools.

After a decade-long effort by the Rhode Island Senate, several lawmakers, businesses, and education leaders attempted to change the state Constitution on this matter. The proposed bill to amend the state Constitution to guarantee "an equitable, adequate and meaningful education" passed in the state Senate but did not pass in the House.[2] Advocates argue that the ability of cities and towns to raise money matched with the low state effort in funding education has made for extremely unequal educational opportunities for students across the state. A team of education funding researchers from Rutgers University identified that spending in Rhode Island's lowest poverty towns would need to increase by $8,626 per student to meet average national outcomes, but in the lowest poverty schools, per-pupil spending was over $7,000 in excess per student to meet those same standards.[3] In short, experts find that school funding does not match the needs of school systems to deliver adequate or equitable educational opportunities and outcomes.

In this essay, we discuss the symbiotic and complex relationship of Rhode Island education and politics to understand how the sociopolitical context affects the K–12 education system and student educational success. We begin with an overview of RI educational demographics and state education funding. Next, we examine recent education reform efforts and their links to political agendas. To close, we discuss anticipated trends in the future of Rhode Island's education and politics.

Education Demographics

Rhode Island's elementary, and secondary public school system (K–12) comprises 32 single school districts, 4 regional school districts, 4 state-operated schools that are available for students statewide, 1 regional urban collaborative, and 23 charter schools that serve 39 towns and cities.[4] Approximately 143,000 students attend the 317 public elementary and secondary schools[5] and 37 public charter schools.[6]

Almost half of Rhode Island students are eligible for free and reduced-price lunch; 8.9 percent are multilingual learners; and 17.2 percent receive special education services. Two aspects of K–12 public school students' race/ethnicity changed dramatically between 2000 and 2018. First, the percentage of students who identify as White decreased from 74.3 percent in 2000 to 56.6 percent in 2018. Second, the percentage of students who identified as Hispanic increased from 14 percent in 2000 to 26.1 percent in 2018.[7]

In the 2020–21 academic year, Rhode Island had a full-time equivalent of 10,660 teachers. The student-to-teacher ratio was 13.05, meaning that for every one teacher employed in Rhode Island there are 13.05 students, slightly lower than the national average of 14.82.[8] The average salary of Rhode Island public school teachers based on 2019 data from the National Education Association was 10th highest in the nation at $67,040, but Rhode Island is the 37th most expensive state to live in (e.g., there are only 13 states in which it is more expensive to live), so teacher salaries are reflective of the state cost of living.[9]

Student Achievement

Rhode Island has been plagued by low student achievement, particularly in its urban core. English Language Arts (ELA) student achievement, as measured by 2017–18 Rhode Island Comprehensive Assessment System (RICAS), results were 40 percent proficiency for students in grade 3, 38 percent for grade 4, 37 percent for grade 5, 34 percent for grade 6, 24 percent for grade 7, and 28 percent for grade 8. Student proficiency in mathematics was 35 percent for students in grade 3, 27 percent for grade 4, 27 percent for grade 5, 25 percent for grade 6, 27 percent for grade 7, and 23 percent for grade 8. RICAS was adapted by the Rhode Island Department of Education to mirror student achievement testing more closely in nearby Massachusetts. In 2017–18, Rhode Island students scored 17 percentage points lower than Massachusetts students in ELA and 20 percentage points lower in mathematics.[10]

Inequalities by race and ethnicity are particularly striking. A report prepared by the Latino Policy Institute at Roger Williams University found that "The Latino-White achievement gaps in Rhode Island are among some of the worst in the country. In both 4th and 8th grade mathematics, for example, the disparities between Latino and White student achievement in Rhode Island are among the 10 largest across states."[11]

School Funding

U.S. school funding policies are set by each individual state. In 2010, the Rhode Island General Assembly voted to revise its school funding formula. This policy, implemented in fiscal year 2012, was revised in 2016, and includes a multi-year implementation plan to allow school districts to prepare for changes to state-supported school funding. Rhode Island's funding formula is student-based, so the money that each school district or school receives from the state is based on the specific number of and type of student in each school. Funding formulas have become a common way for states to deal with inequalities between school districts in terms of how much money towns can raise from local property taxes. This is because towns with lower-priced homes cannot raise the money needed to fund their schools, an issue called tax capacity. Rhode Island's funding formula assigns a cost of education to each student who has no special needs or services, which is referred to as a "base amount." The base amount that Rhode Island's formula assigns to each student was $10,365 in 2022. The formula then increases this amount for education-specific categories of students including English-Language Learners, low-income students, students with high-cost disabilities, and students enrolled in career and technical programs.[12] Unlike some other states, Rhode Island provides no additional funds for gifted and talented students.

While student-based funding is particularly challenging for districts with high administrative costs, and older, more expensive buildings to upkeep, the basic problem is that if a student leaves a school to go to another school, it does not reduce the amount of money that it takes to run the school. The school will still have the same number of teachers, the same principal and number of administrators, and the same building to upkeep. No costs go down with even a fairly large migration of students from a school. As a result, when students transfer to charter schools, and the funding formula has the money following the student, traditional public schools can end up having to do the same work in the same building with significantly less money. As put by the Brookings Institution, "Although such burdens may manifest themselves in higher local tax burdens, the more likely outcome is reduced spending per pupil on educational services—and hence lower educational quality —for students who remain in the district's traditional public schools."[13]

This is a problem Rhode Island has felt particularly because of the large explosion in charter school attendance. Statewide, Rhode Island's public schools lost 4,991 students between 2019 and 2021. But the enrollment drop was not distributed evenly across all schools. Traditional public schools lost 6,554 students, while public charter schools gained a net of 1,523 students.[14] However, the number of students from low-income homes, who speak English as a second language, and who have special educational needs increased during this time. As a result, the fiscal needs of many districts, most notably the urban districts, increased while they were losing students.[15] Overall, the expansion of charter schools in Rhode Island, particularly because it has come at a time of declining enrollments across the state, has meant that many schools are under-enrolled and so shrinking resources are being stretched.

Funding formulas, both in education and in other areas are very political because they must pass through the legislature, which is made up of representatives from across the state and are political institutions. Frances Lee (2000) finds that funding formulas tend to be the product of legislative coalitions.[16] Generally, funding formulas reflect the preferences of those votes in the legislature that are the "cheapest" to get, those unaffected by the new formula, combined with those with the most to gain and large numbers of votes in the legislature. In Rhode Island the urban cities such as Woonsocket, Pawtucket, Providence, Cranston, and East Providence desperately need the state funds due to their tax capacity, but they do not hold enough votes in the legislature to pass a funding formula without the assistance of representatives from more wealthy districts. Since Rhode Island's funding formula had to be passed by the state legislature, many have criticized it for having certain elements that benefit wealthier towns even though the stated objective of the funding formula is to level the playing field between towns with unequal local tax bases. As a result, the funding formula in Rhode Island since 2010 increased the amount the state contributes to education and this funding is largely targeted toward the state's low-income districts. But the school districts in the state with the lowest property values and the largest proportion of students from low-income families "are still among those with the lowest per pupil revenues and expenditures in the state."[17] A team from Rutgers University and the Education Law Center performed an analysis of state funding levels and formula distributions. Rhode Island scored well compared to other states on the amount of money spent on education given the state's ability to generate revenue. However, the state received a "D" grade for how well the money is distributed across districts to provide additional resources for students in concentrated poverty. Only 13 states received lower scores.[18]

The Politics of Education Reform

The Rhode Island Department of Education (RIDE) is the state education agency that oversees Pre-Kindergarten through high school public education and the agency through which state-appropriated school funding is dispersed to the local school districts. The Rhode Island Board of Education, a 17-member board appointed by the governor consists of two councils: The Rhode Island Council on Elementary and Secondary Education and the Council on Postsecondary Education. The Rhode Island Council on Elementary and Secondary Education provides guidance to set policy and to establish strategic plans in collaboration with RIDE.[19]

For the last decade, the politics of K–12 schools have led to an effort to bring about major reform. In 2019, the first Latina and woman of color was appointed to the role of commissioner of education and tasked with spearheading several education reform efforts aimed at addressing several failing school systems across the state, particularly the Providence Public Schools. The commissioner, the governor, and the mayor of Providence brought in the Johns Hopkins Institute for Education Policy to review and conduct a nonpartisan analysis of the Providence Public Schools. Their report, released in June 2019 revealed the disturbing reality of a broken system. In summarizing their findings, the Hopkins team determined that "[t]he great majority of students are not learning on, or even near, grade level. With rare exception, teachers are demoralized and feel unsupported. Most parents feel shut out of their children's education. Principals find it very difficult to demonstrate leadership. Many school buildings are deteriorating across the city, and some are even dangerous to students' and teachers' wellbeing."[20] Moreover, the report found that the District's English-Language learning programs were in violation of the Equal Education Opportunities Act.

The report resulted in the state taking over the school district. However, while there was basically universal agreement that the Providence Public Schools were failing and in desperate need of reform, there is little support from the city for state control and to date, state control has not come with a significant increase in funding. Recent scholarly research has criticized state takeovers, primarily because they have historically been disproportionately targeted at majority-minority districts even when those districts have higher scores than comparable white districts. In these cases, state takeovers take power out of the hands of the Black and Hispanic residents and place power over the schools with white politicians who do not live in the area. Second, recent empirical analyses of the effect of state takeovers on student outcomes find that on average, there is "no evidence that takeover generates academic benefits."[21]

The teachers' unions, particularly those in urban cities like Providence, Central Falls and Woonsocket are a constant target of politicians and the public who blame the unions for blocking efforts to increase school quality. The teachers' unions and their contracts are fairly powerful in the Ocean State, and they argue that the government has failed to give teachers the supports and equipment necessary or provide the resources to adequately pay teachers for additional time and responsibilities that would be required to "turn around" the failing schools. This is particularly important given that teachers are recruited from low performing districts to educate students in higher performing districts, sometimes with higher compensation, in suburban and exurban schools. As a result, many efforts to take power and "punish" teachers for low performance in the state's urban core has resulted in a loss of teachers and a teacher shortage, particularly in the City of Providence. Importantly, because Rhode Island is a unionized state, both the teachers in the high-performing districts and low-performing districts are unionized. As a result, it is unlikely that unions are the reason for the low performance.

Looking Forward: Rhode Island Politics and Education

The rise in organized groups of parents and those from religious and political groups set on abolishing Critical Race Theory (CRT) in K–12 schools is an indication of the intersection of politics and the importance of local school committee governance. CRT is a decades-old theory developed by legal scholars, which posits that race is a social construct that is embedded in legal policies and systems.[22] Discussions of the history of minoritized peoples, such as Black and indigenous people in the United States, have become contentious in school committee meetings. Some state lawmakers argue that teaching about racism and discrimination in grade school is causing discomfort for white children. Others believe that conversations about diversity, equity, and inclusion are necessary at all grade levels.

The confrontation of these polar opposite viewpoints has led to highly emotional, divisive, and disruptive school committee meetings. Some teachers and education leaders have received threats via email, phone, social media messages, and lawsuits. Teacher stress is high for most, and some have chosen to retire earlier than planned or just leave the profession as a result of the conflict over teaching about racism in the United States.

For quite some time—long before the beginning of the COVID pandemic in 2020 and debates on Critical Race Theory in schools—the conditions leading to a teacher shortage in Rhode Island have been present. These include low teacher salaries, oppressive bureaucratic systems, lack of understanding and respect for the profession, and limited teacher autonomy.[23] For decades, Rhode Island administrators had a difficult time filling special education, English Learner, and secondary science and mathematics teacher vacancies. Currently and for the foreseeable future, Rhode Island has teacher shortages in nearly all grade levels and certification areas,[24] which has resulted in an exponential growth in emergency and expert residency certifications for people without an education degree and sometimes without any coursework in the subject they are teaching. Substitute teachers are hard to come by, so principals and teachers fill in as needed. In some schools, classes are simply broken up and sent to sit in another grade's room when a teacher is out because of the lack of substitutes. The racial, ethnic, and linguistic diversity of the Rhode Island teacher workforce has stubbornly remained predominantly white.

The education system in Rhode Island is failing many students. Despite being an overwhelmingly one-party state, there exists no clear plan for increasing performance or improving safety and well-being in the schools. There is considerable in-fighting in the Democratic party over the role the state plays in contributing to and guaranteeing a quality education in urban districts. The design of the state constitution pits towns against each other and the system of private schools available to wealthier families also means wealthy and politically powerful communities fail to put political pressure on elected officials to fix the schools. As a result, the political and social hurdles to meaningful education reform in Rhode Island may prevent needed investment in the schools.

Notes

1. "Educational Rights in the States," American Bar Association, April 1, 2014, https://www.americanbar.org/groups/crsj/publications/human_rights_magazine_home/2014_vol_40/vol_40_no_2_civil_rights/educational_rights_states/#:~:text=Priest%20(1976)%20that%20education%20is,state%20constitutions%20in%20the%201980s.
2. State of Rhode Island General Assembly, Joint Resolution, 2022-S2095, http://webserver.rilin.state.ri.us/BillText/BillText22/SenateText22/S2095.pdf.
3. Bruce D. Baker, Mark Weber, Ajay Srikanth, Robert Kim, and Michael Atzbi, "The Real Shame of the Nation," Rutgers Graduate School of Education, n.d., http://www.schoolfundingfairness.org/.
4. "RI School Districts." Rhode Island Department of Education, n.d., https://www.ride.ri.gov/studentsfamilies/ripublicschools/schooldistricts.aspx.
5. Kathleen O'Leary Morgan and Scott Morgan, in *State Rankings 2020*, 1st ed.(CQ Press, 2020, 119–21.
6. "Elementary and Secondary Information System," National Center for Education Statistics, Institute of Education Sciences, n.d., https://nces.ed.gov/ccd/elsi/tableGenerator.aspx?savedTableID=357854.
7. "Digest of Education Statistics," National Center for Education Statistics, Institute of Education, Sciences, n.d., https://nces.ed.gov/programs/digest/2020menu_tables.asp.
8. "Elementary," National Center for Education Statistics.
9. O'Leary Morgan and Morgan, *Rankings*, 123.
10. "Rhode Island Fully Transitioned to New Student Assessments," Rhode Island Department of Education, n.d., https://www.ride.ri.gov/InsideRIDE/Additional-Information/News/ViewArticle/tabid/408/ArticleId/526/Rhode-Island-Fully-Transitioned-to-New-Student-Assessments.aspx.
11. James P. Huguley, "Latino Students in Rhode Island: A Review of Local and National Performances," Rhode Island Department of Education, The Latino Policy Institute at Roger Williams University, n.d., https://www.ride.ri.gov/Portals/0/Uploads/Documents/Funding-and-Finance-Wise-Investments/Funding-Sources/State-Education-Aid-Funding-Formula/FundingFormula WorkingGroup/AnnaCanoMorales-01.pdf.
12. "FundEd: State Policy Analysis," EdBuild, n.d., http://funded.edbuild.org/state/RI.
13. John Singleton and Helen F. Ladd, "Charter School Growth Puts Fiscal Pressure on Traditional Public Schools," Brookings Institution, May 1, 2018, https://www.brookings.edu/blog/brown-center-chalkboard/2018/05/01/charter-school-growth-puts-fiscal-pressure-on-traditional-public-schools/.
14. Steph Machado, "RI Public School Enrollment down by Nearly 5,000 Students during Pandemic," *WPRI*, February 7, 2022, https://www.wpri.com/target-12/ri-public-school-enrollment-down-by-nearly-5000-students-during-pandemic/.
15. Special Education Expenditures," Data Center, Rhode Island Department of Education, n.d., https://datacenter.ride.ri.gov/Finance/Report?repname=SpecialEducationExpenditures&repgroup=ExpenditureReports.
16. "Senate Representation and Coalition Building in Distributive Politics," *American Political Science Review* 94, no. 1 (March 2000): 59–72, https://www.jstor.org/

stable/pdf/2586380.pdf?casa_token=M_n0a0guMc4AAAAA:W5vuiWpZflWx2s7
Jnb4M92qAZoIKbu2rpU48NXSecS-3axcP7aV7XX1OEBLYm2WNOaiCr4Lui
V3Za5cApU_t4LS8lJHvC82vKG7hRKrmtRELTX6QN80.
17. "Rhode Island's Funding Formula After Ten Years: Education Finance in the Ocean State," Rhode Island Public Expenditure Council, April 2022, https://ripec.org/wp-content/uploads/2022/04/2022_Education_Finance.pdf.
18. Bruce D. Baker, Danielle Farrie, and David Sciarra, "Is School Funding Fair? A National Report Card," Education Law Center, Rutgers Graduate School of Education, February 2018, https://edlawcenter.org/assets/files/pdfs/publications/Is_School_Funding_Fair_7th_Editi.pdf.
19. "Board of Education," Rhode Island Department of Education, n.d., https://www.ride.ri.gov/boardofeducation/overview.aspx.
20. "Institute Leads Review of the Providence Public School District," Institute for Education Policy, Johns Hopkins School of Education, June 25, 2019, https://edpolicy.education.jhu.edu/institute-leads-review-of-the-providence-public-school-district/.
21. Beth E. Schueler and Joshua F Bleiberg, "Evaluating Education Governance: Does State Takeover of School Districts Affect Student Achievement?" *Journal of Policy Analysis and Management* 41, no. 1 (October 4, 2021), https://onlinelibrary.wiley.com/doi/abs/10.1002/pam.22338#:~:text=On%20average%2C%20we%20find%20no,heterogeneity%20of%20effects%20across%20districts.
22. Stephen Sawchuk, "What Is Critical Race Theory, and Why Is It Under Attack?," *Education Week*, May 18, 2021, https://www.edweek.org/leadership/what-is-critical-race-theory-and-why-is-it-under-attack/2021/05.
23. Diana D'Amico Pawlewicz, "Today's Teacher Shortages Are Part of a Longer Pattern," *Washington Post*, November 18, 2021, https://www.washingtonpost.com/outlook/2021/11/18/todays-teacher-shortages-are-part-longer-pattern/.
24 "Rhode Island Educator Preparation Index," Rhode Island Department of Education, n.d., https://tableau.ride.ri.gov/t/Public/views/EdPrepIndex/Dashboard_Summary?%3Adisplay_count=n&%3Aembed=y&%3AisGuestRedirectFrom Vizportal=y&%3Aorigin=viz_share_link&%3AshowAppBanner=false&%3 AshowVizHome=n.

D / Health Policy in Rhode Island

ROBERT B. HACKEY, COLLEEN M. KENNEDY,
AND MICHAELA C. SZYMCZAK

In healthcare reform, Rhode Island lives up to its long-time marketing slogan as "the biggest little state in the union." Rhode Island has been an incubator of health policy innovation for several decades. The state was an early adopter of health planning and rate-setting programs in the 1970s and 1980s. State officials also embraced the implementation of the Affordable Care Act over the past decade. In recent years Rhode Island also developed innovative approaches to transform provider payment from a fee-for-service reimbursement system to value-based payment models. Compared to many states, the state's coordinated response to the COVID-19 pandemic also contributed to a highly successful vaccination campaign. By July 2022, 99 percent of Rhode Islanders were at least partially vaccinated, nearly 85 percent had completed their primary vaccination series, and nearly 42 percent had received a booster.[1] Notably, Rhode Island was one of only four states to achieve a 99 percent vaccination rate among nursing home staff.[2]

Few health policy issues, however, can be 'cured.' Instead, public officials strive to manage a variety of complex and interrelated chronic problems.[3] Under these circumstances, the administrative and fiscal capacity of state policy-making institutions shapes policy-makers' ability to manage difficult health policy problems.[4] During the COVID-19 pandemic, for example, Governor Gina Raimondo exercised broad powers. She declared a public health emergency, imposed statewide mask mandates and social distancing requirements, limited the size of indoor and outdoor gatherings, and required businesses to limit their hours of operation and the number of persons served. In other health policy realms, however, the authority of state officials is contested; a lack of consensus among key stakeholders often stymies action.

Health policy in Rhode Island and in the United States is defined by trade-offs among competing values.[5] Policy-makers can prioritize increasing access to care, improving the quality of care, or controlling the cost of care, but no healthcare system has found a way to realize all three of these goals. Many of the state's most pressing health policy challenges—from ensuring the fiscal stability of the state's hospitals and nursing homes to addressing the worsening opioid epidemic—require sustained (and costly) investments. Until the COVID-19 pandemic provided state policy-makers with a historic infusion of federal funds, Rhode Island struggled with an ongoing structural deficit. Ongoing fiscal constraints, in turn, limited the ability of state officials to manage long-term health policy issues.

In Rhode Island, a strong commitment to ensuring access to healthcare shaped health policy choices in recent decades. The size of the Medicaid program underscores the state's commitment to access as a principal health policy goal. In February 2022, one in three Rhode Islanders—346,545 persons—was enrolled in Medicaid. Rhode Island's Medicaid enrollment increased 81 percent after the implementation of the Affordable Care Act in 2013, compared to a 52 percent increase in the United States during the same period.[6] The growth of Medicaid enrollment in Rhode Island was the 12th highest in the nation.[7] Rhode Island was also one of the first states in the nation to create a state-based health insurance marketplace. Its marketplace—Health Source RI—is widely regarded as policy success in terms of expanding access to—and choice among—affordable insurance for individuals and small businesses.

Beginning in the 1960s, Rhode Island established a national reputation as an early innovator in regulating hospitals and healthcare facilities. Rhode Island became the second state in the nation to enact certificate of need regulation in 1968 to control the rising cost of hospital care.[8] In the early 1970s, state officials also partnered with hospitals and insurers to pioneer a new model of hospital rate setting to determine the allowed annual increase in statewide hospital costs (the 'Maxicap') and negotiated budgets and volume statistics for each of the state's acute care hospitals.[9] In the mid-1970s, Rhode Island's rate-setting approach caught the eye of federal officials in the Department of Health, Education and Welfare, and the state was selected as one of the nation's first federal prospective payment experiments.[10] The Maxicap process remained in place from its inception in 1971 through 2009. During the 1970s, Rhode Island also developed a strong health planning infrastructure, drawing upon federal funds available through the National Health Planning and Resources Development Act (Pub. L. 93-641). In most states, health planning funds were allocated to local health planning agencies but given Rhode Island's small size the state Department of Health was designated as the lead agency. The infusion of federal funds allowed the state to develop a strong planning and data analysis infrastructure in the 1970s and 1980s.

Health Insurance Regulation

Rhode Island's health insurance market is dominated by three major players: Blue Cross and Blue Shield of RI (BCBSRI), Neighborhood Health Plan of RI, and United Healthcare. Neighborhood Health Plan is the state's principal insurer for Medicaid patients. Three insurers (Blue Cross, United Healthcare, and Tufts Health Plan) control the private health insurance market for large groups, but BCBSRI holds a 79 percent market share.[11] Rhode Island established the Office of the Health Insurance Commissioner (OHIC) to oversee the state's health insurance market in 2004. In 2010, OHIC developed new health insurance affordability standards that included extensive consumer protections, payment reforms to transition away from fee for service reimbursement, and limits on insurers' premium increases. OHIC serves a unique role that sets it apart from other state insurance regulators because it capped the reimbursement rate insurers pay to hospitals.[12] In addition, the new affordability standards required insurers to increase their spending on primary care and encouraged insurers to shift towards payment based on the value of services provided rather than volume.[13] As a result of these changes, Rhode Island recorded significant changes in healthcare spending as fee-for-service spending declined by $76 per enrollee from 2009–16, a reduction of 8.1 percent.[14]

Rhode Island also created a statewide expenditure target to limit the growth of healthcare costs to no more than 3.2 percent.[15] According to the Office of the Health Insurance Commissioner (OHIC), "Rhode Island leads all states in the number of mandated benefits required, including benefit, provider, and coverage mandates."[16] These state-mandated benefits—including requirements for insurers to cover autism treatment, hearing aids, home healthcare, intravenous therapy for Lyme disease, among others—were estimated to increase the cost of health insurance premiums by more than 10 percent of the average monthly premium.[17]

The Hospital Industry in Transition

Rhode Island hospitals operate in a difficult environment, sandwiched between two larger healthcare markets—Boston and New Haven—both with larger, well-financed hospital systems that seek to expand their reach into new markets. The hospital industry in Rhode Island is dominated by two competing non-profit hospital systems: Lifespan and Care New England. Since their formation in the mid-1990s, both systems engaged in an on-again, off-again courtship. With five hospitals, including Rhode Island Hospital, Hasbro Children's Hospital, the Miriam Hospital, Newport Hospital, and Bradley Hospital, Lifespan is the state's largest private employer. Care New England's three member hospitals include Women and Infants' Hospital, a tertiary care center for women's health and neonatal care that delivers 70 percent of the state's births; Kent Hospital, a community hospital in Warwick; and Butler Hospital, the state's principal psychiatric hospital for adults. Three hospitals—Roger Williams Medical Center, Our Lady of Fatima, and Landmark Medical Center—are owned by out of state for-profit systems, while Westerly Hospital was acquired by Yale New Haven Health. Only South County Hospital remains an independent, unaffiliated non-profit institution.

Over the past three decades, Rhode Island created one of the nation's most stringent regulatory environments for the hospital industry. The state's Hospital Conversions Act (HCA)—enacted in the late 1990s—subjects hospital mergers or acquisitions to an extensive review by the Office of the Attorney General and the Rhode Island Department of Health. As Attorney General Peter Neronha noted, the state's review process focuses on how any transactions "will impact cost, quality and access to care for the people of Rhode Island."[18] In addition, Rhode Island has some of the nation's most comprehensive and detailed charity care requirements in the nation to ensure hospitals meet their responsibilities to the community as a condition of new or continued licensure.[19]

Lifespan and Care New England engaged in an on-again, off-again courtship since the mid-1990s. After an initial merger attempt in 1998 failed, the two systems returned to the bargaining table in 2007 with a new proposal to create an academic medical center in partnership with Brown University. Once again, however, the merger fell apart.[20] After two unsuccessful merger attempts, Care New England turned to potential out-of-state suitors. However, the prospect of an out-of-state system acquiring Care New England raised concerns among key stakeholders in Rhode Island. Governor Raimondo urged Lifespan and Care New England to resume merger negotiations in 2019, arguing that a locally controlled academic medical center "is in the best interest of Rhode Island, and that it is viable from a financial standpoint. . . . A local AMC would ensure topnotch doctors and care remain in Rhode Island, maintain local governance committed to the community, drive medical innovation and research, and enhance world-class medical education."[21] In the wake of the governor's request, Partners (now MassGeneral Brigham Health) withdrew its bid for Care New England.

After two years of negotiations, Care New England and Lifespan announced plans to create an integrated academic health system with Brown University in 2021. Attorney General Peter Neronha, however, rejected the proposed collaboration in February 2022. In a 150-page decision, issued the same day that the Federal Trade Commission also announced its intention to challenge the merger, Neronha warned that combining the two systems would create a behemoth with "extraordinary and unprecedented" market power. Neronha warned that "When a system is so big, so dominant, that it is the only system that the vast majority of patients will go to for, say, inpatient care, that system no longer has to do the hard work to strive to be better than the alternative, because there is no alternative."[22] This language of the decision—and the FTC's challenge to the proposal—marked the end of more than two decades of strategic negotiations between the two systems. As Lifespan CEO Timothy Babineau noted, "the way it was denied this time—as opposed to prior attempts—it doesn't look like it's going to happen anytime in the near future."[23]

Nevertheless, the financial health of both systems continues to raise concerns.[24] After surviving COVID with the help of federal stimulus funds, the state's two largest hospital systems now face a challenging economic climate defined by staffing shortages and rising costs. In July 2022, Care New England announced it would "pursue a strategy of operating the health system independently" and not seek an out-of-state partnership with another health system.[25] Moving forward, however, it is unclear how hospitals will regain their financial footing and invest in needed renovations and upgrades.

Eleanor Slater Hospital

Eleanor Slater Hospital (ESH)—the state-operated hospital of 'last resort'—has been plagued by concerns about quality of care, staffing, and rising costs over the past decade. ESH operates two campuses—one in Burrillville, the other in Cranston—that care for patients with complex social problems (e.g., substance use disorder), psychiatric conditions, and individuals who require complex, round-the-clock care.[26] The hospital also operates the state's inpatient forensic psychiatry unit. ESH experienced ongoing quality-of-care challenges, and in 2021 the hospital was cited by inspectors from the state Department of Health for significant deficiencies that placed patients in "immediate jeopardy."[27] These concerns were so significant that the state was notified by the Centers for Medicare and Medicaid Services (CMS) that ESH no longer satisfied basic Medicare conditions of participation. The ongoing problems at ESH underscore the chronic nature of health policy issues in Rhode Island.

New budgetary worries also accompanied ongoing concerns about the quality of patient care at ESH. Over time, the hospital's per patient costs increased dramatically. CMS officials questioned whether ESH met the criteria for participation in Medicaid as a long-term care hospital. By 2019, a majority of the patients at ESH no longer qualified for Medicaid reimbursement since they were under treatment for psychiatric or substance abuse conditions (Medicare and Medicaid do not pay for psychiatric care provided in state hospitals). As a result, additional state funds were needed to fill the shortfall. State contributions to support ESH more than doubled in recent years, rising from $55 million in FY 2020 to $115 million in FY 2022.[28] By 2022, the state paid 81 percent of the hospital's total operating cost, compared to 45 percent in FY 2020. The Rhode Island Public Expenditure Council (RIPEC) described the challenges facing ESH as "the most troubling spending issue in state government, with sharp increases in state general revenues, relatively high patient costs, and continuing questions as to future spending."[29] With fewer than 200 patients served by the hospital, the House Fiscal Office estimated that costs at ESH increased by 37 percent in recent years, from $557,000 per patient in FY 2020 to $764,000 in FY 2021.[30]

In the spring of 2022, the McKee administration proposed to construct a new medical facility for ESH and designating the existing hospital in Cranston as a standalone state-funded psychiatric hospital.[31] Solutions to the hospital's quality-of-care deficiencies, however, defy an easy fix in a tight labor market. At the conclusion of the 2022 legislative session, legislators approved the McKee administration's proposal to construct a new $108 million facility on the hospital's Burrillville campus.[32] This investment opens the door for enhanced federal Medicaid reimbursement, potentially generating tens of millions of dollars in cost savings for the state.

The Future of Long-Term Care

Nursing homes in Rhode Island, according to industry groups, "are in the midst of an unprecedented and growing economic and labor crisis."[33] Several nursing homes closed during the COVID-19 pandemic, while many other facilities remain in precarious financial condition. In addition, expenses for long-term care represent a large and growing proportion of the state's budget. In 2021, Rhode Island spent more than $400 million on nursing home care through its Medicaid program.[34] Provider groups, however, argue that Medicaid reimbursement fails to keep up with rising operating costs. A study commissioned by the American Health Care Association found that 95 percent of Rhode Island nursing homes were losing money and 87 percent were at "financial risk"—the highest percentage of any state.[35]

Struggling to rebound from the COVID-19 pandemic, the state's 79 nursing home facilities face significant staffing shortages in a tight labor market. More than 1,900 nursing home positions remained unfilled across the state in 2022. The state's nursing home workforce decreased by 21 percent since 2020. Staffing shortages led nursing homes to either suspend new admissions or reduce their patient census, reducing access to care for frail elders and creating a dilemma for hospitals and families. Occupancy rates in Rhode Island nursing homes fell from 88.6 percent in early 2020 to 80.1 percent in May 2022—a net reduction of more than 600 available beds.[36]

Rhode Island emerged as a national leader in regulating the nursing home industry. In 2021, Governor Dan McKee signed the nation's strictest staffing law for nursing homes. The new law required all facilities to provide at least 3.58 hours of direct nursing care per resident, per day, beginning on January 1, 2022, and also mandated that nursing homes dedicate 80 percent of future Medicaid rate increases to improve wages and benefits for staff. McKee hailed the new law as "a step forward for staff, residents and their families" and declared that "stronger staffing standards and [more] funding for direct care staff will help raise the bar on resident care in our state."[37] This optimistic assessment was not shared by industry groups, however, who argued that the law was simply unworkable. Nursing homes complained that the new law "sets a staffing mandate that requires the hiring of over 800 new employees when our homes already cannot meet existing job demand."[38]

Weeks after the new staffing requirements went into effect, Governor McKee issued an executive order temporarily suspending the minimum staffing ratios. As Senator Josh Miller argued, "we can't have these fines that will cripple nursing homes at the same time we are still struggling from COVID."[39] Supporters of the staffing law expressed disappointment and outrage at the delay, arguing that "the only way to end the nursing home staffing crisis is to improve wages and working conditions and make nursing homes safer for staff and residents."[40] Both sides hoped that the General Assembly would resolve this issue during the 2022 legislative session.[41] Legislators, however, failed to reach an agreement. As Senate President Dominick Ruggerio quipped "We thought we had an agreement on that. Apparently, we didn't.... You know this place; you never know what will happen [until] the last couple of minutes."[42] In 2022, the future of the new staffing regulations—and their financial consequences for the industry—remain uncertain.

Implementing the Affordable Care Act

Efforts to expand access to health insurance in Rhode Island predated the passage of the Affordable Care Act (ACA). HealthRIght, a broad-based advocacy group comprised of businesses, providers, and community groups, formed in 2007 to press for healthcare reform.[43] At the same time Lieutenant Governor Elizabeth Roberts created a "Healthy Rhode Island" advisory group in 2008 and introduced legislation to establish a "Health Insurance Access Hub" modeled after the Massachusetts Health Insurance Connector (e.g., "RomneyCare"). Although the General Assembly did not act upon its own reform legislation before the passage of the ACA in 2010, policy-makers and key stakeholders demonstrated a keen interest in pursuing comprehensive reform.

Rhode Island was well positioned to design and implement the ACA once it became law. After taking office in 2011, Governor Lincoln Chafee asked Lieutenant Governor Roberts to coordinate the state's implementation efforts. Disagreements over funding abortion coverage, however, led to a legislative deadlock over the state's new "health benefits exchange." Governor Chafee established the exchange (now known as HealthSource RI) through an executive order in September 2011 to break the impasse.[44] Over the past decade, all three governors—Lincoln Chafee, an Independent, and Democrats Gina Raimondo and Dan McKee—also embraced the expansion of Medicaid eligibility to previously uninsured individuals under the ACA.

Funding for HealthSource RI emerged as an ongoing concern among policy-makers soon after the implementation of the ACA in 2013. In particular, legislators expressed concerns about the fiscal burden of the new exchange—estimated to cost between $17.9 million and $23.9 million per year—once federal subsidies ended in 2015. Since Chafee's executive order prohibited the use of general revenue funds to finance the ongoing operation of the exchange, policy-makers needed to identify a dedicated funding stream to support the state's new marketplace. Business groups argued that only those residents who purchased coverage through HealthSource RI should pay for its ongoing operations and opposed any proposals to fund the exchange through a fee on all insurance policies or claims.[45]

After the end of the first open enrollment period in May 2014, critics argued that Rhode Island would be better served by transitioning to the federal marketplace (healthcare.gov) rather than incurring the ongoing expense of operating a state-based exchange. Mike Stenhouse, the CEO of the RI Center for Freedom and Prosperity, asked "why should Rhode Islanders pay for an inefficient bureaucracy when a less costly federal alternative is available?"[46] The *Providence Journal* concurred with this assessment and editorialized that "[i]f there is a powerful argument to keep the state program going at a cost of $23 million annually, we have not heard it. If Rhode Island is to move forward, its leaders will have to spend more frugally. This seems one area ripe for cutting."[47] Others argued that additional funding for HealthSource RI would divert resources from other important programs at a time when the state faced a challenging fiscal climate.[48] Key stakeholders, however, including Blue Cross and Blue Shield of RI, Neighborhood Health Plan, and the Rhode Island Medical Society, persuaded legislators and the Raimondo administration to preserve funding for HealthSource RI.[49] To do so, the General Assembly and the Raimondo administration agreed to a surcharge on monthly health insurance premiums for individuals and small businesses.[50]

Rhode Island emerged as a success story in the implementation of the ACA over the past decade. In 2012—the year before the implementation of the ACA—more than 112,000 Rhode Islanders (10.9 percent of the population) were uninsured.[51] By 2018, fewer than 39,000 Rhode Islanders lacked health insurance—a 66 percent decline since 2010.[52] Most newly insured Rhode Islanders gained coverage through the state's Medicaid expansion. In FY 2020, Rhode Island spent more than $3.1 billion on Medicaid including $1.2 billion in state funds.[53] Medicaid consumed 26 percent of total state expenditures in FY 2020, the fifth highest proportion in the nation.[54] Medicaid enrollment increased from 182,000 individuals in 2012 to 253,000 in 2018.[55] The COVID-19 pandemic further expanded Medicaid eligibility by removing requirements for recertification and increasing the federal government's share of Medicaid costs. Since 2013, Rhode Island's Medicaid enrollment increased by 75 percent (143,000 persons), the 11th-highest percentage increase in the nation.[56]

In September 2016, Rhode Island unveiled its long-awaited Unified Health Infrastructure Project, informally known as UHIP. This massive information technology (IT) project, initiated under the Chafee administration in 2011, sought to integrate a disparate collection of aging health and human services data systems. Supporters—and the state's principal consultant, Deloitte—promised the new system would streamline the process of applying for benefits and also improve reimbursement for health and human service providers. UHIP's launch in 2016 was widely regarded as "an epic failure": "Within months, the state had a backlog of 15,000 applications for various forms of public assistance."[57] Deloitte was pilloried for what was described as an "unmitigated, self-inflicted disaster, clogging a system that assists individuals from birth—through medical coverage—to death."[58] The most expensive IT project in state history, UHIP was originally projected to cost $119 million by the Chafee administration, but ultimately cost more than $700 million. In 2021, the McKee administration renewed the state's contract with Deloitte for an additional three years at a cost of $99.4 million.[59]

The UHIP debacle offers a cautionary tale for health policy reform. Rhode Island lacked the administrative capacity and experience with large-scale IT projects to successfully manage such a massive undertaking. Rhode Island's ambitious IT project was "the only eligibility system in the country that integrates more than ten state and federal health and human services programs and a state-based health insurance exchange." Executives from Deloitte—the state's consulting firm and project manager—testified that the state needed "more time, more people, and more training" before its launch in 2016.[60] The state's desire to create an ambitious and pathbreaking model, in short, required far more oversight and expertise than public bureaucrats possessed.

Rhode Island adopted a proactive stance to protect the health insurance coverage gains achieved through the ACA. In 2017, Congress repealed the financial penalty for individuals who did not purchase health insurance coverage with the passage of the Tax Cuts and Jobs Act (TCJA). Since the TCJA was widely regarded as an attempt to repeal "Obamacare," many Democratic-led states—including Rhode Island—adopted new state-level health insurance mandates. The General Assembly enacted a "shared responsibility penalty" for individuals who did not maintain "minimum essential coverage" as defined by the ACA. Beginning on January 1, 2020, uninsured residents faced a state penalty of either 2.5 percent of their yearly household income or $695 per person (and an additional $347.50 per child under age 18), whichever amount is higher. The maximum penalty, however, cannot exceed the total cost of an annual premium for an average bronze plan sold through the state marketplace.

Opioid Epidemic

Unintentional deaths from opioid use increased dramatically in Rhode Island over the past decade.[61] In 2017, state health officials estimated that 20,000 Rhode Islanders were struggling with opioid addiction.[62] Deaths from opioid overdoses more than doubled from 180 in 2012 to 384 in 2020.[63] By 2021, opioid-related deaths reached an all-time high, claiming the lives of 435 Rhode Islanders.[64] Although opioid deaths declined in 2018 and 2019, Rhode Island had the 13th-highest drug overdose mortality rate in the country, and the highest in New England.[65] The COVID-19 pandemic exacerbated the state's ongoing opioid epidemic by limiting access to in-person treatment and rehabilitation services. The state has a long waiting list for treatment beds. In July 2022, all 432 of the state's inpatient behavioral health beds were filled, and 40 individuals were waiting for a bed.[66]

To combat the opioid crisis, Rhode Island embraced a comprehensive harm-reduction strategy. The Raimondo administration sought to improve access to medication-assisted treatment (e.g., methadone, suboxone), and in 2016, Rhode Island became the first state in the nation to provide incarcerated individuals with access to all approved treatments for opioid-use disorder.[67] The state also expanded coverage of medication-assisted treatment under Medicaid for formerly incarcerated persons. Taken together, these policies contributed to a 61 percent decrease in opioid-related deaths among incarcerated individuals—a remarkable policy success.[68] As Governor Raimondo declared in 2018, "we're the only state in America that has a state-supported, state-funded, full range of medically assisted treatment in the prisons . . . and it is working."[69] The state's commitment to harm reduction can be traced back nearly three decades when the legislature first authorized a pilot needle exchange program to control the spread of HIV/AIDS.[70] In 2021, Rhode Island emerged as a national leader in harm reduction by authorizing the licensing of safe consumption sites staffed by professionals trained in CPR and managing overdoses.[71] The implementation of the new law, however, remains a work in progress. As of July 2022, no safe injection sites were licensed for operation in Rhode Island.[72]

Rhode Island also pursued legal action against drug manufacturers, distributors, and other parties that contributed to the growing use of opioids. In 2021, the state received $2.59 million from a settlement with one of the nation's largest pharmaceutical consulting firms to fund expanded treatment, recovery, and prevention programs.[73] In 2022, Rhode Island also reached a $112 million settlement with several drug distributors for their role in fueling the opioid epidemic. State officials pledged to improve access to opioid treatment, needle exchange programs, and safe injection sites.[74]

Reproductive Health

As the most Catholic state in the nation, Rhode Island charted a middle path on abortion rights in recent decades. Most Rhode Islanders are pro-choice, as is the majority of the state's Congressional delegation. In 2019, Governor Raimondo (D) signed the Reproductive Privacy Act (RPA), formally codifying the protections offered by *Roe v. Wade* into state law and the Rhode Island Supreme Court rejected a challenge to the Reproductive Privacy Act in May 2022.[75] The future of abortion rights in many states is now unsettled, but the US Supreme Court's decision in *Dobbs v. Jackson Women's Health Organization* had little impact in Rhode Island. Support for abortion rights is now firmly entrenched among key legislative leaders. After the Court's ruling, House Speaker Joseph Shekarchi observed that "*Roe v. Wade* was codified into state statute, so the women of Rhode Island continue to be able to make the personal decision to access safe and legal abortion. . . . . As a result, no Rhode Islander is losing rights today."[76] Senate leaders declared that "The Reproductive Privacy Act has been law in Rhode Island for three years now and . . . we will not entertain any effort to amend that statute."[77]

Nevertheless, some abortion rights supporters criticized state officials for failing to make abortion more affordable and accessible. Rhode Island currently does not allow for public funding of abortion for state workers and Medicaid recipients. To expand coverage to all Rhode Island women, Governor Dan McKee announced his support for the Equality in Abortion Coverage Act (EACA) in May 2021. For the second straight year, however, the legislation failed to pass. Although legislative leaders promised to take up the EACA again in 2023, reproductive health advocates demanded that legislators convene a special session to consider the bill after the Supreme Court's ruling in *Dobbs*. Senate President Dominick Ruggerio—a pro-life Democrat—dismissed such calls.[78] Governor Dan McKee issued an executive order protecting Rhode Island–based providers who offer abortion services from legal liability in other states and also introduced safeguards for out-of-state patients seeking abortions in Rhode Island. As McKee declared, "Women should be trusted with their own health care decisions and here in Rhode Island we firmly support a right to choose."[79] Improving access to reproductive health services for low-income women will require a fiscal commitment from the General Assembly, as senators noted that "the EACA has financial implications and should be considered as part of the budget."[80] Thus, while the right to obtain an abortion remains secure in Rhode Island, access to abortion services remains unequal.

Health Policy-making in the Nation's Smallest State

In February 2022, Dr. William Binder, an emergency medicine physician and editor-in-chief of the *Rhode Island Medical Journal*, wrote that "the future of healthcare in Rhode Island is at a crossroads. It will take a collaborative effort to solve Rhode Island's healthcare woes."[81] As a small state, Rhode Island has a long history of developing innovative approaches to address difficult health policy problems. Looking ahead, the principal challenge for policy-makers will be to ensure that promising ideas receive the funding and administrative support needed to sustain interventions over the long term.

Notes

1. "Rhode Island Covid-19 Vaccine Data," Rhode Island Department of Health, 2022, https://ri-department-of-health-covid-19-vaccine-data-rihealth.hub.arcgis.com/.
2. Priya Chidambaram and MaryBeth Musumeci, "Nursing Home Staff Vaccination Rates Vary Widely by State as Vaccination Mandates Take Effect," Kaiser Family Foundation, February 17, 2022, https://www.kff.org/coronavirus-covid-19/issue-brief/nursing-home-staff-vaccination-rates-vary-widely-by-state-as-vaccination-mandates-take-effect/.
3. Robert B. Hackey, *Cries of Crisis: Rethinking the Health Care Debate* (Reno: University of Nevada Press, 2012).
4. Robert B. Hackey, "Trapped Between State and Market: Regulating Hospital Reimbursement in the Northeastern States," *Medical Care Review* 49, no. 3 (1992): 355–88, https://doi.org/10.1177/002570879204900304.
5. William Kissick, *Medicine's Dilemmas: Infinite Need and Finite Resources* (New Haven, CT: Yale University Press, 1994).
6. "Medicaid and CHIP in Rhode Island," Medicaid, Center for Medicare and Medicaid Services, 2022, https://www.medicaid.gov/state-overviews/stateprofile.html?state=rhode-island.
7. "Total Monthly Medicaid/CHIP Enrollment and Pre-ACA Enrollment," Kaiser Family Foundation, March 2022, https://www.kff.org/health-reform/state-indicator/total-monthly-medicaid-and-chip-enrollment/.
8. Gerard Goulet, "Certificate-of-Need Over Hospitals in Rhode Island: A Forty-Year Retrospective," *Roger Williams University Law Review* 15, no. 1 (2010): 127–86, https://docs.rwu.edu/rwu_LR/vol15/iss1/5/.
9. Robert B. Hackey, "Setting Limits through Global Budgeting: Hospital Cost Containment in Rhode Island," *Spectrum* 69, no. 1 (1996): 6–16.
10. Hackey, "Setting Limits."
11. "Market Share and Enrollment of Largest Three Insurers—Large Group Market," Kaiser Family Foundation, 2019, https://www.kff.org/other/state-indicator/market-share-and-enrollment-of-largest-three-insurers-large-group-market/.
12. James A. Fanale and Timothy J Babineau. "Opinion/Fanale and Babineau: Status Quo the Biggest Threat to Cost of Health Care," *Providence Journal*, August 11, 2021, https://www.providencejournal.com/story/opinion/columns/2021/08/11/opinion-fanale-and-babineau-status-quo-biggest-threat-cost-health-care/5518852001/.

13. Marie L. Ganim and Stephen Boyle, "R.I. a Leader in Reining in Health Care Spending," *Providence Journal*, July 16, 2019, https://www.providencejournal.com/story/opinion/2019/07/16/our-turn-marie-l-ganim-and-stephen-boyle-ri-leader-in-reining-in-health-care-spending/4678661007/.
14. Ibid.
15. Ibid.
16. "A Review of Rhode Island's Mandated Benefits and Recommendations for . . . ," Office of the Health Insurance Commissioner (OHIC), 2014, https://ohic.ri.gov/sites/g/files/xkgbur736/files/documents/HIAC-Mandated-Benefits-Report-May-2014.pdf.
17. Ibid.
18. Ted Nesi, Eli Sherman, and Steph Machado, "In Stunning Move, AG Neronha Rejects Lifespan-Care New England Merger," *WPRI*, February 17, 2022, https://www.wpri.com/news/in-stunning-move-ag-neronha-rejects-lifespan-care-new-england-merger/.
19. "Rhode Island," *Community Catalyst*, 2021, https://www.communitycatalyst.org/initiatives-and-issues/initiatives/hospital-accountability-project/free-care/states/rhode-island.
20. Jones, Brian. "Lifespan and Care New England sign a detailed agreement to create a massive system that would control nearly two-thirds of the hospital market in Rhode Island." *Providence Journal*, January 30, 1999: A-01. NewsBank: America's News. https://infoweb-newsbank-com.providence.idm.oclc.org/apps/news/document-view?p=NewsBank&docref=news/1525143CE0939980.
21. G. Wayne Miller, "Raimondo Letter: Care New England Demand for CEO's Job Scuttled Effort to Combine with Lifespan and Brown," *Providence Journal*, September 18, 2019, https://www.providencejournal.com/story/news/healthcare/2019/09/18/raimondo-letter-care-new-england-demand-for-ceos-job-scuttled-effort-combine-with-lifespan-and-brown/2634512007/.
22. Nesi, Sherman, and Machado, "Stunning Move."
23. Alexa Gagosz, "Lifespan CEO: Failure of Lifespan-CNE Merger Was a Factor in Decision to Step Down," *Boston Globe*, May 20, 2022, https://www.bostonglobe.com/2022/05/20/metro/lifespan-ceo-failure-lifespan-cne-merger-was-factor-decision-step-down/.
24. Marc Larocque, "With CEO Set to Leave, Care New England at Crossroads," *Providence Business News*, May 20, 2022, https://pbn.com/with-ceo-set-to-leave-care-new-england-at-crossroads/; G. Wayne Miller, "Farewell Message from Lifespan CEO Shows Revenue Wins and Losses for RI's Healthcare Giant," *The Providence Journal*, June 4, 2022, https://www.providencejournal.com/story/news/healthcare/2022/06/04/lifespan-ceo-babineau-final-annual-report-before-retirement/7483305001/.
25. Claudia Chiappa, "Care New England Votes to Stay Independent, Rejects Merger Offers," *Providence Business News*, July 6, 2022, https://pbn.com/care-new-england-votes-to-stay-indepedent/.
26. Katherine Gregg, "Report: Lapses at State Hospital Reached 'Level of Immediate Jeopardy' Last Month," *Providence Journal*, January 25, 2022, https://www.providencejournal.com/story/news/healthcare/2022/01/25/eleanor-slater-hospital-ri-report-lapses-reached-immediate-jeopardy-level/9214225002/.
27. Katherine Gregg, "RI State Hospital Gets 90 Days to Fix Problems That Put Patients in 'Immediate Jeopardy,'" *Providence Journal*, May 20, 2022, https://www.providencejournal.com/story/news/politics/2022/05/19/ri-eleanor-slater-hospital-gets-more-time-fix-problems-that-imperil-patients-state-hospital/9841652002/.

28. "The Governor's FY 2023 Budget and the State's Fiscal Outlook," Rhode Island Public Expenditure Council, March 2022, https://ripec.org/wp-content/uploads/2022/03/2022_FY_2023_Budget_and_Fiscal_Outlook.pdf.
29. Ibid.
30. Shaune Towne, "Eleanor Slater Cost per Patient Balloons to $760K per Year, Report Finds," *WPRI*, March 25, 2022, https://www.wpri.com/target-12/eleanor-slater-cost-per-patient-balloons-to-760k-per-year-report-finds/.
31. Ibid.
32. Nancy Lavin, "House OKs Sweeping New Spending in $13.6B State Budget," *Providence Business News*, June 16, 2022, https://pbn.com/house-oks-sweeping-new-spending-in-13-6b-state-budget/.
33. John E. Gage and James Nyberg, "Opinion/Gage and Nyberg: Now Is Not the Time to Desert Our Seniors," *Providence Journal*, June 4, 2022. https://www.providencejournal.com/story/opinion/2022/06/04/opinion-gage-and-nyberg-now-not-time-desert-our-seniors/9951978002/.
34. Katherine Gregg, "McKee Signs Bill Setting Highest Staff-to-Patient Mandate in Nation for Ri Nursing Homes," *Providence Journal*, May 27, 2021. https://www.providencejournal.com/story/news/politics/2021/05/27/law-sets-highest-staff-mandate-us-ri-nursing-homes/7467080002/.
35. Anthony Vecchione, "Code Red: Amid Closures, Nursing Homes Fight for Survival," *Providence Business News*, June 10, 2022, https://pbn.com/code-red-nursing-homes-now-struggle-for-future-viability/.
36. Ibid.
37. Gregg, "McKee Signs Bill."
38. Ibid.
39. Patrick Anderson and Katherine Gregg, "The General Assembly Session Is Over. Here's What Passed, and What Didn't," *Providence Journal*, June 24, 2022, https://www.providencejournal.com/story/news/politics/2022/06/23/ri-general-assembly-approves-13-billion-dollar-budget-races-toward-end-session/7713060001/.
40. Farzan, Antonia. "What to Know About Reaction to McKee Pausing Law Setting Minimum Staffing at Nursing Homes." *Providence Journal*. January 28, 2022. https://www.providencejournal.com/story/news/politics/2022/01/28/nursing-home-labor-shortage-workforce-staffing-requirements-paused-workers-frustrated/9215354002/.
41. Claudia Chiappa, "Nursing Homes to Get $30M Boost," *Providence Business News*, June 24, 2022, https://pbn.com/nursing-homes-to-get-30m-boost/.
42. Anderson and Gregg, "General Assembly."
43. David S. Rochefort and Marie L Ganim, "Rhode Island: Individual State Report," Rockefeller Institute of Government, October 2016, https://rockinst.org/wp-content/uploads/2018/02/2016-10-RI_Individual_Report_Update.pdf.
44. Lincoln D. Chafee, "Executive Order 11-09," State Coverage, September 19, 2011, http://www.statecoverage.org/files/Rhode_Island_Executive_Order_11-09.pdf.
45. Freyer, Felice. "Business groups say cost of HealthSource RI should be borne by its users." *Providence Journal*. January 21, 2014. https://www.providencejournal.com/story/news/politics/county/2014/01/21/20140121-business-groups-say-cost-of-healthsource-ri-should-be-borne-by-its-users-ece/35376270007/.
46. Mike Stenhouse, "Ruling Dooms R.I. Exchange," *Providence Journal*, July 3, 2015, https://www.providencejournal.com/story/opinion/2015/07/07/ruling-dooms-r-i-exchange/33996161007/.
47. "Join the Federal Exchange," *Providence Journal*, May 20, 2014, https://www.providencejournal.com/story/opinion/editorials/2014/05/20/20140520-join-the-

federal-exchange-ece/35352958007/.
48. Robert B. Hackey, "Robert B. Hackey: Makes Little Sense to Keep HealthSource RI," *Providence Journal*, December 9, 2014, https://www.providencejournal.com/story/news/2014/12/10/20141210-robert-b-hackey-makes-little-sense-to-keep-healthsource-ri-ece/35442884007/.
49. Richard Salit, "Little Support for Bill to Shut down HealthSource RI," *SouthCoastToday*, March 10, 2015, https://www.southcoasttoday.com/story/news/politics/state/2015/03/11/little-support-for-bill-to/35033439007/.
50. Jennifer Bogdan, "The Assembly—Final OK for New $8.7 Billion Budget," *Providence Journal*. June 24, 2015.
51. "Rhode Island Health Insurance Survey (HIS): 2018 Executive Summary Report," HealthSourceRI, Freedman HealthCare, August 2, 2019, https://healthsourceri.com/wp-content/uploads/HIS-2018_Executive-Summary-Report_8.2.19.pdf.
52. Louise Norris, "Rhode Island and the ACA's Medicaid Expansion," healthinsurance.org, December 14, 2021, https://www.healthinsurance.org/medicaid/rhode-island/.
53. "Medicaid Expenditure Report SFY 20," Executive Office of Health and Human Services, 2020, https://eohhs.ri.gov/sites/g/files/xkgbur226/files/2022-04/MedExp%20Rep%20SFY2020_FINAL.pdf.
54. "Medicaid Expenditures as a Percent of Total State Expenditures by Fund," Kaiser Family Foundation, November 2021, https://www.kff.org/medicaid/state-indicator/medicaid-expenditures-as-a-percent-of-total-state-expenditures-by-fund/.
55. "Rhode Island Health Insurance Survey (HIS)."
56. Norris, "Medicaid Expansion."
57. Ellen Liberman, "All You Need to Know about the UHIP Disaster," *Rhode Island Monthly*, September 26, 2017, https://www.rimonthly.com/unified-health-infrastructure-project/.
58. Liberman, "UHIP Disaster."
59. Ted Nesi, "RI Awards Deloitte $99 Million Contract to Keep Running UHIP," *WPRI*, June 28, 2021, https://www.wpri.com/news/politics/ri-awards-deloitte-99-million-contract-to-keep-running-uhip/.
60. Deborah Sills, "Statement of Deborah Sills," WPRI, April 12, 2018, https://www.wpri.com/wp-content/uploads/sites/23/2018/04/20180412225501849_1523587891190_39798257_ver1.0.pdf.
61. G. Wayne Miller, "Drug Overdose Deaths in R.I. Declined in 2018, for Second Straight Year," *Providence Journal*, April 10, 2019, https://www.providencejournal.com/story/news/healthcare/2019/04/10/drug-overdose-deaths-in-ri-declined-in-2018-for-second-straight-year/2634070007/.
62. Arditi, Lynn. "Medical school to pioneer addiction-treatment program." *Providence Journal*. July 10, 2017. https://www.providencejournal.com/story/news/healthcare/2017/07/10/brown-medical-school-to-pioneer-addiction-treatment-program/20290633007/.
63 Brian Amaral, "Fatal Overdoses Spike in R.I. as More Toxic Drugs and Covid Isolation Create 'Perfect Storm,'" *Providence Journal*, September 17, 2020, https://www.providencejournal.com/story/News/coronavirus/2020/09/17/fatal-over-doses-spike-in-ri-as-more-toxic-drugs-and-covid-isolation-create-rsquoperfect-stormrsquo/42635279/.
64. Jack Perry, "'A Crisis': Record Number of Rhode Islanders Died from Accidental Drug Overdoses in 2021," *Providence Journal*, May 2, 2022, https://www.providencejournal.com/story/news/local/2022/05/02/ri-drug-overdose-deaths-set-record-2021-fentanyl-cocaine/9616004002/.

65. Miller, "Overdose."
66. "Rhode Island Behavioral Health Open Beds – Available Beds," Department of Behavioral Health Care, Developmental Disabilities, and Hospitals, 2022, https://www.ribhopenbeds.org/?sort=Filled&direction=desc&status=Filled.
67. Erick Trickey, "How the Smallest State Is Defeating America's Biggest Addiction Crisis," *Politico* magazine, August 25, 2018, https://www.politico.com/magazine/story/2018/08/25/rhode-island-opioids-inmates-219594/.
68. Trickey, "Addiction Crisis."
69. Ibid.
70. Erin Brown, Sarah Biester, Cathy Shultz, Sarah Edwards, Annajane Yolken, Dennis Bailer, Raynald Joseph, and Katherine Howe, "Snapshot of Harm Reduction in Rhode Island (February 2021–January 2022)," *Rhode Island Medical Journal* 105 (April 2022), http://rimed.org/rimedicaljournal/2022/04/2022-04-61-health-brown.pdf.
71. Katie Mulvaney, "Drug Bills Signal Sea Change in Ri's Approach to Opioid Crisis," *Providence Journal*, July 3, 2021, https://www.providencejournal.com/story/news/courts/2021/07/03/ri-could-first-state-in-nation-to-legalize-safe-injection-sites-for-opioid-addicts/7840401002/.
72. Katie Mulvaney, "RI Nets $112 Million in Settlement with Opioid Manufacturer, Distributors. What We Know," *Providence Journal*, January 25, 2022, https://www.providencejournal.com/story/news/courts/2022/01/25/opioid-company-settlement-amounts-ri-johnson-johnson-pharmaceutical-oxycontin/9211677002/.
73. Tom Mooney, "Ri to Get $2.59 Million in Settlement with Consulting Firm That Helped Market Opioids," *Providence Journal*, February 4, 2021, https://www.providencejournal.com/story/news/local/2021/02/04/opioids-settlement-mckinsey-net-ri-2-59-million/4387197001/.
74. Mulvaney, "RI Nets."
75. Katie Mulvaney, Katie. "RI Supreme Court Upholds State Law Protecting Abortion Rights," *Providence Journal*, May 4, 2022, https://www.providencejournal.com/story/news/courts/2022/05/04/ri-abortion-rights-law-supreme-court-ruling-reproductive-privacy-act/9643035002/.
76. Steph Machado, Alexandra Leslie, and Anita Baffoni, "RI Lawmakers End Session without Vote on Bill to OK State Funding of Abortion," WPRI, June 24, 2022, https://www.wpri.com/news/politics/ri-lawmakers-end-session-without-vote-on-bill-to-ok-state-funding-of-abortion/.
77. Alexa Gagosz, "'This Ruling Is Truly Catastrophic'; R.I. Advocates, Politicians React to Roe v. Wade Being Overturned," *Boston Globe*, June 24, 2022, https://www.bostonglobe.com/2022/06/24/metro/this-ruling-is-truly-catastrophic-ri-advocates-politicians-react-roe-v-wade-being-overturned/.
78. Alexa Gagosz, "McKee Plans to Sign Order Protecting Health Care Workers Who Provide Abortion Services to out-of-State Residents," *Boston Globe*, June 27, 2022, https://www.bostonglobe.com/2022/06/27/metro/mckee-plans-sign-order-protecting-health-care-providers-who-provide-abortion-services-out-of-state-residents/.
79. James Bessette, "McKee Signs Executive Order Protecting Reproductive Health Care Access in R.I.," *Providence Business News*, July 5, 2022, https://pbn.com/mckee-signs-executive-order-protecting-reproductive-health-care-access-in-r-i/.
80. Machado, Leslie, and Baffoni, "Lawmakers."
81. William Binder, "Rhode Island Healthcare: Is There Light at the End of the Tunnel?" *Rhode Island Medical Journal* 105 (February 2022), http://rimed.org/rimedicaljournal/2022/02/2022-02-48-commentary-binder.pdf.

E / Overview of Environmental Policy in Rhode Island

Aaron Ley

The Context

Rhode Island's location along the Atlantic coast makes the conservation and protection of coastal land and water resources in the state among the highest of its environmental priorities. Indeed, in 1991-92 a one-time index ranked all US states on the basis of their adoption of pro-environmental policies, and Rhode Island ranked seventh.[1] A more recent, non-academic study that takes into consideration air and water quality, as well as environmental behaviors of state residents, ranks Rhode Island as the 11th most "greenest" state.[2] State spending can also be an indicator of the value that is placed on environmental values. State bonding issues typically go to the voters for approval and if the passage of "green bonds" for large-scale environmental projects is any indication of the public's support of the environment, then the reliable passage of environmental referenda would suggest that support for the environment is strong in Rhode Island. The 2018 "Green Economy and Clean Water Bond" is a case in point. That year Rhode Island voters approved the $47.3 million bonding issue by a vote of 78.9 percent in support and 21.1 percent opposed, while in prior years it was common to see the passage of "green bonds" approved with anywhere from 60-78 percent of statewide support from voters.

The environmental and natural resources of traditional concern in Rhode Island include farms, forests, open space, aquaculture and fisheries, coastal shoreline and beaches, energy production and siting, hazardous waste cleanup, resource recovery, and wastewater treatment. Because Rhode Island is a coastal state with a major tourism component to its economy, the environmental protection of water resources has emerged as a key priority at all levels of government in the state. The primary sources of saltwater resources are coastal ponds, salt marshes, estuaries, and marine waters,[3] all of which form the foundation for the state's aquaculture and commercial fishing industry that produce oysters, shellfish, lobster, calamari (famously designated as the "state appetizer"), and a variety of different fish species. Freshwater resources consist of rivers, lakes, groundwater sources, and freshwater wetlands. A key freshwater resource in Rhode Island is the Scituate Reservoir, which is the state's principal drinking water source and delivers drinking water to about 60 percent of the state's residents.[4]

Many different stakeholders across the state are involved in monitoring compliance with state and federal environmental statutes. Some of the most prominent groups that have historically participated in the formulation and oversight of environmental policy in Rhode Island include Save the Bay, the Audubon Society of Rhode Island, Conservation Law Foundation, Sierra Club, the Environmental Council of Rhode Island (a collection of environmental groups), ecoRI (environmental news reporting), and the Nature Conservancy. Being a home-rule state, another key element of environmental policy in Rhode Island is the local opposition that emerges when local economic or energy development projects are being considered. The hyperlocal nature of public policymaking in Rhode Island provides local opponents a variety of different venues in which they can voice their opposition, including planning boards, zoning boards of review, and town and city councils. Rhode Island's municipalities have also proven to be key actors in the formulation and implementation of environmental policy at the local and state level. On the one hand, towns and municipalities can use general obligation bond sales and operating expenses for projects that improve the environment as well as pursue a variety of grants made available by state and federal agencies to make environmental improvements. On the other hand, municipalities can react against any perception of state environmental overreach or voice their support for distributive state spending on the environment, through the Rhode Island League of Cities and Towns, the lobbying arm of Rhode Island's 39 municipalities.

Key Agencies and Stakeholders in Rhode Island Environmental Policymaking

Section XVII of the Constitution of the State of Rhode Island vests authority in the Rhode Island General Assembly to:

> Provide for the conservation of the air, land, water, plant, animal, mineral and other natural resources of the state, and to adopt all means necessary and proper by law to protect the natural environment of the people and the state by providing adequate resource planning for the control and regulation of the use of the natural resources of the state and for the preservation, regeneration and restoration of the natural environment of the state.[5]

The General Assembly has created a variety of different agencies responsible for executing the state environmental policies that it passes. The key state government and quasi-government agencies with jurisdiction over natural resources include the Coastal Resources Management Council (CRMC), the Rhode Island Department of Environmental Management (DEM), the Office of Energy Resources (OER), the Rhode Island Public Utilities Commission (RIPUC), the Department of Health's (RIDOH) Division of Environmental Health, the Rhode Island Resource Recovery Corporation (RIRRC), and the Energy Facilities Siting Board (EFSB).

Arguably the most important agency for environmental enforcement in the state is the Rhode Island Department of Environmental Management (DEM), which over the years has established a reputation as an overburdened environmental protection agency, although in recent years that reputation has improved. Frustration with DEM reached new levels when Lincoln Almond (R-Smithfield) was governor. During the eight years of Almond's governorship, DEM had undergone dramatic turnover at the highest levels of leadership, beginning with the resignation of Directors Timothy Keeney and Andrew McLeod. During this time period, the US EPA had threatened to take over the agency because of toxic waste mismanagement and the General Assembly had initiated an investigation of DEM to consider splitting it into two agencies. When Director McLeod submitted his letter of resignation in 1998, he cited a lack of political support from the legislature as one of the reasons for his decision.[6] Governor Almond responded by hiring Jan Reitsma, a former Save the Bay employee and administrator at the MA Department of Environmental Protection, to the position of RI DEM Director. Reitsma, a trained attorney, came into the office with the reputation of being an able administrator, "straight shooter," and "problem-solver" who "dealt evenly" with economic and environmental policy concerns.[7] Reitsma had restored some of DEM's reputation by strengthening enforcement of the toxic waste program, reorganizing the agency, and speeding up the environmental permitting process (to this day there remain concerns that wetlands permits take too long to process). Whatever appearance that Reitsma's leadership gave about RIDEM experiencing less turmoil, however, may have been overshadowed by a series of highly public outbursts, investigations, and lawsuits that culminated with Governor Carcieri's acceptance of Reitsma's resignation in 2003. Reitsma would be replaced by Janet Coit, a former director of the Nature Conservancy and aide to Senators John and Lincoln Chafee, who was elevated to the directorship of DEM by Chafee (D-RI) during his governorship. She was kept on after the election of Gina Raimondo (D-RI) and gave steady leadership to DEM for over a decade until joining Raimondo at the Department of Commerce in 2021.

Besides DEM, other prominent Rhode Island agencies include the Coastal Resources Management Council (CRMC), which was formed by legislation in 1971. The CRMC was created to address some of the pressures associated with development along the coast and "is charged with the primary responsibility for the continued planning and management of the resources of the state's coastal region."[8] Given this wide range of responsibility, the agency is responsible for a variety of permitting activities relating to everything from the construction of structures on the coastline to dredging and offshore energy production activities. When issues of coastal concern fall within the boundaries of Rhode Island's many coastal communities, the CRMC commonly seeks recommendations and guidance from local municipalities as part of its decision-making process.

When issues fall within the purview of public health, it is common to see involvement from RIDOH's Division of Environmental Health. A core function of this agency is to ensure that public drinking water is tested and meets federal Safe Drinking Water Act standards. Its other responsibilities include risk assessment for exposure to hazardous and toxic substances, educating the public about environmental hazards, beach monitoring and shellfish industry oversight, and lead hazard mitigation, among a variety of other environmental health functions and responsibilities.

The General Assembly has also created agencies responsible for overseeing energy distribution and the development of energy sources. These agencies include the Rhode Island Public Utilities Commission (RIPUC), a regulatory agency, and the RI Office of Energy Resources, a clientele agency. One of the most important developments in the energy sector occurred in the 1990s, when Rhode Island's energy infrastructure was "deregulated" with the passage of the Rhode Island Utility Restructuring Act of 1996. The passage of this law meant that the distribution of power was uncoupled from the actual production of energy, thus allowing consumers to choose their own supplier. Although the option to choose from a variety of different suppliers exists, the overwhelming majority of distribution is currently delivered by Rhode Island Energy, which is the default supplier, or what is commonly known in the industry as "the standard offer" or the supplier of "last resort." This means that Rhode Islanders can choose their own energy supplier, but if they choose not to (or if the one they choose ceases to exist), then they will be supplied with Rhode Island Energy power. Rhode Islanders are primarily dependent on imported natural gas and petroleum products for energy creation, but the amount of energy being developed by wind and solar has been increasing (Rhode Island Division of Planning, 2015). A variety of laws seek to add to the supply and competitiveness of renewable power on the wholesale market, including the passage of the Renewable Energy Standard in 2004. Renewable Portfolio Standard (RPS) laws work by requiring energy firms to purchase a certain amount of their retail portfolio from eligible renewable sources, which in Rhode Island is targeted to be 38.5 percent from renewable sources by 2035.[9] The General Assembly has also passed laws that provide incentives for homeowners to produce their own power through solar voltaic panels and sell it back to the grid through an arrangement called net metering, and that encourage more offshore energy development (see below).

The agencies and institutional structures in which environmental policy is formed in Rhode Island have led to a variety of unique conflicts that have shaped our built and social environments, which are described in the remaining section. These experiences are sure to provide a window into how Rhode Island will address the future challenges that relate to environmental policy, especially our changing climate.

The Environmental Conflict over Dredging at Quonset Point

One of the most important water-based environmental conflicts to shape environmental policy in Rhode Island emerged in the 1990s during the Sundlun Administration (D-RI). Sundlun was an unabashed supporter of a proposal to use Quonset Point, a former Naval Base deeded to the state of Rhode Island, to create a megaport that would receive large container ships. After Lincoln Almond (R-RI) defeated Myrth York (D-RI) to become the state's governor, opposition began to form against the idea of a major port project at the site. At the time, large panamax container ships were being manufactured to ship products less expensively all over the world, but very few US ports had deep enough water to accommodate these large ships. Rhode Island's Narragansett Bay represented an opportunity for developers to potentially create up to 6,000 jobs by dredging the port by up to 60 feet deep and filling up to 500 acres of the bay with the dredged material. Efforts to build the surrounding infrastructure began in earnest, as this port was considered to have access to rail lines, an air strip, and a state highway. Rail access to the port required 22 miles of upgrades to increase the height of bridges (for stackable freight) and the construction of a third rail (to accommodate both freight and passenger rail).[10] The Almond Administration, along with Rhode Island's congressional delegation, began securing federal funds for the upgrades, which required approval of a $72 million state bond referendum in 1996, $50 million of which went toward the $116 million rail upgrades.[11]

Despite the economic promises made to generate political support for the project, groups began voicing their opposition to the project, and the public never gave the support needed to ensure the success of the plan. When Rhode Island residents were asked whether the project would create jobs, a Brown University poll found that 73 percent agreed; however, 43 percent believed that the port would hurt the bay, and another 63 percent responded that the project would increase noise and traffic congestion.[12] When asked whether the port should be dredged, public opinion was split with 32 percent in support and 32 percent opposed.[13] One of the most active groups that opposed the dredging plan was Save the Bay, at the time led by Executive Director Curt Spalding, who later became EPA's Region 1 Administrator during the Obama Administration. The Sierra Club, the Conservation Law Foundation, and local residents (mostly from North Kingstown) also became reliable opponents of this development. In response to the opposition, Governor Almond (R-RI) formed a collaborative stakeholders group composed of environmental groups, union leaders, business interests, liaisons from nearby towns, and shellfishing interests to reach a consensus on a plan for Quonset Point. After more than a year of meetings, the group failed to reach consensus over the design of the proposed port, and the effort ended when it was announced that Quonset Point was eliminated from consideration to be the delivery site for two of the largest US shipping companies.

Although Governor Almond still hoped that a smaller scale proposal could be considered for the Quonset Point-Davisville site, the 2000 election for Rhode Island Governor featured two major party candidates all opposed to any proposal that would require any significant dredging, Don Carcieri (R-East Greenwich) and Myrth York (D-Providence). Carcieri (R-East Greenwich), a business executive without any formal political experience, was elected and kept his promise to oppose further development of the port, only supporting maintenance dredging of the port to accommodate the existing businesses that used it. When the Environment Council of Rhode Island wrote its end-of-year retrospective about the legislative session, it listed Governor Carcieri's "Vetoing [of] the proposed megaport at Quonset" as one of his early accomplishments as governor.

The Environmental Problem of Nonpoint Source Stormwater Runoff

Governor Carcieri (R-RI) won praise in the environmental community for his opposition to further dredging of Quonset Point, but his administration presided over a massive fish kill during 2003 in Greenwich Bay that quickly shifted the public's attention to an emerging environmental problem related to water pollution in the Narragansett Bay: stormwater runoff and wastewater treatment facility (WWTF) discharges. When Congress passed the Clean Water Act in 1972, it created a statutory framework in order to make the waters of the United States swimmable and fishable. States partnered with the federal government and began developing plans that focused on identifying large point-sources of pollution and requiring compliance with a "permit" for discharged releases. The CWA also contained federal funding that was earmarked for the construction and upgrading of WWTFs.[14] For many years these systems were a major source of pollution when sewerage pipes were inundated with heavy rainfall, causing "combined sewage overflow" (CSO) events. CSOs occur when sewer drains are overwhelmed with stormwater, causing untreated water to be released into the waterways that lead into the surrounding coastal waters, resulting in nutrient pollution that closes shellfishing and recreation activities. While the strategy of focusing on large point sources of pollution ultimately reduced the amount of pollution being discharged into Rhode Island waterways, by the late 1970s attention began to shift to the difficult problem of addressing nonpoint source pollution, the management of which remains a challenge in Rhode Island. Efforts by the environmental community eventually culminated in the passage of state legislation in 1980 that created the Narragansett Bay Commission, which became responsible for the "construction, financing, extension, improvement, and operation and maintenance of publicly owned sewage treatment facilities."[15] The creation of this commission ensured that Providence and its surrounding communities would improve the treatment of its wastewater before discharging it into the Narragansett Bay.

Despite all these efforts, a moment of reckoning that Rhode Island's efforts to address water pollution were falling short came in the form of a massive fish kill in 2003 caused by pollutant-fed algae blooms.[16] It was estimated that one million fish had been killed due to stormwater runoff and combined sewage overflows, which caused a variety of stakeholders at all levels of government to focus on better wastewater management practices and upgrading WWTFs. Despite upgrades to WWTFs in Rhode Island and targeting water pollution control at its source, nonpoint source pollution remains a continuous problem that only promises to get worse as the state confronts the climate change impacts of higher precipitation patterns. Higher rates of precipitation cause more flooding, which causes CSO's and nonpoint source pollution to add more polluted water to the bay and algae blooms that disrupt the Narragansett Bay ecosystem. Stormwater runoff and onsite wastewater treatment systems (OWTS) remain some of the principal sources of nonpoint source pollution in Rhode Island and represent major challenges due to their diffuse origins. Another emerging area of concern for environmentalists includes the regulation of polyfluoroalkyl substances (PFAS), otherwise known as "forever chemicals," that are discharged into surface water and contaminate drinking water sources. PFAS can be found in cosmetics, nonstick surfaces, prescription drugs, and a variety of other products that are manufactured on a large scale.

Environmental Justice and Natural Gas Conflicts at Providence's Fields Point

One important aspect of environmental policy in Rhode Island has proven to be the siting of energy facilities, which is governed by the Rhode Island Energy Facility Siting Act. One particular proposal to create a $180 million liquefied natural gas (LNG) storage facility at Providence's Fields Point in 2015 and another to construct a $1 billion facility in Burrillville tell a tale of two different communities experiencing two different outcomes and provide lessons about the intersection of energy policy, climate change, and environmental justice in Rhode Island.

In 2015, Chicago-based Invenergy applied to build a $1 billion natural gas and diesel energy facility in Burrillville that would create 1,000 MW of power, an estimated 350 jobs, and lower energy prices for New England energy consumers. The small town of Burrillville is located in Northern Rhode Island and in 2020 had a US Census population of 16,158. In order to be completed, a project of this scale would need a variety of permits for wetlands construction, air permits, and approval from the Energy Facilities Siting Board (EFSB). Although the project initially had support from members of the Rhode Island political establishment, including Governor Raimondo,[17] trades unions,[18] and an industry-funded group called Rhode Islanders for Affordable Energy,[19] fierce opposition from local, state, and national groups soon began to form shortly after the power plant was proposed. Some of the prominent groups and individuals to publicly oppose the plant were the Conservation Law Foundation, the Audubon Society, the Nature Conservancy, Save the Bay, and former Governor Lincoln Chafee (D-RI).

Opponents of the power plant collectively raised concerns that the plant would disrupt the character of rural life in Burrillville, that the plant would interfere with achieving greenhouse gas emissions targets mandated by the state's 2014 Resilient Rhode Island Act, and that the cooling water required for the plant's operation would be intensive. For these reasons, in September 2016, the Town of Burrillville filed a motion to the Energy Facility Siting Board to dismiss the request to build the power plant,[20] which was denied.[21] However, one pivotal moment occurred when ISO New England, the non-profit organization that operates the regional grid, reneged on an agreement with Invenergy to purchase its energy (called a "Capacity Supply Obligation"). This signaled to opponents and policy-makers that anticipated consumer demand for the power that would be produced by this plant did not exist, and testimony by a DEM official "that the project poses unacceptable harm to the site"[22] gave the Energy Facility Siting Board no other choice but to reject the project. Ruling unanimously against the proposed power plant, the Energy Facility Siting Board ruled, "Adding a new natural gas plant—even a fast start, more efficient one—does not advance the stated goals of greater fuel diversity, significantly lowered greenhouse gas emissions, or a transformed system.... Adding Invenergy's proposed facility would, at most, perpetuate the status quo."[23]

At the same time that opponents had organized to stop the construction of a power plant in Burrillville, minoritized residents of South Providence's Washington Park neighborhood experienced a profoundly different set of circumstances that led to an LNG facility to be sited in their neighborhood. This proposal entailed the creation of a facility that used natural gas produced through fracking and converted it to a liquid by cooling it at extreme temperatures and reducing its volume.[24] Quick to line up in support of the facility were business interests and labor unions, but opposition had also formed by nearby residents, environmentalists, and local officials, including Providence Mayor Jorge Elorza.[25] The section of Providence being considered for this site also contained "a greater number of polluting facilities than any other zip code in Providence County. . . .[and] some of the highest rates of asthma in Southern New England."[26] In particular, opponents of the proposed plant formed an organization called NO LNG IN PVD to argue that the plant would disproportionately affect the low-income and minority communities already living nearby heavy industry in South Providence and the Washington Park neighborhood.[27] But despite widespread opposition from within the City of Providence, and organized opposition from neighborhood groups, the project did not gain the same attention as the power plant in Burrillville and the project was allowed to move forward after having received approval from the Federal Energy Regulatory Commission.

The Challenges of Climate Change and Sea-Level Rise, and the Promise of Renewables

As a coastal state, Rhode Island is sure to experience a future dominated by the challenges associated with climate change and sea-level rise. So far, the state has sought to deal with these challenges with a combination of renewable energy development and limitations on greenhouse gas emissions. Rhode Island has proven to be on the frontiers of renewable energy exploration by becoming the first state to approve an operational offshore wind farm, called the Block Island Wind Farm, and has a series of additional proposed projects that are underway or are being considered. For all the enthusiasm for renewables in Rhode Island, however, there is a growing awareness of the conflicts that exist between siting of solar renewable facilities and the conservation of open space and forests. That may explain why bills are being considered by the Rhode Island General Assembly to regulate the siting of solar panels in order to preserve woodlands and farmland.

As for state-level legislation, the passage of the Resilient Rhode Island Act in 2014 under the governorship of Lincoln Chafee (D-RI) represents the state's most prominent strategy for addressing climate change. This statute created an Executive Climate Change Coordinating Council and sets targets for greenhouse gas emissions, which featured prominently in the deliberations over the proposed Burrillville power plant. In 2017, then-Governor Gina Raimondo (D-RI) signed an executive order to appoint a Chief Resilience Officer and to develop a comprehensive plan for addressing climate change impacts, which came in the form of the Resilient Rhody report. When then-Governor Gina

Raimondo was nominated and confirmed to be US Secretary of Commerce, former Lieutenant Governor Dan McKee (D-RI) was elevated to the governorship and in 2021 acted quickly to sign in new legislation aimed at making greenhouse gas reductions mandatory and seeking to achieve net-zero emissions targets. Alongside state-level efforts to address climate change, Rhode Island's 39 municipalities are reacting in real-time to climate change and sea-level rise by investing in more resilient local infrastructure to mitigate flooding and other climate-related impacts. One of the most important partnerships between the state and municipalities comes in the form of the Rhode Island Infrastructure Bank's Municipal Resiliency Program, which allows towns and municipalities to become eligible for climate-related grants after having completed a municipal resiliency plan. Rhode Island lawmakers have also supported the tried-and-true strategy of preserving forest, farmland, and open space in order to lessen the worst impacts of climate change and to promote the environmental benefits of land conservation. Most recently this culminated in the passage of the Forest Conservation Act and the creation of a Rhode Island Forest Conservation Commission.

Conclusion

Being a small state on the Atlantic coast, Rhode Island is sure to continue experiencing a large share of environmental challenges as state policy-makers set their sights on the future. Efforts by environmentalists, activists, and municipalities to stop the dredging of Quonset Point and the siting of natural gas facilities have demonstrated their ability to stop development pressures that cause adverse environmental impacts. However, the biggest challenge yet for environmental interests in Rhode Island will be the development of proactive solutions for the environmental impacts already being caused by climate change and sea-level rise. The combination of environmental challenges posed by climate change with the political challenge of overcoming fierce local opposition to state preemption of local rule may pose the greatest challenge yet for the environmental movement in Rhode Island.

Notes

1. B. Hall and M. L. Kerr, *1991–1992 Green Index: A State-By-State Guide to the Nation's Environmental Health* (Washington, D.C. :Island Press, 1991).
2. J. S. Kiernan, "Greenest States," *WalletHub*. April 14, 2021,00. https://wallethub.com/edu/greenest-states/11987.
3. Rhode Island Division of Planning, *Water Quality 2035: Rhode Island Water Quality Management Plan*, October 3, 2016, http://www.dem.ri.gov/programs/benviron/water/quality/pdf/wqmp2035.pdf.
4. M. Grady, "The Secrets of Scituate Reservoir," *Rhode Island Monthly*, October 15, 2012, https://www.rimonthly.com/the-secrets-of-scituate-reservoir/.
5. Rhode Island Constitution, article I, § XVII.
6. A. Sabar, "McLeod Calls It Quits as Almond's DEM Director, *Providence Journal-Bulletin*, November 18, 1998.
7. A. Sabar, "Almond Taps Former Mass. Official to Head DEM, *Providence Journal-Bulletin*, March 31, 1999.
8. Coastal Management Resources Council, n.d., para. 5.
9. Office of Energy Resources, "Renewable Energy Standard," n.d., http://www.energy.ri.gov/policies-programs/ri-energy-laws/renewable-energy-standard-2004.php.
10. W. J. Donovan, "The Real Work at Quonset Point/Davisville Has Just Begun," *Providence Journal*, November 7, 1996.
11. Ibid.
12. D. West, *Rhode Island State Survey*, June 16, 1999. https://watson.brown.edu/taubman/polls/1999/rhode-island-state-survey-june-1999.
13. Ibid.
14. Rhode Island Division of Planning, *Water Quality 2035*, 2–23.
15. RIGL 46-25-2.
16. B. Polichetti, "'Perfect Recipe' for Fish Kill," *Providence Journal-Bulletin*, August 22, 2003.
17. T. Faulkner "No Need: Siting Board Denies Burrillville Power Plant," *ecoRI News*, June 21, 2019, https://ecori.org/2019-6-20-crec-denied/.
18. J. Detz, "Crowded and Rowdy at Power Plant Public Hearing," *ecoRI News*, April 1, 2016, https://ecori.org/2016-4-1-crowded-and-rowdy-power-plant-hearing/.
19. T. Faulkner, "Chicago Developer Helps Fund Pro-Power Plant Group," *ecoRI News*, June 9, 2017, https://ecori.org/2017-6-9-pro-power-plant-group-emerges-with-developers-funding/.
20. F. Carini, "Motion Filed to Dismiss Proposed Power Plant," *ecoRI News*, September 15, 2016, https://ecori.org/2016-9-15-burrillville-files-motion-to-dismiss-proposed-power-plant/.
21. F. Carini, "Burrillville Power Plant Survives Motion to Dismiss," *ecoRI News*, February 6, 2017, https://ecori.org/2017-2-6-power-plant-survives-motions-to-dismiss/.
22. Faulkner, "No Need," para. 16.
23. T. Faulkner, "Energy Facility Siting Board's Written Decision Explains Why Proposed Burrillville Power Plant Wasn't Needed," *ecoRI News*, November 6, 2019, https://ecori.org/2019-11-6-written-decision-explains-why-ri-doesnt-need-burrillville-power-plant/, para. 12.
24. Carini, "Motion Filed."

25. A. Kuffner, "Regulators Approve $180-Million Natural-Gas Plant in Providence," October 18, 2018, *Providence Journal*. [AU: Is URL available?]
26. F. Carini, "Providence's Toxic Avenue Leads to Neighborhood Problems?," *ecoRI News*, https://ecori.org/2019-4-22-toxic-avenue-leads-to-ignored-neighborhood-problems/, para. 21.
27. https://ecori.org/2017-7-14-lng-project-and-public-vetting-draws-anger/.

F / Transportation Policy in Rhode Island

Barry Schiller

We can all see that transportation strongly affects both our day-to-day life and our society broadly. Transportation issues—not just regarding cars but also trucks, buses, trains, bicycling, aviation, water travel too—generate a lot of policy decisions on an ongoing basis. With the influx of federal dollars for improved infrastructure projects, understanding our past practices and considering new alternatives presents an opportunity for updated thinking about transportation in the state.

The Setting

As was the case throughout the United States after World War II, Rhode Island planned post-war development around the automobile. This was already underway even earlier, albeit interrupted by the Depression and the war. An auto-oriented world promised quicker trips, safer rides on limited access highways, and the possibility of quick commutes from suburban greenery instead of from crowded tenements. One might go from Rhode Island to Boston, Chicago, or Miami, without a stoplight! What's not to like?

In the decades following the war, auto-centric development happened. This included building not just the Interstates but also expressways on some or all of the major routes in the state,[1] not to mention supporting local roads, parking lots and garages, and widespread minimum parking requirements.

Though overseeing the design and construction of major highways was largely an executive branch function, it was enabled by the legislature, which provided financing and in 1970 established a strong Department of Transportation (RIDOT), and by voters, who routinely approved General Obligation bonds for state roads. Indeed, even in 1950, when many did not yet have cars, a referendum for state roads had 77.2 percent approval. Since 1982 sixteen consecutive such bonds have been approved. State spending on roads went from about $14 million in 1950 to about $700 million in 2020, a period in which motor vehicle registrations went from 251,000 to almost 900,000.

Yet, over time, concerns grew over various consequences including those related to pollution, land use, mobility for non-drivers, safety, scenic degradation, and nowadays, social justice and climate change. All these issues are still with us. While these concerns sometimes arise from a political leader or agency leaders, transportation touches so much of daily life that issues also arise in the public sphere, where related advocacy organizations sometimes form. Sometimes these organizations are effective, sometimes not, and it can be instructive to understand what makes the difference.

Highway Expansion Then and Now

The Federal Highway Act of 1956 establishing the Interstate system had the federal government paying 90 percent of the cost, so who could resist? But it is important to note that unlike earlier turnpikes, usually tolled and mostly just skirting the cities, Interstates were intended to go right to the city centers and be toll-free. Indeed, I-95 was completed in the Providence metro area before it was finished in southwest Rhode Island. I-95, I-195, and I-295 were built without major opposition despite slicing thru the urban core as well as through Dawley State Park in Richmond. In the 1990s, with little dissent, despite a cost of about $700 million, the state establishment supported relocating the initial I-95/I-195 interchange to facilitate traffic flow and free up land adjacent to downtown that had been taken by the earlier route of I-195.

However, it was quite different for I-84, intended to connect Providence and Hartford. RIDOT really wanted this built, but a group led by residents of western Rhode Island, where the road would go, organized "Stop I-84." With the help of some urban environmental allies, they eventually prevailed when President Jimmy Carter's Council on Environmental Quality rejected the state's environmental analysis related to protecting the Scituate watershed that much of the state depends on for drinking water. Another proposed Interstate, I-895, which would have been an outer beltway slicing across South County and through the center of Aquidneck Island, was also rejected thanks to public opinion in those relatively well-to-do areas. It helped opponents that by then, due to growing opposition to some proposed Interstates around the country, federal law was changed to allow states to "trade in" the federal money for these Interstates to be used on other projects. During this period of opposition to some highway proposals, in 1974 and 1976, voters rejected transportation bonds.

On the other hand, public opposition to some highway projects was unsuccessful. For example, Route 99 connecting Route 146/I-295 to a Woonsocket industrial park was built over some objections from Cumberland and the

Audubon Society of Rhode Island, which were concerned about the filling of wetlands that would be required. In that case, the legislature had to amend the wetlands law to allow the highway, which CVS wanted for access to its headquarters. A big corporation like that makes a difference. Similarly, Sierra Club opposition to the 403 freeway from Route 4 was ineffective against the state's desire for the road to help market the Quonset-Davisville Industrial Park.

Now the highway system is largely built out, and capacity expansions, like widening the I-95 Viaduct in downtown Providence and a section of I-295, and a project to eliminate the one traffic light on Route 146, draw a little opposition from climate activists; they require little additional land, so the opposition is easily disregarded. But they are expensive, about $250 million for the I-95 widening. Another current issue relates to the rebuilding of the Route 6-10 interchange, about a $450 million project. Many see those highways as strangling once vibrant Olneyville, so with some encouragement from Providence city government, some community activists proposed a much less expensive surface boulevard replacement. This process was cut short by the state's decision to proceed with the full rebuild, as existing bridges were deteriorating and a surface boulevard would slow suburban traffic too much. Is a suburban orientation a consequence of an auto-centric culture?

Maintaining Infrastructure Is Expensive

People might think that once a highway is built, that's it, but infrastructure is expensive just to maintain. For example, a project to rehabilitate just one bridge on Route 37 will cost $43 million. Also, debt service was piling up from many years of borrowing to fund the state match, with payments coming at the expense of RIDOT's maintenance budget. As a result, maintenance was too often deferred; hence our many defective bridges and roads, reportedly the country's worst.[2] Groups like the Rhode Island Public Expenditure Council (RIPEC), whose 2002 Rhode Island at the Crossroads report began by saying that "Rhode Island is facing a financial crisis with respect to funding transportation," and again by a 2008 "Blue Ribbon Commission" that tried to warn that the system was on an unsustainable course—we were on course to "sink," in the language of Statewide Planning. Finally, the state acted. First, the Chafee administration and the legislature created a "Highway Maintenance Account," mostly from registration and license fees. The Sakonnet Bridge, connecting Tiverton and Portsmouth, having been poorly maintained, needed replacement, so tolls were to be imposed to help pay for it. The public, used to using the old bridge toll-free, pushed back, at times filling a State House hearing room with angry opposition. That got the legislature to drop the toll.

But tolls remained for some. The Raimondo administration, prioritizing bridge and road repair ("Rhodeworks"), proposed as a significant funding source a toll on heavy trucks, many from out of state, that do a lot of the damage. There was much opposition. The trucking industry threatened and filed a lawsuit. They also told the public it was a tax on consumers, who would ultimately pay the tolls. And some said if tolls were allowed on trucks, cars would be next. Despite this, the Raimondo administration held firm, and the legislature authorized the truck tolls. At the next election truck toll opposition was not a winner. The tolls were bringing in about $42 million/year when a trucking industry lawsuit challenging the constitutionality of the tolls succeeded in stopping the tolling. The state may appeal.

Going forward, maintaining roads and bridges will still be challenging. Borrowing, now shifted to "GARVEE bonds" to be paid back from future federal highway funds, is still a limiting factor; so is public resistance to tolls and gas tax increases. As electric cars become more prevalent, the gas tax itself, largely used for RIDOT maintenance, will decline, and it will be a challenge to replace it.

Safety Is Still an Issue

Increased use of automobiles for travel led to concerns over highway safety as deaths and injuries rose. This was addressed on the federal level with the creation of transportation safety agencies, mandates for seatbelts and airbags, and auto crashworthiness standards. The state and local governments also play a role with road design, traffic safety laws, and enforcement, especially about impaired driving.

Some of this was controversial, such as lowering the legal blood alcohol limit to .08, and making seatbelt violations a primary offense, meaning the police can stop you just for not wearing one. Some felt this was an infringement on their liberties, and some thought it might have disparate impact on minorities. Nevertheless, safety concerns won out on those issues, but not for further tightening of drunk driving laws that several attorney generals have sought, or for motorcycle safety—the state still does not mandate a helmet for drivers.

For a while, highway deaths declined, but around 2010 they started rising again, especially for pedestrians. To deal with this the legislature tightened some laws (such as banning use of handheld cell phones while driving), and the RIDOT has established a broad Traffic Safety Coalition that includes the AAA, Mothers Against Drunk Driving, the RI Bicycle Coalition, insurance, and hospitality industries, as well as police and federal agencies to help with education, legislation, safety-related spending, and now the uncertain effect the legalization of marijuana will have on road safety.

Providence has also taken the step of installing automatic cameras to catch red light runners and speeders at school zones. This too has drawn opposition, including from the American Civil Liberties Union (ACLU), over privacy and due process concerns. Some see it as a money grab rather than a safety issue. Yet, though the city made some concessions, the cameras remain. Going forward, some see a solution in self-driving automated vehicles. That technology is still experimental and would need a regulatory framework if it does materialize.

Land Use

With the building of the expressways, many people, stores, businesses, offices, even parts of state government (e.g., Public Utilities Commission) moved out to where the roads went, and parking was easier. In 1950 Providence and Pawtucket combined had 41.7 percent of the state's population; just 30 years later, they had only 24.4 percent. The resulting urban decline, sprawl, and loss of open space helped lead to the creation of the Statewide Planning Program and eventually a requirement that all cities and towns develop comprehensive plans subject to state approval. In 1998, noting the high cost of providing services to new areas being developed, Grow Smart RI was formed to promote growth in areas already developed with existing infrastructure. Although state planners adopted this as a goal, it is not an easy sell. Indeed, the state itself still facilitates sprawl, for example, by widening part of Route 7 to accommodate Fidelity Investments' move to a Smithfield facility, and by a new I-295 interchange built to facilitate Citizens Bank moving much of its workforce out of the urban area to a new "campus" in the woods just west of I-295 in Johnston. These corporate and governmental decisions inevitably create more sprawl and more vehicle-miles traveled, and if we are to get serious about our land-use goals, we cannot continue such policies.

What Is the Purpose of the Bus System?

In the 1940s the metro area's private United Transportation Company had about 154 million annual rides. Everybody rode! But as the auto age developed, ridership dropped, and the company struggled, cutting service, but then losing more riders. As ridership dropped to about 20 million, in 1964 a decision was made to save the service through a public takeover, and the legislature created the Rhode Island Public Transit Authority (RIPTA.) They began service in 1966 and later took over other private intrastate bus routes, but ridership continued to trend down, to below 14 million in the 1990s. When Governor Lincoln Almond was elected in 1994, he appointed a more activist Board of Directors, which hired Beverly Scott as general manager. At that time, it was unusual for a transit agency to be run by a woman, and Scott was African American, making her position even more remarkable. Scott hired a competent maintenance director whose work included cleaning up the visible diesel exhaust the buses were noted for and ensuring reliable chairlifts so wheelchairs users could access the buses. Scott's vision for improving transit helped increase legislative support. Her team modernized the routes; acquired bike-racks; for some pizzaz instituted rubber-tired natural gas "trolleys" on downtown routes; promoted bus use by RITECARE recipients (a RI variant of Medicaid); developed a "Upass," resulting in most private colleges in Rhode Island supporting transit use for their students; and built a downtown hub and terminal building in Providence's Kennedy Plaza.

In response to lobbying by anti-poverty, senior, and disability advocacy groups, the legislature and RIPTA instituted a program of free rides for low-income seniors and people with disabilities, first just at off-peak times, later at all times. All this grew the ridership to over 25 million in 2007.

It should be noted that facing the usual budget difficulties, Governor Raimondo's administration and the legislature had RIPTA impose a small fare for those groups that had been riding free. This inspired a strong "no-fare" campaign by the Senior Agenda and allied groups. With the state's basic sympathy for seniors and the disabled in mind, the governor and legislature gave in, and their free rides were restored. Indeed, this group grew to about 30 percent of the ridership.

Since 2007, a combination of relatively cheap gas, the decline of downtown Providence (e.g., the empty "Superman" building), the rise of ride-sharing companies, and perhaps the increasing association of bus use with minority and poor populations has resulted in declining ridership. Even before COVID-19, it dropped to about 16 million passengers a year. Rhode Island's commute-by-transit rate, despite relatively high density and corridor development, was reported as only 2.1 percent, far below the national average of 5.2 percent.

Notably, a bill passed in 2008 requiring the Department of Administration to take steps to reduce commuting miles, including offering a bus pass to state employees. It has not been implemented, in part because of state employee union resistance—they did not want to risk their "free" parking. RIPTA has also faced opposition to bus hubs/shelters in some shopping centers and in downtown Woonsocket and Pawtucket, where adjacent property interests associated bus passengers with the poor and minority populations. This is most noteworthy in Kennedy Plaza itself, where it is no secret that adjacent property owners want the buses and passengers relocated somewhere else; a plan for a new bus terminal with parking, restrooms and commercial facilities is gaining support.

The basic issue is that Rhode Islanders, through their legislature, and by direct vote for a 2014 transit bond that passed with over 60 percent approval, support keeping RIPTA going to provide basic mobility for those who don't drive, but few are willing to use it themselves. Yet the state has adopted an ambitious "Transit Master Plan" to greatly improve service, indeed to "take a great leap forward toward a world class transportation system . . . greatly enhancing Rhode Island's attractiveness to employers and residents."[3] Some activist groups support this as a way to help the state's environment. However, financing such a plan so far has largely been put off; it is not clear that Rhode Island will make such an investment or that people will use it in sufficient numbers if it comes to pass.

The Fall and Rise of Rail Transportation

Even into the 1960s, the New Haven Railroad was providing decent service through Providence on the Boston–New York line—for example, it still had a premium dining service on the traditional "Merchants Limited." But with the 1958 opening of the Connecticut Turnpike facilitating trucking, the New Haven could not avoid bankruptcy. In 1968 the line was taken over, reluctantly, by the Penn Central Railroad, which cared little about that service, and in turn, it too went bankrupt. The Providence train station became quite decrepit, some of the freight yards were sold off, additional freight tracks were abandoned (for example the line to Bristol), and though the MBTA (Massachusetts Bay Transportation Authority) was empowered to save commuter trains to Boston, Rhode Island stopped contributing to its operation. All commuter train service in Providence (and Pawtucket) ended in 1981. The railroad station was relocated from its central location to the edge of the State House lawn.

Yet voices rose to try to preserve and improve the declining rail service. Among them was the RI Association of Railroad Passengers, formed in the 1970s. Rhode Island's own Senator Claiborne Pell was one such voice, and his 1966 book *Megalopolis Unbound* laid out a vision for high-speed rail in the Boston-NY-Washington "Northeast Corridor." Though he got some criticism for "playing with trains," Pell's vision came to be largely implemented with the creation of Amtrak in 1970 and later the electrification of the line from New Haven to Boston, which sped up and cleaned up the trips. And though Amtrak still has financial and operating problems—for example, the slow curvy line in southeastern Connecticut threatened by sea-level rise with no obvious solution—it has substantially increased ridership in Rhode Island until COVID hit.

A visionary plan for a high-speed rail line from Boston through Providence, Hartford, New Haven, and then a tunnel to Long Island to New York City has been developed as part of a concept called "North Atlantic Rail" that has gotten some attention, though financing and getting approval to site such a route seem daunting.[4] There is also a "Northeast Corridor Commission" involving state and federal agencies, Amtrak and commuter rail operators, and they too have a plan, albeit more modest, for improved passenger train service along the corridor, with more miles of high-speed track enabling quicker and more frequent service. Hopes for financing the cost, about $117 billion, seem dependent on what the federal government does about infrastructure. However, a 2016 suggestion to take some land in southwestern Rhode Island to straighten a curve to speed up trips was met with fierce opposition; indeed a crowd from the area opposing this filled the State House, leading to Governor Raimondo's opposition, killing the proposal, and revealing yet another obstacle to improving infrastructure.

Commuter rail in Rhode Island has seen a comeback. The business and political community, which once had shown little interest in trains, began to see that our position on the rail corridor was an economic opportunity. So, by 1988, Rhode Island and the MBTA formed a "Pilgrim Partnership" to restore commuter service to Providence (but not to Pawtucket). When weekend service was added, and weekday service was extended to the airport and to Wickford Junction in North Kingstown, ridership grew substantially. Rhode Island is also investing in a new Pawtucket-Central Falls commuter station in hopes it will help revitalize those disadvantaged communities. There are plans to electrify the commuter line, which mostly operates under electric wires that Amtrak uses. Electrification has operational and environmental advantages, but the upfront capital costs and the needed cooperation across state lines makes implementation a challenge. With COVID changing work and commuter habits, there is also doubt about what the future of commuter rail should look like; for example, some suggest less peak service and more service at other times.

Bicycling Gets a Start

Though Rhode Island had long had a recreational bicycle group, the Narragansett Bay Wheelmen, when the state bought the abandoned freight line to Bristol in the 1970s, a new movement began to use the corridor for a bicycle path. That idea had much opposition—from Town Councils, from nearby condominium associations, and from other abutters, including a golf course, a hospital, and a private club; some feared a bike path nearby would threaten increased crime. There was also opposition due to the construction expense, and even from some who wanted the line for eventually restoring rail service. Yet the East Bay Bike path was built, apparently due to persistent local advocates who would not give up (one of whom, George Redman, was eventually honored by having the linear park section over the Seekonk River named after him); however, they had some allies among elected officials, such as Bristol Representative Tom Byrnes, and in key agencies, such as RIDOT Director Ed Wood.

The success of the East Bay bike path facilitated construction of additional bikeways in the Blackstone Valley, West Bay, along the Woonasquatucket

Greenway, and in South County. But opposition, especially from abutters, has blocked some proposed bikeways, notably in Johnston and Smithfield, where fear of crime has remained an issue, and in North Kingstown. It seems those places have not had determined local advocacy or visionary town leadership. In Providence, on-road bicycle facilities have also drawn some opposition when seen to impede motorists or to take up parking spaces, and the first attempt to have a bike-share program there failed due to vandalism and misuse.

Nevertheless, there are active bicycle advocacy groups, such as the RI Bicycle Coalition, promoting what they see as a heathy, emission-free, inexpensive, and often fun way to travel, and in 2020 they helped persuade the state to adopt a "Bicycle Mobility Plan" to promote bicycling all over the state. It remains to be seen how much of the plan actually gets funded, especially as not that many people in Rhode Island regularly ride bikes. (It should be noted "bikeways" are officially multiuse paths, also open to walkers, skateboarders, joggers, as well as wheelchair users.) However, the relatively low cost of bike projects, the enthusiasm of the bicycle community, the increased bicycling during the COVID pandemic, and the need to reduce transportation emissions to deal with climate change may indeed lead to better bicycle infrastructure in the state.

Travel by Boat

Though some in the "Ocean State" might regret that the days of a luxury overnight steamship to New York are long gone, we do have our Block Island ferries. In response to some available federal funding, in the 1990s RIPTA tried to establish commuter ferry between Newport and Providence, but it just wasn't competitive in terms of time or convenience, so it was discontinued. Also using some federal funding, RIDOT now supports a seasonal tourist-oriented Newport-Providence ferry operated by Seastreak that was considered quite successful, at least before COVID hit. With our geography, future ferry operations are always possible but will likely continue to depend on federal support.

Support for Aviation

Rhode Island business and political leaders have long supported air travel as crucial for economic success. TF Green was the country's first state airport when opened in 1931. Post-war expansion led to a new terminal building around 1961. To protect aviation from who-you-know Rhode Island politics, the legislature set up an independent Airport Corporation to manage and promote the airports. As there were residences and schools near to TF Green, neighbors became concerned about its noise and air pollution impacts as well as runoff into the Buckeye Brook watershed, and for a while formed groups to oppose airport expansion. These issues were generally resolved by buying out some property owners and setting up a retention basin for de-icing salts. In the 1990s Governor Sundlun, who had a personal interest in aviation and wanting a new terminal building rather than refurbishing the old one, got that and new highway access roads through the political process remarkably quickly, and without serious opposition, thus showing a Rhode Island Governor can indeed be powerful. In 2021, TF Green was voted as the third best airport in the country.[5]

What About Emissions and Climate Change?

Federal Clean Air Acts going back to the 1960s gradually tightened controls on automobile emissions (not without resistance from some auto makers, who said it couldn't be done!), and Rhode Island did its part by passing an anti-engine-idling law and including pollution control testing as part of its every-two-year inspection-maintenance requirements on passenger vehicles. However, despite decades-old legislation requiring it, the state has not been checking emissions from heavy-duty trucks. This has become a public issue, and the state says it is planning to address it and enforce the law.

The regulations noted above have helped bring Rhode Island into compliance with health-based air-quality standards, but now transportation carbon dioxide emissions are the concern due to climate change issues. Indeed, it is well known that transportation is now the sector with the most such emissions. The state leadership is taking climate change seriously by committing to major greenhouse gas reductions in coming years. There is support in the executive branch for a regional "Transportation Climate Initiative" (TCI), which would use fees to cap the amount of carbon that transportation fuels can emit in the region (in most of New England and the northeast, but this is in flux) and gradually lower the cap. The legislature, fearing this initiative might significantly raise gas prices, has not yet acted on this. But they did implement the Act on Climate in 2021, which updates and monitors climate emission reduction goals to ensure that the state reduces greenhouse gas emissions to net zero by 2050.[6]

The bulk of reductions in transportation emissions are expected to come from conversion to electric vehicles. How to do this, and how fast, and what to do about electrifying the school and transit bus fleet (electric buses are approximately twice the cost of diesel buses) is likely to be an ongoing issue for some time. Although emissions from airplanes are not subject to TCI limits, the aviation industry has successfully restricted regulation of airplane emissions to the national and even international level.

Because there is some history that transportation investments have neglected or hurt minority communities, one of the TCI framework priorities is to serve disadvantaged communities. How this can be implemented is yet another challenge in transportation policy, but it is a priority for the advocacy group TCI for RI.

Those interested in that or any other transportation policy issue should take advantage of Rhode Island's small size and get involved. Agency heads such as the RIDOT Director and RIPTA CEO are remarkably accessible, and besides official public hearings, the RIPTA and Airport Corporation Boards, the State Planning Council, and its Transportation Advisory Committee all allow public comment at their meetings. Numerous public advocacy organizations, some mentioned above, also provide opportunities for involvement. Take advantage!

Notes

1. Routes 4, 6, 24, 37, 99, 114, 138, 146, and 403 were rebuilt as expressways.
2. Rachel Nunes, "Rhode Island Bridges Rated the Worst in The Country," *Patch*, April 2, 2019, https://patch.com/rhode-island/newport/rhode-island-bridges-rated-worst-country.
3. "Rhode Island Transit Master Plan," *Transit Forward RI*, December 2020, https://transitforwardri.com/pdf/TFRI Recs Briefing Book-Final 201230.pdf.
4. "North Atlantic Rail," North Atlantic States Regional Council of Carpenters, http://www.nasrcc.org/wp-content/uploads/2021/05/North-Atlantic-Rail_Legislative-Requests_FINAL.pdf.
5. Paul Brady, "The Top 10 Domestic Airports," *Travel & Leisure*, September 8, 2021, https://www.travelandleisure.com/worlds-best/airports-domestic.
6. Environment Council of Rhode Island, "2021 Act On Climate," https://www.environmentcouncilri.org/bills/2021-act-climate.

About the Contributors

Patrick T. Conley, a retired professor and attorney, is Historian Laureate of Rhode Island and the president of the Heritage Harbor Foundation, the Rhode Island Heritage Hall of Fame, and the Rhode Island Publications Society. He is a former president of the US Constitution Council.

Michael DiBiase has served as president and CEO of the Rhode Island Public Expenditure Council (RIPEC) since January 2020. Prior to his tenure at RIPEC, Michael served for five years as director of administration for the State of Rhode Island. His prior experience includes senior positions in government relations for Fidelity Investments, as well as serving as chief of staff for Rhode Island Governor Lincoln Almond. Michael is a graduate of Boston College and University of Pennsylvania Law School.

Bob Hackey is a professor of health policy and management at Providence College and an Affiliate at the Taubman Center for American Politics and Policy at Brown University. His current research focuses on how partisanship shapes health policy, health policy in popular culture, and the politics of hospital mergers and acquisitions. Bob's latest book, *Today's Health Care Issues: Democrats and Republicans*, was published by ABC-CLIO in 2021.

Rob Horowitz is a strategic and communications consultant who has worked for a broad array of non-profit and business clients as well as candidates and elected officials at all levels. He is an adjunct professor of political science at the University of Rhode Island, where he teaches courses in both media and elections.

Colleen Kennedy is a senior at Providence College with a double major in health policy and management and political science.

Diane Kern is interim director and professor at the School of Education at the University of Rhode Island. She taught for fourteen years in public schools in urban, suburban, and rural school districts in Florida and Rhode Island. Her research interests include bridging the gap between research and literacy teacher education, standards for the preparation of literacy professionals, developing her own and teachers' cultural competence, and increasing access to college and teacher education programs for people who have been traditionally marginalized or under-represented in the profession.

Aaron Ley is an associate professor in the Department of Political Science at the University of Rhode Island and Director of URI's Master of Public Administration Program. He received his PhD in political science from Washington State University in 2011. His research appears in the journals *Environmental Politics, Law & Society Review, Law & Policy*, and *Review of Policy Research*.

Emily K. Lynch is an assistant teaching professor in the Department of Political Science at the University of Rhode Island. She received her PhD in political science from The Ohio State University in 2013. Her teaching and research interests include public opinion, political psychology, political behavior, and political communication, especially in the areas of Rhode Island politics and women and politics. She has publications in the *Journal of Communication* and *Political Behavior*.

Maureen Moakley is professor emerita at the University of Rhode Island. She has published books and articles on comparative state politics, political parties, and Rhode Island politics. She does opinion and political commentary on Rhode Island politics.

Adam S. Myers is an associate professor of political science at Providence College. His research interests are in the areas of state politics, federalism, and political parties/elections. He is currently writing a book about the changing politics of American fiscal federalism from the 1930s to today.

Shanna Pearson is a professor of public policy at the University of Maryland at College Park's School of Public Policy and is currently serving as the associate dean for Faculty Affairs. She studies the politics of public policies and has worked with various government agencies to evaluate social programs. Her work has been published in some of the top journals in political science and she regularly writes for public audiences to help the public access and use policy-research through outlets like the "Monkey Cage" (the *Washington Post*) and the magazine *Pacific Standard*.

Gary Sasse served as the founding director of the Hassenfeld Institute for Public Leadership at Bryant University. He was appointed by Governor Donald Carcieri (R-RI) to head both the Department of Administration and Department of Revenue and was executive director of the Rhode Island Public Expenditure Council (RIPEC). Sasse has had leadership roles in presidential campaigns. He holds a Bachelor of Arts in political science from Florida State University and a Master of Science in public administration from the University of Missouri.

Barry Schiller, a retired professor of mathematics at Rhode Island College, is a lifelong transit rider, bicyclist, and yes, a motorist too. He has served on the RI Public Transit Authority Board of Directors and as a member of the State Planning Council's Transportation Advisory Committee. He lives in North Providence near the #57 bus line.

Wendy J. Schiller is the Royce Family professor of teaching excellence in political science and director of the Taubman Center for American Politics and Policy at Brown University. She has published books and articles on legislative politics and gender and public policy. She is a frequent commentator on American politics for local and national news outlets.

June Speakman is a professor of political science and international relations at Roger Williams University, where she teaches courses on elections, public policy, state and local governments, and national political institutions. After serving fourteen years as a town council member, she was elected in 2019 to the Rhode Island House of Representatives.

Michaela Szymczak is a sophomore at Providence College, majoring in health policy and management and political science.

Matt Ulricksen is an assistant professor of political science at the Community College of Rhode Island. He holds bachelor of arts and master's degrees in history from Providence College and a masters of arts degree in political science from the University of Rhode Island. Formerly active in local and state politics, Matt is a Rhode Island native, has lived in South County almost his entire life, and travels north of the Tower only when he has to.

Index

Note: Page numbers in italics indicate tables or figures.

AAA, 282
ABC, 130
abortion, 17, 49, 58, 59, 96, 111–12, 156, 161n34, 227–28, 257–58, 261
accountability, 101
Act on Climate, 17, 113, 156, 288
Adams, Susan Sharp, 38
Addison, Philip, 205
Administrative Act of 1939, 166
administrative adjudication court, 184. *See also* traffic tribunal
administrative state, 165–68, *169*
Affordable Care Act (ACA), 235, 237, 251, 252, 257–59
African Americans, 4, 204
Africans, 11, 12
agrarian community, 31, 32–33
agrarian debtor revolt, 31
agrarian economy, 32
agrarian population, declining, 32–33
Airport Corporation Boards, 289
Aldrich, Nelson W., 36, 37
Allen, Matt, 135
Almond, Lincoln, 43, 44–45, 74–75, 95, 170, 173, 269, 271, 272, 283
Alves, Stephen D., 117
American Academy of Pediatrics, 120
American Civil Liberties Union (ACLU), 43, 108, 111, 282–83
American College of Obstetricians and Gynecologists, 112
American Federation of County, State, and Municipal Employees, Council 94, 110–11
American Health Care Association, 256
American Lung Association, 113
American Medical Association, 119–20
American Party, 35–36. *See also* Know-Nothing Party
American Rescue Plan Act, 238
American Revolution, 29–31, 163, 203

Ames, Samuel, 36, 164
Amica Insurance, 117
Amtrak, 285–86
Anderson, Patrick, 213
Andrews, Charles McLean, 26
Anheuser-Busch, 117
Anthony, Henry Bowen, 36
anti-Catholicism, 28, 30, 35
anti-discrimination laws, 11, 12
Antifederalism, 31
AOL, 137
Aponte, Luis, 209
Apple, 131
apportionment. *See* legislative apportionment
Aquidneck Island, 3, 4, 26, 213, 280
Arditi, Lynn, 135
Armenians, 12
Arrigan, Robert, 187–88
Articles of Confederation, 30–31, 50
artisans, 32
Asians, 12, 15
Atherton Land Company, 27
attorney general, 190–93. *See also* Office of the Attorney General
Audubon Society, 113, 274, 281
Auto Body Association of Rhode Island, 108, 109, 115, 117, 268
auto body legislation, 105–6, 107
auto insurance industry, 105–6, 107
automatic voter registration, 66
automobiles, 279–80, 282
autonomy, tradition of, 31
aviation, support for, 287–88

Baker v. *Carr*, 200
Bakst, M. Charles, 136
ballot placement, 76
Bally's Corporation, 117
Bancroft, George, 28

Barrington, Rhode Island, 204, 210–11, 214
Bartholomew, Bill, 131
The Barthomewtown Podcast, 131
base-metal industry, 32
Beck, Glenn, 134
Berry, John, 133
Bevilacqua, Anthony, 87
Bevilacqua, Joseph, 42, 183
"Bicycle Mobility Plan," 287
bicycling, 286–87
Biden, Joe, 73, 91, 125, 213–14, 225
bikeways, 286–87
Binder, William, 262
Binning, Helen I., 38
Black, Latino, Indigenous, Asian American Pacific Islanders caucus, 15
Black community, 4
Black Lives Matter, 11, 75, 108
Black Lives Matter PAC, 114
Black River Valley, 145
Blacks, 11–12, 204–6. *See also* African Americans
Black slaves, 30
Blackstone Canal, 32
Blackstone River, 32
Block, Ken, 69, 99
Block Island, 130, 192, 287
Block Island Wind Farm, 275
Bloodless Revolution, 7–8, 37–39, 45, 65, 86–87, 96, 146, 163, 164–66, 170, 173, 180
Blue Cross and Blue Shield of RI (BCBSRI), 253, 258
Board of Education, 167
Board of Public Safety, 200
bond measures, 74
Boston Globe, 125, 126–27, 128, 129, 132
Boston Tea Party, 203
Boyle, Christopher, 117
Bradley Hospital, 253
Brayton, Charles Ray, 6, 36, 37, 146, 164–65
Brayton Act, 37, 39, 146, 164–65
Bristol, Rhode Island, 185, 204
Brown, Matt, 100, 114–15, 139, 224, 227
Brown, Moses, 32
Brown, Steve, 6
Brown family, 11
Brown University, 205, 254, 271
budget, fiscal federalism and, 55–58
Burrillville, Rhode Island, 202–3, 255, 256, 274, 275
Butler Hospital, 254

Calkin, Jeanne, 100
campaign financing, 76–79
Canonicus, 203
Carcieri, Donald, 66, 95, 171–72, 177, 183, 232, 269, 272
Care New England, 117, 192, 253–55
Carter, Jimmy, 280
Caruolo, George, 117
Caruolo Act, 201
Casale, Thomas, 106
Catholic Democrats, 156
Catholic immigrants, 37
Catholicism, 16–17, 111
Catholics, 28, 30, 35
census count, 14–15
Centers for Medicare and Medicaid Services (CMS), 255
Central Falls, Rhode Island, 13, 100, 201, 210, 211, 213–14, 246
Chace, Elizabeth Buffum, 37–38
Chafee, John H., 11, 40, 173, 269
Chafee, Lincoln, 74, 95, 99, 150, 232, 257–58, 259, 269, 274, 275–76, 281
Champlin's Marina, 130
change, 4–6
Channel 6, 128, 130
Channel 10, 128–29, 139
Channel 12, 126, 128–29
Charles II, 27, 30. *See also* Charter of 1663
Charter of 1663, 27–29, 32–33, 35, 44, 46, 52, 64–65, 144–45, 149, 157, 163, 199
charter schools, 244
Cianci, Vincent "Buddy," 6, 8, 207–8, 209
Cicilline, David, 94, 205, 208
citizen engagement, 18–19
Citizens Bank, 283
Citizens Party, 99
Citizens United v. *Federal Election Commission*, 120
city and town news, 136–37
city council elections, property tax paying qualification and, 37
civil liberties, 54
Civil Rights Movement, 12
Civil Service Act, 174
civil service initiative, 166
Civil War, 52, 53, 59–60
Clarke, John, 27
Clean Water Act, 272
Climate Action, 113
climate change, 156, 275–76, 288
Clinton, Hillary, 91
CNN, 125
Coastal Resources Management Council (CRMC), 109, 130, 192, 269–70
Coddington, William, 199

Code of Judicial Conduct, 183
Coit, Janet, 269
College Republicans, 99
Collins, Susan, 221
colonial era, 25–29
"combined sewage overflow" (CSO) events, 272–73
Commission to "Re-Examine the Field of Government Operations, the Cost of Government Services and the Tax Structure of the State," 167
Commission to Study the Financial Problems of the State and Municipalities, 166
Common Cause, 42, 43, 45, 78, 108, 162n40, 179
commuter rail, 286
"conditional grants," 55
Congress. *See* US Congress
Conley, Patrick T., 6, 47n2, 50–51, 145, 164; Constitutional Conventions and Amendments and, 41–42; Separation of Powers Amendment and, 44
Connecticut Colony, 25
Conservation Law Foundation (CLF), 268, 272, 274
Conservative Caucus, 99
Constitution. *See* RI Constitution; US Constitution
Constitutional Conventions, 40–42; Constitutional Convention of 1842, 199; Constitutional Convention of 1951, 200–202
constitutional demography, 32–33
constitutional development, 25–48
Constitution Party, 99
continuity, 4–6
Cool Moose Party, 99
cooperative federalism, 54, 55
Cornwell, Elmer, 175
Coronavirus Aid, Relief, and Economic Security Act, 238
corruption, 13
cotton industry, 32
Council on Environmental Quality, 280
Court Reorganization Act, 39
court system, 183–96, *184*; attorney general, 190–93; district court, 186; family court, 187; federal courts, 193–94; judiciary, 183–96; municipal courts, 189; probate courts, 189–90; superior court, 185–86; supreme court, 185; traffic tribunal, 188–89; worker's compensation court, 187–88

COVID-19, 5, 15, 18, 56, 150, 176, 177, 255; 2020 election procedures and, 68; bicycling and, 287; education and, 247; federal funding response and, 237–38; funds to address, 17; General Assembly and, 157–59; immigration and, 14; judiciary and, 182–83; nursing homes and, 256–57; opioid epidemic and, 260; public transportation and, 284, 285, 286, 287; Raimondo and, 225, 251; vaccinations, 9; voting and, 63, 74, 79; women governors and, 229n11
Cranston, Rhode Island, 143–44, 189, 204, 213, 223, 244, 255
criminal defendants, rights of, 54
Critical Race Theory (CRT), 246–47
Cromwell, Oliver, 27
Cubans, 13
Cuervo, Gonzalo, 209
cultural policy, decentralization of, 58
culture, politics and, 3–24
culture wars, 58–59
Cumulus, 134
Current Population Survey, 72
CVS, 117, 281
cybersecurity, elections and, 69

Davis, Paulina Wright, 37–38
Declaration of Candidacy, 76, 83n49
Deloitte, 259
Democracy Fund, 137
Democratic Governors Association, 225
democratic localism, 31
Democratic Socialists of America, 155
Democratic State Committee, 98, 99
Democratic Women's Caucus, 98
Democrats, 7–8, 35, 37–38, 60, 85–104, 206–7, 221, 223–24; ascendancy of, 39, 40–42, 54, 65, 146; Bloodless Revolution and, 38–39; Constitutional Conventions and Amendments, 40–42; cultural conservatism and, 59; dominance of, 8–9; education and, 247; endorsements and, 77; General Assembly and, 143–62, *148*; gubernatorial race and, 213, 223–25; identity and, 214; interest groups and, 110, 114–15; interstate culture wars and, 58–59; intra-party factionalism and, 154–56; judiciary and, 180; during New Deal Era, 54; state taxation policy and, 57–58; "Trump Democrats," 214; women's suffrage and, 38
demographics, education and, 242
Department of Motor Vehicles (DMV), 66

Department of Youth and Family Services, 18
DePetro, John, 135
deputy governor, 27
Derbyshire cotton industry, 32
DeSimone, John, 155
Diaz, Grace, 223
DiBiase, Michael, 211
Dickinson, Spencer, 224
Dillon, John, 200
Dillon's Rule, 200, 202
DiMario, Alana, 79
DiPrete, Edward, 42, 88, 176
discrimination, 205
disenfranchisement, 64
dissent, 31
dissidents, 3
district court, 186
District Court for Rhode Islands, 192
district courts, 186–87, 189
diversity, 210–11
Dobbs v. Jackson Women's Health Organization, 49, 58, 261
Dominicans, 13
Dominion of New England, 27, 28
Donnis, Ian, 135
Dorr, Thomas Wilson, 33–35, 64
Dorr Rebellion, 33–35, 47n2, 52–53, 59–60, 64, 145, 199
Doyle, Thomas, 206
dual federalism, 52–53, 54, 55

early national period: 1790-1840, 31–33
East Bay, 213
East Bay Bike path, 286
East Greenwich, Rhode Island, 91, 210–11
East Providence, Rhode Island, 244
Economic Development Corporation (Rhode Island Commerce Corporation), 168, 171
Economic Progress Institute, 119
economy, 110–11; economic change, 31–33; industrial, 32; interest groups and, 110–11
Edison Research, 131
education, 58; COVID-19 and, 238, 247; Democrats and, 247; demographics and, 242; General Assembly and, 201–2; looking forward, 246–47; politics of, 241–49; politics of education reform, 245–46; property taxes and, 233–34; RI Constitution and, 241–42; school funding and, 235–36, 236, 237, 243–45; student achievement and, 243
Education Law Center, 245

Edwards, William H., 40
Eisenhower, Dwight D., 90–91, 212
Elazar, Daniel, 10
Eleanor Slater Hospital (ESH), 255–56
election law reform, 82n30
elections, 63–84; of 2020, 68, 143; administration of, 70–71, *71*; city council elections and property tax qualification, 37, 38; cybersecurity and, 69; federal, 90–95, *91*, *92*, *93*, *94*; for General Assembly, 95–97; general state office, 95; gubernatorial, 213, 223–25, *226*, *227*; presidential, 90–92, *91*, *92*; special elections, 73–74; US Congress, 92–95; US House of Representatives, 93–95, *94*; US Senate, 90–93, *93*
electorate, political parties and, 88–90
Electronic Registration Information Center, 88
Elorza, Jorge, 205–6, 209, 226, 275
Emancipation Act of 1784, 30
emissions, climate change and, 288
endorsements, 76
Energy Facilities Siting Board (EFSB), 269, 274
energy issues, 17
English Language Arts (ELA) student achievement, 243
the environment: interest groups and, 113–14 (*see also* climate change; environmental policy)
Environmental Council, 43, 108, 113, 268
environmental justice, 273–75
environmental policy, 167, 267–78; climate change and, 275–76; context, 267–68; General Assembly and, 268–71, 275–76; key agencies and stakeholders, 268–71; nonpoint source stormwater runoff and, 272–73; Providence's Fields Point and, 273–75; Quonset Point dredging and, 271–72
environmental racism, 274–75
Equal Education Opportunities Act, 245
Equality in Abortion Coverage Act (EACA), 261
Equal Rights Movement, 37
Ethics Advisory Panel, 183
Ethics Commission, 42, 43, 179, 185
Euer, Dawn, 113
Europeans, 12
"evergreen contracts," 110–11
executive branch, 163–78; evolution of, 163–72; future executive leadership, 176–77; General Assembly and, 163–66,

168, 170, 177; governors as policy leaders, 170–72; halcyon years of, 166–68; separation of powers and, 168–70
Executive Climate Change Coordinating Council, 113, 275–76
Executive Office of Health and Human Services, 167–68
expectations, rising, 18–19

Facebook, 131, 132, 133
factory workers, 32
Family Court, 182, 183–84, 187
Farmer, Susan, 38, 222
Fatima Hospital, 190, 254
Fay, Thomas, 42, 183
Federal Aid for Highways, 55
Federal Clean Air Acts, 288
federal courts, 193–94
Federal Election Commission, 124n70
federal elections: presidency, 90–92, *91*, *92*; US Congress, 92–95; US House of Representatives, 93–95, *94*; US Senate, 92–93, *93*
Federal Energy Regulatory Commission, 275
Federal Highway Act, 280
Federal Hill, 7
Federal Housing Administration, 205
Federal Indian Regulatory Act, 11
federalism, 31, 49–50, 59–60; cooperative federalism, 54, 55; dual federalism, 52–53, 54, 55; fiscal federalism, 50, 55–58; historical overview, 50–54; transformation of in mid-twentieth century, 54; in twenty-first century, 55–59
Federalists, 31
federal law enforcement agencies, 193
federal system, 49–61
Federal Trade Commission, 254–55
FedEx, 117
Fenton, Josh, 125, 129
Fenton-Fung, Barbara Ann, 143–44
Feroce, Giovanni, 224–25
ferries, 287
Fields Point, 273–75
Fifteenth Amendment, 53
Filippi, Blake, 79
First Amendment, 107, 116
fiscal federalism, 50, 55–58
Fitzpatrick, Ed, 126, 127, 132, 140
Flanders, Robert, 44, 145
Floyd, George, murder of, 10–11, 131
Forest Conservation Act, 276
Forest Conservation Commission, 17, 276

Foulkes, Helena, 227
Founding Era, 50–52, 60
Founding Fathers, 31
Fourteenth Amendment, 53
Fox, Donald, 203
Fox, Gordon, 42, 155
France, 30
Franco-Americans, 38
freehold suffrage requirement, 32–33, 35
freemen, 27, 29, 64
free suffrage, 32–33, 35
French Canadians, 12
Frenemies International Gaming Technology (IGT), 117
Fung, Allan, 77, 224–25, 213, 223

Garrahy, J. Joseph, 177
"GARVEE bond," 282
Gaspee, 30, 203
Gaspee Project, 119–20
Gatehouse/Gannett, 126, 136
General Assembly, 8, 11, 17, 27–30, 36–37, 54, 86–88, 92, 134, 143–62, 162n40, 200, 210, 214; apportionment and, 33, 146–48 (*see also* legislative apportionment); authorized by Charter of 1663, 199; banning of slave trade, 30; as a bicameral legislature, 151–53; Bloodless Revolution and, 38–39; campaign finance and, 77–78; Campaign Finance Annual General Assembly Report, 77; as a citizen legislature, 150–51; Constitutional Conventions and Amendments, 41–42; COVID-19 and, 157–59; Democrats and, 39, 40–42, *148*; development of, 144–48; Dorr Rebellion and, 33–35; EACA and, 261; education and, 201–2, 236, 237, 243; elections for, 95–97; environmental policy and, 113–14, 268–71, 275–76; Ethics Commission, 43; executive branch and, 163–66, 168, 170, 172–77; Grand Committee of, 43, 73, 181; gun legislation and, 112–13, 202–3; healthcare reform and, 257, 258, 259; Hospital Conversions Act, 190; House Finance Committee, 161n24; interest groups and, 105–6, 109, 111–12, 114–17; Joint Committee on Legislative Services, 152; judiciary and, 180, 186; key aspects of modern, 149–59; lobbying and, 115–17; partisan division of, 97; pension reform and, 235; power of, 157–59; property valuation and, 201; ratification of US Constitution and, 31–32; reproductive rights and, 49, 111–12;

Rhode Island Lottery Commission and, 44; RI Constitution and, 241, 268–69; Separation of Powers Amendment and, 44–46; special elections and, 74; spending and, 235–37, 238; strength of, 149–50; as a strong legislature, 149–50; tax policy and, 201, 232–34, 238; voting age and, 66; voting methods and, 67; voting reform and, 70; women in, 221; women's suffrage and, 37–38. *See also* Bloodless Revolution; *specific legislation*
General Court of Trials, 26
general elections, voter turnout, 90
George III, 30
Germans, 12
Giffords Law Center, 59
Gilbert, William, 99
Giroux, Todd, 223
Gledhill, Liz, 85
Goldberg, Maureen McKenna, 44
Goldberg, Robert, 117
GoLocal Live, 129
GoLocalProv, 125, 129, 132
Google, 129, 131
Gorbea, Nellie, 63, 65, 66, 69–70, 77, 88, 116, 139, 226–28
Gorman, Charles E., 37
Gorsuch, Neil, 49
Gorton, Samuel, 26, 199
government: local, 197–217; political parties and, 90
governors, 27; election of first female, 222–25; General Assembly and, 172–77; as policy leaders, 170–72. *See also* executive branch
Granahan, Tara, 135
"Grand Convention," 31
grassroots lobbying, 115–16
Great Depression, 38, 165
Greater Providence Chamber of Commerce, 110, 115
Great Recession, 99, 173, 224, 231, 233, 235, 237
Greeks, 12
Green, Theodore Francis, 7, 38–39, 165, 173
"Green Economy and Clean Water Bond," 267
Green New Deal, 100, 114
Green Party, 91
Green Revolution, 7, 8, 86. *See also* Bloodless Revolution
Gregg, Kathy, 132
Grow Smart RI, 283
gun court, 185–86

gun legislation, 58, 59, 112–13, 202–3

Hale Global, 137
Hannity, Sean, 134
Harrison, Michael, 134
Hasbro Children's Hospital, 253
Hassan, Maggie, 221
Healey, Robert, 223–24
Health and Human Services, 18
healthcare reform, 251, 257–58, 259
"Health Insurance Access Hub," 257
health insurance regulation, 253
health policy, 251–66
Health Source RI, 252, 257–58
Healthy and Safe Families and Workplaces Act, 100
"Healthy Rhode Island" advisory group, 257
Higgins, James, 36
highways, 279–81
home rule, 200–202, 268
Hopkins, Samuel, 29
Horowitz, Rob, 129
Horsmanden, Daniel, 30
Horton v. Newport, 200
Hospital Conversions Act (HCA), 190, 254
hospital industry, in transition, 253–55
"householders" compact, 25, 47n1
House of Deputies, 28, 144
House of Magistrates, 28, 144
House or Representatives. *See* RI House of Representatives; US House of Representatives
Huffington Post, 137
Humane Society, 117
Hummel, Jim, 130–31
Hummel Report, 130–31
Hunt, James, 177
Hurricane of 1938, 207
Hutchinson, Anne, 199
Hutchinson, Thomas, 30

ideology, interest groups and, 114–15
"I know a guy" syndrome, 6, 120
immigrants, 203–4
immigration, 12–15
Immigration Act of 1965, 12
immigration policy, 59
Independents, 221
Indian colonial wars, 11
individualistic political culture, 10, 30–31
industrial economy, transformation into, 32
industrialization, 32–33
Industrial Revolution, 32, 203

infrastructure, expense of maintaining, 281–82
initiatives, 74–75
interest groups, 101–24, 105–24; categories of, 108; Democrats and, 114–15; economic and occupation interest and, 108; economy and, 110–11; the environment and, 113–14; formation of, 107–8, 114; General Assembly and, 114–15, 115–17; gun legislation and, 112–13; ideology and, 114–15; intergovernmental, 108; lobbying and, 115–17; motivation for, 107; pluralist democracy and, 107; political action committees (PACs), 117–18; political tactics of, 115–20; public interest and citizen groups, 108; reproductive rights and, 111–12; resources and tactics of, 109; think tanks and, 119–20
internet, 125, 129
interstate culture wars, 58–59
intra-party competition, 100–101
Invenergy, 274
Irish Catholic Democrats, 36, 38, 206–7
Irish Catholic immigrants, 12, 32–33, 35, 203
ISO New England, 274
Italian Americans, 7, 38
Italian immigrants, 12

Jackvony, Bernard, 74
James, Sidney, 199
James II, 27, 28
Jews, 3, 12, 28, 30
job-training programs, 17
Johns Hopkins Institute for Education Policy, 245
Johnston, Rhode Island, 214, 283
Judicial Nominating Commission, 181
judiciary, 179–96; appointments to, 179–83; court structure, *184*; court system, 183; General Assembly and, 180, 186; reform of, 180–82; streaming of court proceedings, 182–83; technological improvements, 182–83; twenty-first-century, 182–83

Kalus, Ashley, 213
Kaminski, John, 50–51
Kavanaugh, Brett, 49
Keeney, Timothy, 269
Keller, Ed, 133
Kennedy, Patrick, 94
Kent County, Rhode Island, 185
Kent County Daily Times, 136

Kent Hospital, 254
King, Samuel Ward, 34
King Philip's War, 27, 28, 203
Know-Nothing Party, 35–36
Kuhn, Madeline, 221
Ku Klux Klan, 205

labor, power of, 9–10
LaFortune, Nirva, 209
Landmark Medical Center, 254
land use, transportation and, 283–85
Langevin, James, 95
Larisa, Joseph S., Jr., 44–45
Latin Americans, 12
Latinos, 12–14; education and, 243; Latina politicians, 226–28; in Providence, Rhode Island, 209
Law and Order faction, 34
Law Enforcement Officers Bill of Rights, 114
LBGTQ rights, 58, 59
League of Women Voters Rhode Island, 111–12
Lee, Frances, 244
legislative apportionment, 54, 65, 96; apportionment and, 33, 65, 146–48; Charter of 1663 and, 65; malapportionment, 37, 96, 146–48, 200; "reapportionment revolution," 147; US Supreme Court and, 65, 147
legislative patent, 26
legislatures, professionalized, 150–51, 172
Let RI Vote campaign, 70, 79, 81–82n29, 108
LGBTQ community, 99
Libertarian Party, 99–100
Liberty Caucus, 99
Lifespan, 117, 192, 253–55
Lincoln, Abraham, 176
LNG, 274–75
lobbying, 18, 115–17, 124n70
local government, 197–217; early nineteenth century and beyond, 198–99; evolution of state power, 199–200; power shifts and, 207–9; what came before, 198
Locke, John, 30
Long, Melissa, 179
long-term care, future of, 256–57
Luther v. Borden, 35, 53
Lynch Prata, Erin, 179

Machtley, Ronald, 93–94
MA Department of Environmental Projection, 269

Madison, James, 10
Mafia, 6, 7
Magaziner, Seth, 139
magistrates, 181–82
manumission, 30
marijuana legalization, 58, 59, 114, 152–53, 156
Marion, John, 162n40
Martin, Trayvon, murder of, 108
Massachusetts Bay Colony, 25
MassGeneral Brigham Health, 254
Matos, Sabina, 226–28
A Matter of Truth, 205–6
Mattiello, Nicholas, 111, 112, 117, 143–44, 155, 156, 233
Maxicap, 252
Mayer, Nancy, 222
MBTA (Massachusetts Bay Transportation Authority), 285, 286
McCaffrey, Michael, 67, 156
McCarty, Nolan, 153
McClure's Magazine, 37
McConnell, John J., 192–93
McCoy, Thomas P., 38–39
McGowan, Dan, 126, 127, 132, 192
McGrath, J. Howard, 166
McKee, Dan, 9, 14, 70, 77, 106, 131, 136, 158, 176, 213, 226–27; abortion rights and, 261; Deloitte and, 259; environmental policy and, 276; ESH and, 256; marijuana regulation and, 152–53; Medicaid expansion and, 258; nursing home staffing and, 256–57; special elections and, 73–74
McKenna, Keven, 42
McLeod, Andrew, 269
media, 125–41; city and town news, 136–37; new media environment and, 138–39; new online, 129–31; news consumption, 75; newspapers, 126–27, 136–37; policy makers and, 138–39; radio, 134–36; social media, 132–34; television news, 127–29
Medicaid, 167–68, 235, 237, 252, 253, 256, 257, 258–59
Mendes, Cynthia, 227, 228
#MeToo movement, 224
Mexicans, 13
Miantonomo, 203
Milkovitz, Amanda, 126, 132
Miller, Josh, 257
Mills, Janet, 221
mill villages, 32
minimum wage, raising, 100, 156
Miriam Hospital, 253

Moakley, Maureen, 175
Moderate Party, 99, 100
Moonves, Les, 128
Moreau, Chuck, 130
Morgan, J. P., 36
Morgan, Patricia, 224–25
Moshassuck River, 203
Moss, William, 38–39
Mothers Against Drunk Driving, 282
Motif Magazine, 131
motor vehicle excise tax, 233–34, 237
Mowry, Arthur May, 35
MSNBC, 125
municipal courts, 189
municipal governments, 214
municipal taxes, 233–37
Munoz, Luis Daniel, 227
Muravchik, Stephanie, 214
Murphy, William J., 112–13, 117
Myers, Adam, 92

Nader, Ralph, 91
Narragansett Bay, 5, 26, 32, 177, 203, 271, 272
Narragansett Bay Commission, 109, 273
Narragansett Bay Wheelmen, 286
Narragansett nation, 11–12, 25–26, 28, 64–65, 203
National Association for the Advancement of Colored People (NAACP), 205
National Council of State Legislatures, 226
National Education Association, 110–11, 242
National Governors Association, 176
national grants, 55–56, 56
National Health Planning and Resources Development Act, 252
National Organization for Women Rhode Island, 112
National Public Radio (NPR), 135–36
Native Americans, 4, 11–12, 25–26. *See also specific groups*
Native Hawaiians, 15
natural gas, 273–75
Nature Conservancy, 268, 269, 274
"Negro cloth," 204
Neighborhood Health Plan of RI, 253, 258
Neronha, Peter, 77, 190–91, 192, 254–55
Nesi, Ted, 128
Nesi's Notes, 128
New Bedford, Massachusetts, 203
New Deal, 38, 54, 164, 165
New Haven Colony, 25
New Haven Railroad, 285

New London, Connecticut, 203
Newport, Rhode Island, 3, 4, 5, 26, 27, 30, 199, 203, 204
Newport Amusement v. Maher, 202
Newport County, Rhode Island, 185
Newport Daily News, 136
Newport Hospital, 253
New Shoreham, Rhode Island, 192
newspapers, local, 136–37
New York Times, 127
Nineteenth Amendment, ratification of, 37–38
Nipmuck nation, 28
Nixon, Richard, 90–91, 171, 212
Noel, Philip, 87, 171, 173
nonpoint source stormwater runoff, environmental policy and, 272–73
"North Atlantic Rail," 285
"Northeast Corridor Commission," 285–86
North Kingstown, Rhode Island, 272
North Providence, Rhode Island, 201
nursing homes, 256–57
Nursing Home Staffing and Quality Care Act, 110

Obama, Barack, 91, 192, 272
O'Brien, Frank, 105, 106, 120
Office of Energy Resources (OER), 269, 270
Office of the Attorney General, 190–93, 254
Office of the Health Insurance Commissioner (OHIC), 253
Olneyville, Rhode Island, 281
O'Neille, Isabelle Florence Ahearn, 38
one-party control, 96, 101
online media outlets, 129–31
online voter registration, 65–66
onsite wastewater treatment systems (OWTS), 273
Operation Clean Government, 42
opioid epidemic, 260
Oregon, 66
organized labor, 38. *See also* unions
Our Lady of Fatima Hospital. *See* Fatima Hospital

Pacific Islands, 15
Paiva-Weed, Teresa, 222
Paolino, Joseph, 207–8
paper money, 31
Partners, 254
party politics: future of, 101; intra-party factionalism, 154–57; party competition, 153–57; party identification, 89; party in government, 85–86, 90–92; party in the electorate, 85–86, 88–90; party organizations, 98–99; party polarization, 153–54
Pastore, John O., 166–67, 173
Patch, 137
patronage, 166, 180, 181–82, 187
Pawtucket, Rhode Island, 210, 244
Pawtucket Falls, Rhode Island, cotton-spinning frame in mill at, 32
Pawtucket Times, 136
Payne, Kenneth F., 163, 164, 166, 167
PBS, 130
Pell, Claiborne, 223, 285
Pell, Clay, 223
Penn Central Railroad, 285
pension reform, 9, 16, 223, 235
People's Constitution, 34
People's Constitutional Convention, 34, 64
People's Party, 34, 35
personal income tax, 232, 238
Petrarca, Jina, 105
Petrarca family, 106
Pew Hispanic Center, 209
Pew Research Center, 132
Pew Research Group, 137
Philadelphia Convention of 1787, 31, 50, 51
Planned Parenthood Votes! Rhode Island, 111
pluralist democracy, 107, 114, 120
pluralist theory of democracy, 107
Plymouth Colony, 25
podcasts, 131
Pokanoket nation, 198
Poles, 12
"police powers," 58
policy makers, media and, 138–39
political action committees (PACs), 78, 117–18, 120
Political Cooperative, 100, 101
political corruption, legacy of, 6–8
political culture, 9–12, 87
political engagement, 75
political landscape, 8–9
political office, running for, 76
political participation, 75
political parties, 85–104; control of statewide offices, 96; development of RI party system, 86–88; electorate and, 88–90; government and, 90; party identification, 89, 89; party in government, 90–92; party in the electorate, 88–90
Political Question Doctrine, 35, 47–48n13

Politico, 15
politics: culture and, 3–24; current contour of, 16–17; of education, 241–49; women and, 15–16, 221–29
Polito, Jim, 135
poll taxes, 64–65
polyfluoroalkyl substances (PFAS), 273
"popular constituent sovereignty," 33–34
population density, 210
population growth, 146
Port Authority, 171
Portsmouth, Rhode Island, 26, 27, 199, 210–11
Portsmouth Assembly, 26
Portuguese, 12
Posner, Eric, 158
Powers, William E., 41
presidential elections, 90–92, *91*, *92*
primary elections, 87; 2020, 83n51; semi-open, 110; voter turnout, 90, *90*; voting in, 67
Private Equity Stakeholder's Project, 190
probate courts, 189–90
Progressive Era (ca. 1898–1917), 37–38, 53
Property Casualty Insurers of America, 105, 106, 109, 120
property taxes, 37–38, 210, 233, 237, 243
property tax paying qualification, city council elections and, 37, 38
Prospect Medical Holdings, 190
Providence, Rhode Island, 26, 27, 37, 146, 185, 199, 204, 210, 213–14; Blacks in, 204–6; as capital city, 203–4; founding of, 25, 198, 199, 203–4; gets a new form of government, 206–7; growing diversity of, 203–4; healthcare reform and, 258; as industrial leader, 32; Kennedy Plaza, 284; Latinos in, 209; pension reform and, 9; Providence Police Department, 205; Providence Public Schools, 245–46; rebirth of, 207–8; revision of City Charter, 207; school funding and, 244; as slave port, 204; teachers' unions and, 246; threatens secession, 31
Providence Auto Body, 106
Providence City Council, 114, 205, 209, 226
Providence Journal, 6, 36, 106, 120, 125, 128, 129, 130, 136, 138–40, 221; Constitutional Conventions and Amendments and, 40; decline of, 126–27; Separation of Powers Amendment and, 45; traffic tribunal and, 188
Providence Plantations, 3, 4, 46, 143
Providence Renaissance, 5, 8

Providence School Board, 211
Providence v. *Moulton*, 200
Public Finance Management Board, 237
public offices, 29
public safety, spending on, 236–37
Public Square Program, 137
The Public's Radio, 135–36
Puerto Ricans, 13
Puritanism, 10
purposive benefits, 107, 108, 114

Quakers, 3, 30, 31
quasi-independent agencies, 168–70, *169*
Quinn, Robert Emmet, 38–39, 86, 146
Quonset-Davisville Industrial Park, 281
Quonset Point, Massachusetts, 271–72
Quonset Point, Rhode Island, 276

racial history, teaching of, 58
racial injustices, 3–4, 10–12
racism, 204–5
radio, 134–36
rail transportation, fall and rise of, 285–86
Raimondo, Gina, 14, 15, 49, 73, 95, 111, 127, 133, 138, 150, 157, 177, 213; appoints to judiciary, 179, 183; chairs Democratic Governors Association, 225; Coit and, 269; COVID-19 and, 158, 176, 225, 251; elected treasurer, 223; environmental policy and, 274, 275–76; gubernatorial race and, 223–24, 226, 227; hospital industry and, 254; infrastructure maintenance and, 281–82; Medicaid expansion and, 258; nominated by Biden to be secretary of commerce, 225, 275–76; opioid epidemic and, 260; pension reform and, 16, 223, 235; policy process and, 172; reelection campaign of, 224; RPA and, 261; tax policy and, 231, 232; as treasurer, 235; *Truth in Numbers*, 16
Ranney, Meagan, 131
reactionary leadership, 176
Reagan, Ronald, 58, 90–91, 212
recalls, 74–75
Reclaim Rhode Island, 114, 155
Red Alert, 42
Redman, George, 286
Reed, Jack, 94, 192
referenda, 74–75
Reform Caucus, 100
Reform Party, 99
Regulation 36-14-5014, 43
Reitsma, Jan, 269
religious freedom, 51

Index

Rell, Jodi, 221
Renewable Energy Standard, 270
Renewable Portfolio Standard (RPS) laws, 270
renewables, promise of, 275-76
Report of the Commission on Revision of the Rhode Island Constitution, 40
representatives, 27. *See also* local government
reproductive health, 261
Reproductive Privacy Act (RPA), 49, 108, 111, 112, 156, 161n34, 261
reproductive rights: interest groups and, 111-12 (*see also* abortion)
Republicans, 6-7, 8, 36, 38, 85-104, 206-7, 221, 224; ascendancy of, 35-38; Bloodless Revolution and, 38-39; Constitutional Conventions and Amendments, 40-42; Democratic ascendancy and, 39; endorsements and, 77; General Assembly and, 143-62; gubernatorial race and, 223-25; interest groups and, 110; interstate culture wars and, 58-59; judiciary and, 180; state taxation policy and, 57-58; voters in Rhode Island, 212; women's suffrage and, 38
Resilient Rhode Island Act, 274, 275-76
Resource Recovery Corporation, 109
Restoration, 27
revenues, 231-33, 232, 233
Reynolds v. *Sims*, 39
Rhode Island: as birthplace of Industrial Revolution in U.S., 12; communities of, 209-12; federal system and, 49-61; history of legislative dominance, 157-58; home rule in, 200-202; name of, 3, 46, 143; pluralist landscape of, 109-15, 120; population of, 6; voters in, 212-14; women in statewide office in, 222
Rhode Island AFL-CIO, 108, 175
Rhode Island AFL/CIO Labor History Society, 175
Rhode Island Association of School Committees, 108
Rhode Island at the Crossroads, 281
Rhode Island Bar Association, 183
Rhode Island Bicycle Coalition, 113
Rhode Island Center for Freedom & Prosperity, 119-20
Rhode Island Coalition Against Domestic Violence, 112
Rhode Island Coalition Against Gun Violence, 112-13
Rhode Island Coalition for Reproductive Freedom, 108, 111
Rhode Island Comprehensive Assessment System (RICAS), 243
Rhode Island Constitution: Amendments to, 40-41, 43-46; Constitutional development, 1636-2020, 25-48
Rhode Island Council on Elementary and Secondary Education, 245
Rhode Island Democratic Women's Caucus, 85
Rhode Island Department of Revenue, 202
Rhode Island Development Council, 167
Rhode Island Energy, 270; Facility Siting Act, 273-74
Rhode Islanders for Affordable Energy, 274
Rhode Island Firearms Owners League, 112-13
Rhode Island Food Policy Council, 113
Rhode Island Hospital, 253
Rhode Island Infrastructure Bank, Municipal Resiliency Program, 276
Rhode Island Land Trust Council, 108, 113
Rhode Island League of Cities and Towns, 108, 268
Rhode Island Lobbying Reform Act, 116, 117
Rhode Island Lottery Commission, 44
Rhode Island Medical Journal, 262
Rhode Island Medical Society, 108, 119-20, 258
Rhode Island National Association of Social Workers, 112
Rhode Island Political Cooperative (Co-op), 114-15, 155
Rhode Island Progressive Democrats, 155
Rhode Island Public Expenditures Council (RIPEC), 119, 202, 211, 256, 281
Rhode Island Public Television, 130
Rhode Island Public Transit Authority (RIPTA), 283-85, 287, 289
Rhode Island Public Utilities Commission (RIPUC), 269, 270
Rhode Island Resource Recovery Corporation (RIRRC), 269
Rhode Island Retirement and Security Act, 16
Rhode Island Rifle and Revolver Association, 112-13
Rhode Island Right-to-Life Committee, 111, 112
Rhode Island Second Amendment Coalition, 108, 112-13
Rhode Island Shoreline Access Coalition, 113-14

Rhode Island Sound, 17
Rhode Island State Anglers Association, 113
Rhode Island State Association of Fire Fighters, 118
Rhode Island Suffrage Association, 33–34
Rhode Island Utility Restructuring Act, 270
Rhode Island Voting Access Coalition, 70
RI Association of Railroad Passengers, 285
RI Bicycle Coalition, 113, 282, 287
RI Board of Elections, 63, 70, 71, 77, 78, 82n32
RI Center for Freedom and Prosperity, 258
Rich, Robert, 26
Rich, Wilbur, 208
RI Constitution, 96; of 1843, 145–46, 149, 157, 163–64, 180, 185; of 1986, 157; amendments to, 38, 39, 40–42, 43–46, 150, 199, 200–202, 201; Amendment XIII, 201; Amendment XLII, 42; Amendment XV, 39; Amendment XVI, 39; Amendment XX, 38; Article 1, Section 17, 113–14; Article I, Sections 16 and 17, 42; Article II, Section 2, 70; Article III, Section 8, 43; Article IV, Section 1, 42–43; Article IV, Section 9, 41; Article of Amendment III, 36; Article of Amendment XLII, 42; Article of Amendment XXII, 40; Article of Amendment XXIX, 40; Article of Amendment XXVII, 40; Article of Amendment XXX, 40; Article of Amendment XXXI, 40; Article of Amendment XXXII, 40; Article VI, Section 10, 45; Article VI, Section 22, 43; Article VIII, Section 2, 43; Article X, Sections 4 and 5, 43; Article XII, 164; Article XIV, 42; Article XIV, Section 2, 45; Bourn Amendment (Article VII), 37, 65, 199; campaign finance and, 77–78; Constitutional Conventions and Amendments, 40–42; Constitution Conventions and Amendments, 199, 200–202; education and, 241–42; executive branch and, 163–64; General Assembly and, 241, 268–69; Home Rule Amendment (Article XIII), 40, 200–202; recalls, 74; Rhode Island Lottery Commission and, 44; secretary of state and, 82n32; Separation of Powers Amendment, 43–46; separation of powers and, 170; special elections and, 73
RI Department of Administration, 166, 167, 168, 174–75, 284
RI Department of Agriculture and Conservation, 165
RI Department of Budget and Management, 168
RI Department of Business Regulation (DBR), 152–53, 166
RI Department of Civil Service, 167, 174
RI Department of Coordination and Finance, 166
RI Department of Economic Development, 171
RI Department of Education (RIDE), 165, 167, 243, 245
RI Department of Environmental Management (DEM), 167, 269
RI Department of Health (RIDOH), 119–20, 190, 254, 255, 269, 270
RI Department of Health, Education and Welfare, 252
RI Department of Housing, 17
RI Department of Labor, 165
RI Department of Mental Health, Retardation, and Hospitals, 167
RI Department of Motor Vehicles, 184
RI Department of Natural Resources, 167
RI Department of Public Health, 165
RI Department of Public Welfare, 165
RI Department of Public Works, 165
RI Department of Revenue, 168, 211
RI Department of Social and Rehabilitative Services, 167
RI Department of State (DOS), 63, 70, 71, 76
RI Department of Taxation and Regulations, 165
RI Department of Transportation (RIDOT), 279–80, 281, 282, 286, 287, 289; Traffic Safety Coalition, 282
RI district courts, 182, 183–84
RI Federation of Republican Women, 99
RI House of Representatives, 7, 28, 34, 43, 100, 165; education and, 241–42; Fiscal Office, 256; judiciary and, 183; Mattiello/Fenton-Fung race, 143–44; Reproductive Privacy Act (RPA) and, 49; women in, 221, 222; women's suffrage and, 37–38. *See also* Bloodless Revolution; General Assembly
RI Political Co-op, 98, 100
RI secretary of state, 63, 71, 117
RI Senate, 7, 28, 35, 37, 39, 43, 86–87, 96, 165; education and, 241–42; establishment of, 200; judiciary and, 183; malapportionment and, 146, 200; Reproductive Privacy Act (RPA) and, 49;

women in, 221, 222; women's suffrage and, 37–38. *See also* Bloodless Revolution; General Assembly
RI state legislature, 8–9; lobbyists and, 18; progressive agenda of, 16–17
RI State Returning Board, 71
RI Superior Court, 39, 182, 183–86, 189, 192
RI Supreme Court, 7, 16, 37, 39, 43, 87, 180, 182, 183–85, 187, 189; appointments to, 179–80; *Baker* v. *Carr*, 200; Block Island and, 192; Bloodless Revolution and, 86, 165; Court Reorganization Act and, 39; *Horton* v. *Newport*, 200; *Newport Amusement* v. *Maher*, 202; *Providence* v. *Moulton*, 200; resignations from, 42; separation of powers and, 170; *State* v. *Ibbison*, 113–14; *Taylor* v. *Place*, 164; *Town of East Greenwich* v. *O'Neil*, 202; traffic tribunal and, 188; *Xavier* v. *Cianci, Jr.*, 202
RITECARE, 284
Roberts, Dennis J., 167, 173
Roberts, Elizabeth, 222, 257
Rochambeau, General, 30
Rockefeller, John D., Sr., 36
Roe v. *Wade*, 49, 59, 96, 111, 156, 161n34, 261
Roger Williams Medical Center, 190, 254
Roger Williams University, Latino Policy Institute, 243
"Rogue's Island," 31
Roman Catholic Diocese of Rhode Island, 112
Romney, Mitt, 91
Roosevelt, Franklin D., 38, 86, 164
Roosevelt, Theodore, 86
Rosenthal, Alan, 170
Rourke, Jennifer, 100
Royal Charter, 27–28. *See also* Charter of 1663
Ruggerio, Dominick, 111, 156, 257, 261
Russian Jews, 12
Rutgers University, 241–42, 245

Safe Drinking Water Act, 270
safety, transportation and, 282–83
Sakonnet Bridge, 281
sales and use tax, 231–32
sanctuary towns, 202–3
Sanders, Bernie, 114, 214
Sapinsley, Lila, 221, 222, 223, 224, 228
Save the Bay, 108, 113, 268, 272, 274
Schneider, Claudine, 93–94, 222
school funding, 235–36, 236, 243–45. *See also* education
Scituate, Rhode Island, 91–92, 201

Scituate Reservoir, 268
Scott, Beverly, 283–84
sea-level rise, 275–76
Seastreak, 287
Second Amendment, 202–3
secretary of state, 82n32
Section 8 Housing, 55
Seekonk, Rhode Island, 32
segregation, 205
selective benefits, 107, 108
self-government, 198
self-reliance, 31
Senate. *See* RI Senate; US Senate
separation of powers, executive branch and, 168–70
Separation of Powers Amendment, 43–46
Servants of Christ for Life, 112
Service Employees International Union District 1199 New England, 110
Shaheen, Jeanne, 221
Shawomet, 199
Shekarchi, Joseph, 105, 143, 156, 238, 261
Shields, Jon A., 214
Shor, Boris, 153
shoreline access, 18
Sierra Club, 268, 272, 281
Silverstein, Michael, 44, 186
size, 6–8
Slater, Samuel, 32
slavery, 11, 31
slave trade, 3–4, 11, 30, 204
Smiley, Brett, 209
Smith, Al, 38
Smithfield, Rhode Island, 283
Snowe, Olympia, 221
social media, 127, 131; rise of, 132–34
solidary benefits, 107, 108, 114
South County Hospital, 254
South Kingston, Rhode Island, 31
South Providence, Rhode Island, Washington Park neighborhood, 274–75
Spencer, Anna Garlin, 37–38
spending, 231–40, 234; on education, 235–36, 236; outlook for the future, 237–38; on public safety, 236–37
Spotify, 131
state and local spending, 234–37, 234
State and Local Tax Deduction (SALT), 57–58
State Children's Health Insurance Program, 55
State Council of Churches, 43
state employees, 174–76
State Ethics Commission, 150

state offices, elections for, 95
The State of Rhode Island and Providence Plantations, 3
State Planning Council, 289
State Policy Network, 119–20
state power, evolution of, 199–200
states' rights, 50–51, 53
state taxation policy, 57–58
State v. Ibbison, 113–14
Statewide Planning Program, 283
steam power, 32
Steffens, Lincoln, 37, 53
Stenhouse, Mike, 258
Stokes, 204, 205; 2, 204, 205
Stone, Clarence, 208
Stuart Dynasty, Restoration of, 27
student achievement, 243
Student Success Act, 14
suffrage, 64–65; property-based, 32–33, 52, 64–65; universal, 65; women's, 37–38, 65
Sundlun, Bruce, 170, 173, 177, 271
Sunrise Movement, 114
Sunrise Rhode Island, 114
Supplemental Nutrition Assistance Program, 55
Supreme Court. *See* RI Supreme Court; US Supreme Court
Suttell, Paul, 182–83

talk radio, 134–36
Taney, Roger B., 35, 47–48n13
Taveras, Angel, 205, 223, 226
taxation, 57–58
Tax Cuts and Jobs Act (TCJA), 259
taxes, 166–67, 171–72, 210, 231; municipal, 233–37; outlook for the future, 237–38; tax hikes on wealthy, 156; tax revenues, 231–33, 232, 233
Tax Foundation, Business Tax Climate Index, 233
taxing, 231–40
tax policy, 231–33
Taylor v. Place, 36, 39, 164
teacher shortages, 247
teachers' unions, 246
television news, local, 127–29
Temporary Assistance for Needy Families, 55
textile industry, decline of, 38
textile mills, 204
TF Green, 287–88
think tanks, interest groups and, 119–20
third parties, 99–100

Thirteenth Amendment, 53
Thompson, Tommy, 177
Tobin, Thomas J., 112
toll roads, 281–82
topography, 5–6
Town of East Greenwich v. O'Neil, 202
trades unions, 274
traffic tribunal, 182, 184, 187–89
transactional approach to governing, 176
transformational leadership, 176
transgender rights, 58
transparency, 101
transportation: aviation, 287–88; bicycling, 286–87; by boat, 287; bus system and, 283–85; land use and, 283; maintaining infrastructure, 281–82; rail, 285–86; safety and, 282–83
"Transportation Climate Initiative" (TCI), 288–89
transportation network, 32
transportation policy, 279–89
trifectas, 96
Trillo, Joe, 225
Triton Digital, 131
trucking industry, 282
Trump, Donald, 8, 14, 90, 91, 92, 100, 111; administration of, 14; election integrity commission and, 69; election of, 155; presidency of, 224; supporters of, 98, 125, 212, 214, 225
Tufts Health Plan, 253
Turnpike and Bridge Authority, 109
Twin River, 117
Twin River Casino, 172
Twitter, 127, 132

undocumented immigrants, 14
Unfair Claims Practices Act, 106
Unified Health Infrastructure Project (UHIP), 259
unions, 9–10, 38, 174–76, 274; pension reform and, 16; teachers' unions, 246; trades unions, 274. *See also specific organizations*
United Healthcare, 253
United Transportation Company, 283–84
universal healthcare, 100
Urban League, 205
US attorneys, 193
US Census, 72
US Census Bureau, 15
US Congress, 52, 53; Clean Water Act, 272; elections, 90–95

US Constitution, 31; Fifteenth
  Amendment, 53; First Amendment, 107,
  116; Fourteenth Amendment, 53;
  Nineteenth Amendment, 37–38;
  ratification of, 31–32, 51–52, 180; rejection
  of, 31; slavery in, 31; states' rights and,
  50–51, 53; Thirteenth Amendment, 53
US Court of Appeals, Circuit 1, 192
US district courts, 192, 193
US Election Assistance Commission, 63
US Environmental Protection Agency
  (EPA), 269, 272
US House of Representatives, 14–15;
  elections, 93–95; federal elections, 93–95,
  94; women in, 221. *See also* US Congress
US Senate, 36, 39, 225; elections, 90–93;
  federal elections, 92–93, 93; federal judges
  appointed by, 192–93; women in, 221. *See
  also* US Congress
US Supreme Court, 35, 39, 52–53, 192;
  abortion and, 49, 111, 156, 161n34;
  apportionment and, 65; *Citizens United* v.
  Federal Election Commission, 120; *Dobbs
  v. Jackson Women's Health Organization*,
  261; federalism and, 52–53, 54–55;
  interstate culture wars and, 58; New Deal
  and, 54; Political Question Doctrine, 35,
  47–48n13; "reapportionment revolution"
  and, 147; *Roe v. Wade*, 261

Valicenti, Gene, 135
Valletta, Paul, 118
Valley Breeze, 106, 136–37
Vanderbilt, William H., 166, 173
Vermeule, Adrian, 158
Violet, Arlene, 99
voter registration, 65–67, 88, 89, 102n15
voters, 212–14
voter turnout, 72, 90; general elections, 90;
  primary elections, 90, 90; registered voter
  turnout, 72–73; by voting method, 64
voting, 63–84; 2020 election procedures,
  68; methods of, 67–68; politics of, 69–70;
  in primaries, 67
voting age, 66
Voting Rights Act of 1965, 65

Walmart, 117
Wampanoag nation, 27, 28
Ward, Samuel, 29
Warren, Elizabeth, 221
Warren, Rhode Island, Town Council
  of, 198

Warwick, Rhode Island, 26, 27, 199, 201
Washington County, Rhode Island, 185
wastewater treatment facility (WWTF)
  discharges, 272–73
water pollution, 272–73
waterpower, 32
water resources, 267–68, 270–73
Weisberger, Joseph, 44
Wesberry v. Sanders, 39
West, Phil, 45
Westerly, Rhode Island, 204
Westerly Hospital, 254
West Greenwich, Rhode Island, 37, 146
Westminster Consulting, 117
West Warwick, Rhode Island, 40, 204
Weygand, Robert, 74, 95
Whigs, 34, 35
Whitehouse, Sheldon, 93, 170, 192
WHJJ, 135
Williams, Anastasia, 209
Williams, Frank, 189
Williams, Roger, 3, 4, 25, 26, 28, 29, 47n1,
  198, 199, 203
Wilson, Woodrow, 86
wind power turbines, 17
Winthrop, John Jr., 27, 47n1
WNRI, 135
women: election of first female governor,
  222–25; in General Assembly, 221; legacy
  in Rhode Island politics, 221–29; politics
  and, 15–16; in RI House of
  Representatives, 221, 222; in RI Senate,
  221, 222; rise of Latina politicians, 226–28;
  in statewide office in RI, 222; in US
  House of Representatives, 221; in US
  Senate, 221; women's suffrage, 37–38, 65
Women, Children and Families Caucus, 99
Women and Infants' Hospital, 253–54
women's suffrage, 37–38, 65
Wood, Ed, 286
Wood, Gordon, 10
Woonsocket, Rhode Island, 210, 211, 244,
  246
Woonsocket Call, 136
Workers' Compensation Commission, 187
worker's compensation court, 182, 183–84,
  187–88
Working Families Party (WFP), 98, 100,
  101, 115
World War II, 54
WPRI, 158
WPRO, 130, 131, 134, 135

Xavier v. *Cianci, Jr.*, 202
Yale New Haven Health, 254
Yale v. *Curvin*, 87
Yates, Elizabeth Upham, 38
York, Myrth, 95, 271, 272
Yorke, Dan, 135
Young Republicans, 99

Zurier, Sam, 101